Law in West German Democracy

Studies in Central European Histories

VOLUME 66

The titles published in this series are listed at *brill.com/sceh*

Law in West German Democracy

Seventy Years of History as Seen through German Courts

By

Hugh Ridley

BRILL

LEIDEN | BOSTON

Cover illustration: Finger zeigt auf Paragrafen. Zoonar GmbH / Alamy Stock Photo.

Library of Congress Cataloging-in-Publication Data

Names: Ridley, Hugh, author.
Title: Law in West German democracy : seventy years of history as seen through German courts / Hugh Ridley.
Description: Leiden ; Boston : Brill, 2020. | Series: Studies in Central European histories, 1547-1217 ; volume 66 | Includes bibliographical references and index.
Identifiers: LCCN 2019032224 (print) | LCCN 2019032225 (ebook) | ISBN 9789004410602 (hardback) | ISBN 9789004414471 (ebook)
Subjects: LCSH: Trials—Germany (West) | Trials—Germany. | Law—Germany (West) | Law—Germany. | Justice, Administration of—Germany (West) | Justice, Administration of—Germany.
Classification: LCC KK65 .R53 2019 (print) | LCC KK65 (ebook) | DDC 349.4309/045—dc23
LC record available at https://lccn.loc.gov/2019032224
LC ebook record available at https://lccn.loc.gov/2019032225

Typeface for the Latin, Greek, and Cyrillic scripts: "Brill". See and download: brill.com/brill-typeface.

ISSN 1547-1217
ISBN 978-90-04-41060-2 (hardback)
ISBN 978-90-04-41447-1 (e-book)

This book is printed on acid-free paper and produced in a sustainable manner.

Contents

Preface IX
Acknowledgments XII
List of Abbreviations XIII

Introduction: The Historical Situation of Law in the Federal Republic 1
0.1 Politics and the Law 4
0.2 The Centrality of Law after the Collapse of 1945 7
0.3 Institutional Structures in German Law: Basic Law and the Federal Constitutional Court 12
0.4 Statute Rather Than Common Law 16
0.5 Anomalies in a Changing Legal Code 20
0.6 History and the Law in the Federal Republic 23

1 **The Trial of Friedrich Flick** 26
1.1 Understanding the NS State 30
1.2 Who Was Flick and on What Charges Did He Appear? 32
1.3 Legal Issues 35
1.4 The Sentence 39
1.5 Assessing the Verdict 41
1.6 The Repercussions of the Flick Trial 42

2 **Adjusting the Political Landscape: Banning the KPD** 49
2.1 The Banning of Political Parties 50
2.2 Outlawing the KPD 52
2.3 The Deliberations of the BVerfG 56
2.4 The Legal Consequences of the Ban 59
2.5 Reflections on Constitutional Courts and Politics 62

3 **The Lüth Case – at What Price Freedom of Expression?** 67
3.1 The Starting Point: Artists and Nazism 67
3.2 The Call for a Boycott 70
3.3 The Decision of the BVerfG 71
3.4 Repercussions 74

4 **Four Murders, and Reflections on Court-Reporting in the Federal German Press** 79
4.1 Reporting the Law 79
4.2 Precedents in Weimar 85
4.3 The Federal Republic 88
4.4 A Routine Murder 89
4.5 Rosemarie Nitribitt 92
4.6 Two Women in Court 95
4.7 Hetzel's Campaign for a Retrial 97
4.8 Conclusions 102

5 **Personal Matters in Court: Homosexuality and Abortion** 106
5.1 The Legacy of the Past 108
5.2 Post-War Shifts of Policy 111
5.3 The Frankfurt Homosexual Trials 112
5.4 § 218 in the Federal Republic 118
5.5 'It's Not You, Doctor, Who Have Offended Me, but the Judges' 119
5.6 The Campaign against § 218 Moves Forward 125
5.7 The Last Razzia 127

6 **The *Spiegel* Affair** 130
6.1 The Dimensions of the Affair 132
6.2 Old Antagonisms 134
6.3 The Principal Legal Issue: Military Secrecy 137
6.4 A Brief Consideration of the BVerfG Judgment 142

7 **The Frankfurt Auschwitz Trial** 146
7.1 At Last the Silence Is Broken 147
7.2 The Implications of the Eichmann Trial 149
7.3 Auschwitz-Birkenau 150
7.4 Preparing for the Trial 152
7.5 Gathering Momentum 158
7.6 A New Type of Trial 160
7.7 Individual Moments from the Proceedings 163
7.8 Sentencing and Final Considerations 168
7.9 Final Comments 174

8 **The 1970s: The Campaign against Radicals – Ideology Becomes the Crime** 177

8.1 Prologue 177
8.2 Background to the 1970s 180
8.3 The Legal Basis of the *Berufsverbot* 185
8.4 Three Individual Cases 187
8.5 The Legal Issues 191
8.6 The BVerfG Judgment 195
8.7 Dissenting Judges 199
8.8 Final Thoughts 201

9 Chasing after Sympathizers – Threats to the Rule of Law 204
9.1 Reactions to an Act of Terror 210
9.2 An Unwanted Requiem 211
9.3 Sympathizing with Terror? 212
9.4 The Knives Come Out 215
9.5 A Chequered History of Controlling Free Speech 218

10 The Rub of the Green – a Range of Environmental Cases 224
10.1 Historical Prologue 224
10.2 Environmental Protection in the Federal Republic 226
10.3 Violence among the Trees 230
10.4 Chemical Pollution – 'Everyone the Loser' 231
10.5 Reflections on a Small Victory for the Environment 236
10.6 Problems of Atomic Power: Atomkraft? Nein Danke 243

11 Danger from the Right 252
11.1 Post-heroic Law 252
11.2 Ten Murders 256
11.3 The Origins of Racist Violence 257
11.4 The Role of the Extreme Right 260
11.5 Institutional Failures 262
11.6 Back to the Crimes 269
11.7 Problems with the Trial 270
11.8 The Trial 271

Appendix: Background Notes 277

Bibliography 294
Index 310

Preface

This book gives an account of the history of the Federal Republic of Germany as seen through a series of significant trials conducted in the country between the end of the war and 2017. It explains how these trials came to take place, the legal issues which they raised, and their importance to the development of democracy in a country only just emerged from twelve years of a murderous and criminal régime. By analyzing the actions which led to these trials and the judgments of the courts, the book holds up a mirror to the central issues of this new republic, as it tried to build a democratic state on the ruins of Hitler's Germany. Crime, as a celebrated German minister of justice remarked, can be seen as 'the reverse image of any political system, the shadow cast by the social and economic structures of the day'.[1] It is natural therefore to use court cases to illuminate the eventful history of the Federal Republic's first seventy years thus – in the words of the editor of a recent volume – 'unlocking the power of criminal trials as historical sources'.[2]

The book offers the general reader an original account of the course of West German history, in which – by the very nature of court procedures – major issues of social policy, politics and social history are made both concrete and personal. It makes accessible important material and discussions otherwise not available in English. At the same time, it offers an important guide for students embarked on legal, historical and business studies involving Germany.

The court cases discussed here cover a wide range. Some are criminal, some of them matters of constitutional law, crucial to the establishment of a western democracy. Others highlight the country's dealing with its NS past – most famously the Auschwitz trial of 1963–65 –, with press freedom (here the notorious *Spiegel*-Affair of 1962 is the centre of attention), with left-wing urban terrorism, with environmental issues and with neo-Nazi violence. Four celebrated murder cases serve to illustrate the shifting moral climate at the end of the 1950s, while the story of homosexual rights and women's right to abortion is told across a number of trials from 1950 to 1988. The courts which heard these cases range from local and state courts to the highest court in the country, the Federal Constitutional Court. Where appropriate, comparisons are made to practice in Irish, British and American courts.

The book assumes no knowledge of the German language, but it offers extensive bibliographical guidance to the field in both languages and the

1 Werner Maihofer (1978, p. 328).
2 Richard F. Wetzell (2014, p. 21).

court-proceedings at its heart are translated, but referenced directly. I thus acknowledge and lament 'that the international academic debate seldom notices literature in the German language'.[3] The chapter background notes in the Appendix supply the information needed to follow up the individual arguments. These notes are extensive: they contain both a general survey of the literature on the particular topics – from abortion to official secrets – and specific references to material quoted in the text, but the text can be read without reference to the notes.

In the middle of my work on this book came the Brexit referendum in Britain. Whatever its outcome, the debate has shown beyond any doubt the pressing need for information and understanding about post-war Germany. Indeed, an objective understanding of German law and history is more urgently needed than ever before. For my Irish readers the new landscape means that Ireland represents the only member state in which English is the everyday language, and we may look forward to an intensification of student and academic exchange in consequence and a strengthening of cultural and legal relations.

My generation has grown up with the Federal Republic, and when we look at its history we look into a mirror of our own selves. The superficial consumerism of the 1950s, the idealism of the 1960s, the sense of life's bitter realities in the 1970s and 1980s; the difficulty of believing in the better world after the Berlin Wall came down, the awareness in the last few years of dimensions of problems which had somehow not been included in our generation's various agendas – these are both personal and general reactions. But we have seen too an enormous change in Germany from the rather threadbare remnants of a military past still visible in the early 1950s to a confident anti-militarism; from an often self-important bureaucracy to a more open society, with challenging values and newly established traditions; from a society in which women had to find their fulfilment solely in what the Germans used to call 'the three Ks' – kids, kitchen and church. That change has enriched Europe, as it has also enriched Germany. This book maps out some of its steps.

I have confessed to being older than the Federal Republic of Germany, and I must also confess that I am not a lawyer. For all the fascination which the material possesses and the respect which I have for the legal mind, I have little wish to turn into a lawyer and none whatsoever to present myself here as one. I have approached this subject as a historian, and as a non-lawyer I have handled the specialized legal material of this study with two principal thoughts in mind.

3 Pünder & Waldhoff (2014, p. vii).

The first is to accept a general truth about all inter-disciplinary work. Often the topic in question must either wait for an ideal author, who meets every requirement of expertise and professional experience, or the topic must be understood as preliminary, as asking questions of specialist groups who, for the most part, have not yet realized its importance. That is certainly how this book appears to me. As a number of academic lawyers in Germany have recognized, the historical dimension of the law does not feature prominently enough in the study of law, and yet this topic is of paramount importance, seldom more so than over the last seventy years of the Federal Republic.

Some of the cases covered by this book may appear to be pre-eminently lawyers' topics. That is to say that they focus on issues which have been exhaustively discussed by generations of academic lawyers and that they raise principles which have long occupied the best legal minds. This is not to say that such cases – *Lüth* or International War Crimes, for instance – have not been nor still are directly influential on the lives of ordinary German citizens. In no way does their place in specialist discussion diminish the importance of their historical dimensions. Other cases seem to lie naturally within the orbit of anyone interested in public policy, while it is not just the murder cases of Chapter Four which have become legally significant thanks to the efforts of journalists and cultural historians rather than because of the distinctive work of legal professionals. Not just legal history, individual cases too have been enriched by the intervention of other disciplines.

So much for the book's interdisciplinarity. My second thought is less modest. Not only do I believe that an understanding of German law is essential to those who concern themselves with that country: I am convinced that, while the professionalization of the law is crucial to the fairness of the law, the accessibility of the law to ordinary citizens is no less important. We can recognize this idea as a campaigning slogan: behind it stands justice for Dreyfus or for the Birmingham Six, and in the following chapters this stance demands justice for among many others – Hans Hetzel, Axel Dohrn and Silvia Gingold. There's no outcome to be obtained from campaigning at the present time for justice in these cases, for they lie many years in the past, but they show how pointless it would be to present German law as if it were a closed system, requiring merely the technical expertise of lawyers for an outcome to be achieved. Without a desire for justice, the law is a meaningless ritual. German law is interesting not just for its systematic character: it is fascinating for being embedded in a historical society which possessed its own strengths and weaknesses. To recognize the distinctiveness of that society and to see the way in which its development is reflected in the workings of its legal system and yet remains open to the search for justice, is a more than worthwhile activity, and one in which wider circles than lawyers should participate.

Acknowledgments

I have besieged friends for years on this project. I cannot begin to list the help which I have received, but I owe everything to it. I would mention first the encouragement I have received from the former journalist and prize-winning crime-fiction writer Ulrich Ritzel – his fierce commitment to justice in both writing modes has been inspirational. I would like to thank the very gifted students of Law and German in Trinity College Dublin and University College Galway for engaging in discussion. Thanks are due to Stephen Mennell for advice and guidance on sociological matters. Bill and Sheila Bell sorted me out on the Dreyfus Affair. Dick Jones was a steadying hand in Chapter Five. Mary Cosgrove set my view of Auschwitz. Hannes Krauss guided me through the intricacies of Chapter Eight. Gilbert Carr read me through the Environment, while Richard Ullmer not only breathed green air into Ireland, he put me in touch with Herr Matthias Möller-Meinecke of the Rechtsanwaltskanzlei EDIFICIA in Frankfurt who gave me wonderful material taken from his own fight for the environment. Deirdre Byrnes, Jeanne Riou and Caitriona Leahy lent their wise heads to the enterprise. Dickson Ensonrae, LLB, LLM made himself available for wide-ranging discussions of points of law, and Tim O'Neill – a fine barrister and finer colleague in University College Dublin – helped me to see what the law is and can do. My friend, the late Colin Seymour-Ure, gave me access to his unrivalled understanding of the workings of the press. Other conversations which have taken place over the years in Crivitz, The Maharees and Zehlendorf have helped and cheered me in this project more than I can say. With some of the books listed in my bibliography I feel I have lived as with friends, and I thank their authors warmly, just as I thank those kind and forbearing people who have helped me to find books in the Staatsbibliothek zu Berlin, the Cambridge University Library and the British Library. I would like to put on record my appreciation of the skill and charm with which the editors of this series and Brill's editorial staff – especially Gerda Danielsson Coe and Wendel Scholma – welcomed my book into their world. Also at Brill, Thalien Colenbrander helped me through the technical aspects of the book's production with unfailing patience and expertise. Otherwise, as ever, I have gratefully exploited the time, patience and expertise of Jenny, Guy and Simon, Suzanne and Eva, to all of whom this book is dedicated.

Berlin, Dublin and Canterbury May 2019

Abbreviations

AGIT		Alternative Press to the K-Groups
APO	Außerparlamentarische Opposition	Extra-parliamentary opposition
BfV	Bundesamt für Verfassungsschutz	Federal Office for protecting the constitution
BGB	Bürgerliches Gesetzbuch	Civil Code
BGH	Bundesgerichtshof	Federal Court of Justice
BGH St	Entscheidungen des BGH in Strafsachen	Record of BGH decisions in penal cases
BKA	Bundeskriminalamt	Federal Office of criminal justice
BND	Bundesnachrichtendienst	Federal Information (secret) Service
BRD	Bundesrepublik Deutschland	Federal Republic of Germany
BVerfG	Bundesverfassungsgericht	Federal Constitutional Court
BVerwG	Bundesverwaltungsgericht	Federal Administrative Court
CASTOR		Registered trade name of atomic waste flasks
CDU	Christlich-demokratische Union	Christian-democratic union (Party of Adenauer)
COMECON		Council for Mutual Economic Assistance
CSU	Christlich-soziale Union	Christian-social union
DKP	Deutsche kommunistische Partei	German Communist Party
DM	Deutschmark	
DVU	Deutsche Volksunion	German People's Union
DWK	Deutsche Gesellschaft für Wiederaufarbeitung von Kernbrennstoffen	German Society for the re-processing of nuclear fuel
ECHR		European Court of Human Rights
EDC		European Defence Community
EU		European Union
FAZ	*Frankfurter Allgemeine Zeitung*	[Major national newspaper]
FDJ	Freie deutsche Jugend	Free German Youth
FDP	Freidemokratische Partei	Free Democratic Party (Liberals)
FIFA	Féderation Internationale de Football	
FRG		Federal Republic of Germany
GA	Goldammers Archiv für Strafrecht	Leading legal journal
GDR		German Democratic Republic
GEW	Gewerkschaft Erziehung u. Wissenschaft	Education and Science Trades-Union
GG	Grundgesetz	Basic Law
IAK	Internationales Auschwitz Komittee	International Auschwitz Committee

IED		Improvised explosive Device
IG-Farben	Interessen-Gemeinschaft-Farbenindustrie Aktiengesellschaft	Conglomerate tried at Nuremberg for the production of poison gas for Auschwitz
IM	Informelle Mitarbeiter	*Stasi* informer
IMT		International Military Tribunal
IRA		Irish Republican Army
KGB		[Soviet secret service from 1954–1991]
KPD	Kommunistische Partei Deutschlands	Communist Party of Germany
LG	Landgericht	State Court
NJW	*Neue Juristische Wochenschrift*	Major Law journal
NPD	Nationaldemokratische Partei Deutschlands	National-democratic party of Germany
NS		National Socialist
NSDAP	Nationalsozialistische deutsche Arbeiterpartei	National Socialist German Workers' Party
NSU	Nationalsozialistischer Untergrund	National Socialist Underground
OLG	Oberlandesgericht	Higher State Court
ÖTV	Gewerkschaft öffentliche Dienste, Transport und Verkehr	Public transport and communications union
PDS	Partei des demokratischen Sozialismus	Party of democratic socialism
PKK		Kurdistan Workers' Party
PLO		Palestine Liberation Organization
RAF	Rote Armee Fraktion	Red Army (Section of Baader-Meinhof)
REP	Republikaner	Republicans (Party)
RGB	Reichsgesetzbuch	NS law code
RM	Reichsmark	Forerunner of the DM
RSHA	Reichssicherheitshauptamt	Reich Head Office for Security
SA	Sturmabteilung	Early militia of the NSDAP
SDS		Students for a democratic society
SED	Sozialistische Einheitspartei	Socialist Unity Party
SIPO	Sicherheitspolizei	(Nazi) Security Police
SPD	Sozialdemokratische Partei Deutschlands	Social Democratic Party
SRP	Sozialistische Reichspartei	Socialist Reich Party
SS	Schutzstaffel	Hard-core organization of NSDAP
Stasi	Ministerium für Staatssicherheit	Security police of the GDR
StGB	Strafgesetzbuch	Penal Code
StPO	Strafprozessordnung	Penal trial code
THS	Thüringer Heimatschutz	Neo-Nazi organization in Thuringia
UNWCC		United Nations War Crimes Commission
VEB	Volkseigener Betrieb	Publicly owned factory in GDR

INTRODUCTION

The Historical Situation of Law in the Federal Republic

This book is a history of the Federal Republic of Germany – or West Germany, as it was usually known before unification in 1990 –, told through a representative selection of court trials. The trials are taken from across the seventy years of the Republic's life, from its foundation in 1949 to the present. Each chapter gives an account of the trial itself, focused on the legal and historical issues which the trial raised, while also filling in the historical and political background of its time. Some trials are made by history, others make history. I hope I have included both in this book.

There are not many histories of jurisprudence in the Federal Republic, fewest of all on that aspect on which my account here is built. Few indeed expand legal history by exploring, beyond the formal changes in individual laws, the patterns of political, social and intellectual history into which these changes fit, and these few histories tend to take a long-term view of changes in judicial practice, rather than to see the series of crises in the Federal Republic's development as in themselves causes of change. Nevertheless, my purpose in this book is not the history of German law-making and practice, but the impingement of that history on the generations which experienced it.

The question of generation is anything but incidental. While everyone's experience of history depends on the generation they belong to, in few countries has that truth been more important than in Germany. In the twentieth-century attention has focused on the 'Front Generation' (born roughly between 1880 and 1900) – the generation decimated by the first world war. The focus then shifts to the generation too young to fight in the second world war and, if they were lucky, too young to be indoctrinated by NS youth organizations. (Chancellor Kohl – 1930–2017 – famously spoke of 'the blessing to have been born late'.) Another generation got drafted into the anti-aircraft batteries towards the end of the war – the so called *Flakhelfergeneration* – but did not die on the eastern front. We have the '68 generation, and the post unification generation. When we meet someone from Poland or the former German Democratic Republic who can't speak Russian, we know that they belong to that generation. The Greeks believed that character determined one's fate: it seems rather that fate is the generation one is born into.[1]

1 See Linda Shortt (2015).

Those in my generation (born during the Second World War, between 1939 and 1945) have more or less grown up with the Federal Republic. We have watched the Federal Republic too grow up, and as observers we have passed through phases of hope and despair similar to those which the country itself has undergone during its development. We got to know that history as if it were our own. It follows that, as I give an account of aspects of that history through the activities of its law-courts, elements of the story are personal, bound up with the generational memories of stages in an individual and national life. These events are inseparably connected with feelings of justice, injustice and *fairness*, as they affected members of our generation. For other, younger generations, some familiarity with the legal system of the Federal Republic will have come through other routes, whether through trade and employment (even a summer job can teach one much about the law), through study at a German university or through the move towards an integrative European legislation. In these cases, however, familiarity with the law may not be accompanied by knowledge of the history which it so closely mirrors. This book aims to help readers by supplying another pattern and another set of facts in which to situate their knowledge.

Law is not just for specialists. Not simply because a legal system is the water in which all citizens swim or sink, but because the law reflects the way in which any country is constituted and the way in which it behaves. In contrast, for instance, to Britain, the Federal Republic operates through a codified legal system and constitution: the word *Rechtsstaat* defines that, making clear that the laws of the Federal Republic *are* the country. No less than its culture, a country's laws define it, and the behaviour of its courts should be a reflection of the better and more reflected aspects of that country's life.

In every age writers have endeavoured to inform their readers about the activities of the law. As early as the seventeenth century a series of books presenting famous cases of the day was published in France, known and imitated throughout Europe under the general title *Pitaval*. From the beginning, such books – together with the much later newspaper and other media reporting on current cases – had two principal rationales. The first has been a concern for justice itself, for strengthening the rule of law against the arbitrary exercise of power by secular and religious despots, and for monitoring and improving the efficiency and fairness of the courts. The second rationale has been the sensational content of many of these cases. Long before such material naturally found its way into novels and other forms of entertainment, court reporting, whether in book or newspaper form, was the staple diet for readers seeking excitement and sensation. Beyond these motives, however, throughout the centuries writers have believed that by bringing court-proceedings to the attention of a wider public they were holding a mirror up to their system of government and to the condition of their society.

This aim is shared by the present book, both in a specialist and in a more general way. Jurisprudence, focusing on the evolution of systems of laws through time, has a historical dimension wider than its specialist content. The changing treatment of particular crimes within the law – being hung or deported for stealing a sheep, for instance, or the prosecution of particular acts of violence as 'hate crimes' – reflects accurately the values and concerns of a particular society, or, at least, of its law-givers. But the crimes themselves, their motivation and how they are carried out, show no less of the realities of a particular age, and can be a strong accompaniment to historical understandings. The all-too human, timeless element of crime is invariably admixed with features which are particular to one society and one time, and which may act as a guide to the temper of a particular age. It follows that some of the cases discussed in the following chapters will reflect the particular circumstances of the political development of the Federal Republic, while others will relate to more general phenomena across the globe as they affected Germany. But both categories amount to crucial threads in the Federal Republic's history.

It's this feature of the historical presence of the law which prompted me to write this book and which, I hope, will make it of interest to wider circles than lawyers alone. If, as a famous novelist commented on perhaps his greatest work, it is possible to write a love story in such a way that could happen only in one particular period of history,[2] then how much more possible is it to understand the history of the law not as the evolution of an abstract system of statutes, but as a focused part of one essential and unique human history .

'For some years now', wrote a young court-reporter in 1926, Gabriele Tergit,

> the Moabit court in Berlin has been the fountain-head of all attempts to understand our age. It's not the isolated actions of individuals, the scandals of a complacent and saturated economy, or the timeless human passions [...] which demand our attention, but the most typical features of the age, of our epoch, *res gestae* are on trial. It seems arbitrary which particular individuals are sitting among the accused.[3]

Her remarks hold true for all the cases in this book.

---

2 Gustave Flaubert's letter of October 6 1864 discussing *L'Éducation sentimentale*.

3 Tergit (1999, p. 138). In Chapter 4 below there is a fuller discussion of the role of court-reporting in the justice system. *Res gestae*: the legal term referring to the events, circumstances, remarks etc. which relate to a particular case, especially as constituting admissible evidence in a court of law.

0.1 Politics and the Law

If I suggest that a history orientated to court-trials sheds light on important political processes of a country, I do not wish to be misunderstood. The Federal Republic, like other Western democracies, operates a separation between the judiciary and the legislature, and even in those trials where the wishes of politicians for one particular outcome were identified and, worse still, directly articulated, we find examples where these intentions were explicitly frustrated by the judiciary. Such cases highlight the purpose of the separation of the powers. Yet it is no less clear that, in all judicial systems, courts are sensitive to the general wishes of government. As a distinguished academic lawyer, Michael Stolleis, insists: a praxis-oriented jurisprudence acts as a 'mediation between the political and legislative systems'.[4] The issue is the extent to which this mediation involves a damaging compromise with political power.

At all events, legal systems have little option than to be sensitive in this way, since their administrators must see in elected governments and the laws they pass an expression of the public will, and they wish, like governments, to be part of the fabric which advances the stability of society. If this reasonably describes a balancing act required in all societies, the Federal Republic faced a particular problem in the relationship between politics and law, a problem which was the direct result of Germany's dark past. The theme of the role of the law in a new democracy, therefore, remains in the foreground of this whole book.

Between 1933 and 1945 the law conspicuously failed to distance itself from Nazism, and the risk after 1949 was that the 'depoliticizing' of the law would seem a necessary and attractive option. In a democracy, however, not only does the insistence that the law identify itself with democratic principles seem essential, but the detachment of the law from those principles seems dangerous. By 'democracy' of course its advocates mean no mere formalistic identification with the state – i.e. loyalty to the state as state, represented, for instance, in the executive –, but a commitment to the explicitly democratic features of the state and a readiness to identify potential democratic deficits in the law and to overcome them. Conservative elements in the legal profession will interpret such attitudes as a politicization of the law and therefore warn against them. The danger of the Constitutional Court's *Lüth* judgment (see Chapter Three) was that the court's commitment to the Basic Law could be seen as a mere formula, not as a recognition of the need for the law to embark on a process of democratic action. In particular Chapter Eight discusses a series of cases in

4 Stolleis (2001, p. 145).

which tokenism of this kind can be seen at work, and where 'democracy' was defended by means of legal instruments which were clearly not in the spirit of the Basic Law.

Such considerations lie behind the wide range of the trials dealt with in this book. Overtly political cases (involving basic human rights, freedom of political opinion and the right to form political parties) rub shoulders with criminal cases and those celebrated actions which have established the rights of homosexuals and women's right to abortion. In these areas the law had to catch up the considerable democratic deficit left behind by the NS years. Across the whole range, however, we can identify a further common feature, namely the distinctive situation of the Federal Republic, placed in the middle of Europe on the geographical fault-line between the Communist world and Western liberal capitalism. This shaped many of the trials, just as it marked the whole of the post-war period.

The relationship between the law and the government of Chancellor Konrad Adenauer constantly shows up the difficulties brought about by the Federal Republic's geopolitical situation. Adenauer was the strong man of the first fourteen years of the Federal Republic (1949–1963), responsible for forcing through the Republic's integration into the West and building up its economy on largely traditional lines. For the first years of his Chancellorship the German legal code had to co-exist with the considerable legal powers of the Allies, conferred by the Statute of Occupation. Under this statute the Allies had the power of direct intervention in the legal affairs of the state. Yet, even long after the Statute had lapsed, the Federal Republic's international position continued to colour the administration of justice.[5] We see this, for instance, as social tension rose during the late 1960s in the generational conflict between those born in and just after the war and those whose adult experience included the NS years. It recurred in the deep polarization of society caused by urban terrorism and by the spread of a type of socialism with affinities to the official ideology of the German Democratic Republic, on the other side of the Iron Curtain.[6] Without the position of the Federal Republic in a divided Europe, these local crises would have looked very different.

As we suggested above, some of the trials analyzed in later chapters demonstrate the participation of the Federal Republic in trends common to many

5 The Allied Control Commission laws can quickly be traced in Wikipedia. The Soviet Union withdrew from the Commission in March 1948. See: Benz (2009, pp. 199–208).

6 Dirk Blasius (1983, p. 8 f) argued (at a sensitive time for such a topic, when left-wing critiques of the system were prevalent) that the justice system's relationship to crimes against the state 'is one of the taboo areas in legal history'. As we shall see in later chapters, there are many possible explanations.

western countries. But that fact is not without significance: it amounts to an important symptom of deep historical change in Germany. One of the principal motivations represented in the foundation of the Federal Republic was that, perhaps for the first time in their history, the Germans accepted their country's participation in general movements and ceased to wish to be a special case, outside European norms. This acceptance represented a significant political and cultural change and was reflected in the intense debates which took place from the mid-1950s on the topic of modernity. These were not just cultural or artistic discussions, but a struggle for the soul of the country.[7]

A major symptom of change is the way many German thinkers stopped categorizing democracy as 'un-German': in other words, they abandoned Germany's special route in history, the *Sonderweg*. Although this might seem an obvious requirement for the Federal Republic's survival, the topic was raised constantly during the so-called *Historikerstreit* in the 1970s, when the resistance to this change was particularly visible.[8]

Notwithstanding the Europeanization of German thinking and culture, the trials in this book raise issues distinctive, if not exclusive, to the Federal Republic. It is unthinkable that this book would not include two trials concerned with the crimes of the NS past: the first conducted by the victorious Allies (including the Soviet Union) in Nuremberg from November 1945; the second represented by the famous Auschwitz trial in Frankfurt am Main in 1963, at which for the first time, if belatedly, German authorities faced up to their responsibility to prosecute those actively engaged in running the death-camps and hence to confront the involvement of ordinary Germans in the genocide. Environmental law features in a later series of cases (Chapter Ten), while the final trial focuses on the efforts of the law to come to grips with the violence of the neo-Nazi right, which has become so prominent since unification. Regrettably, however, neither environmental threat nor neo-Nazi violence is a problem confined to the Federal Republic.

To approach the law from a historical perspective brings out a particular paradox. On one hand the law presents itself as a hermetic institution, whose development through time seems to be distinct from that of other institutions. It's hardly surprising that the great student of self-contained systems, the sociologist Niklas Luhmann,[9] has devoted so much energy to the study of the law. It follows that, when one chronicles the development of the law over the

7 See: Kießling (2012, esp. pp. 313–58). Dahrendorf (1968) is often seen as the authoritative statement of the change in FRG identity.

8 See: Kocka (1988).

9 Luhmann (2008).

years of the Federal Republic, what emerges is a story whose outlines roughly match those of a conventional historical and political survey, but which at times shows a different momentum and different emphases. The story of the law includes the initial continuity with Nazism, followed by the gradual dying out of old Nazis in the judiciary and the justice ministries – a process, however, which did nothing to weaken the inborn conservatism of the legal profession as a tradition-conscious social elite. It's not necessary to argue for the existence of an unbroken authoritarian tradition of law in Germany. We need to observe what Richard F. Wetzell calls 'more complex continuities in German legal history'.[10] The attitudes of the legal profession continued largely undisturbed by the pressures of the world outside. Many of the political slogans of these years – from de-nazification to the call for reform and Willy Brandt's demand for 'more democracy' – had greater impact outside than inside the legal profession. Lawyers and judges managed to justify their conservatism by arguing that the objectivity and impartiality of the law required that it be defended against all change, particularly change of a 'political' kind.

At the same time, as we shall see, the law is not self-contained. It possesses an extraordinarily wide area of contact with all aspects of life and society. From the normal to the exceptional circumstances of an individual's life, from private to collective and corporate action, in good and in bad times, the law is involved in every life, from the cradle to the grave. The historical study of the law writes the history of a particular time by showing how an existing corpus of law and legal procedures has dealt with the varied historical and political events of the time. Such history does not neglect significant reforms and innovations within the law as system, but its main focus will lie on observing the relationship between a more or less stable institution and the cases which come its way. If we were to take up an image often used by observers of the law, we would say: the way in which the machine of the law processes its raw material – the pile of outcomes which is its product – amounts to a history of the period, and it is this history we tell here.

0.2 The Centrality of Law after the Collapse of 1945

The history of the Federal Republic depends more closely on the behavior of its courts than we might claim for other western democracies. This is due in part to the fact that the state began its life in the most unfavorable of circumstances,

10 Wetzell (2008, p. 15).

and that a crucial element in the survival and consolidation of the state was the strengthening of its formal structures.

The Federal Republic's initial problems lay in every area of its activity. Politically the Federal Republic tried to make itself the spokesman of all German territory (this was the so-called Hallstein doctrine), consistently rejecting the claim to sovereignty and representation put forward by the German Democratic Republic, the state created by the Soviet Union out of its zone of occupation in the east of Germany. By doing so, however, the Federal Republic all too easily became identified as the successor-state to the thirteen years of NS rule, a regime discredited throughout the world for its wars of aggression and its genocides.[11]

Unsurprisingly the first significant post-war acts in that part of Germany occupied by the three Western Allies which was to become the Federal Republic were trials, rather than summary executions or simple retribution. By staging the Nuremberg trials, at which some of the most important NS war-criminals were sentenced, the centrality of law was indelibly marked. Dealing with the toxic legacy of Nazism was, initially therefore, a legal matter, international in character, but nevertheless held on German soil. Not only was Germany a pariah state – in modern parlance, a 'failed' state –: it seemed to possess little chance of changing its status. The Federal Republic inherited no democratic parliament or party system, little enough experience in administering a democracy, no free press and only restricted opportunities for regional democracy, following the Nazis' radical centralization of the country. The political outlook was not good when the Federal Republic came into being.

Economically, West Germany appeared in ruins in 1945. Hitler's deliberately chosen policy of total war had brought about not only military defeat on an unimaginable scale, but the physical devastation of the country and its cities; massive civilian as well as military casualties, further depleting a work-force propped up during the war-years by slave-labour drawn from the occupied territories, while the scientific establishment had been fatally weakened by the antisemitism and intolerance of the Hitler state, which had driven world-class researchers into exile in the UK and the USA and had greatly weakened Germany's economic prospects.

Culturally, the twelve years of Hitler's rule had been a period of all but complete sterility, devoid of creativity and lacking thinkers capable of working outside the worthless clichés of NS ideology. The talents which had made the years of the Weimar Republic (1919–1933) a time of exciting cultural and intellectual innovation had been forced out of the country, and it was far from clear

---

11 See: Perels (2008, p. 136 f).

after 1945 that many of them were in any way anxious to return. Culturally the Federal Republic had a difficult birth.[12]

The situation at the end of the war is often described as the *Stunde Null*: a zero hour. This is understood as a moment of such negativity that history came to a standstill and had to be started afresh. Above all, Germany needed stabilizing institutions. With the approval of the newly formed parliament and more importantly with the consent of the occupying powers (France, Britain and the USA) the Federal Republic gave itself a provisional, make-shift constitution – the *Grundgesetz*, Basic Law –, set up by the all-party Parliamentary Council, but after that it was the responsibility of the forces of law, the police and the courts, together with the whole legal profession and the parliament, to restore the law to its proper place as such a force of stability in a democracy.

This was never going to be easy. Before 1945 the apparatus of the law had not only faithfully implemented the little legislation enacted under Hitler – such as the Nuremberg race laws of 1938 – and had not only massively encouraged the imposition of death-penalties on 'enemies of the state', giving to the so-called People's Court the function of a propaganda show-case for the equation of the law with the 'will of the Führer', but the apparatus of the law had wilfully shut its eyes to the operations of the secret police and to the administration of the concentration camps, and had foolishly imagined that, in doing so, it had preserved its own integrity. What happened in these dark places was explicitly ignored by the law, while the fact that many day-to-day features and practices of the law continued unchanged after 1933 did little more than provide an alibi function for a regime which despised and openly flaunted all the basic principles of the law. So there was a great need, but little realistic expectation – Frei speaks tellingly of 'an indolent justice system'[13] –, for the law to find the power to reform itself after 1945 and to play its part in the transformation of West Germany. An unfortunate light was shed on the seriousness of such reform with the appointment – as late as the mid-1960s – of Eduard Dreher, one time judge in a NS 'special court', to head up the commission for criminal law reform in the 1960s. It's understandable that the legal historian Requate describes the legal profession as one of the few 'winners' in 1945.[14] The trials discussed in this book illustrate, perhaps in less blatant ways, the success and the failures of aspiration in its battle with inertia and self-interest.

12 More details of Germany's cultural difficulties in the Third Reich and their effect on the Federal Republic are given in the course of Chapter Three.

13 Frei (1999, p. 23).

14 Requate (2008, p. 28). Also: Wittmann (2006, p. 212). Diestelkamp points out that not a single NS judge was punished in a Federal German court (1988, p. 133).

The second effect of taking an historically based approach casts an unusual light on a familiar critique of the law. Its implications are by no means confined to Germany, for it goes back to the mid-nineteenth century and to Karl Marx, and under other names much further back. The concept of class-justice – *Klassenjustiz* – has been repeatedly used during the Federal Republic to characterize many of the cases we discuss, and, although the word itself perhaps grates in a post-Communist world, its truth remains quite unproblematic. Indeed, it reflects something obvious, a position shared by anyone with experience of the law. In the midst of the student unrest of the 1970s, for instance, the Nobel Prize winning Catholic novelist Heinrich Böll characterized the situation in Germany in a striking way, which exactly illustrates my argument here. Böll described a violent street demonstration, such as was routine in these years: on one side we saw the 'radical' students protesting about 'class-justice' on angry placards, which the police struggled to confiscate as they cleared the streets. On the other side stood the ranks of the police force, some ninety percent of whom – according to a survey which had recently been published in the magazine of the police union – were convinced that the rich got off more lightly in court. It seemed as if the forces of law and order were no more persuaded of the positive social effects of the law than were the students. What divided society at that point, Böll therefore argued, was words, not realities. Rather than fighting 'Marxist' students, the police should have made common cause with them in the name of democracy and overcome the bias built into the law.[15]

Marx took the view that the law was part of the superstructure of society, reflecting the power relations at society's base and therefore affirming those relations and lending them permanence. Like religion and culture, the law reinforced and legitimized existing structures of power. This is a perennial argument, and I've expressed it simplistically here; I hope, however, not as simplistically as the Baader-Meinhof group, who murdered judges and lawyers in protest at what they called class justice.[16] We need to remember, however, that during the 1960s and 1970s the revival of Marxist thinking – which happened both in Europe and in the USA (to say nothing of Latin America), but regrettably not in the Soviet Union – was accompanied by far more subtle arguments than the truism that the rich get off more lightly in court. A sophisticated left-centred critique of the law characterized the generation of lawyers which came out of the student revolt of 1968, and was reflected not only in the person

15 Böll (1973, p. 243 f).

16 The reference is to the murders of Drenkmann and Buback (see Chapter 9). In the early 1970s some courts imposed fines on defendants who referred to class justice in their defence. See: Requate (2008, p. 270).

of radical lawyers such as Horst Mahler who became actively involved with the Baader-Meinhof group, but in many lawyers whose involvement was with the human rights' issues involved in the so-called 'terrorist trials': here names such as Heinrich Hannover, Kurt Groenewold and Otto Schily come to mind. The history of Marxist thinking is also part of that of the Federal Republic and is reflected in some of the cases discussed here.

Nevertheless, combining legal and political history, as I try to do here, means that the stabilizing property of the law is seen in a positive light which risks becoming uncritical. Not only was the law one institution with the power gradually to pull the Federal Republic out of the chaos of the *Stunde Null*: it was possible for the law to bask in that role and not to reform itself. No-one has done more to expose the unreformed state of the law in the early years of the state than the historian Norbert Frei, yet he shows clearly how – beyond the rather depressing re-installation of 'the economy and the military' – 'restoration' (the term used to emphasize the failure of radical change after the NS period) was in fact 'a many sided, bitterly ironic consequence of the *Rechtsstaat*'.[17] In other words, the restoration of the rule of law inevitably brought with it a restitution of the basic features of a class-society, as well as the re-establishment of a type of abstract authority which did not depend on its service to the public good. This is reflected in a typical remark by a law professor in the late 1940s. 'As we look over Germany's fate in the last twenty years,' he wrote, 'it is clear that we need a powerful system of penal law which respects moral values.'[18] The authoritarianism of the remark and its potential distance from democratic law needs no further comment.

At various times in the development of the Federal Republic, there were different reasons why this trend was not more vigorously opposed. We might point to the compromise made in Bad Godesberg by the SPD when they revised the party programme in 1959 and thereby accepted significant features of western capitalism, or to the spectacle of the supposedly Marxist state in the East corrupting the law into merely legitimating the interests of a narrow power clique represented in the party hierarchy. The circumstances of German unification in 1990 were also hardly conducive to a rethink of the direction of West German development. Confronted with these trends, the public found the students' response to class-justice less than attractive and dreams were left unfulfilled.

---

17 Frei's (1999, p. 93). The remark on the restoration of the economy and the military is from the journalist Eugen Kogon from 1962 (the time of the *Spiegel*-Affair), quoted in: Kießling (2012, p. 287).

18 Quoted in: Herbert (2002, p. 25).

In any event, as is illustrated clearly by the trial discussed in Chapter Two, there are more pragmatic reasons to question the function of law than simplistic arguments about the superstructure. In the course of that case, it became clear that major legislation aimed at banning oppositional political parties – pre-eminently the Communists – was less effective in achieving the goal of the Adenauer government than administrative measures. Since these measures were not fully debated, they operated under the radar of parliamentary reflection. On one hand this tactic brought less embarrassment to Adenauer than major legislation, which would easily be portrayed as 'repressive'. On the other hand, it is a reminder to the historian to look closely at the relationship between laws controlling big issues and the actual smaller-scale administrative practice of state institutions. It's not just making laws which affects the lives of citizens – it's the small print of official policies and the way these are administered. Sadly it is much easier to change a law than to erase the continuities with an undemocratic past which exist within the administrative style of a successor state. We can see this with particular clarity in the behaviour of the police and secret services at least during the 1950s and beyond, as a number of the trials discussed in this book will make clear.

0.3 Institutional Structures in German Law: Basic Law and the Federal Constitutional Court

The Basic Law itself, for all its novelty and short evolution, was deeply rooted in previous German constitutional law. It was the product of a small group – spun-off during the founding of the so-called Parliamentary Council, the all-party body which was responsible for establishing the Federal Republic. The Council was made up of representatives of the federal states and the political parties (including, incidentally, the Communists) and it convened a group out of its own numbers, with the addition of legal experts and a number of senior civil servants, with the explicit task of developing what was defined from the start as a temporary constitution, waiting for German re-unification before a more permanent constitution was created. Their initial work took a mere thirteen days, from August 10 1948. This group was evidently not working from a blank sheet – many features of the Basic Law can be found in the Weimar Constitution and in the earlier constitutions of individual federal states –, but in a remarkably short time the group had produced a document which was subsequently approved by the military governors, by the Parliamentary Council itself (with amendments) and by the federal states – with the exception of Bavaria. (The habit of the Bavarian state government to oppose

Federal government measures – even those proposed by Adenauer's CDU, which has remained coalition partner to the Bavarian CSU – is a feature not just of recent times. It goes right back to the days before the foundation of the Federal Republic.) The Basic Law gave particular prominence to the rights of the individual citizen and created the institution which became the Federal Constitutional Court, the *Bundesverfassungsgericht* (subsequently referred to here as the BVerfG). The precise details of the court were subsequently established by the first elected parliament of the Federal Republic, and the court began its work on September 7 1951.

Nothing better illustrates the central place of the law in the early years of the Federal Republic than the role and function of this court. It was to be situated in the city of Karlsruhe – a move to the provinces in which some commentators see an early (and ultimately unsuccessful) attempt by Adenauer to prevent the court from assuming too much political prestige. Since the BVerfG was explicitly charged with judicial review – i.e. testing the constitutionality of the decisions of the federal and regional legislatures and of the lesser courts (including the courts of the individual federal states) –, the court occupied a crucial position in the rebuilding of the West German state. Its prestige was not merely a result of constitutional arrangements, but was increased by the fact that it was a new court, untainted by participation in the events of the NS years.

The power of judicial review had been only a minimal part of the mandate of the *Reichsgericht*, the supreme court in Leipzig during the Weimar Republic, and it had never fully been incorporated into the wider traditions of German law. The *Reichsgericht*, as legal historians point out, had on occasion expressed the need for such review (it would have been interesting to see how it might have reacted to the emergency decrees by which Brüning had governed after 1930), but it had lacked the power to carry through its wishes. So it's possible that, without the hiatus of the NS years, the German legal system might have introduced some form of judicial review anyway.

It's important to mention that fact because, although the US Supreme Court – along with the Austrian Supreme Court, whose structure the BVerfG followed in not taking on full appellate function – obviously served as a model for many features of the BVerfG, the court was by no means alien to German judicial traditions. Despite much criticism of its existence and judgments during its subsequent history, the court was seldom regarded either as an American imposition on the country or as an unconsidered over-reaction to Germany's humiliation during the NS years. Despite controversies, the BVerfG steadily gained acceptance across the political spectrum, as well as from those levels of the judiciary whose position and power had been diminished by the creation of the new court. Historians are agreed in seeing the *Lüth* judgment, the third of the cases in the following chapters, as the moment when the BVerfG established its primacy.

Since the 1970s there has been much discussion as to whether the BVerfG has become too powerful in the Federal Republic – the phrase 'Karlsruhe Republic' is sometimes used to indicate that and to suggest that the court's power tends to overshadow more central elements of democracy, such as the elected parliament. It has not been helpful for the image of parliament or of the court that the opposition got into the habit of threatening to appeal to the BVerfG any government policy which it did not like, rather than trusting the elected legislature to resolve conflicts of interest and opinion by parliamentary means. The fact that the BVerfG's judgments cannot be appealed has also tended to undermine the position of regional courts, and especially that of the federal appeal court, the *Bundesgerichtshof* (Federal Court of Justice, BGH). This court, founded in 1900, would have expected to be the senior court of the Federal Republic.[19]

As in the US Supreme Court, the nomination of the judges to the BVerfG was subject to parliamentary control – in this case such control was mediated through the *Bundesrat*, the Federal Council, which was made up of representatives of the Federal parliament and of the individual states. It followed that, just as in the American example, the process of achieving a balance of opinion among the judges became contentious at various points in the life of the court, seldom more so, for instance, than at the start and during the abortion debates of the 1970s. But already on many occasions in the 1950s the Federal government was in major disagreement with the BVerfG, notably when it had been formally requested by the President to rule on the constitutionality of Germany's rearmament, initially in the context of the proposed European Defence Community.[20] The then minister for justice, Eduard Dreher (FDP), was openly contemptuous of the court, challenging its right to scrutinize government policy. In view of such controversies, the court itself was mindful of the need to gain acceptance, not merely from the public at large, but from other parts of the judicial system, and from the political institutions of the

19 The BGH had a profound effect on the prosecution of NS criminals, as we examine in Chapter 7. Another example of their power was their deliberate sabotage of the first case brought by ZSL. See Weinke (2008, p. 32). Also: Godau-Schüttke (2008).

20 After about two years during which the BVerfG worked nearly full time on the issue, the French national assembly rejected the proposed EDC anyway. Similar issues were raised by the Federal Republic's proposed entry to NATO in 1955. It was in the earlier context that Dreher's immoderate attacks on the BVerfG were made.

state. The court did not wish to be marginalized as an outsider in the determination of the nation's future.

Gradually, with reluctant compromises by a number of the parties, a working relationship was established. It's interesting to observe that, as the court's position became more secure, the fact that the CDU had managed to get a majority of its nominees in both divisions of the BVerfG seemed less important than in the early years. By then, the court had developed its own momentum, and its judges assumed a more risk-taking attitude towards the court's relationship to the political establishment: in 2001, for instance, a distinguished BVerfG judge, looking back over the first fifty years of the court, could proudly emphasize the difference between the constitution, as the court interpreted it, and the law, for which other courts were responsible. He argued that, by increasing the gap between the two through its judgments, the BVerfG had in fact been able to create a much wider area for legitimate political debate and action than in a situation where there would have been no tension between the constitution and the legal codes. In this way, the court had intervened in the political sphere, but its intervention had been productive of democratic debate. That is an argument typical of an established and consolidated court, not of a court in its infant stage.[21]

Whatever else the history of the BVerfG shows, the terms of its establishment demonstrate the danger of excessive promises of overnight democratic change. An impossible burden of cases afflicted the court's business from the start: not just the continual need to test the decisions of a new state for their constitutionality, but the fact that every citizen was given the right – without needing to go through a solicitor or any preliminary legal steps – to bring a complaint of unconstitutional treatment (*Verfassungsbeschwerde*) to the court's attention. Very shortly after its foundation, therefore, the court was overwhelmed with work and in consequence often unable to respond even to major issues in less than five or six years. Despite the luminaries sitting on the benches of its two divisions, its actual judgments often depended on the work of junior, sometimes temporary legal staff.

The title 'constitutional court' indicates the centre of gravity of the BVerfG's work. But we need to remember that, although the *Grundgesetz* does not include specific reference to all features of the law (notably excluding criminal and commercial law), the clear intention of its formulators was that it should represent a new spirit which would permeate all areas of national life and

21 Grimm (2001, p. 314): 'If the difference in level between the constitution and the law is ever surrendered, then the room for manoeuvre in the political field is narrowed by the same degree'.

therefore all areas of the law. The BVerfG therefore found itself involved in a huge range of issues which, in other legal systems, might not be identified as constitutional, including for instance: the internal regulation of universities and the acceptability of nuclear power. Justin Collings' detailed history of the court illustrates that range across the court's first sixty years. In fact, the BVerfG intervened directly in no less than six of the cases in this book, and indirectly in three others. But I don't wish to repeat Collings' work and while, understandably, at the very start of the Federal Republic's existence, constitutional law is the emphasis of the trials which we consider, my focus consciously moves away from formal constitutional issues. The first two trials discussed here which were eventually heard before the BVerfG (Chapters Two and Three) belong together, not because of their intrinsic subject-matter, but because they illustrate two strikingly different basic positions which the BVerfG adopted and from which one can generalize for much of the Republic's life-time. I repeat, however, that this book is not an institutional history of the BVerfG.

0.4 Statute Rather Than Common Law

These unusual developmental factors took place within a system which already possessed features which may be unfamiliar to English-language readers, in that the system significantly differs from the judicial structures of Britain, Ireland or the USA. American readers will have no difficulty with the structures of a judicial system within a federal state and will be familiar enough with the potential for conflict between federal and regional courts. The Federal Republic comprised eleven federal states before unification in 1990 (after unification the number rose to sixteen), each with its own legislature, courts and legislation. These federally based courts ranged in both constitution and specialization, from criminal and civil courts to labour and administrative courts. At a federal level, the BGH represents a final criminal court of appeal for the whole of the Republic, and the federal labour and administrative courts operate as appeal courts within their specializations.

This complex structure has an immediate consequence. Both before and after unification there has inevitably been a much higher number of judges in the Federal Republic than might be expected from comparisons with similarly sized countries. As a result, perhaps too because they appear to act like a grade of the civil service, judges do not always enjoy the same prestige and respect as in other systems. Furthermore, because they have not risen through the ranks, judges often lack any fellow-feeling with the attorneys they encounter in court, and may have no experience of practice. All this means that judges tend to be of a conservative frame of mind, thinking more of the paragraphs of the law than of the realities of the human situations played out before them. We might think of their attitudes as 'minimalist', supine: untrained in the responsibility involved in judge-made law. Some legal historians have suggested that the career structures for judges mean that they tend to stay close to their political masters and thus 'encourage adaptations to the reigning political climate'.[22] If this is so, however, it is far from unique to judges in the Federal Republic.

We will refer to other, less important particularities of the Federal Republic's legal system as we go along, but at this point a fundamental difference between many English-language law systems and the German tradition should be identified: that between common and statute law. These differences will emerge from my account of individual cases, but they are so fundamental that they should at least be named here. Indeed, formal accounts of the German legal system invariably begin with such a discussion.

The ambition of the Federal Republic was, as I said earlier, to re-establish itself as what is called a *Rechtsstaat*. This concept has a double meaning. It means first a state in which the rule of law prevails, i.e. a constitutional state. In its worst nineteenth-century forms the word describes a state in which law replaced democracy. Secondly it refers to a state in which codified law exists for all areas of life. This understanding of the law has implications which reach far beyond the observation that the Federal Republic possesses, in contradistinction to Britain, a written constitution, for it influences not only the self-understanding of the courts and of judges in particular (as we shall see in the chapters which follow), but also everyday life in the country.

I will never forget the sight of my friend, a university administrator, sitting at his desk with several volumes of Bavarian University Law on a shelf behind him. That metre of law-books was a direct sign of the *Rechtsstaat* operating as a 'gapless' system of legal propositions. Without implying that British or Irish universities operate beyond the law (although many of them hold to the erroneous view that it is their prerogative to make law for their own institutions, as if they operated outside existing legislation), it is inconceivable that a university administrator in these countries would understand his or her relationship to the law in the way my friend did – still less likely that such an administrator would be able even to *find* bound volumes of law about the university system in which he or she worked. Common law operates on the basis of a fundamentally different assumption, whereas the statute law practised in the *Rechtsstaat* operates on the basis that all areas of business or public life need to be ordered by a codified system. For that reason a high percentage of public servants in

22 Cit. Prantl (1996, p. 360).

the Federal Republic are former students of law – and for just that reason German universities' law departments study much more administrative law than is the case in educational systems which see the study of the law primarily as a training for the professions of solicitor and barrister. (Incidentally, that distinction is one which the German system does not recognize, and judges follow a separate career structure.)

Within this system a further important development took place in the work of the BVerfG. In the course of the years the court saw something approaching a seismic shift in function of its judges. The general tradition of codified German law is that the administration of justice consists of the identification and implementation of existing laws and of their application to individual cases. Accordingly within such a system judges apply the law and seldom develop it, let alone make new law.

Opinions are divided about the desirability of this tradition of legal positivism. Some historians have claimed that it was responsible for the readiness of judges and lawyers to administer the NS legal codes despite the manifest injustice of those codes. It was argued that, since their job had never been understood as involving anything other than the application of a set of laws, regardless of their content, German judges were well prepared for that dishonourable role. 'Obedience to the law had made the judges defenceless', Michael Stolleis wrote in his authoritative study of the legal system in the Third Reich.[23] The law had not required judges to take overall responsibility for a wider and all-embracing understanding of the law. (Other historians regard this explanation as little more than an excuse: in their eyes, so many German judges supported Nazism because they were profoundly conservative and agreed with most of what the Nazis wanted.)

Whatever the truth of such claims, the positivism of the judicial system has had a major influence on the legal education offered in German universities, a tradition which seemed almost mechanistic to observers from the American-English system, and which until the end of the 1960s had hardly changed since the nineteenth century. It is significant, for instance, that the study of individual cases was far less prominent in German legal education than in other systems and the historical-social dimension of the law remained greatly underrepresented. Only the events of 1968 began to introduce significantly new elements into legal education, both in the curriculum and more importantly in the overall approach taken by a law degree. Obviously such innovations take time to affect the practical working of the legal system itself.

---

23 Stolleis (2005, p. 297).

The BVerfG required more from its judges than the positivistic application of existing codes. § 93 of the Basic Law explicitly empowers the court to measure individual laws with greater authority than what was merely recorded in the criminal and civic codes.[24] They were to act in their own responsibility. This conferred on the judges the task of creating unity and cohesion within the new constitution, recognizing that their position involved them not merely in a process of logical application, but in an activity with an explicit constructive purpose which went beyond the existing paragraphs. The court was challenged to mould its judgments so as to give substance to the constitution. In the specialist literature this task is identified as a *teleological* activity, not just a interpretative one. Its judges were expected to look at the Basic Law not as a mere *corpus*, like the BGB or the penal code: their function was to bring the Basic Law into reality. The novelty of this requirement underlines the reason why judicial review had never formed part of the German tradition. Once a law was there, judges were not used to looking beyond it.

The more the BVerfG developed, the more the judges were obliged to *make*, rather than merely to implement law. In the immediate post-war period there were excellent reasons to be wary about such an enhancement of judicial power. The vast majority of legal personnel in post-1945 Germany had been positively involved in administering NS justice, and in the meetings of the Parliamentary Council the SPD had expressed an understandable unease at the creation of a court in which judges with such questionable personal histories were to be given still wider powers. The party demanded that the BVerfG should therefore have the possibility of issuing dissenting opinions (on the American model), for they saw such a measure as a safeguard against the likely railroading of decisions by an ideologically suspect majority on the bench. The Party's demand was rejected – a sign of insecure times, for it was believed to be so essential for the BVerfG to establish its authority that it should always speak with only one voice. In practice, however, the SPD's worries did not materialize. It proved possible considerably to reduce the percentage of judges serving the BVerfG who were compromised by their NS past. As judges returned from the exile in which they had spent the NS years or from the retirement into which their 'ethnic status' had forced them, the percentage inside the BVerfG of judges with a questionable past remained low, and in consequence the background of the BVerfG judges seldom raised problems with their judgments. When they were controversial, it was for going beyond the letter of the law.

24 The BVerfG is governed by a number of paragraphs of the GG – the *Spiegel* series in the midst of the crisis of the 1970s listed esp. §§ 18,21,41,61,93,98,100 (not including provisions for the constitutional complaint). *Der Spiegel* 45/1978, p. 78 f.

0.5 Anomalies in a Changing Legal Code

The embedding of legal thinking into the administration has one further important effect beyond that of simply making the system more rigid. It causes problems in managing change, which show themselves in two areas of the law. Everyone can see the importance of precedence in forming legal judgments – although it is accepted that statute law does not recognize 'any binding rule of precedent'.[25] The very concept, however, depends for its plausibility on a certain continuity of legislation and on social stability. Legal security, the eminent sociologist Norbert Elias writes, 'depends partly on the law's resistance to change'.[26] This feature of the law is thrown into question in times of radical political change. The history of West German jurisprudence after 1949 highlights the existence and the importance of anachronistic and anomalous elements within the written code.

In stable societies anomalies of this kind are unimportant. Although new legislation will normally include provision for the annulling of previous legislation, departures from this practice will not have serious consequences. Indeed, many legal systems draw prestige and occasionally some humour from those redundant elements which remain within them as anachronisms, usually dormant. These elements seldom feature actively in any litigation process, but, never having been repealed, they can emerge suddenly in certain circumstances. It can become clear, for instance, that an ancient society still has the right to drive sheep down a public highway, and in occasional cases it becomes clear that the law has not been adjusted to meet modern circumstances, for instance from the many cases when legal definitions of intellectual property rights are turned on their head by yet another advance in software technology. A similar cult of anachronism happened when, in a famous London trial in 1990, a learned judge demanded petulantly of defence counsel to know 'Who are the Beatles?'.[27]

In societies which have enjoyed great stability for a long period of time such anomalies are merely amusing – and lawyers have always exploited these anomalies, just as they have enjoyed chronicling the process by which centrally determined laws are 'adapted' and subverted by provincial communities. However, where societies have been subject to radical and violent change

25 Dainow (1966/67, p. 426).

26 Elias (2009, p. 585).

27 Judge Pickles in 2010. The occurrence of legal anomalies in English law was the basis of much of A. P. Herbert's writing (e.g. *Uncommon Law*). For (an occupying power's view of) Irish anomalies see the now all-but forgotten classic accounts of the English 'resident magistrates' in Ireland: Somerville and Ross (1899).

the hiatus of archaic law surviving into a different regime is not amusing, but threatening.

This certainly was the case in Germany, which in the twentieth century experienced three such times of radical change within forty years: the change in 1919 from the authoritarian rule of the *Kaiser* to the unstable and short-lived Weimar democracy (all this happening in the wake of a catastrophically lost war). This was followed in 1933 by the radical shift from democracy to the totalitarian state of the Nazis, which was in turn followed by the abrupt shift to a modern democracy externally imposed on an occupied and divided country, hopelessly defeated in global war. In all these situations chunks of legislation survived the turn-round, and while – regrettably – it does not matter if democratic paragraphs survive into a totalitarian society (for they are simply ignored by a legal system happy to bend all law to the will of the dictator), the survival of authoritarian paragraphs in an age struggling to implement democracy contains real dangers.

In addition, the situation in federal state legislation is still more confusing. The various states had different legislative bases – the *Allgemeines Landrecht* of 1794 had been an attempt to unify the law only in Prussian territories: what happened in other states could be radically different, dependent on the wishes of their individual rulers. We often think of Bavarian law as eccentric, perhaps reactionary, but in some respects it was more liberal than that of other German states, although only for the first half of the nineteenth century. Hitler dissolved the federal states (*Länder*) in 1933: the Allies insisted that the *Grundgesetz* restore a wide measure of autonomy to them. It can be imagined what scope all these changes afforded for anomalies within the legal codes.

In a revolutionary change such as Germany experienced in 1945 one might expect people to be determined to tear up the laws of the old and discredited system and to make a fresh start. (We would not expect that from people in whose eyes the old system had not been discredited, but that's another matter.) In fact, from the start of their occupation of Germany after the war, all the Allies insisted that any legislation which had been used to advance the NS system had to be taken off the books: that was the stipulation of Article 1 of the Allied Control Council, formulated on 20 September 1945 and valid in all four zones of occupation. In the early years of the Federal Republic the wishes of the Allies had to be followed to the letter, and offending chunks of legislation were duly deleted. But this happened reluctantly in some cases, and the attitudes behind the NS legislation often remained unchanged.

The (at times deliberate) confusion existing concerning the validity of old laws is well illustrated in the case of Heinrich Tillessen.[28] Tillessen was

---

28 See Etzel (1992).

arrested as a member of the NSDAP when the Americans occupied Heidelberg in May 1945, but it emerged during his subsequent interrogation that he had been actively involved in one of the most scandalous political murders during the Weimar Republic, that of the Centre politician and minister Matthias Erzberger. (Erzberger's 'crime' in the eyes of the violent right wing had been that he had signed the Treaty of Versailles on behalf of defeated Germany.) Erzberger's murderers had returned from abroad in 1933 and were immediately amnestied by Hitler, and when Tillessen was put on trial for murder in Freiburg in the early autumn of 1946 the court dismissed the charge on the basis of that amnesty, a judgment which was in direct contravention of the Allied Control Council's provisions. The French occupation authorities accordingly dismissed the Freiburg judge and a fresh trial took place in February 1947 in Konstanz, at which Tillessen was duly sentenced for murder and for a crime against humanity – an offence established by law 10 of the Allied Control Council. By 1952, however, his sentence had been suspended and in March 1958 he was pardoned. His case shows the resistance to change on behalf of the NS legal system after 1945 and makes clear that undesirable attitudes would live on in the judicial system of the Federal Republic. The only reason that judicial scandals of this type were not more numerous still was – as Requate soberly comments – that the system completely stopped prosecuting Nazis in the first place. No trials, no scandals.[29]

It is easy to become indignant about such cases, and Norbert Frei's detailed account of the speed with which the Federal Republic passed laws granting amnesty to huge numbers of people found guilty of crimes during the NS years offers almost unlimited cause for such indignation. However, experience suggests that, desirable it may sound, it is neither necessary nor feasible to change every feature of a discredited legislation, least of all to change it all at once. Certain crimes – murder, for instance, or theft and perjury – will need to be similarly identified in any society which wishes to avoid anarchy. It may be that a state does not penalize these crimes in the same manner as its predecessor, or that it offers particular groups of people immunity from prosecution (not to say explicit encouragement and reward) when they commit these crimes against particular sections of the population, but there is little point in changing their actual codification.

Other, essentially political offences sound as if they could not be compatible with different systems of government, but even very different types of society turn out to need a similar definition of these offences, and actually changing the text of the law can seem redundant to a new system. In particular, those

29 Requate (2008, p. 57).

laws explicitly aimed at protecting the state will appeal to all types of political system: an elected politician will wish the law to offer the state protection against treason no less than will the lackeys of a dictator. That's a less than balanced way to describe how in 1951 Adenauer looked to strengthen the legislative armoury of the new republic by re-introducing a range of measures from earlier systems with the intention of protecting both the existence of the state and public order. These measures were incorporated in the first *Strafrechtsänderungsgesetz* (law changing the penal code). The rationale and the practical arguments for this measure, which, as it were, deliberately *created* legal anomalies in the penal code, contained elements which were eminently reasonable. In several of the trials which follow, however, we shall see that these anachronisms, incorporated into a rigidly codified system without regard to the radical nature of the historical change which the Federal Republic had undergone, threatened democratic freedoms (see especially Chapters Eight and Nine).

0.6 History and the Law in the Federal Republic

In many societies there seems to be an automatic affinity between the study of history and the law. In some cases – one thinks of Britain, or the United States – this seems to be due to the historical continuity of a particular legal and political culture. The historians take from the study of the law a sense of the principles on which their society appears to remain founded; the lawyers appreciate the polishing and refining of a legal instrument first formulated centuries before. This seems natural, yet it is impossible to consider the legal system of the Federal Republic without being struck by the dominance of discussions of historical issues taking place within the courts. Already in the last pages we have briefly touched upon the long shadow which the Hitler years cast over jurisprudence in the Federal Republic and the success of the Republic has at least in part depended on its ability to deal with that legacy, however shamefully and slowly that process began. Yet history cast a still more disturbing shadow over the last seventy years: namely, the shadow of the catastrophic failure of the Weimar Republic.

There is scarcely a chapter in this book in which either the legal instruments or the individual judgments of Federal German courts were not influenced by explicit reflection on that historical failure. Those reflections were distinct from any rejection of Nazism as such: the problem which disturbed judges and legislators was the failure of democracy to sustain itself between 1919 and 1933 and the need to work out what part the law played in that failure.

In consequence, legal and political debates, legislators, judges and counsels repeatedly focused on that failure. From the first of the trials in this book onward the work of the courts was focused on the questions: how did the Weimar Republic fail and how could the Federal Republic avoid the same failure? In particular, the BVerfG's deliberations often resembled nothing more than a historians' workshop, and their often lengthy judgments can read like a paper given to an academic conference.[30] Sometimes Michael Biddis' differentiation between the court's duty – 'an historical exercise of judgment' – and an academic 'exercise in historical judgment' can get blurred.[31]

This may seem a paradoxical claim to make. After all, the unmistakable lesson of Weimar appeared to be that democracy's greatest enemy was Nazism. Certainly for the Western Allies there was no more important task than to use the law to put an end to Nazism, and, as we saw, one of their most abiding interventions in Federal German political structures was to strengthen the power of the federal states, as a bulwark against any future totalitarian centralization. One might think that a post-war legal system preoccupied with learning the lessons of the past might have followed that example, for instance by making a more determined effort to remove ex-Nazis from the administration of justice. Yet history seldom teaches lessons unambiguously. From its first Chancellor on, the Federal Republic was obsessed with the danger to democracy from the left, rather than the right. The achievement of the *Rechtsstaat*, of which the early politicians were so proud, has often been parodied to mean not a state governed by law (the word *Recht* means both law and right as opposed to left), but a right-wing state. That this was so reflected the geopolitical situation of the Cold War, but it was also a feature of a system trapped in the double bind of excessive historical reflection. We shall watch this process unfold in the chapters which follow.

The German philosopher Nietzsche, as a young classical scholar writing about the purpose of studying the past, suggested three modes in which it might be productive for succeeding generations to approach the history of

30 Irish readers will be put in mind of the great Foyle Fishery Case, which ran for forty-eight days in the winter of 1947–48, and at which distinguished historians crossed academic swords, enjoying the fact that the lawyers had little option but to follow their arguments. But historians' and legal judgments do not always coincide. In Chapter 8 we examine a range of cases where the distinguished historian from whom an interpretation came – Karl-Dietrich Bracher – was unconvinced of its legal relevance (See Bracher 1976, 1978. Also Duve 1976).

31 Biddis quoted in: Bähr, Drecoll, Gotto, et al. (2008, p. 569).

their world.[32] His ideas apply equally to the acquisition of knowledge of the law. History can have first what Nietzsche calls a 'monumental' aspect, inspiring the present by the greatness of the achievements of the past. There are epic and great legal cases just as there are epic and monumental decisions of state, and these can inspire as much as their military equivalents. The great legal breakthroughs – on slavery, women's rights or justice for Dreyfus – have their place with Willy Brandt on his knees in the Warsaw ghetto or the fall of the Berlin Wall. Law too has its monumental and heroic aspects and people rightly wish to live up to them.

There is a second approach, Nietzsche wrote: something which he called 'antiquarian' history. This is made up of a sense of personal identity with the continuities of the past, a feeling of being rooted in that infinity of small things which build up a community or a profession. For lawyers, the sense of familiarity with particular problems faced in the past, of delight in the subtleties and delicacies of legal thinking and formulation, the sense of sharing a common habit of mind with the lawyers and traditions of the past – these are all part of what Nietzsche meant by the antiquarian. They too can be an inspiration to a younger generation.

But there is finally a type of history which Nietzsche calls 'critical' – the courage to re-think, to redirect tradition into a different course, in a modern phrase to 'move on'.[33] The challenge for the Federal Republic was to move on from Nazism without – as for instance so many of the immediately post-war historians were anxious to – forgetting to deal with the regime's crimes. We shall see aspects of this dilemma in the history of the Federal Republic and its legal system, just as we shall see failures to move on. But it would be crucial to understand German history since the Second World War not just as an unbroken period of success and conformity, or as a German re-conquest of Europe by economic means, but to appreciate the critical potential of which the German legal tradition finally proved itself capable – a potential which had been present in the *Kaiserreich* and in Weimar: a spring which had only half unfolded[34] –, and to take such enthusiasm for challenge and reform into other situations and histories. These positive achievements belong to the law no less than to other sides of human endeavour.

---

32 Nietzsche (1874). I can find no reference to the translator here – a pity, for it is a magnificent essay which should be widely appreciated.

33 The 'moving on' of the early post-war historians, such as Friedrich Meinecke, is discussed by Herbert (2002, p. 19 f); and with special reference to the Holocaust, by: Berg (2002).

34 Cf. Blasius (1983, p. 140).

CHAPTER 1

The Trial of Friedrich Flick

The Nuremberg trials were not conducted according to German law – whatever that phrase may have meant at the end of twelve years of lawlessness. Nevertheless, their history is inseparable from that of the Federal Republic. They hardly mark the end of the malign influence of Nazism in Germany, nor do they stand as the beginning of a period. They were the product of the no-man's-land. But they do mark a frame within which the Federal Republic in its early years related to the Third Reich, and, as we shall examine later in this chapter, the Nuremberg International Military Tribunal marked an important stage within the development of international law. The Tribunal's profound historical importance must ensure its place in this book as the first of a series of significant German cases – the last to be conducted under the aegis of the four occupying powers.

At least in the medium term, the circumstances of the trials did not help to generate any German enthusiasm for the task of coming to legal terms with the legacy of the Hitler years. A significant military defeat can provide the trigger for major social and political change. It was military failure that brought to an end the Romanovs' power in Russia, just as the defeat of 1918 cost the Emperors of both Germany and Austro-Hungary their crowns, and the Allied legal team had hoped that something similar would happen this time.[1] The capitulation of 1945, however, seemed to have been too total to provoke a similarly active response from the German people. Instead, it was left to the victorious allies to take the first moves. They were more than ready for the task, seeing it – in the principal prosecutor Robert H. Jackson's deputy Telford Taylor's idealistic phrase – as a chance 'to give meaning to the war against Germany'.[2]

For some years before the end of the war, the four allied powers had begun to discuss what to do with the leaders of NS Germany. There had been little unanimity as to how to proceed. The differences of opinion reflected less the extent to which the various countries had suffered during the years of the war, and much rather diverging understandings of the effectiveness of legal action in dealing with the wide-scale criminal actions of the NS state. Since everyone was determined that Germany would never again become a threat to the peace of Europe, the treatment of the crimes of the NS state was not merely seen

1 See Taylor (1993, p. 30).

2 *Ibid.* p. 50.

from the point of abstract justice, or even of retribution, or compensation: it had to make sense as part of a re-education of the German people. The need to re-educate the Germans was common to all the allies, even though the Soviet Union and the West hardly agreed on the principles according to which any re-education should take place.

These disagreements had contributed to a feeling among certain allies that the best way to deal with the NS leaders and their crimes was not by means of the formal law, but by summary executions. As late as 1945, for instance, this was the considered opinion of the British War Cabinet and Foreign Office. Stalin was anxious to execute between fifty and one hundred thousand leading figures in the regime. The French were consistently in favour of retributive justice, while the Americans were in two minds. On the one hand the notorious Morgenthau plan envisaged the reduction of the entire German territory to a pre-industrial state and advocated whole-scale executions of all NS leaders – the executions to be carried out by 'firing squads composed of solders of the United Nations'. On the other hand, President Truman and the military command were determined to conduct forensically thorough and judicially correct trials of the figures responsible for the crimes of the NS regime, and to do so in public. In a strange alliance with the Soviet authorities (perhaps looking for a replay of their own Show Trials: it was said that Stalin liked trials so long as someone got shot) this came to be the common policy.

In this consensus, various legal positions were agreed between the allies. The Moscow Declaration of October 1943 'concerning the responsibility of Hitler's followers for atrocities committed' was followed by the London accord of August 1945 'concerning the prosecution and punishment of the major war-criminals of the European Axis powers', and finally by the statues of the Allied Control Commission. These agreements delivered the legal instruments on the basis of which the International Military Tribunal was set up in Nuremberg and confirmed by the United Nations. Here, from November 1945 until October 1946 onwards, the trials of twenty-four prominent leaders of the NS state and military took place. These trials were concerned with major war-criminals, but the list of defendants was oddly unbalanced. There was no trial for the head of the Gestapo (Hermann Müller),[3] while the virulent, pornographic antisemitic journalist Julius Streicher (who from 1940 at the latest had been excluded in disgrace from Party inner circles) stood in dock. There were four counts on the indictment: of criminal conspiracy, crimes against peace, war crimes and of crimes against humanity, as defined in Article 6

3 Müller had vanished at the end of the war, but so had Martin Bormann, and he was sentenced at the IMT.

of the Charter of the International War Tribunal. By and large these trials of major war-criminals achieved results. Many leading figures of the regime were executed, and Hitler's long-time deputy, Hermann Göring, escaped execution only by taking his own life.

Three particular features marked these trials and left behind questions and problems not merely for resentful or revanchist opinion in Germany, already inflamed by the loss of extensive former German territories in the East and West, but for any future German legal system if it were one day to take on the task of bringing to justice the crimes of the NS period. The first question concerned the actual legal basis of the court and its judgments. Naturally, the defence and individual defendants, such as Robert Ley (head of the Labour Front), used every opportunity to question the legitimacy of the Tribunal. In the so-called follow-up trials, which took place a year or so after that of the major war-criminals, these problems became more tangible. In fact, not only the defence but the judges themselves were conscious of the limitations on the court's authority, and their judgments explicitly respected those limitations. The sentencing frequently made clear the existence of a tension between the prosecution's attempts to extract the widest applicability from the legal instruments of the Tribunal, and a much narrower ruling from the bench. Public opinion in America had begun to discuss matters of legitimacy fully before the Tribunal had been established, but in Germany it was not until the early 1950s that the issue of legitimacy was seriously raised in the public sphere. At the time of the trials themselves, the German public had other matters on its mind.

A second, perhaps more grievous problem was that the principal victims of German war crimes were not given a voice in the Nuremberg trials. Both the American and British legal systems are adversarial in structure, based on the opposition of prosecution and defence, rather than explicitly on the establishment of fact as in the inquisitorial system. This meant that neither survivors of the Holocaust, nor the victims of the pillage and destruction which German expansion brought to so much of Europe, nor the huge number of German victims of NS policies had their day in court. In particular, the Jewish people of Europe and what had happened to so many millions of them, were in a certain sense less than central to both phases of the Tribunal's work. Thirdly: since the principal charges against German leaders were that they had conducted a war of aggression against the nations of Europe and had frequently broken the rules of war, as drawn up in the Geneva and Hague conventions (most recently in 1926), the focus of these trials tended to underplay not only the victims, but also the genocide itself. In any case, while a survivor of Treblinka gave testimony to the court, awareness of Auschwitz itself (which Frank claimed to have been outside his jurisdiction) was more limited, even though Rudolf Höss (commandant in Auschwitz) appeared briefly as a witness in Nuremberg, incredibly for the defence.[4] Knowledge of Auschwitz became more widespread after Höss' arrest, trial and execution in April 1946 in Poland.

A final shortcoming of Nuremberg was that, by focusing on major war criminals and on the upper echelons of the NS state, these trials did little to clarify broad questions of the culpability of 'ordinary citizens' within a fundamentally criminal regime. Since this, of all issues, was essential to any meaningful process of re-education, it amounted to a significant failure.

The remainder of this chapter will be concerned with one of the follow-up trials. The International Military Tribunal conducted follow-up cases after the first spectacular sessions at which major war-criminals were tried. After trials dealing with the doctors who carried through NS policies and experimented on concentration camp inmates, and with the lawyers who had been prominent in NS courts, especially in the occupied territories, Nuremberg conducted sixteen further trials: one of them concerned the industrialist Friedrich Flick.

Not only had this second wave of trials to live with the unresolved legal issues of the first, but the political climate in which they were conducted had begun to change significantly. The growing alienation of the two blocs of East and West meant that western powers were increasingly concerned to ensure that any future German state became allied to the West and aligned against the Communist bloc. This meant that the western allies became less interested in punishing many of the functionaries of the military and industrial systems of NS Germany and concerned rather to recruit them to the cause of the West. This happened most markedly in the case of police and security personnel and in the field of military technology, as the career of Werner von Braun shows, with his seamless move from being the inventor of the v1 and v2 rockets to his role as the central figure of US missile and space programmes. Paradoxically, one of the central tenets of the NS state – its anti-communism – had become a defining principle of the western allies, and showed itself in Nuremberg in the attitudes of Jackson. The extent to which these macro-political issues affected the work of the Tribunal has often been debated. Nothing one reads from the trial, however, suggests that the court was consciously following this mission.

4 See Taylor (1993, p. 362). Höss was called by Kaltenbrunner's defence team.

1.1 Understanding the NS State

Some of the deficiencies of the trials against prominent NS war-criminals will re-emerge in other trials discussed in future chapters of this book. In general, however, it was not surprising that the phenomenon of National Socialism was not fully understood before these trials took place. The prosecutors thus faced a particular difficulty: not only that of interpreting actions initiated by a country which was unfamiliar to most of them, but that of interpreting an entire social and political situation which, before the trials began, had lain outside American experience and which had, by virtue of its abrupt collapse, become historical before the trials started. Whatever forensic skills the court required, it also needed to bone up on its historical understanding.

In the years immediately after the war there was a genuine shortage of reliable historical literature interpreting the structures of German fascism. People read two works by defectors from the ranks of the Nazis: Hermann Rauschning (1938), and Franz Neumann's (1942).[5] Neither of these offered a guide to judging the culpability of individuals such as Flick, although Neumann had argued strongly for the general culpability of industry for the rise of Hitler. Among socialist theories of fascism, the most celebrated had been Stalin's disastrous idea that fascism was a natural and essential step in the preparation of the proletarian revolution.[6] Trotsky had been murdered by Stalin's agents for pointing out the fallacy of this theory, which had led to the failure of the Communists and Social Democrats to combine against Hitler before 1933, as well as to the Non-Aggression Pact between Hitler and Stalin in 1939. None of these interpretations of fascism enjoy much credibility today. Any shortcomings in the historical understanding underpinning the prosecution's case were therefore widely shared.

As far as victims were concerned: it would take considerable shifts in attitude before the many types of victims within Germany were identified, let alone felt to be worthy of representation in court. In attitudes towards homosexuals, for instance, (who had constituted a significant number of the victims of the concentration camps) the 1952 prosecution of Alan Turing in Britain would show that the allies were not necessarily more sympathetic or their laws more finely tuned than in NS Germany, even if the severity of the sanctions

5 Neumann directly advised the prosecution team of the IMT. Otherwise much US writing on the Third Reich focused on its intellectual and cultural 'origins' and did nothing to explain the place of people like Flick (or the average civil servant behind their desk) in the NS machine. See for instance: Peter Viereck (2003^2).

6 See: The Tragedy of the German Proletariat (March 1933) and: The German Catastrophe (June 1933), in: Leon Trotsky (1975, pp. 379 f, 397 f).

against homosexuals lay on a different scale. As I mentioned before, witch-hunts against socialists and Marxists (another significant group in the concentration camp population) could hardly be taboo with the opening salvoes of the Cold War being exchanged as the trials proceeded and with McCarthyism on the increase in the USA.

The existence of the state of Israel from 1947 would gradually bring those pressures to bear which made the fate of the Jewish peoples of Europe a matter for the German and European courts: it must be said that, not always for defensible reasons, the allies had done little to initiate action in that direction. The NS campaign against the gypsies was another matter to which European governments were noticeably slow to turn their attention. But there were two areas of German society too important to be ignored – not from the standpoint of the victims (though these were numerous enough), but from the standpoint of their importance to a war of aggression. The first was the military.

The military's importance in the war-crimes cases tried at Nuremberg increased the higher up the hierarchy one looked. While the individual rules of war had most commonly been breached at a subordinate level, the responsibility for that war could be understood only as residing at the top. And in terms of planning, there was clearly a distinction to be made – most of all by the lawyers in military uniform who prepared and conducted the trials in Nuremberg – between high-ranking professional officers who conducted individual military campaigns, performing their duties within traditional guidelines, and those officers who had personally compromised with the killers and ideologues who directed the National Socialist movement and worked most closely with Hitler. It was for that reason that Admiral Dönitz, Raeder and Keitel found themselves on the same bench as Kaltenbrunner (representing the SS), Streicher and Göring.

The second group was the complementary part of what – in an entirely different situation – Eisenhower was to call the 'industrial military complex': namely the industrialists themselves. Just as even the Nazis could not have fought aggressive wars without the support of a professional army, so the need for weaponry, transport and the raw material on which both depended turned allied eyes towards the industrialists as co-equal collaborators with Nazism. Ever since Bismarck had described the foundation of the German Empire in 1871 as being based on 'blood and iron', the dependence of modern states on this industrial-military complex was a truism of social analysis. It had become a journalistic commonplace to see a link between major armament magnates like Krupp and the murderous arsenals which sustained the First World War for so many years, and it was a small step to regard such industrialists as equally responsible for the wars which were fought out with their equipment and which provided them with enhanced profits. Krupp himself had originally been scheduled for trial in the first round at Nuremberg, together with several other industrialists, but the British ruined the plan, in part by muddling up the given name of the Krupp who was indicted. Rather than the active son Alfred, the prosecution charged Gustav, whom everyone knew to be too senile to stand trial.

The view of the responsibility of the industrialists was general across the political spectrum. For socialist thinkers, the seemingly uncontrolled expansionism of industrial capitalism was a natural counterpart to the territorial expansion and war practised by states. After all, the lessons of colonialism in the nineteenth century had pointed to the inseparable link between territorial acquisition and commercial expansion, particularly in the exploitation of raw materials, and the twentieth century appeared to confirm this. For American, British and French patriots the role of Krupp and his ilk in aggressive warmongering needed no further proof.[7]

The Americans had a further reason to put Krupp in the dock. They were too familiar from their own history with the necessity to control the expansion of industrial giants: their long history of anti-Trust legislation (in which the chief prosecutor, Robert H. Jackson, had been deeply involved before the war) was a natural cause of their turning their attention to the massive Trusts which had run essential German industries before and during the war. It was only later on that even American public opinion was made aware that the legal battle against the Trusts placed their lawyers in a similar position to that of the Communists in the East.

But for all that, the trial against Flick was a start, however fumbling. And its inadequacies set the points for much that was to follow.

1.2 Who Was Flick and on What Charges Did He Appear?

Friedrich Flick (1887–1972) was a magnate whose huge empire (known as the 'concern', *Konzern*) crossed the boundaries of the coal, iron and steel industries. His name was less well known than that of Krupp or Thyssen for a simple reason. His empire was a product of the twentieth century, rather than of the nineteenth, and he lacked the social status enjoyed by members of the old

7 Louis Lochner (1954, 188f) gives an interesting counterview of Hitler's connections to German heavy industry. Using Telford Taylor as a source, he suggests that Hitler was uninterested in Flick's support. In any case, Lochner argues, industry is not interested in war: peace and exports are more profitable. The true sycophant to Hitler on this account was Krupp (p. 51f).

elite. As a result, his name was less familiar to European and American observers. Indeed, he was something of an upstart. He bought and dealt his way into a dominant position in the key industries and made the Flick-*Konzern* one of the real power-brokers of the last century.

Flick found himself in the dock at Nuremberg because of his prominence in industries which had been essential to the German war-effort. Energy, munitions, rolling-stock – in all these key areas, without which no modern war could be conducted, the *Konzern* worked its way into dominance. He was seen by the Allied (in this case American) prosecutors as the epitome of the industrial power which had supported Hitler's rise to power and made possible his wars of aggression.

Flick, together with three of his most influential senior managers and one of his cousins, was accused on five charges:

1. active participation in the programme of forced (or slave-) labour, in the course of which large numbers of foreign workers and concentration camp prisoners were drafted into Flick's plants;
2. plundering of factories and natural resources in the occupied territories;
3. active participation in the persecution of Jews through the forced expropriation of Jewish properties;
4. giving financial support to the SS;
5. membership of the SS (a charge brought against only one of the accused, Flick's right-hand man Otto Steinbrinck).

Interest in the Flick case has not been confined to legal historians, nor was the importance of his career diminished at the end of the trial. Flick's influence, and in particular that of his money, has been observed behind a number of party-political scandals throughout the years of the Federal Republic, and for many people his name has remained associated with the darker elements of German politics and industry in the twentieth century. The Flick scandal still reverberates in CDU and SPD circles. Recent historians have successfully untangled the immensely complicated corporate and financial structures on which the *Konzern* was built – a mammoth task in itself and one barely manageable for the prosecutors in the eighteen months at their disposal before the trial opened on March 13 1947. It is possible to look over the stages and strategies of the *Konzern* during its rise to prominence during the years of the Weimar Republic (that is: before Hitler's accession to power in 1933), its mushrooming during the years of NS rule leading up to the outbreak of war in September 1939 and the still greater expansion during the first five years of the war. We cannot reproduce this story here, and even the trial itself – with its 10343 pages of transcript – cannot be treated in any detail: only general principles can be discussed.

Yet to present this trial properly, we must start with a factor which was crucial to the whole event, even though it was based on a presumption of guilt which the court was not obliged to follow. Namely, that on the face of things, no-one could have been more appropriate to face these charges than Flick and his team, especially after the trial of Gustav Krupp had come to nothing. If one were looking (as the Americans and Russians were undoubtedly looking) for a person to epitomize the worst features of German industry across twelve years of NS rule, then they could hardly have been a better example than Flick himself.

To list *the prima facie* case against Flick on these charges makes clear the sense of the prosecution team that they had selected the right target:

1. On slave labour: in individual Flick plants the percentage of slave-labour in the work-force grew from under 1% in February 1942 to some 42% in August 1944. Among this element of Flick's work-force were Italian, French and Polish internees and deportees, Russian prisoners of war and concentration camp inmates. These facts were clearly and explicitly known to Flick and his associates.
2. On plundering: the Flick empire was massively augmented by acquisitions of industrial plant and resources in the wake of German military conquests. Under Flick's control both the Rombach plant in occupied Lorraine and Dnepjr, in the Soviet Union, were committed to German war-production.
3. On the expropriation of Jewish property: in an amazing coup Flick took over the major steel and lignite empire of the Petschek family in Czechoslovakia in 1937–38. He exploited his own personal contacts with Hermann Göring, who had responsibility for the Four Year Plan (a crucial element in the economic preparation for war); he deliberately channelled the antisemitism of the state into pressurizing Petschek to sell his companies, emphasizing that the seizure of his works by the state was the only alternative to a sale to Flick, and he used the international situation – in particular the *Anschluss* of Austria and the threats to Czechoslovakia contained in Hitler's policy on the Sudetenland – to force the Petscheks' hand. At the end of complex negotiations, conducted on Flick's instructions 'with extreme brutality', Flick commented that he had acquired one of the biggest industrial empires in the eastern part of central Europe 'for nothing'.
4. Flick and Otto Steinbrinck were members of the group: Friends of Heinrich Himmler. After a visit to Dachau in 1942, organized by Himmler himself, Flick personally made a contribution of 100 000 RM to the group.

5. Steinbrinck – a highly decorated U-Boot commander from the first world war – was a member of the SS from 1933 to the collapse of the Third Reich. He appears to have been the conduit for collaboration between the SS (responsible, generally, among other things, for the concentration camps) and Flick, both personally and organizationally.

I repeat: if one wanted an identikit picture of an industrialist whom the victorious allies would wish to take to court and make an example of, to act as representative of the sinister alliance between big industry and the Nazis and whose fate would serve as a lesson to re-educate the Germans – in such a search, one would not have to look further than Flick.

1.3 Legal Issues

As legal historians have gone over the case, a number of major questions have been identified. Some, but not all, were clearly identified during the trial; some hung over aspects of the proceedings without being explicitly mentioned, others took on importance only subsequently. But the most immediate had to do with the conduct of trials in the various jurisdictions represented in Nuremberg.

We identify here by way of introduction some of the significant differences in procedure between the traditions of German law and the practices adopted in the Nuremberg trials.

First, the defendants had no right of appeal to a higher court. This was partly a result of the fact that there was no higher court, and partly a product of the fact that the International Military Tribunal was an Allied institution (broadened by the UN into an international dimension), not rooted either in the German national system or in the systems of any of the allies. After sentencing, Flick tried – as Field-Marshal Werner Milch had before him – to appeal to an American higher court, but the American courts refused to recognize their competence in such an appeal. After the principal Nuremberg sentences had been passed they were sent to the Control Commission for ratification, but this was clearly a political, rather than legal or truly appellate body. The absence of a jury in these trials departed from Anglo-American practice, but not from the German legal tradition.

Secondly, there was no consensus concerning the relationship between international law and the individual. International law was traditionally understood to bind *nations* to certain codes of behaviour. The basic question of how a national, collective guilt could be transferred to individuals who were not part of that state had not been resolved. In general, the behaviour of individuals was not regarded as an appropriate topic for international law. Furthermore, the rules of war as traditionally formulated did not envisage the situation universally prevailing during Hitler's wars: namely that not just military personnel, but also non-combatants could commit war crimes. The fact that, in any case, Hitler had had nothing but contempt for international law, did nothing to prevent Flick's legal team from trying to argue from international law, insisting, for instance, that, since the Soviet Union had not been a signatory to the Hague convention on the rules of war, there was no framework of international law which could be applied to the events taking place during the Russian campaign. More questionably still, the defence insisted that only Hitler could be held responsible for the crimes of those years, and that he should have protected his subordinates: 'whoever establishes legal obligations must protect compliance with them', defence counsel Dix argued. The court, however, acted according to the so-called 'Nuremberg Principle', which established that immunity from prosecution could not be based on the mere fact of acting on superior orders. Responsibility had to be more closely considered.

Furthermore, there was a major question about retroactive legislation. *Nullum crimen sine lege*. This long established legal principle concerns retroactivity, and insists that no-one should be accused, let alone punished, without a clear legal definition of the crime itself – crucially, one which had been formulated before the committing of that crime. No accused person should be surprised at the terms of an accusation levelled against him or her and, most importantly, no piece of criminal legislation should be applied retrospectively.

In attempting to resolve this issue, the prosecution argued that crimes against humanity were so obviously criminal that they required no legislation for the offender to be aware of the action's criminality. The prosecution argued that it was not necessary for membership and support of the SS to have been declared criminal at the first round of the International Military Tribunal for intelligent citizens like Flick and Steinbrinck to have known *at the time* that the SS was guilty of repeated and outrageous crimes against humanity. Flick's argument – fluctuating between the argument from necessity (i.e. that in a dictatorship he had had no alternative but to follow the state's expectations, on pain of personal and commercial threat) and the claim that his actions had been in conformity with the law as operating at the time – was weakened when it came to light that, some time before the end of the war, he and his senior managers had systematically tried to destroy all documentation relating to the *Konzern*'s relations with the NSDAP and the Gestapo. At the very least, this showed that Flick and his associates knew exactly how the Allies would judge their activities during the Third Reich. Far from being retrospective legislation, therefore, the prosecution claimed that the system under which the defendants were being judged amounted to no more than the confirmation of what they already knew.

No less problematic was the concept of criminal conspiracy.[8] Traditionally, the charge of conspiracy has been available to prosecutors in UK and US courts. It is familiar in the present day as part of the 'war on terror', as an instrument to apprehend criminals before an actual criminal act has been carried out. In the UK it has offered a way of generating non-specific offences into indictments (for instance, in ending political 'sit-ins' which might in themselves otherwise have not constituted indictable offences). In the Flick trial, as in the main hearings, conspiracy was seen as a catch-all device to tie the accused and their associates in with the general and manifestly criminal activities of the NS state. In particular, conspiracy charges involved the fundamental assumption that Flick was involved with the Nazis in initiating and pursuing a war of aggression.

Whatever the truth of that assumption may have been, the charge of conspiracy raised a legal problem. In common with French and Soviet law, German law not only did not interpret the offence of conspiracy with the breadth of application common to UK and US law (though the Federal Republic would introduce it in the face of the urban guerrilla movement of the 1970s), but the judges – as well as the defence – at Flick's trial made clear their suspicion of the idea of conspiracy as a catch-all device.

In addition to these legal questions, two general assumptions significantly influenced Flick's team as they set about his defence.

The first of these was that there was a profound difference between 'white collar' crime and crimes of violence. In the eyes of the accused the management of large-scale factories on the basis of slave-labour could not be compared to the direct personal ill-treatment and murder committed by others accused at Nuremberg. In 1946, for instance, a member of the Flick family (initially arrested and imprisoned but not ultimately indicted) complained at having to be imprisoned in the same prison as Otto Ohlendorf, a leader of one of the *Einsatzgruppen* who had admitted killing 90 000 people in the course of the invasion of the Soviet Union. Such company was 'rather disturbing' to well-mannered and urbane industrialists. In a very similar vein, Flick – who was the only one of the accused to make use of his right to a final statement

8 The use of the category of conspiracy is discussed in Overy (2003, p. 1 f).

before the court[9] – focused his remarks on a determined defence of the *professional* honour of German industrialists. 'I stand here,' he declaimed, 'as the proud representative of German industry [...] I refuse to allow German industrialists to be pilloried in my person in the eyes of world opinion as slave-holders and robbers'. If he was charged as a representative, he at least defended himself as such.

Finally there was the issue of coming to equity with clean hands – and avoiding the charge of *tu quoque*. This approach was hardly likely to be used openly before the court, though the final address to the court by Frank's defence team made great play of the argument, for it challenged the legitimacy of a court not on the grounds of its formal constitution, but on the grounds of its moral right to stand in judgment over a particular case. While it was left to the media to question the right of the same military authorities who had participated in the carpet bombing of German cities to judge the propriety of NS activities against civilians, the possibility of including among NS war crimes the indiscriminate slaughter of civilian populations was in no way ignored by the prosecution, but the charge was certainly restricted to war-time activities.[10] In addition, Flick's defence team and the American public knew too much about the behaviour of Soviet troops and authorities (to say nothing of Stalin's purges in the 1930s or of the Soviet Union's invasion of Poland and Finland) for the accusation 'But you do the same' not to hang almost tangibly in the air during parts of the trial. It was not surprising that, as the anti-communism of the Federal Republic became more pronounced, such arguments became more common in the media, and we must assume that they would have been prominent in any appeal which Flick might have been allowed to make against his sentence. It was common, for instance, to compare the Allied internment camps with the NS concentration camps.

---

9 Flick's final speech, discussed in Frei u. Ahrends et al. (2009, p. 425 f) and Bähr, Drecoll et al. (2008, p. 640 f). There more detail on Dix and his intimidation of witnesses (ibid. p. 638 f). The trials of Hjalmar Schacht (not guilty) and Alfred Speer (20 years) – the ultimate technocrats of the Third Reich – focused entirely on such issues. It's no coincidence that Flick appointed Rudolf Dix, Schacht's successful defence counsel in the first round of the Nuremberg trials, as the head of his own defence team.

10 The closest the IMT had come to open discussion of this point was the establishment by Admiral Dönitz' defence team that his U-boat policy in the war had been identical to that pursued by Admiral Nimitz on the US side. See Taylor (1993, p. 592). In a much wider historical framework, leading FRG historians embarked in the so-called 'historians' dispute' (*Historikerstreit*) on an examination of the relation between the atrocities committed in the Soviet Union and NS Germany: the question which came first was dismissed i.a. by the sociologist and philosopher Jürgen Habermas.

1.4 The Sentence

The verdict of the court was announced on December 22 1947. In pronouncing sentence the judges restated the principles which they had followed: principles, as they said, 'familiar to anyone who knows the Anglo-American judicial system'. These were the need to establish personal guilt, rather than passing sentence on the grounds of any collective guilt. This personal guilt was to be established beyond reasonable doubt, and the presumption of innocence was to be safeguarded. While this had been the spirit in which Robert Jackson had declared that no court should be trying a man 'if you are not willing to see him freed if proven not guilty', it clearly flew in the face of the determination both to use the trials as part of the re-education of the German people and in the person of Flick to make an example of the whole of German industry for its collaboration with Hitler. The burden of proof lay with the prosecution, and – the judges remarked finally – in cases of doubt the court should find in favour of the accused. No element of German law, and certainly no aspect of the NS justice system, could have been more favourable to the accused than these principles.

On the first charge (slave-labour) two significant points were accepted by the judges. First that the slave labour programme was initiated by the NS state, not by the industrialists themselves, and that, secondly, resistance or non-compliance with the programme by the industrialists would have been regarded as sabotage and therefore incurred severe penalties. The judges cited Wharton's *Criminal Law*, Chapter xiii, to the effect that 'when an irresistible physical compulsion is present, the action carried out cannot be seen as corresponding to the intention of the individual'.[11] Perhaps more significantly still, the court decided that membership of the two official national councils for coal and for iron – councils concerned with the implementation of national policy in these industries, including of course slave-labour – did not involve the individual member (i.e. Flick) in any responsibility for aspects of that policy.

While they dismissed the defence's argument that slave-workers in Flick's plants had not been maltreated by the plant (in any case, responsibility for their out-of-hours treatment lay with the army or with the SS), the judges properly insisted that slave-labour existed even if the workers had been well housed and fed. Nevertheless, the court accepted that responsibility for any ill treatment lay with the staff and management of the individual plant rather than with more senior figures. (This was an obvious case where the non-representation of the victims was greatly to the advantage of the defendants.) Flick himself,

11 Judges quoting Wharton, in: Thieleke (1965, p. 384).

sitting in his Berlin office, could not be held responsible for what happened in the plant. He was therefore in the happy position of being responsible *neither* for the policies implemented by the commissions on which he sat *nor* for the realities of those policies played out on his own shop-floor.

Nevertheless, since on one occasion one part of Flick's *Konzern*, the Linke-Hoffmann plant in Saxony, had put in a request for extra workers from the slave-labour programme and had done so in order to increase its production, rather than as a response to a direct order from the state, the court found Flick, together with Bernhard Weiss, guilty as charged.

On the second charge (plundering in the occupied territories) Flick was largely exonerated. As far as the Dnepjr works were concerned, these had belonged to the Soviet state and, the court found, it was part of the to and fro of war that Flick should have taken over the works – the judgment referred to the circumstances in which this had happened as a 'military necessity'. Thus, as the German forces retreated, the works should have reverted to the Soviet Union, as in fact happened, the works being in good working order when abandoned by Flick's managers. In the Rombach works, however, which had been in private hands at the time of the German invasion of Lorraine, the court ruled that Flick had made no effort to take into consideration either the interests of the French owners or the restitution of the works as the German armies retreated. As a result, Flick was found guilty on that charge.

The third charge – expropriation of Jewish property – was dismissed as lying outside the competence of the court. The Petschek case had taken place before the outbreak of war and did not therefore come under any of the paragraphs of the Hague convention, which concerned only activities carried out in a time of war. In a further move, the judges discussed the possibility of regarding Flick's action as a 'crime against humanity', but, as they reviewed official attempts to define such crimes (most recently at the conference of international jurists held in Brussels on July 10/11 of that year), they found it impossible to define a crime against humanity in any way which involved damage to another person's *property*, rather than to that person's life and limb. It was an unusual decision, in that in sentencing the major war-criminals Frick and Seyss-Inquart, the International Military Tribunal had recognized that the economic disadvantaging of the Jewish populations was an essential part of the removal of all legal protection from them and that this 'meant nothing less than ordering their destruction'. In the Flick trial, however, the judges held it to be inconceivable that the IMT could ever have contemplated, let alone made a principle out of, the idea that 'anyone could be guilty of a crime against humanity merely by the exercise of antisemitic pressure applied with the purpose of acquiring industrial wealth from Jewish ownership'. Later in the same judgment they pronounced: 'to covet something may be a sin in the light of the Ten Commandments, but it is neither an infringement of the Hague declaration nor a war-crime'. No clearer separation could have been made between economic behaviour and the law.

The fifth point of the indictment – membership of the SS – was uncontentious. Steinbrinck had indeed been a member of the SS and he was found guilty. He and Flick were also found guilty on point four, on the grounds of their membership of the Friends of Heinrich Himmler. The court was contemptuous of the idea that money donated to this circle was destined for 'cultural purposes' only. The court doubted whether, particularly after 1939, the SS had devoted much of its attention to cultural matters anyway. Nevertheless, the court rather bizarrely suggested that it was not an offence to be in attendance at meetings at which Himmler might appear as the 'Gentleman and friendly host'. This view appeared to lie some way outside the spirit of the decision that the SS was a criminal organization (a decision taken in the first round of the IMT and passed on to subsequent trials). Nevertheless, the judges determined that it was 'unimportant whether [Flick's] money went towards SS salaries or towards poison gas' and found him guilty of being an accomplice of the SS.

Flick was sentenced to seven years imprisonment, Steinbrinck to five and Bernhard Weiss to two and a half. In fact they were all released long before the end of these periods.

1.5 Assessing the Verdict

There are at least three ways to view the sentence passed in Flick's case, and it is an open question as to which should be regarded as the most plausible. The first would be to regard it as an all-but complete exoneration of the role of German heavy industry in the rise and expansion of the NS state. The prosecution failed to persuade the court on the most serious of the charges brought against Flick and his associates, and where he was found guilty it was for the most part on the lesser elements in the charges. Certainly every element of the charge of conspiracy was dismissed. It was as if major industrialists had never helped Hitler to power or supported him in his aggressive and expansionist wars. The court had not been impressed by Flick's claims to have been a 'resistance fighter' against Hitler, but it had only tangentially tied him in with the national and international crimes of the regime. In the Soviet occupation zone, the court's verdict was roundly condemned: the court had been too lenient. Its leniency was explained by the left as the result of the Americans' lack of interest in exposing the structural links between capitalism and National Socialism. Even neutral historians see it as 'a fiasco for [Telford] Taylor and his team'.[12]

A second view would be to identify in the trial a disproportionate relationship between the modern state and the concepts and the legal instruments which might stand in judgment over it. While, as we briefly outline in the next section of this chapter, the international community responded to Nuremberg by attempting to forge better and more appropriate laws to deal with national crimes, German practice tended to move away from general concepts and to approach crimes against humanity simply by seeing them as normal crimes which should not be turned into a new category simply by virtue of their numerical repetition and particular brutality, thus ignoring the innovations in international law for which Lemkin had fought. The legal and political circumstances in the Federal Republic, under which this took place, were, however, hardly favourable to the success of any other approach.

Finally, it might be possible to see in the sentences a testimony to the scrupulous fairness of the judges and an outstanding achievement of an adversarial court-room. While the judges' opinions on the crimes committed against humanity represented the opinion of the morally committed outside world, their understanding of the conduct of a criminal trial meant that these opinions found little expression in their sentence. The judges' dilemma, and the very scrupulousness of their judgment, pointed repeatedly to the difficulty of applying to complex modern societies the necessity of reaching an unambiguous guilty/not guilty verdict. When historians invite us to admire the 'fine-tuning of degrees of culpability' displayed by the judges,[13] they are in danger of failing to match that fine-tuning to the real situations in modern societies in which major crimes are committed.

1.6 The Repercussions of the Flick Trial

The judgments of the International Tribunal in Nuremberg still echo strongly in legal circles, both inside Germany and in the wider world. Their initial effect was to highlight the inadequacies of international law in the field of crimes against humanity and genocide, and to point international lawyers in the

12 Quoted in Weinke (2006, p. 86).

13 This was a comment on the follow-up trials conducted against the NS doctors involved in the human experiments: Louise Harmon (2006, p. 172).

direction of the improvements which in more recent years have been seen in the legal response to the genocides in the former Yugoslavia and in Rwanda.

In particular, the complexity of major state-sponsored actions such as genocide has been recognized, the idea of complicity has been clarified and strengthened (to the extent that even silence, or non-action can be classed as complicity) and crimes against humanity have been defined so as to separate them from the state of war. They are – in the words of Andrew Clapham – 'self-standing crimes'.[14] In addition, international law has recognized the necessity (on occasion) of interfering in the internal affairs of sovereign states in order to prevent genocide. Another clear lesson from the short-comings of Nuremberg has been to provide easy routes for the prosecution of crimes against humanity by the national courts of the countries involved. Richard Overy's summary of the Tribunal's work perhaps overstates the initial ambitions of the Tribunal's founders, but certainly expresses well the longer-term effects of its work: 'the central purpose of the Tribunal was not to conform to existing principles in international law but to establish new rules of international conduct and agreed boundaries in the violation of human rights'.[15] But there were effects on national, as well as international, legal thinking. We shall meet these arguments again in reflections on the Eichmann trial in the early 1960s.

A general significant shift after Nuremberg has been noted in American legal thought.[16] Before 1945 the dominant mode of American legal commentators had been so-called 'legal realism'. By its empty formalism this movement relativized understandings of the relationship between the law and society, suggesting – sometimes in an absurd fashion – a disconnection between the sentence of courts and the motivation, origin and even the perpetrators of crime. Nuremberg, as Rodger Citron argues, changed the orientation of American law back to a view closer to morality and ideas of natural justice. The appalling nature of the crimes tried at Nuremberg reminded lawyers of the primary function of the law: to identify and to punish wrong-doing and to deter future crime.

German approaches were less focused on the strengthening of international law, although the Federal Republic has been a staunch supporter of all moves to build up the legal framework of international law, particularly after it became a member of the United Nations. Instead, the ostensible wish of enlightened prosecutors has been to find ways of bringing the law to bear on the so called

14 Clapham (2003, p. 43).

15 Overy (2003, p. 23).

16 For the responses of the US legal system to the revelations of Nuremberg see the essays of Citron (2006) and Brown (2006).

'desk-top murderers' (as they were called in the jargon of Nuremberg) – that is, to uncover the people inside the processes which made the final solution possible. The Frankfurt Auschwitz trials showed this wish clearly. It is also clear that German legal thinking could not simply revert, as American lawyers did, to a more ethically based notion of the law. Indeed the various attempts by German courts to reinforce 'natural justice' have needed to be resisted strongly. When judges used arguments taken from 'natural law' – for instance on issues of homosexuality or gender equality – they lapsed all too readily into the language of NS ideology. Recognizing German law after 1949 as a 'normative' construct, we may with Lloyd Weinreb 'be inclined to exclude from its range the 'natural' feature of our lives, which just happen'.[17]

The German legal system needed more than natural law to re-establish itself, and it was not helped in this by an all-but total failure to purge the legal profession in Germany of former Nazis after 1947.[18] While we can see the immediate results of this failure in the scandalous conduct of individual trials, commonly in the 1950s but continuing as late as the 1970s, it is the statistical picture which is the most disturbing. Apart from the execution of those lawyers whose elevated office and political prominence had focused world attention on them – among them Hans Frank, for instance, governor of the *Ostmark* (i.e. what the Nazis left behind of Poland) and Roland Freisler, sadistic and histrionic president of the *Volksgerichtshof* in Berlin: the former executed at Nuremberg and the latter killed in an Allied bombing raid – virtually every judge who had been in post during the Third Reich was back in office after 1946. In the Nuremberg sequence of the lawyers' trials only sixteen judges were tried. Most of the ten found guilty had been released by 1951 and enjoyed long retirements on generous pensions in the Federal Republic.[19]

This is not the place to argue that different sentences should have been passed, but we should reflect that the failure to prosecute the NS judges all but made it impossible for at least twenty years to identify and punish the 'desk-top murderers'. After all, in the German system judges are in effect civil servants, *Beamte*, and they therefore held an identical position within the NS systems of persecution and total war to those of other civil servants, who had belonged to chains of command and decision which were essential to the

---

17 Weinreb (1987, p. 234).

18 On the failure to clean up the legal profession after 1945 see: Distelkamp (1988), pp. 131–49. For the RSHA fiasco see Ralph Giordano: *Perfekte Morde* in: http//www.zeit.de/1999/37/Perfekte_Morde.

19 A frightening statistic: of the original suspects on the IMT lists 28 000 remained 'relevant' (i.e. unprosecuted) until their deaths (Weinke (2008, p. 154 f). See also Weisbrod (2008, p. 247).

smooth operation of NS war-crimes. Like these civil servants, the judges had every interest in keeping open the argument that – like Flick and his associates in the slave-labour organization – they had had nothing to do with the creation of the system, and could not therefore be indicted for the system's crimes. They were merely its technical administrators. No less damaging to the pursuit of further justice was the continuation of ex-Nazis in positions of state prosecutor (in the *Staatsanwaltschaft*) – let alone in the levels of justice lower than the courts, namely the police. While the German Democratic Republic's record was massively flawed too on this point, the Federal Republic's tolerance of an ideologically (and criminally) flawed justice system contributed greatly to its later difficulties.

Only when a younger generation of lawyers grew up (though they were trained by the generation contaminated by the past) could the stranglehold of the past begin to be broken. One cannot understand the violence associated with the student movement of the 1960s without comprehending the size of the task with which reformers were confronted and their frustration at the barriers which the contamination of the judiciary placed in the way of reform. The shift in American legal thinking towards a new moralism could not be reflected in Germany while the legal system had more or less in its entirety been transferred from the Third Reich into the Republic in this manner. Someone else had to drive this reform. While the first chancellor of the Federal Republic, Konrad Adenauer, appointed to high and influential positions in his cabinet and administration people who had held high and influential posts in the NS regime, he – if not they – was at least susceptible to public mandate and had to be re-elected every four years. For the judiciary, however, neither political mandates nor the available legal instruments held any terrors. They were independent of the former, and they and their fellow travellers with Nazism held the legal instruments in their own hands.

One final crucial decision showed the near impossibility of reforming the NS legacy of German courts. In the early to mid 1960s a major public debate was inflamed on the subject of the statute of limitation: the infamous *Verjährung*. Without a change in the law all prosecutions on serious charges would have become statute barred in 1965 (i.e. twenty years after the collapse of the Third Reich). As a result of pressure from parliament and public opinion this was extended to 1969 (twenty years after the founding of the state). Subsequently, after more heated debate, this was extended to 1979 and then 1989 and after that indefinitely.

Two major trials stood in the shadow of these debates. The first was the 1963 Auschwitz trial in Frankfurt (fully examined in Chapter Seven); the second was hardly less significant – the attempted indictment of the RSHA staff.

(The *Reichssicherheitshauptamt* had been responsible for the administrative organization of the Gestapo, of the concentration camps and of the notorious mobile murder squads, the *Einsatzgruppen*. Its director had been Reinhard Heydrich.) Although the prosecution had been planned in co-operation between the authorities in East and West Berlin, at the trial which opened in Berlin in 1958 no convictions were achieved. When it was re-opened in 1969, it turned out that the charges came under the statute of limitation. No-one could now be indicted as an accomplice of murder unless it could be proved that they had acted out of personal 'base motives'.

For a bureaucracy like RSHA, many miles away from the activity of mass murder, that ruling amounted to a virtually automatic acquittal. No group of civil servants merely carrying out their appointed tasks would fall under this provision. The potential defendants were working within a bureaucracy which – though it required a fundamental inner identification with its ideology: no room for liberals, Jews or communists in the NS civil service – had turned inhumanity into a series of technical procedures. How could bureaucratic efficiency be labelled 'a base motive'? While elements in the judiciary claimed that the various amendments to the statute of limitation were purely technical, relating to clearing a whole series of trivial matters from the machinery of the law, it is now widely accepted that the device had the explicit intention of putting an end to any further pursuit of NS criminals, except those 'monsters' whose prosecution helped to make the 'desktop murderers' appear still more innocent. The RSHA case confirmed that view. The desk-top murderers were safe. The fact that Eduard Dreher, who was in charge of the commission for law reform in the 1960s, had himself been a prosecutor in the NS 'special courts' confirmed the essentially corrupt nature of that legislation. Its effects at the time are beyond dispute.

Flick's sentence was characterized not only by his relatively speedy release and by his early resumption of control of his industrial empire. These facts together with his personal determination to rescue the reputation of German industry at large point to the early years of the Federal Republic as being a restoration, rather than as a period involving any serious reckoning with the NS years. When the SPD leader Kurt Schumacher spoke contemptuously of the Federal Republic as 'a nature reserve for yesterday's capitalism',[20] Flick's success made the point still more eloquently. We saw that even the 'Economic

20 On Schumacher see Pirker (1965), p. 72. Other *bons mots* showing Schumacher's extraordinary intransigence include his references to the Federal German police as 'Himmler's police' (p. 52) and his description of the Catholic Church as 'the fifth occupying power' (p. 108). SPD views of IMT were hardly more favourable (cf. Weinke, 2006, p. 106).

Miracle' might be interpreted not as the product of the newly released energies of a nation finally free under democracy, but merely as the continuation into peace-time of the extraordinary intensity of production in German industry at the height of total war.

In terms of public perception, the Flick trial certainly demonstrated the inability of the law to deal with the involvement of the 'industrial-military complex' in a criminal and genocidal state. Indeed, the trial itself – encouraged by the defence's successful approach as they argued for the defendants' lack of individual responsibility within the bureaucratic machinery of a totalitarian state – went in the opposite direction. Despite the ideological divide which would scar the world at least until the collapse of the Soviet Union in 1989, the post-war political developments moved increasingly towards a view which stressed the primacy of the technical handling of the economy (a view which made possible the many left-right coalitions in post-war politics) and that regarded technical efficiency rather than the active consent of its members as society's principal goal.

Again, one could argue that inadequate historical understanding continued to vitiate the case which could be brought against German industry. If the prosecutors at Nuremberg had been obliged to rely on Neumann or Rauschning to interpret the world in which Flick had exercised such power, the post-war was still more strongly in the grip of similarly organizational models of the modern state. In particular, James Burnham – influenced in part by the economic centralism of Roosevelt's New Deal and its imagined parallels to the centralization of planned economies such as Hitler's Germany and the Soviet Union – saw ever closer links between the systems of the three great power blocs of the time. For him, the differing ideologies of these blocs were all but irrelevant: the world for him represented a *Managerial Revolution* (1941), in which concepts of morality, democratic consensus or individual responsibility were dwarfed by the imperatives of a technical world.[21] The best known expression of these ideas (and warning against them) was contained in George Orwell's novel *1984*, first published in 1949. Orwell feared that the tendencies epitomized, in our example, in Flick's relationship to Nazism constituted the future of the entire world, and that the expansion of states and their parasitic industrial combines would continue unchecked, at untold cost to humanity. Long before the word 'globalization' had further impoverished alternative perceptions of economic development, Orwell believed that the expansionist wars of aggression which would in future be waged by faceless military-industrial complexes would make Hitler's campaigns seem almost harmless in comparison. The possibility

21 James Burnham (1941). See also Orwell's pamphlet (1946).

for law, national or international, to prevent or even check these developments appeared derisory in face of such visions of the future.

In short, it is arguable that it was Flick who emerged from his trial and in 1950 from his prison-cell as the figure of the new age. His judges, with their scrupulous 'fine-tuning' of degrees of culpability, appeared as representatives of an archaic liberal conscience, whose relevance to modern technocratic states was under serious challenge. The sentence of Nuremberg was in danger of being turned against those who attempted to pronounce it. The new republic would not only have to deal with the legacy of a horrendous past: it would suffer from the wounds inflicted during the years of its birth.

CHAPTER 2

Adjusting the Political Landscape: Banning the KPD

It's a marked feature of the history of both German states that stability was so quickly established after 1945. In terms of foreign policy, the presence of the Western powers and the Soviet Union on German territory had a positive effect, for it identified clear spheres of influence and created a framework within which stability could be achieved, even at the cost of dividing the country and diminishing its territorial extent. This stability was more influential than the agitation which the GDR continued to practise against the FRG. It did much to contain the pressure to regain 'lost' territories, which had been a particularly toxic legacy of the first world war thirty years before.

The path to economic stability was, however, very different in the two parts of Germany. In the West the Marshall Plan, the rapid merging of the three zones of occupation and the Currency Reform of 1948 were the obvious bases of economic stability. In the east, Soviet policies – notably that of demontage (the dismantling of industrial plant, rail track and the like and their export to the Soviet Union) and the start of the nationalization of the means of production – exacerbated the difficulties of the half of the country, which was not merely considerably smaller than its western pendant, but predominantly agricultural rather than industrial. These measures meant a longer period of shortage and destabilization for the East. Politically, however, stabilization occurred at similar speeds and in different forms, but in ways which determined the future shape of the two emerging German states.

In both states the courts played a significant role within the pre-ordained shape of development, and nothing illustrates better the place of the courts in the early years of the Federal Republic than the role and function of the Federal Constitutional Court. In this and the following chapter I wish to examine two particularly significant cases which the court had to decide within the first eight years of its existence. They belong together, not because of their subject-matter, but because they illustrate two basic positions which the court adopted – conformity to prevailing political opinions and the courage to move towards new ideas.

The first of these two cases presented a particular challenge to the new court. In particular, it raised the likelihood that the judges would be challenged on the grounds of their past. This was especially likely since the majority of denunciations of ex-Nazis in the judiciary came from the German Democratic Republic – these people were always referred to as 'Adenauer's blood-judges' – and, in banning the KPD, any suspicious figures on the bench of the BVerfG would have immediately been exposed. In fact only one such complaint was made, and the system seemed to work.

This trial illustrates judicial approaches to the problem of political extremism – approaches which were significant in the early years of the Federal Republic and which, like extremism itself (in different forms), made a spectacular return in the late 1960s and once again in the early years of the new millennium. The second trial was less dramatic, but the way in which it was embraced by the court as one of its major achievements gives it special prominence in the history of post-war justice. Taken together they show clearly the balance which the BVerfG attempted to establish within the Federal Republic between the rights enshrined in the Basic Law and the provisions and constraints located in the civil and criminal codes, and they also show the ambiguous position of the court towards the Adenauer government.

2.1 The Banning of Political Parties

The decision to outlaw a political party is a hot potato in all democratic systems. Inevitably, in German consciousness the issue is inseparable from the unending discussion around the dilemma of the 1920s: whether it would have rescued the Weimar Republic (and, rather more significantly, whether it would have saved the lives of over twenty million citizens of countries other than Germany – matters of this kind are not simply issues of academic constitutional law) if the National Socialist party had been declared illegal, and by these means prevented from coming to power. Not only that dilemma haunted German law-makers after 1949: the Nazis' immediate outlawing of the Communist Party (KPD) in the first weeks after they came to power in 1933 presented a most unwelcome precedent for the decisive intervention of the courts into the party-political landscape. Those with longer memories recalled Bismarck declaring not only Social Democrats but the Catholic Church itself to be enemies of the state. No democratic post-war German state would wish to go down that route lightly.

After 1945 there was an obvious need to ban certain types of political activity. As we saw in the Flick trial, membership of the SS had been immediately declared criminal by the Allies, but simple party membership was too widespread to be written into post-war legal instruments, even if it had been politically possible. But that was by no means the full extent of the problem. There were millions who had voted for the NSDAP and stayed loyal to the Party to the end (even without Party membership), and after 1945 it was hardly conceivable that none of these citizens would wish to continue the policies and ideology of Nazism, albeit under a different name. The de-nazification policy was agreed at Yalta and confirmed in Potsdam and in the Control Council Laws, but it was constantly subverted by the government and legal establishment in the early years of the Federal Republic. The occupying powers held on to the power to deal with ex-Nazis and thus to prevent National Socialism passing on its legacy into the post-war period. The questionnaire handed out in 1946 by the American occupation authorities (the infamous *Fragebogen*) was an attempt to deal with the individual aspect of the problem, but all too soon the Allied powers' enthusiasm for getting rid of ex-Nazis in public office gave way to a more pragmatic recognition that efficient government and administration in post-war Germany would be impossible if every follower of the old system were swept out of office. The infant Federal Republic was left to take responsibility itself without being purged of ex-Nazis.

The historical dilemmas relating to the Nazis' twelve years of one-party rule were made concrete in the explicit insistence of the Basic Law on the rights of political parties. The Weimar constitution had said next to nothing about parties – reflecting, it is often claimed, the ultra-liberal distrust of political parties as a distortion of both the individual conscience and the public will. The lack of organizing provisions in the constitution had allowed the chaos of unstable parliamentary coalitions, including cabinets led by a chancellor who had been sacked from his own party.[1] In contrast, the Basic Law paid close attention to ensuring the conditions under which the political parties could play a positive role in parliamentary democracy, for instance in its insistence on the constructive vote of no confidence. The Basic Law explicitly protected political parties, and the provision that only the BVerfG was to have the power to ban a political party was aimed to ensure that such a decision should have an exclusively constitutional, rather than political character. In considering cases of this kind, the judges of the BVerfG have always been conscious of the unpromising historical precedents for such decision and emphasized that a ban could be imposed only if a particular party represented a threat to what were seen as absolutely core elements of the democratic system: human rights,

1 Understanding the role of the parties was an important part of Karl Dietrich Bracher's highly influential work on the dissolution of the Weimar Republic (1955). In its analysis of the failure of the party system in Weimar it offers a classic example of the role of historians in shaping constitutional law in the Federal Republic. For instance, the constructive parliamentary vote of no confidence insists that a vote of no confidence in a government can be held *only* when, should the motion be carried, the proposers of the motion are able to form a government with a parliamentary majority. Such arrangements were manifestly not part of the Weimar constitution.

the sovereignty of the people, the multi-party system and the independence of the courts.

One of the first cases to which the BVerfG had to respond was the outlawing of the SRP (*Sozialistische Reichspartei*).[2] This party was an explicitly Nazi organization, with some forty thousand members (this was not an insignificant number: it amounted, for instance, to half the membership of the Liberals at the time). It achieved percentages of up to 30% in individual constituencies in local elections. The Federal government, as was its right, banned the paramilitary wing of the SRP (the so-called *Reichsfront*) in May 1951, but to ban the party itself the government had to make a formal request of the BVerfG. In response to this request, the court's judgment banning the SRP was announced on October 23 1952 and party members excluded from the *Bundestag*.

The ruling was problematic neither to the court, nor to the larger political scene – indeed, those parties trying to recruit disaffected Nazi supporters (especially the DP and, surprisingly, the FDP) were glad to see the competition reduced. The word 'socialist' in the party's title was as much of a lie as it had been in the National Socialist party, but the more serious dilemmas confronting both the government and the court would come from the party with a more legitimate claim to the word: the Communists. In November 1951 Adenauer's government requested the court to report on the compatibility of the KPD with the constitution (thus balancing its hostility to both left and right), while shifting onto the court's shoulders the need to solve the acute sensitivities contained in historical precedents which the case awoke. When the court announced its decision in August 1956 it must have felt that it had done someone else's dirty work.

2.2 Outlawing the KPD[3]

In the early 1950s, no-one looking at the recent history of the Soviet Union would have been reassured that Communism was any respecter of the core elements of the democratic system: human rights, the sovereignty of the people, the multi-party system and the independence of the courts. From Stalin's purges to the Show Trials, Moscow's record was disturbing. The problem for

2 Full details of background to the SRP ban in Frei (1999, pp. 326–60).

3 *Kommunistische Partei Deutschlands.* This title was that carried by the Communists in Germany from 1919 onwards. It should be distinguished from the DKP (*Deutsche Kommunistische Partei*), which was established formally in 1968 and laid a different claim to the historical legacy.

the BVerfG would lie in deciding not only to what extent the Soviet Union had moved away from these events (Khrushchev's secret speech denouncing Stalin in 1956 was an important element in such consideration[4] – though not necessarily for the court), but also to what extent the western communist parties had distanced themselves from these practices. And if they had distanced themselves, was there any guarantee that, once in power, they would not behave similarly themselves?

These were not easy questions to resolve. After 1945 the grass-roots German and European Communists had every right to present themselves sympathetically as victims of NS terror, and even if KPD policy leading up to 1933 had not been a shining example of democratic beliefs in action, no-one could deny that the Communists had opposed Nazism, any more than they could deny the immense contribution of the Soviet Union in defeating Hitler. Nevertheless, there were strong reasons why the Federal government would wish to ban the German Communist Party.

Most obvious was the close identification of the KPD with the Soviet Union, the West's decisive ally in the military battle against Hitler, but increasingly identified as the West's enemy in the Cold War. The leadership of the KPD had gone into exile in the Soviet Union almost immediately after Hitler's seizure of power, and those who had survived Stalin's purges had returned with the Red Army and taken up responsible positions in the Soviet occupation zone, which was subsequently to become the German Democratic Republic. Their attitudes and policies were dictated from Moscow and there was neither evidence of nor opportunity for any significant independence from Moscow on behalf of any of the so-called satellite states. Indeed, events in post-war Yugoslavia, where Tito had managed to distance himself from Moscow, caused Stalin to insist on still greater loyalty to Moscow from the European Communist parties, and in particular from the Germans. For Moscow there was to be no 'German road to socialism'.[5] Everyone had to travel on the same road, dictated by the Soviet Union.

This meant that the KPD was closely identified with the German Democratic Republic. This was not just a question of overall ideology, but of the physical location of the party leadership, as well as of funding and resources available

---

4 Nikita Khrushchev, On the cult of personality and its consequences: speech made to the 20th Congress of the Communist Party of the Soviet Union on February 25 1956.

5 The phrase 'German road to socialism' has a long history, being used in the late 19th and early 20th century to distance the SPD from orthodox Marxist teaching and its commitment to revolution. During the years of the Soviet Union it indicated Moscow's rejection of any separatist tendencies among the satellite states. For some of its early history see Carl Schorske (1983).

to the KPD in the West. On the other hand, as the Federal Republic drew further apart from the GDR and the Cold War intensified (to say nothing of the suppression of the uprising in East Berlin in 1953) the electoral appeal of the KPD in the West suffered. This meant that, while the GDR's challenge to the Federal Republic's claim to be the representative of the whole of Germany (the Hallstein doctrine) might be an offence to the Federal Republic and an occasional diplomatic nuisance, the attitudes and behaviour of the GDR made the Party an ever more insignificant factor in West German politics. Pragmatism and principle pointed in different directions for the government in determining its policy towards the KPD.

The KPD did itself no favours by challenging the entire legitimacy of the Federal Republic, arguing on occasion that the state was set up merely on the basis of the Statute of Occupation, which had no legal validity once the occupation ended.

Still more unacceptable, finally, was the KPD's strong opposition to Adenauer's central policy: the integration of the Federal Republic into the western alliance, both politically (in the East-West divide), militarily (after the start of the FRG's rearmament this crystallized in the Republic's proposed membership of the European Defence Community and then of NATO) and economically. The Republic's economic policy was reflected not just in the restoration of capitalism which saw Flick back at the head of his *Konzern* by 1950, but in the string of treaties which finally produced the European Union. While it was evident that the KPD would campaign vigorously against these policies, Adenauer stressed his economic plan as a 'social market economy' (i.e. a lightly modified form of capitalism). In any case the gap in consumer goods between the Federal Republic and the GDR (and the unbroken stream of defectors coming West out of the GDR) took most of the sting out of the KPD's arguments.

While these were significant points of tension, the fear of the KPD which was expressed by the Federal Republic's established parties was surely exaggerated. Although the principal heavy industries, from which the radical left had traditionally drawn much of its strength, were situated in the Federal Republic and it had been from these areas, especially the Ruhr, that the KPD had recruited most successfully, there were in fact relatively few Communists left in the West after the war. Hitler had smashed the party and its organization and murdered large numbers of its members. (So, for that matter, had Stalin.) After 1945, electoral support at national level reached a peak of 7% – only just over the five percent hurdle needed for representation in parliament. Certainly the considerable support which the Communist parties enjoyed in France and Italy had no real equivalent in Germany, for that support derived in large part from the significant role which the Communists in these countries had played in resistance to German occupation during the war. In comparison, rather unjustly, little heroic legacy attached to the German Communists: indeed, as Trotsky maintained until his murder in 1940, Stalin's tactics leading up to the NS take-over in 1933, by splitting the opposition from the left, had significantly contributed to Hitler's assumption of power. To this day, memories of the resistance to Hitler inside Germany are more associated with middle- and upper-class figures than with the politically conscious working-classes, and this perception further weakened the KPD in the immediate post-war years.[6]

It's here that the issue of proportionality arises. The BVerfG action against the KPD represented a sledge hammer used on what was, by 1956, a relatively small problem. It could be argued that the Party's attitudes discredited the Party itself far more than they damaged Adenauer. Indeed, for much of the early 1950s, the KPD represented the kind of opponent any political leader would choose to have, and certainly posed no threat whatsoever to the democratic order.

In many ways the Party's impotence was less a product of its actual policies – these were little more than an ill-defined continuation of the Popular Front[7] – and rather a direct consequence of its failures of tactics. In particular, the Party fell out spectacularly with the two social groups with whom it might have co-operated in order to further its goals: the SPD and the trades-unions. The first failure stemmed in part from the merger of the SPD and the KPD to form the SED, the ruling party in the Soviet occupation zone. This was hardly a recommendation to any party in the west to work closely with the KPD. No less important was the fact that the SPD leader, Kurt Schumacher, was a veteran SPD man, scarred by Gestapo torture and by the hostility between the KPD and SPD in the latter years of the Weimar Republic, and as a result quite unforgiving of the KPD for having, in his view, let Hitler in.

The second failure came from the KPD's insistence on engaging in a trial of strength with the West German trades-unions, as a result of which the unions decided that Communist membership was incompatible with union membership. As a result of the confrontation, the members of the unions – forced to choose between the Party and the union – almost unanimously settled for the union.

---

6 The great novel *Ästhetik des Widerstands* (1975) by Peter Weiss amounted to a heroic, if not always widely shared attempt to alter this state of opinion.

7 The Popular Front was the policy of forming a common front with other parties and countries in order to fight against fascism. It was exemplified in the Soviet Union's engagement against Franco in the Spanish Civil War, conveniently forgotten in the NS-Soviet Pact of 1939, but hastily revived when Hitler invaded the Soviet Union in 1941. My generation started to learn of these things through the magnificent study of the history of the left: Wilson (1940).

With tactics like this the KPD was well on the way to self-destruction. It may well not have survived the shattering blow which the Soviet Union delivered to communists across the world (but especially to the European communist parties) when the Red Army brutally suppressed the Hungarian uprising in October 1956. Nevertheless, to raise the issue of proportionality (*Verhältnismäßigkeit*) is not simply to indulge in idle speculation. One of the questions raised by the banning of the KPD is the extent to which the measure was the state's legitimate self-defence mechanism against a genuine enemy to democracy, or to what extent the ban amounted merely to the *post hoc* legitimation of an ideological tradition of anti-communism, widespread in western Europe at the time, but also a principal point in the discredited NS ideology. Any question of the appropriateness of the ban has to involve an assessment of its motivation: democratic survival or ideological prejudice. Wesel is not alone in arguing that the KPD ban was a personal vendetta by Adenauer.[8]

2.3 The Deliberations of the BVerfG[9]

The KPD fought its case vigorously – among its defence counsels was Friedrich Kaul from East Berlin, whose hostility to the Federal Republic reappeared in the Auschwitz trial some seven years later (see Chapter Seven). Its leaders made significant appearances in Karlsruhe. They argued two fairly obvious points and one which may read strangely to modern eyes. The first argument was that the Marxism-Leninism at the Party's heart was a science, not a political programme. As a science, the Party argued, it fell under the protection of GG § 5 – the right to freedom of opinion – and the Party could not therefore be declared unconstitutional. The second argument was that the Potsdam agreement[10] had explicitly recognized the KPD as a democratic party and that the KPD had subsequently signed up to the free democratic basic order of the Federal Republic and was determinedly working within that framework in

8 Wesel (2004, p. 90). Somewhat paradoxically he also praises the court's judgment for its clarity and concision (p. 92).

9 The judgment of the BVerfG can be found in the usual source for BVerfG's reporting: *BVerfG E* 5, p. 91 f. The KPD judgment was also published separately, ed. Dr Gerd Pfeiffer (1956). The full text of the judgment runs from p. 581 onwards. Quotations from recent KPD pamphlets pp. 670 f, 691, 696; on the 'overall style' of the Party's literature, pp. 738–44; on issues of re-unification, p. 713.

10 The Potsdam Agreement was signed on August 1 1945 between the three principal Allies in the Cäcilienhof; this was the peace treaty effectively bringing the Second World War to an end, superseded by the Final Settlement of September 12 1990.

order to achieve the maximum benefits for the German proletariat. The Party was therefore both *de jure* and *de facto* constitutional.

The third argument was closely linked to the offers to create a framework for German re-unification which were held out to the West by the Soviet Union at various times during the 1950s. The Party argued that banning it would make any future re-unification of Germany impossible. Since the re-unification of Germany was a *prima facie* goal of all West German political activity, the KPD's argument – even if it might lack specificity – required being taken seriously: at least in a political dimension. It was not clear to what extent this argument was based on any point of law.

The BVerfG announced its decision to ban the KPD on August 17 1956. The grounds for this decision were explained in over one hundred and fifty pages of closely argued text. The document is not only excessively long, however: it often reads less than convincingly. The court had clearly spent much energy combing through the classic works of Marxism-Leninism, including a number of essays and speeches by Stalin himself, in order to examine the Party's claim to be a disinterested science. The BVerfG was not a forum in which the early philosophical works of Marx himself were known or would have been read with appreciation, but in fact these works would have offered a much easier way to answer the question the court had posed itself. The outcome of all the judges' reading would have been accessible at any time to anyone walking into the entrance hall of the Humboldt University in East Berlin: carved there on the stone stairs is Marx's celebrated eleventh thesis on Feuerbach: 'Up to now, philosophers have only interpreted the world differently: our task now is to change it.' From that moment on Marxism (and all the add-ons which came from Lenin and Stalin) was about that change and not about the philosophers' interpretations. Perhaps the Party manifestos occasionally watered down the explicit need for immediate revolutionary change, but the argument that Marxism-Leninism was a disinterested science and not a programme for action had always been specious and remained so after 1949.

The KPD's tactical acceptance of the free democratic basic order carried no greater conviction for the court. Not only was the court persuaded that at some future date the Party would not hesitate to resort to revolutionary violence in order to achieve its ends. It was also convinced that behind the utopian images of peace and brotherhood after Communism had been established lay both the dictatorship of the proletariat and the elimination of other classes and parties. The KPD wished to be the sole party – that was its purpose in describing itself as a 'unity party' (*Einheitspartei*). For these reasons the court refused to accept that the Party's tactics of working within the free democratic basic order made it constitutional. Its description as a democratic party in the Potsdam Agreement referred, the court judged, to nothing more than its opposition to Nazism.

The court finally considered the issue of re-unification. Its finding was that the KPD understood unification merely as the means to destroy the Federal Republic (perhaps even in 1956 one can see traces of the counter-view: that re-unification was simply to be the extension of the Federal Republic into the whole of Germany). The court did concede however that, in the case of elections being held on a two-state basis across Germany, the ban on the KPD would not prevent a Communist party putting forward candidates. In the realistic view of the West German establishment, however, there was no remote possibility of elections taking place on such a basis, and the concession (definitely political, rather than legal in character) was cheap to make. In 1990, however, the court's decision on the conduct of the first all-German elections showed that the BVerfG had meant what it said in 1956.[11]

One final issue should be mentioned. The court clearly had not enjoyed ploughing through the classics of Marxism-Leninism, or the political speeches and propaganda leaflets of the KPD. As we follow the judgment in its account of this reading, it's impossible not to be dumbfounded by the arrogance and self-confidence of the more recent documents which the judges had had to consider. The KPD leaders wrote and spoke as if the Party's victory were just round the corner; their rhetoric became more extreme as their political chances tended towards zero. 'The German people will bring down the Adenauer regime' the court had to read – this at a time when, for the first time in the twentieth century, a democratic party (Adenauer's CDU) had gained an absolute parliamentary majority. Desperation made the 'insults and invective' of the party leaders ever more violent. Another pronouncement even read: 'Hitler and Adenauer: the same words, the same policies'.

It's worth pausing on this phrase. The slogan of the KPD (dictated by Stalin) in the early 1930s had been that there was no difference between Chancellor Brüning, as he ruled by the emergency decrees signed by the President, and Hitler. That was one of the reasons why the KPD did not oppose Hitler as forcibly as its considerable power would have made possible. Once again, it was Trotsky who pointed out that equating Hitler and Brüning had cost the lives of thousands of KPD members. Whatever else Brüning had wanted, it did not include the physical liquidation of his political opponents. It was disgraceful that the KPD should repeat the slogan and use it against Adenauer.

At one moment in their judgment it seems as if this all had got too much for the judges. 'The attack on the "Adenauer regime"', we read in the judgment,

---

11 Judgment in *BVerfG E* 82, p. 322 f.

'is an attack on the entire free democratic basic order of the Federal Republic'. Party invective had gone on so long that for the judges it had become anti-constitutional. They had had enough by this point and seem to have made a conscious decision to take the Party's empty rhetoric seriously. In the general principles which the court published to accompany its decision, the judges wrote that a party is not necessarily anti-constitutional 'when it fails to acknowledge the highest principles of the free democratic basic order', but that when it takes 'an actively hostile, aggressive attitude to the existing order' then that party is an enemy of the constitution. The judges' patience had clearly broken at that point, and the Party paid a high price for its rhetorical exaggeration.

2.4 The Legal Consequences of the Ban

So the ban on the KPD had been achieved and publicly justified, and the political establishment was content. But it was a kind of Pyrrhic victory for the BVerfG. Notably, it was the last time the court took any decision in that area of law. It did, for instance, not get asked to rule on the constitutionality of the DKP (founded in 1968 – a party which even moderate opinion saw as 'a branch of the SED in the West'[12]), even though its 1956 ruling had explicitly included the outlawing of any follow-up organizations of the KPD. Later the court refused – on the grounds of disproportionality – to reach judgments on two minor extremist parties at the end of the 1980s and, most significantly, a major split in the ranks of its own judges meant that in 2003 the BVerfG refused to consider imposing a ban on the neo-Nazi NPD. Some of the consequences of this decision emerge from Chapter Eleven below.

The reason for this shift of activity had nothing to do with any ambiguous sympathies held by the court. In the case of the NPD, the disagreement among the judges was the direct result of the involvement of the security service in the NPD's organization. It's a tactic familiar to all countries which have to deal with violent clandestine groups: the security forces infiltrate undercover agents into such groups at the highest possible level. In the case of the NPD this tactic led a number of judges to believe that they had no proper basis to reach a decision on the constitutionality of the party, since significant elements of its actions and policy might have been influenced by agents infiltrated by the security forces. (The British government is still having to struggle with the problems caused by their own undercover agents working within the para-military

12 On the DKP see Chapter 8. The quotation is from Uwe Wesel (2002, p. 109).

groups of Northern Ireland.[13]) These were significant problems for the BVerfG itself. But there were still more basic problems coming from the standpoint of the government.

The KPD ban hardly amounted to glory days for the court. It had taken them five years to reach a judgment, and elements of the presentation of that judgment did not convince – perhaps the judges insisted too loudly that their decision was exclusively legal in character and lacked any political calculation. In any case, it was the government which moved away from the use of the court for the purpose of banning a party. Governments want clearer and more efficient procedures to deal with problems than the BVerfG was able to provide.

In fact, the SRP case had already made clear that the Federal government possessed more efficient procedures which it could use without having recourse to the BVerfG. The legal instruments which could be mobilized to put a party out of business were (with the exception of GG § 9) situated in the criminal code, not in the Basic Law, and were unlikely to be challenged by the BVerfG. GG § 9 concerned the basic right to form associations – as distinct from political parties –, but it expressly permitted the Federal Minister of the Interior to outlaw an association: it was in that way that the Communist youth organization, the FDJ, got outlawed in the Federal Republic, thus delivering a serious blow to the KPD's chance of widening its appeal. Other, no less effective procedures were used at a lower level. Early civil service legislation had made it possible to exclude KPD members from any level of the public service, including as manual labourers. It was much easier for Adenauer's government to use these less exalted legal instruments in order to pick off individual party members than to ban the party itself: it was also possible to penalize firms and prevent them from placing advertisements in Communist newspapers (hence cutting off funds to the party), and to block the frontier to East Berlin whenever the GDR was holding a youth festival or some other 'propaganda' meeting. These and other measures enabled government, in short, to strangle a party, rather than to dispatch it outright.

We must conclude that the fact that only the BVerfG possessed the power to declare a party illegal offered no guarantee for a party's continuing in existence once the government wished to be rid of it. Events in the 1970s showed that government had learnt that lesson from the KPD ban. From 1972 onwards the state was to demonstrate the effectiveness of discriminating against individual members of a party, while taking no steps to have the party itself declared illegal. Its measures took place under the ideological umbrella with

13 On the complications of covert operations (not just in Northern Ireland) see: Porch (2013, p. 268 f). On NPD see: *NJW* 2003, 1577, 95, 340.

which various societies have subsequently become all too familiar: 'We must sacrifice freedoms in order to preserve freedom'[14] (an early *bon mot* of justice minister Dreher), but they could be carried out far more effectively without taking the cumbersome and potentially provocative route through the BVerfG. In all these areas *old* laws proved much more useful than new ones, for they could operate comfortably without a conflict with the Basic Law becoming apparent and without waiting years for the court's decision.

Following the little noticed measure announced in September 1950, many of these old laws had received a major revitalization in August 1951, as we saw, with the passing of the first of a number of laws amending the criminal code – the so-called *Strafrechtsänderungsgesetz*. This was a substantial piece of legislation, bringing up to date a series of measures long present in the criminal code but in their previous forms too explicitly tied to past forms of government to be immediately applicable to the post-war situation. The list of topics covered included treason, damaging the national interest, and the insulting of high-ranking office-holders (here the only change needed was to put the Federal President into a form of words which previously had mentioned only the *Kaiser*) or the defacement of symbols of the nation. It moved on from these matters to laws relating to demonstrations, trespass, political leaflets, and concluded with the laying down of prison sentences for persons either founding 'an association whose purpose or activities are directed towards the carrying out of criminal activities' (StGB § 129) or 'being a member of an association' such as one which 'the Federal Administrative Court (*Bundesverwaltungsgericht*) or the most senior court of a Federal state has found to be a banned organization in accordance with GG § 9, Art. 2' (StGB § 129a).

These were highly significant provisions, and not just for the political parties. The Basic Law had, for instance, failed to concede a universal right to strike, and – although the working population of the Federal Republic had other things on its mind in the early 1950s than to go on strike – the *Strafrechtsänderungsgesetz* made sure that the well-known positive elements within the Basic Law (for instance, the explicit encouragement of trades-unions, the institution of co-determination and the central idea of an economic system which offered protection to the labour-force from the brutalities of unfettered capitalism – all these featuring strongly in the positive image which the Federal Republic gave of itself) were, if need be, more than balanced out by elements within the criminal code.

14 Dreher's attacks on the BVerfG can be found in any of the usual sources. The quotation in Brünneck (1978, p. 77). On the EDC: Kommers (1976, p. 284 f).

This was heady stuff. By means of these instruments the government was able to achieve at a stroke virtually all that the BVerfG had achieved after five years of deliberation. It was a clear indication of the power of this minor legislation that, when the KPD leader and another member of the Party's executive had come to Karlsruhe to argue the case against the ban on their party, they had already been in custody for some of the offences mentioned above. They had experienced the individual aspect of the party ban long before it had been institutionally formalized. In short: it was one thing for the BVerfG judge – as we saw in the Introduction – to praise the gap between the constitution and the legal code as having created a fruitful latitude within which the political process could operate: his view should be complemented by the recognition that such latitude also allowed the government to erode significant elements of the constitution, and that aspects of the BVerfG's work could easily be side-lined by the government. Banning the KPD merely put the seal on what had already been the substantive moves in the case.

2.5 Reflections on Constitutional Courts and Politics

Not surprisingly, the judgment of the BVerfG was severely attacked both at the time and subsequently. It represented, in a title of a book from the left, 'a disgraceful blot on the record of the court'.[15] This was the moment when, in the view of some observers, the court showed itself to be little more than the lapdog of Adenauer. It's a harsh attack, but not solely rooted in the political ideology of its authors. It was not only communists who worried lest the BVerfG had joined Adenauer's political establishment. Perhaps that makes it a suitable moment to raise here some more general issues.

In particular we should hesitate before being too critical of a decision which appears to have been political rather than legal in origin. First we might recognize that there is a general pattern here, often observed by legal historians: that the higher the authority of the court, the less narrowly 'legal' the basis on which it reaches its judgments. Similar observations, if less starkly, have been made about the recently constituted British Supreme Court. But for a more specific comparison with the practice of the BVerfG in the 1950s, we might look briefly to the behaviour of the Supreme Court in Washington, and to the subsequent assessment made by jurists of its decisions at the time, taking as our example the decision on School Segregation in 1954 – an issue as radical for the USA as de-nazification or anti-Communism was for the Federal Republic.

15 The GDR's attacks on the judgment e.g. in: *Das Schandurteil von Karlsruhe* (1957).

We cannot go into the whole debate, but briefly summarize two subsequent views of the judgment, starting with Alexander Bickel's classic account of 'the Supreme Court at the Bar of Politics'.[16]

In its judgment the Supreme Court unambiguously established the unconstitutionality of segregation, but it made no moves whatsoever to force immediate change in the practice of segregation – in terms either of taking steps to enforce its decision in Kansas (from where *Brown vs. the Board of Education* had proceeded), or of insisting on the repeal of the smaller administrative instruments on which day-to-day segregation was based. (We recall the relationship between constitutional and administrative measures in the KPD case.) The apparent passivity of the Supreme Court could have led observers to conclude that the Court had been ineffective, or – more seriously – that, like the BVerfG in the KPD case, it was too close to right-wing elements in the establishment. Some ten years after the judgment, however, Bickel reached a very different assessment.

In particular, Bickel insisted on the absolute need for the Supreme Court to respect the political realities of the country. He accepted that the Supreme Court was 'an organ of government' at large, and that its critics must be aware of the fact that 'the law proposes, but, for a time at least, the facts of life dispose'. In Bickel's opinion, no other balance was acceptable between 'authoritarian judicialism and the practice of democracy'. The Court was not 'a synod of bishops', he wrote (although since his book appeared even synods of bishops appear to have lost some of their power to do whatever they wish), nor 'a collective poet laureate', building beautiful thoughts in the world of ideals, with no regard for political realities.

Bickel therefore put forward the view that the Supreme Court was right through its 'inactivity' to undertake no steps to stop segregation immediately. The Court had done its work, its judgment had ensured that, in the medium term, segregation was finally going to cease to exist – as Lincoln had said of slavery, 'it is in the course of ultimate extinction'. In the interim, however, the Court's function was not to force confrontation, but 'to seek and foster assent'. For Bickel and for the Court itself this form of patience was the lesson of history. Across the centuries of the American Constitution the debate on judicial review – launched by and still focused on *Marbury vs. Madison* – they

16 Alexander M. Bickel (1986^2, esp. pp. 244–72). *Marbury v. Madison* (1803) has become – not without controversy – a founding judgment of the Supreme Court in establishing the practice of judicial review. Federalists such as Hamilton argued that 'the Constitution ought to be preferred to the statute, the intention of the people to the intention of their agents'. Other authorities objected to this as meaning the subordination of the elected legislatures of the federal state to the central Court.

could see a battle repeatedly played out between the 'defenders' of the federal Constitution and the consensual evolution of the constitution and practice determined by parliament in the individual states. In the interests of the latter, the court should not be overly authoritarian in insisting on immediate obedience to its judgment.

In his study of *The Empire of Law*, published at some twenty years greater distance to *Brown*, Ronald Dworkin does not dissent from this broad and pragmatic view of the relationship between the Court and the politics of the moment and – although he is critical of the actual judgment of the Supreme Court in *Brown*, for it 'proved to be a charter for obstruction and delay' – nevertheless he argues in the segregation issue for the Court's duty to ensure 'a stately and gradual process of change' and to avoid impatience.[17] Among other things, Dworkin regards it as essential that the Court put the people on notice about what the law is going to require of them; for in that manner the court allows time for social consensus to catch up with its judgments. The preservation of public order and consensus is also, in Dworkin's opinion, an important feature of the law.

In his recent comparison between the Supreme Court and the BVerfG Alfred Rinken is comfortable in taking a similar approach. He interprets the BVerfG's relationship to the political process positively, and in similarly gradualist terms, while drawing attention to a potential endangering of constitutional procedure which might occur 'if the constitutional judicature emancipates itself from a mere control organ to become an active political decision maker'. Even if it is far from clear that the BVerfG ever had the ambition of being 'a mere control organ' – Grimm's comments, quoted in the Introduction, strongly suggested that this was not the case –, Rinken's approach was responding to criticism of judgments such as the KPD ban simply on the grounds of the court's conformity to government's wishes. Gradualism and balance were, in Rinken's view, the key to the court's success.

The BVerfG's more controversial decisions not only laid the court open to the charge of a lack of political independence: they raised a question of consistency. In particular, it seems difficult to reconcile the judgment on *Lüth* (discussed in the following chapter) with that on the *Radikalenerlass* (Chapter Eight), in which concepts clearly championed by Nazism (notably the absolute loyalty of the public servant to the state) remained unchallenged by the inactivity of the BVerfG. Freedom of opinion seems in one case to have been declared absolute while in the other it was heavily compromised. One must

---

17 Dworkin (1986, p. 391). Rinken (2012, p. 80). As I suggest at various points, Otto Kirchheimer's analysis of 'political justice' overlaps at many points with Rinken's arguments.

ask whether a reconciliation can be achieved by taking the longer-term perspective which Dworkin and Bickel apply to the Supreme Court.

In the German situation, however, one of the bases of Dworkin's argument certainly deserves greater reflection. Discussing with approval the gradualist work of the Supreme Court, Dworkin quotes the celebrated Austrian political economist Otto Neurath's 'happy image'. We can only, Dworkin comments on the improvement of constitutional law, 'reform our settled views the way sailors repair a boat at sea: one plank at a time'.[18]

This may well be a happy description of the Supreme Court in its third century of existence, but it seems questionable whether Neurath's analogy can be applied to a legal system which, far from sailing the oceans, had within living memory publicly smashed upon the rocks. In any case, the BVerfG judgment came after the effective outlawing of the KPD and confirmed, rather than initiated, a shift in the political climate. 'One plank at a time' may well be a good idea implemented at the wrong time: perhaps gradualism of this kind was less than appropriate to the situation of the 1950s. And in particular the *Strafrechtsänderungsgesetz* of August 1951 ought more appropriately to be compared to loading heavy armaments onto a ship at a time when it is hardly able to float. As we look in this and two other chapters more closely at the judgments of the BVerfG we shall certainly notice the court's determination to remain close to political power, and therefore (staying with Neurath's metaphor) not to rock the boat, but we may suspect that the court's performance is less well described by Rinken as a sophisticated balance between radical and conservative decisions. Instead, we may be struck by the insecurity of these early decisions, revealed in a rather erratic mixture of abject conformism and defiant independence: in short, these were judgments of a constitutional court less than certain of its ground. I return to this point briefly at the end of the next chapter.

In both the Federal Republic and the USA it is easy for those people disappointed in elements of their country's achievements to focus on the roles of their respective constitutional courts. Whether – to take my examples more or less at random – the McCarthyism to which the Federal Republic was in danger of succumbing in the 1970s, or the dominance of money in funding American election campaigns, explicitly authorized by the Supreme Court in *McCutcheon v. Federal Election Commission* (2014),[19] will be seen by future generations as temporary deviations from the road leading inexorably to tolerance

18 Dworkin (1986, p. 111).

19 In fairness, we should point out that the BVerfG's judgment on party finances had almost the identical effect as the Supreme Court decision (cf. *BVerfG E* 8, p. 51f).

and equality; whether these disturbing circumstances prove to have been no more than temporary anomalies which, in Lincoln's words, are 'in the course of ultimate extinction' – such questions are not for this book to decide. But we cannot tell the stories of these trials without making clear that the BVerfG raised issues of this seriousness in those of its judgments which appear to declare allegiance to governmental policy in the Federal Republic. There are better ways to question such allegiance than, as the Baader-Meinhof movement attempted to, with guns and bombs. But in the light of the ban on the KPD it could not be said that the BVerfG had managed to break with all features of the past and to establish itself in the public mind as an organ of state truly above the prejudices which swirl round the political scene.

CHAPTER 3

The Lüth Case – at What Price Freedom of Expression?

We have noted the slowness with which the Federal Republic came to terms with ex-Nazis in the legal profession. Among other factors it was a heavily pragmatic approach which led the Allies to relax de-nazification in favour of getting an administrative system functioning once more in the West. Perhaps it's not easy to see how the legal profession could have been treated in a fundamentally different way, though decisions on sensitive individual cases should not have been left in the hands of a compromised judiciary. But the treatment of artists and intellectuals compromised by their support for Hitler's regime – the starting-point of our case in this chapter – raises altogether different issues.

3.1 The Starting-Point: Artists and Nazism

Artists, intellectuals and philosophers present the law with the difficulty of judging the culpability of ideas in themselves. The so-called party ideologue, Alfred Rosenberg, author of a large volume of turgid NS philosophy, was executed in Nuremberg not for his writings (though they were offensive enough), but rather for his activities when in charge of part of the occupied territories. A couple of levels down the hierarchy, Hanns Johst – one of the principal writers involved in the bureaucracy of Hitler's cultural system, and an officer in the SS, thanks to the support of his personal friend Heinrich Himmler – was interned and subsequently found guilty of being a 'Mitläufer' (fellow-traveller) in the de-nazification trials, but even he was back again in the literary profession by the early 1950s, albeit in obscurity. The bigger talents to have compromised with the Nazis – the philosopher Martin Heidegger, the poet Gottfried Benn and the essayist Ernst Jünger – all continued to publish after the war, and, although Benn suffered a brief ban on his works appearing in the French zone, none of them had any difficulty in re-establishing themselves in the cultural scene of the Federal Republic. Any further de-nazification of writers seemed to be left in the hands of a small number of amateur critics with a sense of personal mission – generally the legal apparatus of the Federal Republic showed no interest in pursuing writers and artists on the grounds of their past ideas.

The only noticeable achievements of the Third Reich in the arts lay in the area of film. The major films of the Third Reich were, however, not only technically sophisticated: they made significant contributions to the propaganda of the regime and were seen by many millions of people both inside and outside Germany – one thinks of the world-wide impact of Leni Riefenstahl's films *The Triumph of the Will* (1934) and *Olympia* (1938). Riefenstahl's major public profile made it more difficult for her, having been classified as a 'Mitläuferin', to establish herself in the post-war film industry, and she seems to have accepted that as a fact. Other compromised figures found it much easier to renew a post-war career.[1]

Our case initially concerns the director of the most obnoxious film providing propaganda for the regime's antisemitism, Veit Harlan. His film *Jud Süß*, scripted and directed by Harlan himself, was released in 1940, at a time when the state's persecution of the Jewish populations of Germany and Europe was already well advanced, and about to get massively worse. The film's twenty million strong audience was explicitly encouraged in its antisemitic attitudes and programmed by the film to welcome further murderous actions against the Jews.

In the light of his public profile in the Third Reich, Harlan's route through de-nazification was little short of a scandal. In his first hearing the defence argued that there was a distinction between 'artistic antisemitism' and 'criminal antisemitism'. One sees at once the difficulty of trying artists for their ideas, and an expert witness appearing at Harlan's hearing explicitly denied the existence of 'an *abstract* propensity of artistic material to encourage criminal behaviour'. What he meant was that even an antisemitic propaganda film was not capable of encouraging antisemitic behaviour in real life. For that reason, not even making *Jud Süß* could, the defence argued, constitute a criminal offence.

The more familiar line followed by Harlan's defence was, however, that Harlan had been powerless to refuse to direct the film. Since Harlan's defence lawyers had had their own successes at the Nuremberg trials (ten years later the Nuremberg defence teams were once again ready for the Frankfurt Auschwitz trial with the same disingenuous arguments), Harlan's principal contention was the same as Flick's: namely that his non-participation in the film would have involved direct disobedience to Goebbels' wishes – in other words a one-way ticket to the concentration camps. Unlike the Nuremberg trials, these de-nazification courts did not collect their own evidence, but relied on the accused's testimony for the evidence, so, fortunately for him, Harlan's claim remained untested. At all events, the first hearing in April 1949 – at

1 There is little point in blowing the dust off the petty denunciations and feuds of the early years, but a good overview of the film industry is offered by: Josef Wulf (1963).

which Harlan was accused of 'crimes against humanity' under Article 10 of the Control Council Law – acquitted him.[2]

The judgment was bizarre, particularly since it came relatively soon after the Nuremberg trials, and some sources suggest that it was only under explicit pressure from the British military governor that Harlan was re-tried in the Supreme court of the British zone, on the charge of 'being an accessory to persecution'. At this trial the earlier not-guilty judgment was upheld (no need to ask about the background of the judges in that appeal). The defence had been strengthened by the first of Adenauer's Amnesty Laws which was approved on December 31 1949, but of greater help to Harlan's case was the fact that the Jewish witnesses for the prosecution had already emigrated to Israel and were not willing to return to Germany to testify in court – in view of the sort of judges they might face there, that was hardly surprising. This was a pity, since experience from the concentration camps had established that there was an immediate increase in personal violence against the Jewish detainees after the staff had been shown Harlan's film. This was true in Auschwitz too, where one might have imagined that nothing could have been capable of increasing the violence to Jewish detainees. Nothing, that is, except *Jud Süß*.

Nevertheless, the argument which most persuaded the court was once again that Harlan had been forced to work on *Jud Süß*; that he had not been a free agent, but had directed the film under duress. He was therefore free to return to his profession and to start making films again. His next film – *Unsterbliche Geliebte* – was due to open the Hamburg film festival in December 1950. Germany was ready to present herself once more to the world's cultural elite, with of all people Veit Harlan as its figurehead. It was a grotesque but by no means unique epitome of the 'restoration'.

By this time, the already high level of public acceptance of the inadequacies of de-nazification had risen still further. Even for those who cared, it was hard to think what to do about figures like Harlan when the legal hindrance which might have prevented his further activities had been definitively blocked. The idealist amateurs exposing the NS past of writers, musicians and artists had no other method at their disposal than the occasional public denunciation. Otherwise they confined their activities to publishing academic books and lengthy encyclopaedic works documenting their subjects' involvement in the NS period, moving the debate from a legal to a moral level. It's clear that none of these activities had any impact on the ex-Nazis themselves, or damaged their subsequent careers.

2 It's debatable whether the terms in which Streicher was found guilty at the IMT might have applied to Harlan: the judgment stated that 'persecution on political and racial grounds [...] constitutes a Crime against Humanity' (cit. Taylor 1993, p. 590).

3.2 The Call for a Boycott

Erich Lüth, however, an SPD member of the Hamburg senate, was so incensed at the decision of the appeal court to acquit Harlan that he tried a new approach. He called for a public boycott of Harlan's new film. We should explain that this was some time before society had got used to the kind of boycott familiar in the late 1950s, for instance, through the boycott of South African oranges and sherry during the apartheid era. At the time of Lüth's appeal to the public, the principal boycott known in Germany had been the boycott of Jewish shops in the NS period, which had been a preliminary to further, lethal measures against the Jewish population. So Lüth was fighting fire with fire, and it can have been no surprise to him that a legal reaction followed swiftly.

Lüth was charged by the production and distribution companies of *Unsterbliche Geliebte* for damaging their legitimate business, citing § 823 of the BGB.[3] More significantly, he was found guilty under BGB § 826 of damaging Harlan in the exercise of his personal freedom, in – as the paragraph explains – 'a manner contrary to public morals (*gute Sitten*)'. In addition, the court had been far from impressed by Lüth's description of Harlan's de-nazification process as having amounted to 'a legal acquittal, but a moral condemnation'. The judges felt that Lüth's remark had shown too little respect for the courts. An injunction was served on him prior to the principal trial, in order to prevent him from repeating his call to boycott Harlan's film. Lüth appealed the injunction, but at the end of February 1950 this appeal too was rejected.

Finally, in November 1951 Lüth lost the principal hearing of his case, and then almost immediately embarked on what was one of the first instances of a *Verfassungsbeschwerde*, a personal constitutional complaint addressed to the BVerfG.[4] The Basic Law laid down the right of citizens to make such an appeal in a case where one of a number of personal injustices was claimed to have taken place, for instance, those relating to GG § 103 (the right to a fair hearing) and GG § 104 (powers of arrest). In fact, however, the complaint – prepared by the principal lawyer of the SPD, Adolf Arndt, and circulated widely among the leading legal circles of the time, thus combining a political campaign with a constitutional intervention on Lüth's behalf – focused on the claim that the court's judgment had infringed Lüth's right to freedom of expression, basing on § 5 of the Basic Law. At the time the BVerfG was a new institution and was only gradually finding its feet. More significantly, it was grossly overburdened

3 The BGB is the extensive codification of German civil law, which came into force originally in 1900, and has subsequently been much modified.

4 See Gusy (2006) on this procedure.

with the need to consider the ban on the KPD as well as to deal with President Heuß' request for clarification as to whether or not German rearmament was compatible with the constitution. So it was a number of years before Lüth's complaint could be addressed. One might argue that the judgment was irrelevant to the individual case long before it was issued.

With this delay the Lüth case separated out fundamentally from the issues which Lüth had initially begun by addressing. In the intervening years Harlan's career developed a momentum of its own. His new film was shown across the Federal Republic, accompanied in many places by protests and demonstrations, especially from students. The protests were met with inappropriate strong-arm measures from the police. In the course of these demonstrations, much to the shame of the Federal Republic, crowds shouting antisemitic slogans added their encouragement to the police violence. Still greater is the shame of leading politicians who took these protests as evidence of how greatly Lüth's campaign had offended the views of 'sensible and fair-minded citizens'. Perhaps not surprisingly, this level of public attention turned *Unsterbliche Geliebte* into a considerable box-office success. The film satisfied the elements of the population, who had positively enjoyed Harlan's *Jud Süß*, although more on the grounds of the symbolic significance of its screening than because of the later film's actual content. Those who do not believe that boycotts work would be encouraged by the outcome of Lüth's campaign.

3.3 The Decision of the BVerfG

By contrast, the Lüth case itself had effects which in their own sphere were far more significant. The decision of the BVerfG was not reached until January 1958, but it is generally hailed for having ensured as a principle the pre-eminence of the basic rights legislation of the Basic Law over the provisions of other elements of the civic and criminal codes – in other words a major and permanent victory for the court's power of judicial review. The judges of the BVerfG themselves were in no doubt as to the importance of what they had achieved. We cite once more the opinion of one of these judges, Dieter Grimm. 'No judgment', he wrote in 2001,

> has more decisively widened the protection of basic rights than the *Lüth* judgment of 1958. Through its finding, the court gave fresh recognition to the view that basic rights are not merely the subjective means by which the individual can defend himself against the state, but are at the same time objective principles which give to a legal system its proportionality

> and direction. In *Lüth* the BVerfG concluded that the demands of basic rights must not only be respected by the law-makers, but must also be taken into full consideration in interpreting and applying [existing and future] laws. By means of that decision, the protection of basic rights was brought onto the level of the general application of the law. Laws which limit basic rights, or in a particular application have the effect of restricting basic rights, must in consequence be interpreted afresh in the light of these restrictions. In the case before the court this meant that the civil courts – in the process of interpreting and applying the provisions of the BGB – were obliged to take into consideration the fact that Lüth's actions took place within the protected area of the basic right to freedom of expression.[5]

Grimm went on to claim that it was the basic rights which gave unity to the entirety of the Basic Law (this was the 'teleological' function which the court was to assume towards the *Grundgesetz*) while at the same time preserving their 'subjective' property of being able to prevent 'the over-expansion of the state'. Grimm's views are typical of the self-confidence which the BVerfG subsequently gained, but there is no doubt but that the judgment has generally been hailed as a watershed in the legal history of the Federal Republic – what one might call German law rising from the ashes, through a return to fundamental rights.

As we read the judgment of 1958 it's easy to understand Grimm's enthusiasm. A study of the evidence submitted to the court makes clear the considerable extent to which it was Arndt's submission – with its passionate appeal for a positive reading of the place of basic rights and their influence on the interpretation of other pieces of legislation – which lay behind many of the court's pronouncements. Particularly significant was the fact that Arndt's submission in a matter of civil law was based exclusively on constitutional law, and all but entirely ignored the paragraphs under which Lüth had been originally found guilty. Collings summarizes that *Lüth* 'constitutionalized all jurisdictions'.[6]

What is refreshing in the judgment is the insistence of the BVerfG that freedom of opinion has to include the freedom for opinions to be active within society. Freedom of opinion is held to be not just the right to think something

---

5 Grimm (2001, p. 307). His critique of the lack of a referendum after reunification: (p. 299 f).

6 The relationship between the BVerfG's judgment and Lüth's constitutional complaint is examined in: Arne Riedlinger (2005, esp. 176–860). The politician's comments on Lüth causing offence to right-minded citizens was explicitly criticized in the BVerfG judgment (see *ibid.* pp. 174–75). Collings quote (2015, p. 61).

and to do nothing with one's opinions. Freedom of opinion must mean the freedom to act on one's opinions. For the BVerfG judges, the freedom to hold passive, socially non-effective opinions was not the point, and did not represent that personal space which the law should defend.

This was an approach which shows how far legal debates have moved on since, for the judges in 1958 appeared not to be at all concerned to uphold freedom of thought in the face of a society which sought to control everyone's thoughts in the spirit of Orwell's *1984*, or in the face of (to quote Vance Packard) the 'hidden persuaders'.[7] That is of course the emphasis which recent discussions of surveillance have brought to the topic, but it was entirely absent in Karlsruhe in 1958. Instead, for the BVerfG the principal fear was of less sinister measures and attitudes which might nevertheless prevent opinions from becoming active in a democratic society.

In the judgment of the court, Lüth therefore was entitled not merely to hold opinions about Harlan, or about antisemitism, but he was entitled do so something with those opinions, including publicizing them and calling for a boycott of Harlan's film. Democracy had to be understood as the active conflict of opinions – a conflict described as 'the living element of the free democratic basic order'. Freedom of thought could not simply be defined as the mere coexistence of ineffectual opinions.

Out of such considerations, the BVerfG judged that the courts which had found against Lüth had failed to recognize that those elements of the law which they were interpreting in reaching their decision against Lüth had themselves to be interpreted in the light of the basic rights paragraphs: the courts should have seen that, by enforcing those paragraphs without reference to § 5 of the Basic Law, they were bringing about an infringement of those basic rights. Accordingly, the injunction on Lüth was lifted and the verdict in the earlier trial was reversed. All this took place explicitly in the name of encouraging a society in which each individual is to be the 'exponent of the Basic Law' and to be supported in carrying through the implementation of rights even in ways (such as the proposed boycott) which quite properly lay outside the range of measures permitted to the state itself.

Of course, the BVerfG had to come back to the Veit Harlan case itself. Taking its own evidence (including, for instance, reading the self-important memoirs Harlan had published during the Third Reich), the court defended the rights which Harlan too enjoyed under the Basic Law, but conceded that the public policy interest in Lüth's campaign against Harlan was of fundamental

7 Packard's text (1957) arrived in Europe in the late 1950s as a harbinger of new, subliminal American advertizing techniques.

importance to the fabric of the Federal Republic's democracy. Lüth's intention had not been part of any personal vendetta, but had come from an all-embracing political vision of democracy, including – among other things – the restoring of friendly relations with the state of Israel and making clear to the rest of the world that the Federal Republic had once and for all left behind the legacy of Nazism. Lüth's motives were issues of central political importance to the whole community.

The court therefore found that the reference of BGB § 826 to Lüth behaving in 'a manner contrary to public morals' was entirely inappropriate. We spoke in the first chapter of the difficulty which post-war German courts experienced in responding to the Nuremberg trials – as American practice was to – by reverting to the value-orientated concepts associated with natural justice. In *Lüth* this question arose specifically in the court's critique of the appeal to public morals contained in BGB § 826 (and, as we shall see, elsewhere) and its mobilization against the defendant in 1951. The natural justice approach to Lüth's case had focused on the argument that individuals should be free to develop their personality without interference from boycotts and the like, but the BVerfG judgment explicitly corrected this tendency. It insisted that a *political* understanding based on the essential features of a democracy had priority over 'natural' sentiments.

Finally, the court even explicitly defended Lüth's description of the result of Harlan's de-nazification hearings ('a legal acquittal, but a moral condemnation'). It pointed out – perhaps a little disingenuously – that, as a non-lawyer, Lüth could not have been expected to find entirely appropriate language in which to express what the BVerfG clearly regarded as an accurate assessment of Harlan's position in 1950. It would be impossible to think of a more complete vindication both of Lüth's fight against Harlan and of Lüth/Arndt's plea for a wider interpretation of the constitutional right to freedom of expression.

3.4 Repercussions

It is, nevertheless, hard to escape the sense that this outcome might have been too good to be true. As Henne and Riedlinger's work has shown, the court was strongly influenced by the phrasing of Lüth's submission, and many of Arndt's formulations are echoed in the judgment. Nevertheless, so soon after the NS years it seems inconceivable that the Federal Republic could claim to be in possession of a constitution in which every law was to be read in the light of its effects on basic rights. We saw in the previous chapter that freedom of expression had fared less well in the ban on the KPD. Such scepticism about the

Basic Law was not held simply by those on the far left, for whom all forms of the bourgeois state tend towards the totalitarian. Chapter Eight examines a judgment of the BVerfG eighteen years later, which makes elements of *Lüth* seem highly questionable – indeed, in the eyes of the left, these cases seemed to prove clearly that their cynicism about *Lüth* had been well-placed. More impartial constitutional historians too have their doubts concerning this euphoria about basic rights. In his study of the creation of the Basic Law, published in 1958 (i.e. before *Lüth*), the American historian John Ford Galay commented:

> Absolute statements of rights and theories tending to establish the absolute or extra-historical character of such rights appear to have had little effect on the actual sphere of freedom enjoyed anywhere.[8]

In other words: the enshrining of basic rights in a constitution (something which famously characterizes the American constitution) offers no guarantee that those rights will actually be enjoyed in that society; indeed, it is the way in which society operates, rather than any abstract principles, which creates the scope within which basic rights may become a reality. The issue of press freedom illustrates his point well: not anchored in the constitution, it had to rely on general rights paragraphs for realization. In just the same way – to complete Galay's argument – it is specific, historically identifiable circumstances which restrict human rights and which, one might suggest, the Basic Law and certainly the Adenauer government could have been more explicit in bringing under control. While tensions are always likely to arise in the relationship between *static* laws and a dynamically changing society, the question as to the foundation on which basic rights are best predicated remains unanswered. It was for that reason that, in BVerfG judge Dieter Grimm's opinion, a significant opportunity was lost when the Basic Law was not put to a referendum following German unification in 1990. Such an endorsement by the new population of the Federal Republic might at least have begun to overcome the 'absolute' and 'extra-historical' quality of basic rights in the German constitution. As it is, Galay's reservations will continue to be germane.

Grimm's euphoria about *Lüth* had one other dimension – his personal euphoria about the BVerfG itself. For there is no doubt that critiques of the court were to become more common after *Lüth*, and that these critiques had

---

8 Galay's scepticism about absolute declarations of human rights: (1964, p. 160). This view is taken up by Peter G. Sack, who writes: 'English language tends to reify 'law' as an operational system which *produces* the rights of individuals, whereas German tends to reify these rights themselves' (1996, p. 66).

a much wider and more complex basis than the ideological critiques from the left which we touched on at the end of the last chapter. They surfaced both as an expression of opinion among constitutional lawyers and as a judgment by political scientists about the potential weakening of parliamentary democracy by an over-active constitutional court. *Lüth* – and its subsequent praise – is characteristic of that attitude, one which Alexander Bickel in his remarks on the American Supreme Court labelled 'authoritarian judicialism'.[9]

Particularly intense discussions were unleashed by a remark of Chancellor Schmidt in the mid-1970s, when he spoke of 'the necessity for self-limitation' which all organs of the state should respect, 'including the constitutional court'.[10] Much later in his life Schmidt expressed his criticism more trenchantly, but in the difficult situation of the abortion debates of the 1970s he remained moderate. 'Not everyone can set out to expand their sphere of influence to its absolute limit,' Schmidt went on, 'the constitutional court must recognize that'. The background to Schmidt's remarks was that the BVerfG had almost made a habit of reaching rulings which not only implicitly or directly contradicted statute law, but which also ran counter to the declared wish of the nationally elected parliament. The right to judicial review had been exercised, Schmidt felt, without regard to the need for self-restraint. The court's judgments on the German-German treaty of 1975, for instance, and – as we shall see in Chapter Five – in the abortion case, offered clear examples of this tendency. In settling conflicts of interest between central government and the federal states, the BVerfG had already set itself above the established processes of democratic decision-making. It's not surprising that not only disgruntled politicians, but serious academic constitutionalists were worried lest the court was making itself – rather than being the 'protector of the constitution' – the 'absolute ruler of the constitution'. At a lower level of debate the media spoke of Karlsruhe as 'the real extra-parliamentary opposition' and described relationships between Bonn and the court as the 'real Cold War'.

All institutions tend increasingly to believe themselves more important than other institutions. It was a result of this tendency that the initial fear of CDU dominance in nominating judges to the BVerfG had diminished considerably by the 1970s, for it was the judges' loyalty to the institution of the court, rather than their original political orientation which had become problematic.

9 (1965, p. 214).

10 Schmidt's remark from the mid 1970s is quoted in the *Spiegel*-series on the BVerfG (1978), p. 38. In the same article the comments on the 'real' cold war (p. 48) and the anxieties about the court as the 'absolute ruler' of the constitution (p. 49). See also Rinken (2012, p. 74 f) and Wesel (2004, p. 213f), who sees the solution to be the recognition that the BVerfG is a political institution, but not party-political.

Yet even when this problem was publicly discussed, the fact remained that the judges had all the cards on their side of the table. The prestige of the Basic Law was the foundation of their power; this was reflected, as we saw in the Introduction, in the public opinion polls, which invariably rated the court more highly than any regional or national parliament. Furthermore, the right of every citizen 'at no expense and without reference to a lawyer' to address petitions to the court appeared to offer a guarantee of individual representation such as parliamentary democracies find hard to achieve. Much in the same way, it could be argued that referenda can disrupt effective democratic parliamentary government, although they appear to promise greater democracy.

In fact, as *Lüth* and the KPD-ban already showed, the court's effect on political life was on occasion less than constructive. Its decisions sometimes came long after the situation they should have resolved had become irrelevant. The enormous numbers of individual petitions meant that the court risked failing to live up to the promise of its statute. Yet these disadvantages remained unimportant and the court survived the critiques unscathed, for the reason that it built its prestige essentially on reversing the features of the NS system, an activity which made it all but impossible to argue against the court on fundamentals. As one commentator pointed out, 'the more dictatorially an issue had been handled in the past, the greater determination the court showed to expand its jurisdiction into that area'.[11] It was clear that the court derived its understanding of its mission from the immediate past of the Federal Republic, and its determination to practise 'wehrhafte Demokratie' (militant democracy: see also Chapter Eight below) was defined in those terms. This attitude was of course entirely admirable, provided that, in making itself the 'fourth power' in the state, the court did not stand in the way of the other powers learning both the principles and the practicalities of sustaining a democracy.

For all the satisfaction with which its judges looked back on *Lüth*, we cannot ignore the fact that this case had given the court a glory day an experience which it would be slow to repeat and which would occasionally cast into shadow other aspects of its work.

A postscript to the case was offered by the judgment of the European Court of Human Rights in 2004.[12] Princess Caroline of Monaco had lost her case in the German courts, when she tried to prevent a photographer publishing

11 *Der Spiegel* (1978, p. 52).

12 On the case of Princess Caroline: Thomas Henne (2005, esp. pp. 149–50). The claim that the case is a catalyst for widespread reform of the law: Rainer Wahl (2005). A more cautious, technical discussion of the case (stressing the BVerfG's reservations about the ECHR judgments acting as 'a guide to the interpretation of German basic rights') in: Schilling (2010, pp. 17–21, 252). See also Collings (2015, pp. 291–305).

intimate photographs of herself. In reaching their judgment, the German courts accepted that, as a figure well-known to the public, the Princess could not argue that the publication of the photos was not in the public interest. The ECHR however reversed the judgment, contending – and thereby, legal commentators argue, correctly picking up the essence of the *Lüth* judgment – that the question to be resolved was not one of public *interest*, but that of the *political* importance of the issues raised. In effect, the ECHR held that Lüth's motivation had been fundamental to the BVerfG's judgment, since he had been concerned with the essential functioning of a democracy and this idea had priority over any ill-defined 'public interest' in the princess's photographs. Lüth's case had been won because his freedom was being exercised and defended in the interests of a better and more democratic society: in calling for a boycott, he had been acting out of political-democratic reasons. No such case could be made for the photographer, the European Court found, and he therefore lost the case. That judgment has subsequently found its way back into German clarifications of the significance of the *Lüth* judgment.

It is not surprising that in England the adoption of the European Human Rights legislation and its integration into English law had long before June 2016 at various times given rise to controversy, so much so that at the time of writing the British government is determined to remove the ECHR's jurisdiction over the country (although there is a general failure to differentiate that court from the European Court). The impatience of successive British ministers of the interior has focused, for instance, on the fact that they could not deport 'trouble-makers' as they saw fit. This criticism has had its origin not simply in local scepticism about the European project, or the quality of legal advice available to British administrations, but it reflected the standpoint of the particular legal tradition of England, profoundly different from the German tradition which we examine here. Rainer Wahl's enthusiastic comparison of English and German practice on this point (2005) goes too far in assessing English experience in the light of the *Lüth* judgment. It is certainly now fanciful to see *Lüth* as a turning-point for any jurisdiction other than the German. But, as later chapters suggest, it may also be premature to greet it as a once-and-for-all turning-point in German jurisprudence. Not only the unalienable freedom of speech enjoyed by the individual was an outcome which it might be hard to sustain in the times of religious and political terrorism, but a hardly less great freedom of jurisdiction came to be enjoyed by the BVerfG, and it was not clear how either outcome would look in changed circumstances. Events in the 1970s were to offer serious challenge to both.

CHAPTER 4

Four Murders, and Reflections on Court-Reporting in the Federal German Press

In this chapter we examine a case which, without ever dominating national headlines, remains familiar to many West Germans. The principal trial which we discuss contained an important issue of law, and the resolution of that case, albeit in a minor respect, represented an unusual positive effect of the co-existence of two judicial systems in divided Germany. But the case is also important because it raises questions fundamental to all legal work, inside and outside the courts: namely, the relationship between the administration of the law and the wider public. It shows that justice depends on the courts' being embedded in a network of democratic communication. In a democracy the mediation of the law to a lay public through the work of free and responsible media rightly shares something of the prestige of the law itself – in short, justice is too important to leave to professional lawyers.

4.1 Reporting the Law

At the beginning of the Federal Republic considerable efforts were made to familiarize the population with the law, especially of course with the new, the Basic Law. There were strong political reasons for this. In order to build respect for democratic law, German schools had the task of passing on basic constitutional knowledge to the young, a practice which has more or less continued into the present, if for changing reasons. At the same time, embassies and cultural services were provided with copies of the Basic Law, translated into the languages of the world, in order to make clear to an international public the democratic credentials and commitment of the new republic. Commercial law was of course also regarded as important, if to a more specialized circle. Other branches of the law, however, and the criminal law in particular, remained reserved for those either wishing to build their career around it, or unwittingly becoming entangled in it, and was much less well mediated by the state. Other forms of mediation were required.

Among the institutions which traditionally have mediated between the law and the public none has been more important than the press. The roots of the press's involvement with reporting the law are to be found in the late eighteenth century and were explicitly political in intention. As modern societies developed, the law gradually ceased to be the expression of the will of absolute rulers and of the churches; it became codified and increasingly operated as a form of social contract. It became the medium in which social conflicts were resolved and an expression of the general will. In view of this function, it was essential that the administration of the law took place in public and – to use the modern term – transparently.

Newspapers began to report regularly on court proceedings. The proprietors were determined to guarantee that the law was administered in this open way. They initially employed professional lawyers as their legal correspondents, hoping not only to ensure the seriousness of the reporting and to bridge the gap between everyday language and the all but incomprehensible language of the court, but also in order to raise the low esteem in which lawyers were generally held at the time. With the massive increase in the circulation of newspapers, however, proprietors became aware that crime-reporting sold newspapers, and that it was the skills of the reporter rather than of the lawyer which would boost their circulation figures. This shift of emphasis meant that the papers concentrated ever more strongly on sensational cases: the public interest of a court case rather than its legal niceties was the crucial factor. At a time when newspapers were sold on the street by newspaper boys shouting out headlines, few news stories were as effective as a brutal murder, ideally involving a celebrity. Northcliffe exhorted his editors: 'Give me a murder a day'. Such sensationalism, however, did not necessarily represent a break with the progressive origin of the whole practice: it remained important for the press, for instance, to draw attention to miscarriages of justice or to the unreasonable behaviour of judges and prosecutors, perhaps particularly so in sensational cases – indeed they were proud to contribute 'more than all the police in Europe' to tracking down fugitive criminals.[1]

The book-market offered another channel through which the activities of the law-courts were mediated to the lay public. Here crime-reporting and fiction soon became all but interchangeable. I mentioned earlier the tradition of the *Pitaval* stories. Such works anticipated the popular press of the late nineteenth century in their preference for melodramatic contrasts between innocence and guilt, as well as in their almost exclusive focus on murder and other crimes of violence, and from the early nineteenth century on fiction was anxious to exploit the popularity of these topics.

---

1 A selection from the extensive literature on the mediation of the law through the press and by fiction is listed in the general notes to the Introduction. Northcliffe's comment is quoted in Rowbotham (2013, p. 103). The 1870 remark of an English detective (*ibid.*, p. 110 f).

Among the works deriving from the *Pitaval* tradition and from the popular press was the classic detective story, a genre most strongly associated with France, Britain and the USA. While the genre includes points of law only marginally, it reinforces a general familiarity with the law. Detective fiction has expanded massively in recent decades into the crime and detective stories which now dominate the TV channels of the world. The urban – usually big-city – setting of the majority of these works suggests important elements of their origin: an Enlightenment concern for justice further down the social ladder, and a nineteenth century fascination with the law as a social mechanism regulating 'the jungle of the cities'.

Another highly significant contribution of the novel to the mediation of the law was the fascination of many serious writers with the criminal mind, in particular with the mind of the murderer. We note that – just as Sherlock Holmes acted as one conduit for forensic methods to reach the police – professional lawyers eagerly took up fiction's concentration on criminal psychology. This interest is clearly reflected in the work of the celebrated law-reformer Erich Wulffen, whose name became widely known outside Germany. Wulffen's publications reflect the links between professional and amateur in this field. From the early 1900s he published extensively in two closely related fields. Parallel to his professional works on criminal psychology – in which his focus was on sexually motivated crime –, Wulffen also wrote popular crime fiction and in addition published widely-read accounts of the criminal mind as revealed in literature.[2]

Finally, we should mention the fashion for court-room dramas, played out on stage and subsequently on the larger and smaller screen. Whether Perry Mason (for a very old generation) or Rumpole (for a moderately old generation): such series have an abiding place in popular entertainment. The heroic highpoint in media's treatment of court procedures – Sidney Lumet's dazzling film *Twelve Angry Men* (1957) – has, however, scarcely been emulated.

It would be hard to point to structural differences between the power and role of newspapers in the Federal Republic and in other national cultures. The effects of sensationalist reporting have not differentiated themselves

2 The background to Wulffen and his links to prominent figures in the progressive jurisprudence of the years before 1914 and of the Weimar Republic (especially Gustav Radbruch) is given in: Schönert (1991a). On the increasingly technical nature of court proceedings see Rückert (1991), who expressly discusses the 'de-dramatization' (*Entdramatisierung*) of the courts, also citing Foucault. A German approach to these matters will have in mind the classic court-room comedy of the early nineteenth century, Heinrich von Kleist's *Der zerbrochene Krug* (The Broken Jug, 1806), in which the principal dialogues take place between the judge and the accused.

significantly across the systems: Heinrich Böll's denunciation of the *BILD* newspaper in *The Lost Honour of Katharina Blum* is little different to the various campaigns waged against the Hearst or Murdoch presses. Nevertheless, differences between the various national legal systems have shaped the forms in which the mediation of the law has taken place. The widespread use of the jury system in English and American law, for instance, has furthered the involvement of ordinary citizens in the administration of justice, while the adversarial structure of English and American courts has allowed great scope for the dramas of the court-room, starting from the sense that the jury and the public represent an audience before whom the lawyers have to *perform*. Paradoxically, fiction took over the drama which had once been natural to the courts at precisely the time when in reality, as the law became more technical and judges more like civil servants, drama was vanishing from the courts.[3]

By contrast, although German fictional writing does not lack colourful legal figures, the German court system, through its preference for the bench-system and a more restricted use of lay members, has been less dramatically portrayed than English and American courts. There's a preference for the drama of cross-examination, conducted between judge and defendant – a tradition which goes back at least to the early nineteenth century. But there are other, still more significant aspects of the German judicial system which have exercised influence on the reporting of trials, both fictional and real.

In the Introduction we identified some of the fundamental differences between the judicial practices in a *Rechtsstaat* and a common-law system, such as the English and American. We noted a tendency for the German system to understand the courts as possessing a limited technical remit, namely to apply existing laws to the circumstances of individual cases. As a result, the *Rechtsstaat* tends to develop far less interest in the activities of counsels and judges than in the Anglo-American tradition. On the one hand German judges are in a career grade, reached, often at a relatively young age, by means of academic and administrative achievement, rather than by experience – still less by a life outside the courts. This has had the effect of somewhat reducing public interest in the business of the courts, even of senior courts, for their

3 A sidelight on the 'colourful' characters produced by English adversarial courts: R. W. Cooper's account of the IMT, strongly orientated to the British legal team in Nuremberg, is clearly entranced by Mr G. D. 'Khaki' Roberts, K. C. with his 'sense of fun'. He sees him as 'one of the most popular personalities of Nuremberg' (1947, p. 35). Telford Taylor gives a highly critical view of Roberts' usefulness to the prosecution. He 'oversimplified problems' and was 'not good on paper' (1993, p. 84). The adversarial lawyer did not fit in to a system different to the Old Bailey.

dealings have become bureaucratic, and innovation or originality has not often been at a premium.

We saw, for instance, that it took a number of years before even the BVerfG grew beyond merely implementing laws into the role of shaping laws and using judgments in individual cases to create a coherent system of justice – in other words (although we are mindful of Dworkin's rejection of a distinction between 'interpretive' and 'non-interpretive' judgments: all justice is interpretation) *making* the law rather than simply applying it. This contrasts strongly with the focus of the media in the Anglo-American systems on how individual judgments have been reached. As a consequence of this, to take one further example, the election of judges to the US Supreme Court remains a matter of massive public attention. (By contrast the election of BVerfG judges, though it has not lacked controversy, was shifted from open parliamentary sessions into a committee structure.) Next to such dramas outside the courtroom, the English and American press have regular and extensive Law Reports (these, however, have not included criminal cases), and the rationale of a court's judgments is rightly seen as being no less newsworthy than the lives and pronouncements of celebrity counsels, or the 'human story'. Specialist court reporting may have declined a little since the days of the barrister-journalists of the mid-nineteenth century, but it certainly has not gone away.

I don't wish to overstate the argument. Of course the BVerfG's judgments are fully reported, and on occasion other courts – more or less consciously, and often in order to assert themselves *vis à vis* the BVerfG – have seen for themselves a shaping and interpretative function well beyond the letter of the law. At various stages of the *Berufsverbot* cases, for instance, as is clear from Chapter Eight below, specialist courts adopted distinctive approaches which went beyond the mere application of the legal paragraphs. The administrative courts and the labour courts in particular felt challenged as a matter of principle to *develop* existing legislation towards a particular view of the general good, and in the course of this development they took up very different sides in the legal arguments. At least in the years between 1972 and 1980 their judgments took on a wider, extra-judicial function, and the press responded accordingly. But this remained an unusual situation in the Federal German court-landscape.[4]

The law is both a technical matter for specialists and a crucial medium in which all citizens have to move. The more it is understood as the former, the greater is the tendency for the business of the courts to be recorded merely

4 On the labour courts and the *Berufsverbot* see Chapter Eight. The individual judge who best illustrates that independence was Hans Carl Nipperdey (1895–1968). See: Requate (2008, p. 64 f).

in specialized journals and in language all but inaccessible to the public and where (although this is a small matter) cases are identified by means of volume number and shelf-mark rather than by means of the defendant's name.[5] German legal records certainly look impersonal. By contrast, a system based on case law lends itself to more committed court reporting, and while it is not by definition easier to follow than codified law, it has tended to offer more and more explicit points of entry for the socially engaged reporter.

My argument in this section will seem particularly obvious to Irish, English and American readers: of course, the newspapers report on the law and knowledge of the business of the courts is an integral part of citizenship in a democracy. However, the Federal Republic's circumstances in 1949 remind us that the role of the press is the result of particular historical developments in jurisprudence and that such developments cannot simply be taken for granted or grafted seamlessly on to a system with a different past. At all events, in the early years of the Federal Republic there was an extremely weak tradition in this respect, and a massive deficit in the practice of court-reporting. The reasons for these shortcomings were both simple and complex: simple, in that the Federal Republic was the new-born baby at the end of a period of totalitarian dictatorship, in which the administration of the law was not merely continuously brutal and unjust, but much of it unreportable and all of it beyond criticism: complex, because traditions have to be established before they can be broken and they take time and chance to evolve. For whatever reasons, not only was the judicial system compromised by the years of NS rule, but the link between justice and the public had been all but completely broken.

In order to understand the break which German law suffered, and which the Federal Republic had to overcome before it could become at home with the law in a way familiar to other Western democracies, we need to take a brief backward glance at the relationship between the public and the German courts, and the Weimar Republic is the place to begin.

5 For the German system of identifying cases see Horn, Kötz, Leser (1982, p. 58). On court-reporting during the Weimar Republic: Isabella Claßen (1988). Claßen also gives an interesting account of Egon Erwin Kisch and his reporting of the notorious spy trial of Carl von Ossietzky (pp. 139–46 – see Note 3 to Chapter 6). On the process of adaptation through which the post-war German press had to go in order to leave behind its NS past, see: Christine von Hodenberg (2002).

4.2 Precedents in Weimar

We start with an essay by the writer Heinrich Mann published in the early months of the first world war.[6] His essay compared German and French intellectuals in their engagement in issues of justice. Mann wrote this essay because he was upset by the failure of German intellectuals to exercise any restraining influence on the enthusiasm for war which was sweeping Germany in 1914: unfortunately for his argument as well as for history, the French intellectuals were hardly more restrained in their drive for war than were their German counterparts. Mann selected as his two examples the most notorious miscarriages of justice in French legal history. His first example was taken from the mid-eighteenth century, with the religious bigotry which led to the sentencing and execution of Jean Calas for the murder of his son; the second was the still recent Dreyfus case, in which a Jewish army officer was wrongly found guilty of spying for Germany by a military tribunal held *in camera*. In the Calas case justice was finally achieved, if only posthumously, in 1764 through the persistent intervention of the writer Voltaire; as everyone knows, justice was eventually arrived at for Dreyfus in part through the intervention of the novelist Émile Zola and his famous pamphlet *J'accuse* (1898).

Mann wished to see a similar involvement of public intellectuals in questions of justice in Germany. While he seriously underestimated the ability of democracies to whip up that chauvinism and antisemitism which had turned the Dreyfus Affair into such a divisive case, Mann was certainly correct in arguing that the opportunities for the involvement of the public in the judicial process were far greater in a democracy than in an authoritarian monarchy. What Mann did not appreciate was that it would take much more than exhortation to create forms of medial activity which would be capable of bringing judicial issues regularly and objectively into public consciousness.

Democracy arrived in Germany four years after Mann's essay in the shape of the Weimar Republic, and gradually the administration of the law began to move in the direction Mann had looked for. It was not celebrated novelists like Zola who got themselves involved in the fight for justice. On one hand the reformist lawyers of the pre-war years, close to the SPD, found themselves in power – the most notable being the legal philosopher Gustav Radbruch

6 Heinrich Mann (known outside Germany not just for being Thomas Mann's elder brother, but for the book behind the classic early film *The Blue Angel*, directed in 1930 by Josef von Sternberg, in which Marlene Dietrich starred): Zola (1981, p. 218 f). Note how for Wesel (1997) the Dreyfus Affair occupies an absolutely decisive place in the evolution of the European law.

(1878–1949), who became justice minister in the early years of the Republic and was responsible for major changes, including the admission of women to the judiciary. (Unfortunately these changes could not balance out the effects of the continuation in office of the old guard of judges with no interest in reform and still less loyalty to democracy.) Another positive development was in the field of legal journalism. The most prominent figures were the journalist Paul Schlesinger, writing under the by-line *Sling*, and the journalist Gabriele Tergit. The work of both journalists had its focus in the Moabit court in Berlin.[7]

Sling wrote for the mainstream daily newspaper, *Vossische Zeitung*. As he himself admitted, when he had started out, he was relatively unfamiliar with the law, but his expertise increased over the years, and with it the respect in which the legal profession held his work. While modest about his own achievements, he held strong opinions about the importance of court-reporting. Sling saw his function as important for two reasons: the first was that justice – 'that machine [...] which can crush each one of us' – could not be allowed to run its own publicity. Justice was too important to leave to the professionals: it needed to be mediated by lay-people and outsiders. Sling was also concerned about many areas in which the courts got things wrong, not just in their failure to speak and understand the same language as most of the people passing through them, but also – and this was Sling's second focus – in the utter disregard which so many judges showed for the democratic principles of the state and therefore of the law itself. The commitment to democratic justice was behind every article Sling wrote. 'The public nature of court proceedings', he wrote, after one judge had proposed that cases should regularly be held *in camera*, 'is the only air in which the law can thrive'. Sling was a true successor to Pulitzer, with his belief that 'there is not a vice which does not live by secrecy'.[8]

Tergit's reporting in newspaper articles (primarily the *Berliner Börsen-Curier, Tageblatt* and *Die Weltbühne*) focused on the business conducted daily in the law courts of Berlin. She gave more attention than Sling to the minor and insignificant cases which came to court. Her explorations were what sociologists would class as a 'walk on the wild side', conducted without legal training, and they were initiated in part out of a flaneuse's interest in exploring the underbelly of her city. But they were not sensationalist. Tergit followed the numerous 'unimportant' trials in which the 'little people' of the city got involved, and she recorded the injustices and unreasonableness with which such people were confronted, while observing with quiet irony and occasional anger that

7 Gabriele Tergit's work is sampled in (1999). I have used the reportages in Sling (1929), to which the celebrated law minister Gustav Radbruch wrote a complimentary forward.

8 Quoted in: Lotz (1991, p. 4).

discrepancy between the instruments of the law – both police and judges – and those people to whom the law should be a protection. After 1933, exile cut Tergit off from her subject, from her public and from her function within society. It was not until the mid-1980s that her name re-surfaced and her work was published in book form. In the meantime her ideals were trampled over by the Nazis and her example to journalists all but forgotten.

One other writer was notable in the Weimar Republic for opening the law to the public, albeit in a much more restricted area and more polemically than Tergit or Sling. The documentary writer and novelist Ernst Ottwalt – belonging to a much more left-wing political background than Tergit – produced with *Denn sie wissen, was sie tun* (1931) what has become the token 'justice novel' of the German twentieth century, often reprinted during the years of the Federal Republic by those anxious to argue that little has changed or improved in the justice system since the declining years of the Weimar Republic.[9] Ottwalt's novel strings together some of the most notorious examples of class justice in the Weimar Republic into the fictional biography of a successful right-wing judge. The title of the novel – *For they know what they do* – refers to the words of Jesus spoken on the cross, but it reverses those words and claims, persuasively, that the injustices and miscarriages of justice during the Weimar Republic were the deliberate and direct product of the reactionary ideology and careerism of members of the judiciary, who saw little reason to use the law to support democracy and still less reason to restrain their prejudices out of respect for fair procedure or for the law itself. Judges, such as the novel's 'hero' Dickmann, do know what they are doing, and the destruction of the Weimar Republic is their long-term intention, rather than merely the by-product of their incompetence or (as some historians argued after the event) of the excessive liberalism of the law itself.

Ottwalt too went into exile in 1933. As a prominent Communist he left Germany more quickly than Tergit and went on to face the disillusionment to his ideals of justice in the Moscow Show Trials from 1936 onwards. He died in 1943 in the Soviet Gulag, one of Stalin's countless victims. Nevertheless, the anti-Communism of the Adenauer years meant that his name remained forgotten until well into the 1960s – and, of course, also in the German Democratic Republic, where, even after Khrushchev's denunciation of Stalin in 1956, opposition to Stalinism continued to have a very mixed reception from the state.

9 Ottwalt's novel has at various times been available in a series of more or less alternative presses. In literary circles it is known because of the criticism which its publication provoked from the eminent Stalinist critic Georg Lukács. On these (and other) forms of fictional writing on justice, see: Erhard Schütz (1986, pp. 18–20, 154–159).

Despite the work of these writers, the Weimar Republic was only just beginning to develop democratic law-reporting. As a historian of the period has written, 'there remained a striking discrepancy between the number of court judgments and their public reporting'.[10] The Federal Republic would have much to learn.

4.3 The Federal Republic

The Federal Republic was slow to develop new social forms appropriate to a democratic society. In its early years the state had major and urgent problems to address, none of which prioritized the extension of democratic engagement in the law – issues such as the rebuilding of housing and food-supplies, the improvement of public health following the hunger-typhus epidemic of winter 1947, and the resettlement of many millions of refugees from the eastern part of the former German empire, as well as of those fleeing from the Russian zone. In political and economic terms stabilization did take place, and often quickly, but the numerical preponderance of NS judges presented significant problems, both within the actual administration of justice and, no less importantly, in the embedding of that system into the new democratic society. While the press soon got into the habit of cultivating and discussing a healthy distrust of Adenauer's authoritarian and manipulative style of government (Chapter Six discusses the most prominent manifestation of an increasingly personal tension between the government and the media in the *Spiegel*-Affair of 1962), it took a long time before the legal profession consistently formulated its own critical legal opinion, and still longer before this debate extended beyond specialist circles and into the columns of the daily press.[11] A sign of the underdeveloped state of such discussion was the fact that at the end of the 1950s Adenauer had the temerity to put forward proposals for a government-controlled TV news network – a proposal struck down by the BVerfG. Only very gradually did the changing generations erode the legacy of the Hitler years in this regard. The remainder of this chapter is concerned with a particular case which showed the importance of solving these problems.

10 Claßen (1988, p. 164).

11 In discussing this problem, Requate also draws attention to the early legal work of the journalist Ernst Müller-Meiningen in the *Süddeutsche Zeitung* (2008, p. 73 f). On legal correspondents see also: Kommers (1976, p. 255 f).

4.4 A Routine Murder

On September 3 1953 a sales representative, Hans Hetzel, driving on business a short distance through a rural part of southern Germany, stopped to pick up a young woman who was hitch-hiking. It shortly became clear that the woman was out for an adventure and Hetzel soon forgot his business trip and drove the woman on a scenic tour round the Black Forest before stopping in a lay-by in the woods, where consensual intercourse took place. After a pause for a cigarette, the woman – known to him only by her first name – demanded to resume intercourse. This duly happened, more vigorously this time, perhaps *a tergo*. During this second round and at the height of a climax, the woman died.

Hetzel panicked. Knowing that the area had been used twice recently by a serial killer, the so-called motorway killer, he put the dead woman's naked body into his car and drove her to a place close to where the motorway killer had disposed of his victims' bodies, laid the body in the grass and went back to his wife and family as if nothing had happened. Only three days later, when the woman's husband had reported her missing and after the newspapers had reported the finding of the body, was she identified as Magdalena Gierth, a married woman, with two children, and only at that point did Hetzel – at the time briefly in a police cell on an unrelated minor charge – go to the police with his story.

Meanwhile the autopsy had been conducted. Nothing was found which did not confirm Hetzel's story. Frau Gierth had suffered heart failure, possibly brought on by the extreme excitement of the sex-act. Her general health had not been good, in particular the effects of a recent unsuccessful abortion were evident to the pathologist. Since there were no inconsistencies between the results of the autopsy and Hetzel's statement, the body was released for burial and it played no further part in the case. Indeed, all that was available to future forensic examination were the photographs of the body and of the place where it was found, and these – owing to the illness of the regular police photographer they had been taken and developed by an inexperienced and barely competent amateur – were next to useless.

Despite the lack of any compelling forensic evidence, the state prosecutor brought charges against Hetzel, and eventually the case came to trial in the early months of 1955. Perhaps it was not improbable that Hetzel would be charged, for his record hardly spoke in his favour. There had been clear indications that, during his earlier training as a butcher, he had taken some pleasure in killing animals less humanely than the law required. These and other minor offences were on his record. The fact that he was well over six feet tall and the dead woman petite and delicate corresponded to a certain negative stereotype, and as the details of their sexual activity became public (partly due to the indiscretions of the senior pathologist) they led to every kind of alarmist fantasizing about a serial killer and to prurient speculation in the press. All this meant that Hetzel was fitted more and more closely into the stereotypical pervert murderer, the *Lustmörder* of fear and imagination. In a rather touching dependence on one of the clichés of the detective story – the idea that a murderer always revisits the scene of his crime – the police were convinced that Hetzel was in fact the motorway murderer they had been unsuccessfully hunting, and their enthusiasm for a prosecution was considerable. By his behaviour and statements Hetzel offered the police considerable assistance in forming this negative image, with the singular exception that he consistently denied either having committed the motorway murders or having killed Frau Gierth.

The trial itself appeared to run smoothly, and – although such an outcome was going to disappoint the police by leaving unanswered the question of the motorway murders – the evidence from the pathologist who had conducted the autopsy seemed destined to lead to an acquittal. Possibly a general distaste for Hetzel's person played a role in bringing about a different outcome: the career ambitions of the prosecuting counsel also affected events in court, but evidence was evidence and could not easily be gainsaid, even if the chief forensic pathologist (who had himself not conducted the autopsy) insisted on his view that Hetzel was a pervert and a sadist who should be punished. At this point, however, the prosecution called its star expert witness.

The star expert witness is a figure which has existed in most judicial systems over the last couple of centuries. Sometimes such witnesses draw their authority from their position in a national forensic laboratory. (Dr Frank Skuse who played such a crucial role in the Birmingham Six trials was one such example in Britain; in another generation Bernard Spilsbury.) It is characteristic of the German system that the expertise of such witnesses is often taken from their status within a profession which at that time was quite unused to challenge and incapable of rethinking: namely, the university professor, the so-called *Ordinarius*. Professor A. Ponsold had established himself, by authoring a standard text book on forensic medicine, as *the* authority on such matters, and he was presented to the court as an unimpeachable expert witness. Quite unexpectedly and inexplicably – for his conclusions were based neither on an examination of the body itself, nor on anything other than smudged amateur photographs – Professor Ponsold informed the court that Frau Gierth had been killed by strangulation and that the marks seen on the photographs of the body were consistent only with that explanation. The evidence from the *post mortem* was swept aside, heart failure was entirely ruled out; Hetzel's evidence was claimed to be a tissue of clever lies.

In this case, details of sexual position were of crucial importance. The body not only required a more complete forensic examination than it had received, but the facts of Frau Gierth's position during intercourse were absolutely central to explaining the markings found on her body. The prosecution failed to conduct that part of the examination thoroughly and the court did not hear any debate on the markings, so that the 'expert' opinion remained unchallenged. The reason for this second failure (and perhaps the first too) was unambiguous: the court was embarrassed to undertake such a debate, since to have done so would have been to discuss 'unnatural' sexual practices in public. The 1950s were not a time when sexual matters could easily be discussed publicly, least of all by public officials. The hang-ups caused by war and twelve years of Nazism had left many walls of silence which it would prove difficult to break down, so a crucial element of the evidence was passed over and its significance for the truth of Hetzel's story ignored.

This silence extended far beyond court-proceedings. We may, however, identify a possible clue in an unrelated field. A marked feature of the immediate post-war years – only recently examined by historians – was the number of mail-order catalogues, dealing in sexually explicit material and distributed in huge numbers. These catalogues not only met an urgent need for the contraceptive devices which NS racial policy had wished to keep out of 'the family', but they offered an anonymous forum in which more complex sexual matters – including most notably the idea of sexual pleasure – could be discussed. Although these catalogues repeatedly contravened much of the archaic legislation concerning obscenity and pornography (for the relevant legislation had been taken over in 1950 almost unchanged from the NS period) there were remarkably few prosecutions of the distributors. It has been suggested that the reason for the failure to prosecute lay in the fact that the prosecuting authorities knew that in any trial they would be obliged to read out to the court the sexually explicit passages on which the prosecution case would rest, and they were reluctant to do that.[12] If personal inhibitions were strong enough to hold prosecutors back from bringing winnable cases to court, then it was extremely unlikely that a provincial court would manage to overcome its own inhibitions and follow through 'embarrassing' aspects of a case, especially when such evidence might benefit a defendant whom the court found unsympathetic. It was much easier for the court to work under the protection of the language of

12 Discussion of sexual repression in post-war Germany is found in two rather disparate sources: Atina Grossmann (1995, esp. pp. 136 f, 189 f). Particularly fascinating in Elizabeth Heinemann (2011). I have used her argument here and later in the chapter. The wider study is Sibylle Steinbacher (2011, quotation p. 347).

'perversion' and to leave unraised just those questions which might in this case have made justice for Hetzel possible.

Reactions to the Hetzel case highlight a general feature of the 1950s, to which Sibylle Steinbacher's extensive study of the sexual attitudes of the time has drawn attention. The public's prurient interest in sex, fed by the Hetzel case, coexisted uneasily with the determined efforts of influential sections of the public to set a rigid code of morals at the heart of Federal German society. We shall see in the following chapter something of the influence of these individuals and organizations as guardians of public morality when it came to legislation on matters of sexual orientation or birth-control, but the ambiguous attitudes revealed in the Hetzel case make evident the uneasy coexistence of a repressive morality with sex-catalogues. Steinbacher writes of the juxtaposition of 'a fight for public morality and a boom in erotica'. Hypocrisy may not have been on one side alone, but it was a feature of the whole age, and Hetzel's case shows its negative effects.

The defence missed an important trick when it failed to request a further expert opinion.[13] However, as we shall see, it would have been difficult, if not impossible, to find any expert willing to dissent from Ponsold's opinion. As a result, Ponsold's arrogant self-confidence dominated the proceedings and secured a conviction, while major elements of the evidence were simply ignored. Ponsold's certainty that he was right was a sign of the expert witness's special relationship to the courts. Perhaps Ponsold himself reacted allergically to any suggestion of 'perversion', or perhaps his dogmatism had its origin in older and more political power-structures. However that might be, he intimidated the court and ensured that Hetzel was found guilty of first degree murder (no evidence was adduced concerning the two bodies previously found at the spot Frau Gierth's body had been dumped) and sent to prison for life. The matter was closed.

4.5 Rosemarie Nitribitt

Hetzel's case had hardly been a celebrity trial. It took place in the provinces, with no wider reporting than the local newspapers. It received no national attention and Hetzel was dispatched to prison well away from the light of publicity. Yet, as the fifties moved on, Hetzel's case – or more properly we should say:

13 According to Arnau, in many courts defence had no option to nominate its own expert witness (1973, p. 21).

Frau Gierth's case – began to occupy a greater position in public attention. The way in which the court had considered what had happened to her came to be seen differently, and a significant role in this shift was played by a more spectacular murder. This crime did take place under the spotlight and in a big city synonymous with Germany's post-war prosperity, Frankfurt am Main. It was the case of Rosemarie Nitribitt. Her life and death turned her – in the words of *Der Spiegel* – into 'one of the mythological figures in the history of the Federal Republic'. Her case was to be influential for the Hetzel re-trial.

Rosemarie was a high-class prostitute, who approached her career with the same principles in mind as drove the successful German industrialists with whom she consorted: money. Not unlike Christine Keeler a few years later in England, selling her services simultaneously to the British minister for defence and to the Soviet military attaché in London, Rosemarie had rapidly moved up the social ladder.[14] The clients she received in her luxurious flat in an expensive area of the city included not merely many of the great names of German heavy industry but highly placed politicians – including, it was rumoured, a future Chancellor. Rosemarie's character exemplified in technicolour the same world which Gabriele Tergit had illuminated in some of her reports from the grey of Moabit: an indifference to traditional morality, the radical abandonment of all conventions and hypocrisy, and the conviction that, in a world which had lost its certainties, money and sex represented the sole things to live for, but only in that order. Frau Nitribitt conducted her business openly, driving around Frankfurt in her famous black Mercedes with red-leather seats, flaunting her celebrity life-style without shame. The only drawback for her was that *probably* – the forensic evidence was greatly confused by the fact that Rosemarie's luxury flat had under-floor heating, thus making it almost impossible to ascertain the exact time of death – on the night of October 29 1957 she was murdered. Her body was discovered on the heated floor of her flat on November 1.

The investigation of this murder took place in the full glare of publicity. The police authorities made repeated mistakes and the disappearance of a whole series of files showing the involvement of major public figures in Rosemarie's life (for, like any successful business operator, Rosemarie kept detailed customer records) immediately aroused suspicions of a cover-up. A suspect was acquitted at trial in July 1960 – otherwise, speculation, dead-ends and technical errors dogged the entire investigation, and the case was closed, only to

14 Christine Keeler's story can be followed in any number of web-sites, as can Lord Justice Denning's report on the whole Profumo scandal.

blossom in a string of press articles, best-selling books and films on Rosemarie, which continues into the present day. She had provided the grateful media with a spectacular scandal, but no less importantly she had held a mirror up to her society and had expressed in her life some of the home truths on which that society was based, but which had been papered over by clichés more palatable to the moralizers. Her murder remained unsolved, and the dilemmas which her life had exposed continued to haunt her society.

There were many contrasts and differences to Frau Gierth's case. Nevertheless, two elements should be mentioned here. The first was that the public verdict on the 'immorality' of these female victims was significantly different. Frau Gierth had not been a sex-worker and the indications that she had actually sought out and enjoyed sex had had a hostile reception in the provinces. In the climate of those years, this fact and her apparent life-style indicated an immoral woman, the more so in that Frau Gierth, a refugee from East Germany, had not gratefully accepted the opportunities for work which the state offered her but had hung around idly in a transit camp for refugees from the east. She seemed not only to have rejected the values of the Federal Republic, but was felt to be downright immoral.

Frau Gierth and Rosemarie may have been different, but the attitudes which had played a part in Hetzel's trial – in particular that sense of prurient fascination, combined with the desire to sweep sexual details under the carpet – was inevitably affected by the open admiration with which Rosemarie's life was viewed by the national public. The search for Rosemarie's killer was never completed, but it made the public eagerly interested in such cases and it shifted sympathies. It would be some years before what historians quaintly call *the* sexual revolution would shake that society to its foundations in the late 1960s. Nevertheless, Rosemarie's case made public the ambiguity of the sexual attitudes of the time and prepared the way for fresh approaches to the Hetzel case in which prudery and cheap condemnations might no longer be dominant.

Rosemarie's case also highlighted how life-stories such as her own came about. Born in 1933 – her childhood therefore spent in Hitler's Germany, when her father abandoned the family – she experienced the chaos and brutality of the post-war years as a young girl. Since her mother was often in prison, Rosemarie passed through children's homes and foster families, having been raped at the age of eleven by a *Wehrmacht* soldier, and was forced while still a minor to find her own way and to earn money for herself – by prostitution. But her life, elevated to the headlines and the glossy magazines, suddenly seemed not a failure, but some kind of success, a subject for grudging admiration, not condemnation. She at least had not deserved to be killed.

4.6 Two Women in Court

No account of controversial murders during the late 1950s and early 1960s would be complete without an account of the Vera Brühne case. While Rosemarie Nitribitt was the celebrity victim, Vera Brühne was the woman whose trial for murder turned her into a celebrity, almost replacing Nitribitt in the headlines. A study of the case published in 1970 went so far as to call it 'the Federal Republic's Dreyfus-Affair'.

On April 19 1960 a Munich doctor Otto Praun and his companion *cum* housekeeper Elfriede Kloo were found shot dead in Dr Praun's villa. The police hastily reached the conclusion that they were dealing with a suicide pact, and it was only when Dr Praun's son insisted that the bodies be exhumed that it was discovered that Praun had been shot twice in the head – something which should have been noticed at once and which cast considerable doubt on the suicide verdict. One year later a previous companion *cum* housekeeper of Praun's, Vera Brühne, was arrested on suspicion of the double murder, together with her companion, Johann Ferbach, who had been involved with Frau Brühne ever since he had pulled her out of a collapsing house during an air-raid. The police saw the motive for the murders in the fact that, in his will, Praun had left Frau Brühne his Spanish villa. The assumption was that Brühne had been worried lest, now that he had a new companion *cum* housekeeper, Praun might change the terms of his will. Brühne was assumed to have incited Ferbach to carry out the murders before Praun had time to make the change.

Three factors made the case notorious. The first was that – as a TV documentary revealed – Praun had in fact for many years been involved with work for the BND and specifically been associated with secret negotiations on behalf of Defence Minister Franz Josef Strauss concerning a new battle tank. It was alleged that the order for this tank had been connected with large-scale corruption, in short: another Starfighter affair. With the *Spiegel*-Affair on everyone's mind (see Chapter Six) it was inevitable that links were made between Franz Josef Strauss and the murders. It seemed a natural suspicion, and was real enough for Strauss to be obliged publicly to deny any involvement in the murder.

Secondly, the incompetence of the Bavarian police and prosecuting authorities, when it became public, was so extraordinary that it seemed deliberate. Establishing the exact time of death might be complicated – although this played a crucial part in discrediting the alibis offered by the accused –, but not noticing that Praun had been shot twice really did seem suspiciously stupid. Not subjecting a number of other objects at the crime scene to any form of forensic examination also seemed willful. A full ashtray offered forensic investigators important material on the people who had been in the villa at the time of the murder, but evidence was simply not collected and no investigation was carried out.

Most significant, finally, was the opinion which the court reached about the woman defendant. It was hardly surprising that the popular newspapers focused on Vera Brühne's appearance and that of her 'glamorous' daughter (who gave evidence against her mother and then retracted it), rather than on her evidence, but it was the judge who took this condescension to unacceptable limits. He argued explicitly that for an unmarried woman like Vera Brühne – as he pointed out, on the wrong side of the menopause – the only chance she had in life was to hoover up a rich man. It followed in the judge's opinion that the fear of losing such a catch was ample motive for murder. It was as simple as that, and Ms Brühne got life.

In 1962 the journalist Ulrike Meinhof poured scorn on the judge's degrading view of women and on the readiness of male-dominated courts to stand in judgment on all women, with their claim to 'know better than the woman herself what it's like to be a double-murderer – just as they knew in the case of Maria Rohrbach'.

By linking Brühne's situation to that of Maria Rohrbach, Meinhof made clear that she thought Brühne innocent. In a sensational trial in Münster in 1958 Rohrbach had been found guilty of poisoning her husband: as in the Hetzel case, the court had relied on the amateurish testimony of an 'expert witness'. Rohrbach had been fortunate in that – her sentence having depended on the theory that she had burned her husband's skull in the stove – the missing head turned up in one piece, thus throwing the prosecution's case into disarray. In 1962 the appeal court paid her back for the system's own errors by refusing to pronounce her innocent, and Meinhof made clear both her sympathy for Brühne herself and her contempt for the legal system itself and its indifference to ordinary people. In fact, other observers – among them Gerhard Mauz, who was to play a prominent part in obtaining justice for Hetzel – reached a different conclusion about Brühne's innocence, and even the *Spiegel*'s editor, Rudolf Augstein, certainly not a person to believe in Strauss' integrity, refused to believe that Strauss had had Praun killed in order to cover up a scandal.

Speculation about Strauss' involvement never went away, nor did that about Brühne's guilt. In the wider context of justice in the Federal Republic, however, the case brought about a profound scepticism concerning the court-system, for once not on the basis of the NS background of so many of the judges, but in terms of the legal system's other-worldly, ultra-conservative and arrogant attitudes such as had been revealed in the judge's comments. The massive publicity which the case attracted, in both serious and popular entertainment magazines, certainly contributed to a change in the balance of power in the Hetzel case, although as we shall see this shift was slow to show itself. As for Vera Brühne herself, sentenced to life imprisonment, her appeals for a retrial were regularly turned down, before in 1979, at an unusually early stage of her sentence, she was pardoned by Strauss, by then, having shaken off the failures of the 1960s, First Minister of Bavaria. Those who had suspected political motives for the original verdict and for the rejection of Brühne's appeals for a retrial were quick to point out that, through this pardon, Strauss had ensured that there would be no further trial and that the possible miscarriage of justice – let alone the disturbing loose-ends of the case – would remain permanently out of sight.

4.7 Hetzel's Campaign for a Retrial

Hetzel had been in prison for some seven years before the efforts to obtain a retrial began to surface. His original defence counsel had routinely lost the first appeal, but gradually the defence began to assemble expert voices which might succeed in challenging the damning opinion given by Professor Ponsold. Nevertheless, appeals for a retrial were turned down in 1962, 1965 and 1967.

German law on appealing a judgment has been fairly stable, its provisions going back before 1914. The NS years saw no necessity to tinker with the law on this point, since the prosecution would never feel the need to appeal an already harsh sentence – in any case the concentration camps were formally out of the reach of the law – and defendants had no chance of appeal. Appeals had the reputation, not just in the Hetzel case, of being hard to achieve. As one lawyer wrote, they were harder than winning the lottery,[15] especially for lifers. The grounds on which an appeal could be granted were in themselves unremarkable: a witness found to have made a false statement in favour of the guilty party; statements not on oath needed to be deliberately false to be appealed by the prosecution, whereas it was sufficient to prove that a falsity on oath was the result of negligence rather than ill-will. As one would expect, the

15 Judex (1963, p. 204). Not until 1925 could decisions of the Bavarian *Volksgericht* be appealed at all. A successful appeal was thought to endanger the state's reputation (*ibid.* 1963, 193, 75). Appeal legislation was 'the most backward legislation of the century'.

principal grounds for appeal were when new facts or evidence could lead to an acquittal or a reduced sentence, and this was where Hetzel's lawyers hoped for movement.

The third rejection of Hetzel's request for a retrial was particularly scandalous. A group of five forensic pathologists was commissioned by the authorities to provide an opinion, yet they unanimously confirmed every detail of Ponsold's findings. They reached this verdict despite the fact that their opinion stood in direct contradiction to the evidence produced in authoritative forensic textbooks, which had demonstrated, for instance, the fact that certain marks on a body could be produced *after* death. (This was hardly new science and had first been established in 1860.) The acceptance of such evidence would – even without considering sexual position – have opened the possibility that the marks which Ponsold had read as signs of strangulation had in fact been caused by the subsequent treatment of Frau Gierth's body, either by Hetzel himself as he transported the body in his car, or by the investigating authorities. As we saw, Ponsold's reading of the markings was simply not challenged in the trial, and the group of five did nothing to alter this. Still more outrageously the group's opinion ignored scientific evidence recently published – including by the five pathologists' own academic departments! In other words, not for the first time, the medical profession had closed ranks and Hetzel remained in prison.

By this point, however, a regular journalist with *Der Spiegel*, Gerhard Mauz, had entered the story. A series of articles appeared in the magazine outlining the original case which had been brought against Hetzel and highlighting the reasons for a retrial. These articles are remarkable neither for their dramatic rhetoric (indeed, Mauz writes in the rather mannered style which had already become a trade-mark for *Der Spiegel*) nor for any Zolaesque revelation of corruption or conspiracy, even though such conspiracy theories had been massively encouraged by the death of Rosemarie Nitribitt. It was a remarkably principled intervention by Mauz. Frau Gierth's death had no notoriety; as a person she had little to offer the press by way of sensationalism. It was a banal and uninteresting death. Nor was Hetzel himself – as Mauz' articles made explicit – a remotely positive figure. When Mauz therefore, without adopting Zola's famous sentence, moved on to make accusations, it was the justice system itself, as system, on which his attention was focused. Some elements of his attack, as in Tergit's reporting, related to the view of the system as an impersonal 'machine', which, starting slowly, gains momentum and cannot be halted as it indiscriminately crushes those who come into its path. But other aspects of Mauz' criticism were more specific and related to the principal theme of this chapter: the separation of the justice system from the lives of ordinary people. Mauz campaigned for a retrial not only narrowly, but on wider grounds, identifying Hetzel's sentence as a contravention of democratic justice.

In his articles Mauz, like Sling before him, argued passionately against the 'closed system' of German justice. For him the words with which sentence is confirmed in German courts – 'In the name of the people' – could not be allowed to remain a mere phrase. It conferred on the people, Mauz argued, on 'us', the responsibility for the decisions of the courts, since these decisions are taken in our name. Hetzel had not been tried before a jury, but there had been six lay people sitting with the judges. Yet their presence could not exonerate the public for what was done in its name. No-one could wash their hands or be indifferent when manifest injustice was occurring, as in the refusal of the system to allow Hetzel a retrial.

But one must ask what 'democratic' justice could mean in a society where – for instance in regard to the sexual issues at stake in this case – the public was at once prudish and judgmental, led by strong prejudices against the accused (and prudish indifference to the victim). After all, in the NS courts, the same phrase – *Im Namen des Volkes* – had been used to sanction blatant travesties of justice and to cover up the state's violence to its own citizens, and all too often those verdicts had been acceptable to wider sections of the public than it's comfortable to admit. (Post-war reactions to the film director Veit Harlan, which we briefly mentioned in Chapter Three, showed that such strong prejudices changed only slowly.) The problem Mauz faced was hardly new. What could democratic justice mean for Zola, for instance, when popular antisemitism had been exploited by chauvinist groups in order to turn wide sections of public opinion against Dreyfus? It was hardly reasonable to equate 'democratic justice' with public opinion. Mauz' articles appear to offer three general and unassuming answers to these questions.

First, Mauz suggests that 'democratic justice' has to respect individuals. It should not allow the prosecution to bully witnesses. Mauz means this practically and specifically, for he draws attention to the fact that not until the campaign for a retrial had begun did a witness come forward to complain at the bullying which he had received in a previous case at the hands of the public prosecutor who had directed the Hetzel case. This witness had himself not been part of the Hetzel trial, but he felt that the bullying by the prosecution had been strong enough in his own situation to cast doubt on the conduct of the Hetzel case. Such evidence should have been accessible before Hetzel's original trial. So too, Mauz implies, the prosecution should not have been able to publish an article in the local press detailing the reasons why Hetzel should be sentenced as a pervert. Also the senior medical expert's complete lack of respect for the work of his junior colleague in conducting the autopsy had seriously prejudiced the original trial, and his attitude to the defendant should not have been expressed in public statements labelling Hetzel a pervert and a sadist. All these were failures of democratic respect.

The central issue, however, remained the use of unchallenged expert witness opinion. Even if the court procedures allowed the defence to call another witness, the real difficulty – as the experience with the group of five had shown in 1967 – lay in the untouchable authority of the professional class from which the particular witness, and other witnesses too, were drawn. It would be some years before the student revolt tried to shake the power of the professors, but whatever success may have been registered in other faculties, the position of the medical professor was to remain largely unchanged. In the early 1960s, the only chance to question medical authority had to come from an independent voice, a rational critique from outside.

Hetzel's newly appointed defence counsel, Dr Gross, was clearly an example of the outsider figure in legal circles: often abrasive, rude and disrespectful. As we shall see, he was regarded with disdain by the legal establishment. Most significantly, however – and perhaps this was the cause of the establishment's suspicion of him – in a recent prominent case he had successfully defended Maria Rohrbach. Gross had humiliated the original 'expert' witness (Ponsold had also given evidence in that case[16]) and obtained an acquittal, but he had achieved this by breaking with the unwritten conventions of the legal system, thus – as Mauz commented – revealing 'a scandal in German justice'. For Mauz, the commitment to finding out the truth had higher priority than merely ensuring that the justice machine ran smoothly. Only outsiders could achieve that.

One element of Mauz' series of articles on the need for a retrial made that point bluntly. In 1966 the expert witness Professor Ponsold had contributed an article to an Italian law-journal on the subject of 'high prestige expert opinions'. Instead of offering any reflection on his own function in having Hetzel unjustly consigned to a lifetime in jail, Ponsold's essay was an attack on the practice of defence counsels in calling their own expert witnesses. The practice deeply offended his feeling of self-importance. The only function of expert witnesses called by the defence, Ponsold claimed, was 'to contradict a previous expert opinion'. He argued that such opinions were the product of 'mere vanity'. The defence did not share the same 'honourable' purpose as the court, for it was concerned only for its own prestige and for winning the case. The behaviour of defence counsels thus 'represents a great threat to the discovery of the truth and is a serious burden to major criminal trials.' By putting Ponsold's biased and arrogant remarks onto the public record in *Der Spiegel*, Mauz' contribution to strengthening the argument for Hetzel's retrial was clear. He did this explicitly for the sake 'of the reputation of the German judicial system and

16 Arnau (1967, p. 118).

of forensic medicine'. His campaign was legal, and not – to the extent that one can differentiate – personal.

A third area of Mauz' perceived task consisted of his explicit effort to change the public, democratic, perceptions surrounding the Hetzel case – in other words, to bring the virtues of enlightenment to bear on it. In particular Mauz attempted to reduce the element of prejudice which existed towards the sexual practices (and therefore towards the accused) hinted at, but never explicitly discussed by the prosecution.

Elizabeth Heinemann has summarized the situation – we referred briefly to her argument earlier concerning the failure to prosecute the sex-catalogues in the 1950s. 'The taboo of speaking of sex', she wrote of the failure of the prosecutors in that situation, 'was so strong that it made it difficult to do so, even when the purpose was to combat indecency'.[17] How much more likely was it that the court would lack the necessary openness, when its purpose would have been to argue for a retrial for an unattractive defendant convicted of a sexual murder. To obtain a retrial Mauz would have to break this silence.

Assumptions of abnormality had been essential to proving Hetzel's guilt. In order, therefore, to move the discussion away from ideas such as 'perversion' (the only terms in which the original court could place Hetzel's sexual behaviour), Mauz had to go back to basics. On the one hand his articles drew on the findings of the recently published Kinsey Report, from which it had emerged that a much wider range of sexual practice was in everyday use in society than the narrow range referred to as 'normal'. In a more conventional spirit Mauz also wrote of the German national poet Goethe's explicit references to his own sexual practices, including intercourse *a tergo*. If Goethe's behaviour was 'normal', Mauz argued, then perhaps anything goes. As well as demanding a properly informed reconsideration of the evidence in the Hetzel case, therefore, Mauz was determined to undermine the condemnation of Hetzel out of a false sense of 'the normal'. All this was important preparation for a retrial.

Eventually the pressure to re-open the case became irresistible, and at the retrial Gross called the distinguished forensic pathologist Professor Otto Prokopp from the Humboldt University in East Berlin as expert witness. It would have been hard to find anyone more of an outsider in West German legal circles – even entering the Federal Republic was as controversial an action on Prokopp's part as it was for East Germans to be invited to highlight a miscarriage of justice by a Federal German court. Prokopp was joined by experts from other parts of the Federal Republic and from Switzerland, and together they demolished Ponsold's evidence. An expert on photography dismissed the

17 Heinemann (2011, p. 48).

'marks' on which Ponsold based his evidence as being probably no more than smudges on amateurishly produced photographic prints. The matter was so unambiguous that the prosecution quickly asked for an acquittal, and after fourteen years in jail Hetzel was a free man. The retrial did not end, however, without the court shuffling off any sense that things had gone wrong in the previous handling of the case. The president of the court implied that the court system bore no responsibility for the miscarriage of justice, which had been Hetzel's own fault, because 'he had not had the courage to tell the whole truth'. As Mauz' final article on the case concluded: not only did the system refuse to accept its responsibility for the way the case had been handled, but it had from the start been the court itself which had lacked the courage to face the truth. Nowhere, incidentally, did Mauz imply that his own journalistic work had contributed to the achievement of justice.

4.8 Conclusions

From start to finish, this case lacked the glamour to have become one of those European *causes célèbres* which Heinrich Mann had called for. It was made up of banal details and crude misjudgments, all this acted out among unremarkable people. Only Gross and Ponsold possessed any of that charisma which Mann's argument had seemed to crave. Mauz was right to suggest that a need for charisma was symptomatic of a problem with the law, rather than a desirable ideal in its practitioners. The Hetzel case did not change the practice of expert witnesses – if anything, the Rohrbach case had begun to achieve that in 1959. But the Hetzel case showed two things which this chapter wishes to emphasize. The first of these was the extraordinary importance of the process of mediation of the proceedings of the court outside the charmed circles of the legal profession. Mauz was not the only hero of the story, but he was a significant one, and so was the writer Franz Arnau, with his interest in highlighting miscarriages of justice in the Federal Republic. Secondly, this case shows the ability of banal and unglamorous court trials to encapsulate the spirit of an age, to reveal that the underbelly of a particular society, shown in its crimes, is an integral part of the dazzling colours of its upper scales.

The first truth is emphasized in a significant follow-up to the case.[18] In 2001 Thomas Hettche published a book (halfway between crime fiction and

18 Thomas Hettche's fictionalized account has the title: *Der Fall Arbogast* (2001). If one were to pursue the origin of the name Hettche gives to Hetzel, Erich Wulffen published a novel with the title: *Die Kraft des Michael Argobast* (Dresden, 1924), which belongs in the context

historical reconstruction) which gave a detailed and almost entirely accurate account of the Hetzel case. Only the names, and occasionally the dates, are altered. In addition, for his own – not especially convincing – reasons, Hettche replaced the figure of Professor Prokopp with a woman forensic pathologist from the Humboldt University who comes to the West to act as expert witness, a character who, as the story progresses, is revealed to possess similarities in personality to Frau Gierth. Hettche was continuing the earlier tradition of exploring the criminal personality, and it is striking how successfully he combines that interest with a commitment to the progressive nature of such writing.

Hettche's motives in writing *The Arbogast Case* were multiple and complex. The book can be compared to Truman Capote's *In Cold Blood* (published in 1966, Capote's work tells the story of a multiple murder in rural Kansas in 1959), but, unlike Hettche's text, Capote's narrative is structured round the enquiries which the author *cum* narrator makes in the area of the murders gathering his own material. By contrast Hettche is not concerned to include himself in the account, although he does constantly draw attention to the role of journalists in bringing justice in this case. A freelance crime writer and chair of a human rights organization is prominent (Arnau), so too the figure of Mauz himself (disguised as Tietz). Writing about justice – whether reporting in the local papers or the national media or through fictional writing – is shown by Hettche to be an integral part of democratic justice. Since this novel was responsible for the mediation of the Hetzel case to later generations, the angle from which Hettche presents the case is also of some importance to the case's interpretation and to its place in legal history.

A significant part of the purpose of Hettche's 'docu-fiction' was to set the Hetzel case in a historical and legal context.[19] Without – as I have in this chapter – including the other cases which make the historical dimensions unmistakable, Hettche repeatedly underlines those aspects of the story which were typical of that period. His story emphasizes the dislocation typical of

of German Naturalism's interest in the criminal mind, with strong overtones of the now forgotten socialist philosopher Bruno Wille. The transposition of letters in Hettche's title might well be an acknowledgement of Wulffen's text (but not of his story). Film buffs will recall that Arbogast is the name of the detective in Alfred Hitchcock's *Psycho*.

19 An interesting, lawyer's perspective on Hettche's novel in: www.juristischer-Gedankensalat.de/2009/10/29/lesetipp-der-fall-arbogast. A summary of Maria Rohrbach's trial can be found in Wikipedia. Also: Arnau (1967, p. 200 f). Arnau notes that the utterly unreliable 'expert witness' in the Rohrbach case had immediately after that case been taken on as head of a laboratory in the security services – hardly an encouraging step for the forensic reliability of those services.

people like Frau Gierth, rootlessly moving not only across different historical times as the chaos of war leads to the division of Germany and then to peace, but crossing physical borders too, value systems, ideologies and life expectations. Hettche's approach was in that respect similar to that of Erich Kuby writing on the Rosemarie affair some forty years earlier. Both were sharply criticized by the right-wing press of the time, which was determined to present only the positive side of the Federal Republic under Adenauer, and to stress the restoration of German statehood and the new state's economic pre-eminence. There was resistance to seeing the age summed up in less flattering terms. 'It is difficult', the *Deutsche Zeitung* wrote primly of Kuby's book, 'to present the story of a prostitute as the portrait of a whole society'. Similar remarks could be made about the Christine Keeler affair. The trouble is that, at least in retrospect, it is hard not to see both stories in that way.

For all its provinciality, the Hetzel case highlighted in significant areas the smug complacency of the whole of Federal German society. Hetzel showing off his new car, his unthinking hedonism, the uneasy mixture of fascination and condemnation shown in public reactions to the crime, the timid acceptance of authority – these hardly seem the trappings of historical analysis. Yet they spoke crucial truths. The age had feet of clay and the actors in Hetzel's story reflect its unheroic dimensions, but behind these banal lives was the edge of a hardly dormant volcano. Despite its scared prudery and complacent consumerism Federal German society in the mid-1950s bore deep scars from the violent times through which Germany had so recently lived. The country had only apparently moved on from the years in which Germans were first the perpetrators and then the victims of mass rape, plunder and violent death. These situations could not merely be wiped away and forgotten in the excitement of the economic 'miracle'. The intensity of Hetzel and Frau Gierth's physical passion, so distasteful to the society which enjoyed its salacious details, is portrayed by Hettche as 'an eruption, a violent thunderstorm, the last remnants of the war which suddenly exploded'.[20] Gabriele Tergit's understanding of that explosive, disorientated time between the war of 1914/18, the Revolution and the hyperinflation was essentially the same, and she too sees the aftermath of cataclysmic events in the featureless cases coming daily before the Moabit court.

While sharply focused on the historical dimension of the case, Hettche was drawn to the court – as Tergit had been before him – because of the timeless raw passions which its cases can display. Tergit's headline for a particular case had been: 'Who shoots out of love?' – a question which has the ring of classical tragedy to it. As a celebrated dramatist remarked in the nineteenth century,

20 Hettche (2001, p. 340).

one does not need to be a princess to have a tragic fate: the Moabit court can compete with Elsinore or Colchis when it comes to passion and tragedy. Is the tragedy less acute when Medea kills her children than in those everyday cases when despairing teenagers find themselves charged in court for offending against § 218? Similar passions drive ordinary people to extreme actions, and the paragraphs of the law offer both an inadequate safety-net and an inappropriate substitute for the Furies. Hettche's question is less than criminological in character: 'What does it mean to die in the act of love?'. There are psychological depths and overtones in this question such as Tergit did not wish to investigate, but the question shows once again the power of the court to cross-examine and indict not only the individual, but the age and life itself. Such trials break the fetters of the provincial and of the historical. They are acted out against the widest of horizons, but they are also, whether we like it or not, part of history.

CHAPTER 5

Personal Matters in Court: Homosexuality and Abortion

We hear arguments for natural justice in many of the trials presented in this book, but so far they have not proved impressive. In the preliminary hearings of the Lüth-Harlan case it was felt natural that the economic interests of the maker of a notorious antisemitic film should be protected against an individual boycott. The Hetzel case took a wrong turn at the moment when natural feelings about sexual matters led to the accused being labelled a pervert before his trial had opened. As we mentioned in the Flick trial, while American judicial thinking responded to the Nuremberg trials by moving away from the abstract view of justice adopted in 'legal realism', German political and moral concepts had been so corrupted by the NS years that democracy and justice could not trust 'natural' feelings any more.

For at least its first twenty years, natural law was recognized as the preserve of the Federal Court of Justice (BGH). The court set out from the start to oppose the BVerfG, and it used natural law as the device with which to challenge the BVerfG's ideal of the *constitution* as the inspiration of the law. Generally the appeal to natural law implies a court's distance from the social attitudes of the present, and on occasion the BGH used it not only to avoid meeting the conditions of the GG, but directly to exonerate NS criminals. For traditionalists natural justice appealed to the determination of German legislators to bring stability and morality back into German law. When we consider cases in which these sentiments played a part, however, it seems as if natural feelings are invariably those furthest from justice and reflection – and thus from what must be called true humanity.

In few areas of the law were debates and trials conducted more regularly on the basis of 'natural' sentiments, in a powerful alliance with Church dogma, than in those concerned with the two laws which are the subject of this chapter – those most easily recognized from their number in the penal code: § 175 and § 218, criminalizing respectively homosexual acts and abortion. The impact of these laws on the Federal Republic has been considerable, as they have been in the other European countries whose penal code enacted similarly criminalizing laws. The assumption that few things are more 'natural' than heterosexual activity and uncontrolled reproduction has appeared to give arguments from natural law a *prima facie* relevance to both legal issues.

Germany, and especially the Federal Republic before 1989, is a country untidily divided between Catholicism and Protestantism. Not for nothing were the bloodiest religious wars of the seventeenth century fought out inconclusively on German territory, and the proliferation of states in the succeeding centuries left behind distinctly Catholic regions, such as the Rhineland and Bavaria, predominantly Protestant states (e.g. Hessen and Lower Saxony) and strongly mixed regions, like the Ruhr District and Baden-Württemberg. This diversity provides one of the reasons why the Basic Law attaches such importance to the sovereignty of the federal states in matters of education and culture. Furthermore, in distinction to many European states, two major political parties in the Federal Republic (CDU and CSU) advertize in their title their Christian status. To do so is perhaps a defiant restatement of traditional values; perhaps too it reflects the competition of the religious traditions as to which emerged with less shame from the NS years. It's far from sure, however, that it was an inevitable consequence of the religious complexion of the Federal Republic that §§ 175 and 218 remained so controversial. In addition, the Nazis' cynical mobilization of 'natural sentiments' in favour of its eugenic and racist programme undoubtedly left deep scars on public attitudes, and this chapter will provide much evidence of this scarring.

The two paragraphs are placed together in this chapter, however, for reasons other than their relationship to supposedly natural law, or because of their closeness to issues of gender and self-determination, or indeed because they represent extreme moments of the state's interference in the private activities of its citizens. Were those to have been my criteria, then this chapter would have had to spend time on trials in which – to name but a few out of a long list – prostitution, domestic violence, 'illegitimacy' and gender equality in divorce played a central role. Of all these areas one could claim, as campaigners against § 175 did, that they acted as a 'seismograph for the well-being and condition of society'.[1] It's striking to note that, without the efforts of Justice Minister Gustav Heinemann between 1966 and 1969, adultery and extra-marital sexual activity would have found their way into the penal code.[2] The two paragraphs on which this chapter is focused belong together because the trajectories of these areas of jurisprudence follow such similar lines across the years of the Federal Republic. It is no coincidence that the principal trials I wish briefly to present are both drawn from the 1950s and

1 Schlemmer (2012, p. 232). A discussion of the place of natural law 'above' the constitution can be found in: Requate (2008, pp. 38, 48, 128).

2 On the draft legislation including adultery on the criminal code (the so-called 'E 162') see: Requate (2008, p. 47); Steinbacher (2011, p. 279 f); and Kindora (2002, pp. 387–89).

early 1960s, for the focus of the theme lies more in the reform of these laws than in their implementation.

In giving this early focus to my topic I mean no disrespect to those long-term victims of § 175 (or of what some conservative voices regarded as its natural successor: AIDS) in later generations, nor to the women cornered between a state concerned with the unborn only up to the moment that the embryo's life in society begins and a church determined to protect its dogma more securely than the children it forced into unhappy life and certainly with greater insistence than it protected those children who were to become the object of the sexual predations of its own rogue priests. Writing at a time when English legislators see no requirement to go beyond 'pardoning' the victims of their own anti-gay legislation (reminiscent of the retrial judge in the Hetzel case who said that none of this would have happened without *Hetzel*'s faults), I wish simply to stress that this book is not about being judgmental. I want the events to tell the story, not the author.

5.1 The Legacy of the Past

There is much historical continuity in both issues, but for the most part that continuity takes the shape of repeating – at various intervals, under different political systems – more or less the same arguments. We can take it for granted by now that progressive voices during the Weimar Republic had argued passionately for a reform of both laws, and that similar voices could be heard from the time of the *Kaiser*. After all, with the notorious Eulenberg scandal involving the *Kaiser* himself in suspicion of the sexual practices which his legal code condemned, it would be extraordinary if the issue of homosexuality had not been discussed at the time, even if such discussion remained unproductive and the threat of *Lèse-majesté* hung over them. The analysis of certain prominent literary figures of the time – notably Walt Whitman, the poet of American democracy – kept the topic of homosexuality in the public eye,[3] but (as so often in the field: after all, it was Oscar Wilde not Lord Alfred Douglas who ended up in Reading Gaol) class justice ruled. In most cases, the defenders of homosexuality operated at a level of social acceptability and intellectual

3 A characteristic account of this aspect of Whitman's personality is: Karl Knortz (1911). Knortz' neologism 'Edelurning' referred to the type of aesthetic homosexual familiar to cultural circles at that time. On the Eulenberg scandal and the trial of the journalist Maximilian Harden, who first launched the story, see: Norman Domeier (2015).

inaccessibility which kept most of these involved, including of course (if for other reasons) the *Kaiser*, out of the courts.

As in so many other areas, the Weimar Republic proved unable to carry through the liberal reforms which its democratic wing desired (once again Gustav Radbruch was at the fore of efforts to reform § 175). As a result, the law had not changed when the Nazis came to power in 1933. The so-called Röhm-Putsch in June 1934, when Hitler purged the revolutionary wing of the Party under the guise of combating homosexuality within the SA, was a turning-point. It gave Himmler the justification for establishing a special section of the SS to deal with § 175. The Nazis did not need to pass any new legislation in order to turn their own prejudices into law, but in June 1935 the law was tightened up, so that it included not just penetrative homosexual acts, but other activities (including 'erotic glances') on the list of forbidden activities. Indeed, as one critic has commented, it seemed that the Nazis were afraid that homosexuality was contagious.

Despite this new legislation, however, enforcement was uneven, and depended on local leadership. There were plenty of other 'moral' issues to take up Gestapo time, and in any case an ambiguity about homosexuality remained at the heart of Nazism. The cult of masculinity, for instance, which Nazism furthered not simply in the military but in the uniformed ranks of the Party militia, certainly touched on areas of sentiment and behaviour close to gay practice, and contrasted strongly with the prudish attitude of many of the Party hierarchy to sex. This is to say nothing of the opportunities for gay exchange provided by the intimacy and danger of military action. As Dagmar Herzog has shown, both 'great wars' offered particular opportunities for gay servicemen.

In some administrative districts, however, – Hamburg, Berlin and particularly Düsseldorf – local Gestapo chiefs waged war on the gay community, with hundreds of trials each year. Other forces spent their energy on bringing to court men and women found to be in a sexual relationship with Jews (the so-called 'race defilement') and § 175 was less rigorously enforced. Nevertheless, large numbers of homosexuals ended in the concentration camps, where they were identified as the 'pink triangle' prisoners. For those anxious to emigrate in order to get away from this danger, the fact that after 1936 the Soviet Union was hardly less active in persecuting homosexuals (inevitably it was known there as 'a fascist perversion') hardly made their chances better.

It was largely due to the fresh interest which the generation of 1968 took in the NS years that the repression and imprisonment of homosexuals was first clearly identified by academic historians. Furthermore, it's evident from Sybille Steinbacher's work how many of the groups actively resisting the liberalization of § 175 during the first thirty years of the Federal Republic had their institutional and personal origins in the Third Reich. While such groups publicly deplored the 'chaos and disorder' of Nazism, in fact their own repressive attitudes had been part of Nazism itself. Steinbacher shows in particular how the bitter attacks on the Kinsey report (in other countries a milestone in the acceptance of homosexuality) were conducted in the traditional anti-American language of Nazism. In this way the battle for sexual enlightenment had to involve coming to terms with the NS past, and, while it had previously been unfashionable and damaging to one's academic career to research into the history of homosexuality,[4] post-1968 work finally broke the taboo surrounding the topic. This was shown in 1985 when President Weizsäcker spoke publicly of NS persecution of homosexuals and commemorated its victims.

For women, of course, § 218 was only one of the grievances from which they had suffered since the foundation of the Empire. Within the area of human reproduction, for instance, the Weimar Republic had seen both a major campaign for making contraception widely available and at the same time an increasing conflict between the proponents of contraception and those campaigning for the abolition of § 218. In a significant judgment on March 11 1927 the *Reichsgericht* in Leipzig had ruled that abortion was permitted when the woman's health was threatened. At the time of increasing mass unemployment and insecurity an unwanted child was a catastrophe for many women, and illegal abortions were running, it was claimed, at over a million a year. The most prominent campaign took place in 1931, under the slogan 'Your Body belongs to You'. This followed the notable success of Friedrich Wolf's play *Cyankali* (Cyanide, 1929) which portrayed the legal and physical dangers to women through the practices of illegal abortion.

The Gestapo was quick to take over not only all those institutes working for a liberal understanding of sexuality and therefore tolerant of homosexuality, but also the counselling agencies which had been campaigning for birth-control to be made more available.[5] (At various times, even during the Weimar Republic, either the advertising of contraceptive products or their supply had been prosecuted.) In the NS state the activities of these agencies were redirected towards eugenics and public health. Contraceptive advice was rapidly phased out. The provisions of the *Reichsgericht* decision remained in force, however, and to these were added a number of 'eugenic' measures legitimizing abortion, on explicitly racial grounds. It was not until 1943 that the NS state enacted in

4 On the damage which researching into homosexuality could do to an academic career, see: Introduction to Domeier et al. (2015, pp. 8–11).

5 On the birth-control movement in Weimar and through the NS years, see: Grossmann (1995). Details of 'Your Body belongs to you' (pp. 78–106).

law its insistence on the state's interest in 'protecting' the unborn. On pain of death, pregnant women and the medical profession were compelled to ensure that any unborn child should arrive in life in order that it could serve the state as cannon-fodder and cheap labour. One might suggest that the Nazis had unwittingly done the opponents of § 218 a considerable favour by revealing the precise nature of the state's interest in the protection of the unborn.

5.2 Post-War Shifts of Policy

Following the capitulation in May 1945, § 218 underwent a massive transformation and weakening. The number of German woman raped by the occupation forces has been estimated well into seven figures.[6] This was a time before public consciousness had begun to confront the fact that rape was not an incidental by-product of military conquest, but a direct policy of the conquerors. The revenge nature of much of this behaviour – revenge, that is, for the behaviour of German forces in the occupied territories – meant that it was difficult for the matter to be discussed openly. At all events the demand for abortions rose dramatically, and in fact the grounds found acceptable by the NS lawyers and doctors – namely impregnation by eugenically and racially 'undesirable' elements – could be seen as matching the situation of the women who had been raped by foreign soldiers. For this reason (as well as on general grounds of compassion and common humanity) no legal barriers were put in the way of the women seeking abortion. The so-called Marburg resolution of May 1945 was the crucial legal instrument in this policy.

This policy was practised even in that part of Germany where rape was not only alleged to be more prevalent, but where the violations were carried out by members of a state – the Soviet Union – which, having been the object of loathing and fear under the Nazis, was now being declared the welcome liberator of Germany from the curse of fascism and true friend of the German people. In the course of the next fifty years, however, practice in abortion differed considerably between the two German states, and even after re-unification the legal situation of women in the then defunct German Democratic Republic

6 Reading the literature one becomes wary about the figures quoted during the various campaigns, whether concerning the number of homosexuals in concentration camps or the number of illegal abortions at any one time. This is not to question the sincerity of those who put forward these figures, but historians of the field encourage their readers to be sceptical. Cf. Jensen (2005, p. 328f) and Gante's excellent survey (1993, esp. p. 188 f). Dr Dohrn's team believed there were two million abortions and some 40,000 resultant deaths each year in the Federal Republic. Such statistics inspired both Dohrn's actions and those of his legal team.

was important in determining legal arrangements in the reunited German state: nevertheless, both states set out from the same starting-point.

Both states were also quick to move against the 'liberalization' of abortion forced upon them by the events of the capitulation. In Weimar the KPD had campaigned for the reform of § 218, but policy in the Soviet Occupation Zone and then in the German Democratic Republic reflected instead the fact that the Soviet Union had radically tightened up its law on abortion in 1936 (certainly with a view to ensuring a rise in the population). Such considerations were anything but irrelevant at a time when the GDR was losing population to the West. It was not until 1972 that the GDR re-legitimized first trimester abortions, eleven years after the Wall had been built.

In the West many factors came together after 1949 to ensure the speedy re-criminalization of abortion. The search for stability was conducted under the tutelage of a party explicit in its allegiance to Christianity – historians speak of a 're-Catholicization' of the country[7] –, and family values were emphasized the more strongly for their supposed opposition to the collectivist and atheist values of the east. Furthermore, since the trend of historical writing about the NS state was to emphasize its freakish departure from bourgeois morals (whereas in so many respects Nazis followed the shell of this morality exactly), the proponents of § 218 argued that abortion was soulless and technological – a carry-over from the eugenic practices and euthanasia policy of the NS regime. Their paradoxical attitudes became clearer in the Dohrn trial, which we consider later in this chapter.

5.3 The Frankfurt Homosexual Trials[8]

Returning to § 175, our model trial concerns the city of Frankfurt am Main, in what had shortly before been the American sector. In the city centre, with the knowledge and tolerance of the police, a small number of gay-clubs had become established. Here men could enjoy a drink together and dance with one another. This peaceful situation came to an abrupt end. In July 1950 a young male prostitute was arrested for same-sex prostitution, and the prosecution service threw itself with alarming energy into using him as an informant on

7 The phrase 're-Catholicization' is discussed by Sybille Buske (2002, p. 339). Also: Requate (2008, p. 48). The principal organization insisting on a particular form of Catholic sexual morality was Michael Calmes' *Volkswartbund* – especially mentioned for state support in Hitler's Concordat with the Vatican. (See Steinbacher, 2011, p. 36 f and *passim*).

8 For the Frankfurt trials see: Eine Million Delikte, in: *Der Spiegel*, Nov. 29 1950. The Wikipedia article *Frankfurter Homosexuellenprozesse* contains useful details and further references.

some seventy of his former clients. Enjoying his power and the fact that the prosecutor believed every denunciation he made, and benefitting from plea-bargaining arrangements which were in fact not permitted under German law, the informant widened the scope of his denunciations so profitably that the authorities did everything possible to protect him, for instance crucially ensuring that his evidence was never tested in cross-examination. Their only problem was to decide whether to proceed against other rent-boys whom his testimony had identified, or to increase the number of prosecutions on the basis of these boys' further evidence against their alleged former clients. Eventually nearly five hundred investigations were undertaken, some one hundred arrests were made and charges were brought against over a hundred men.

At that time any investigation on the grounds of § 175, let alone an arrest or a trial on that count, was about the worst thing that could happen to the man concerned. A large number of the men charged were in heterosexual marriages, with most of the features of 'normal' marriage, such as trust, love and children. In view of the general homophobia, such men were liable to lose their jobs when their situation became known, and for those who did not lose their jobs, relationships at work would be, to say the least, seriously compromised. The action of the prosecution service had laid all men, homosexual or straight, open to blackmail, since the random accusations which were at the basis of all the investigations could without difficulty be made against anybody. It was easy for the rent-boys to threaten anyone with denunciation – to wife, work-colleagues or to the police. Any of these steps would have had severe consequences.

There was another factor in this wave of litigation: the wild enthusiasm for § 175 prosecutions shown by the prosecution service, and, still more shamelessly, by the judge. The driving force in the prosecution service was problematic in himself: the judge, Dr Kurt Ronimi, not only had a background of energetic prosecutions of homosexuals in the late 1930s, when his enthusiasm had sent hundreds to face concentration camp, castration and death – but he ensured that all § 175 prosecutions were channelled through his division of the Frankfurt *Landgericht*. (Such an arrangement was explicitly excluded by GG § 101.) In his own court he conducted the cases on a strict reading of the 1937 text of the law. It is not interesting to speculate on why judge and prosecutor should have felt this messianic zeal to deal with these cases. The philosopher Theodor Adorno classed their behaviour under the rubric of the 'Authoritarian Personality', in which he saw a central element of the rise of fascism – explaining their zeal as a mixture of ideology and personality disorder.

In virtually all cases the evidence presented was unambiguous and the sentences were passed at great speed, efficiency and without any general social purpose. Although the prosecution presented itself as being concerned with the problem of blackmail, no such charges were brought against any of the people involved. The local newspapers courageously echoed the 'natural' sentiments of a majority of their readers, and lent the trials their support. Gradually however attitudes changed, partly because of the number of suicides among the accused, partly too because of the intervention of the American Civil Liberties Union. Within a short period of time the trials had become an embarrassment to Frankfurt. Judge Ronimi was moved sideways to a less prominent court, where, unsurprisingly, he continued his private vendetta against homosexuals, while the Frankfurt authorities discreetly dropped charges against over a further hundred accused. The key witness – the rent-boy whose arrest started the whole avalanche of cases – was himself charged with perjury, and the episode served to warn prosecution services of the dangers of launching into large-scale action on § 175. As *Der Spiegel* pointed out in November 1950, casting a critical eye over the trials, it could safely be assumed that in Frankfurt alone one million homosexual acts took place each year. Did the prosecution service really imagine that it could deal with them all and trace their perpetrators?

The problematic elements in the Frankfurt trials, however, did nothing to change the law itself, as was demonstrated some six years later in the by now familiar form of a judgment of the BVerfG.[9] An individual, referred to in the documentation as R., had submitted an individual petition to the court on the grounds that § 175 was in contravention of the Basic Law.

The grounds for the appeal seem unproblematic to the eyes of today: R. argued that § 175 offended against the equality paragraphs of the Basic Law (though it is debatable whether GG § 3.3 in its reference to gender, *Geschlecht*, had actually been intended to include sexual orientation – equality for women was a contentious enough issue at that time and it had been quite an achievement to enshrine that basic equality into the *Grundgesetz*), and against GG § 2 which insisted on the citizen's right freely to develop their personality. It was hard to know what this provision could mean if it did not include a citizen's sexuality.

We don't need to spend long on the judgment in which the court rejected the appellant's arguments, for it was traditional and conservative in tone, concluding the (highly confusing) justification of its decision on the dual grounds 'that homosexual activity offends the moral law and that it is not unambiguously evident to the court that there is no general public interest in punishing it'. (All the negatives cannot disguise the actual meaning of that sentence: that

9 The judgment of the BVerfG in *BVerfGE* 6, pp. 389–441. Principal quotations on pp. 389 and 414 f.

the court saw a lot of moral disapproval aimed at homosexuals and did not wish to take a different view.) The reference to the moral law meant that the court found itself arguing in the same terms as advocates of natural law. The problem was that the Basic Law included – right in the middle of § 2.1's guarantee of an individual's right freely to develop their personality – the proviso 'provided that [he] does not offend the rights of others and does not breach the constitutional order or the moral law'. The moment when – in a state of near moral anarchy – the Basic Law appealed to the moral law would be the moment at which natural law re-entered the BVerfG's armoury.

The court followed other authorities in trying to provide the law with the function of offering a comforting certainty in a world shaken to its core by the war. Nowhere was this more evident than when the court turned to the appellant's highly reasonable argument that § 175 had been part of the NS state's repressive legislative armoury and should therefore have been annulled when the Third Reich had come to an end. While admitting that NS violence had delegitimized many laws, the judges rejected the claim:

> Yet we cannot simply reject all laws passed by the National Socialist government without examining them closely and considering whether they are regarded as valid by the citizens of the state. To do so would ignore the fact that even unjust legislation, which would be repudiated by a more enlightened standpoint, may acquire validity by reason of its inherent ability to create order. Such legislation at least creates a firm legal order (*Rechtssicherheit*) and, provided that its range of application is firmly limited, it represents the lesser evil in comparison to complete legal chaos among those subject to the law.

In this extraordinary judgment, homosexual rights were sacrificed on the twin altars of an unquestioned and largely compromised moral code and of an all but entirely arbitrary belief in the usefulness of law – any law! While it's known that lawyers prefer bad laws to the absence of law, the court's decision wilfully shut its eyes to the radical changes in society since 1945 and certainly ought to have included a message to the legislators to rectify the anomaly. Because it omitted to do this, the BVerfG's decision ensured that reform of § 175 remained unlikely, and, though the blatancy and scale of the Frankfurt trials were not repeated, the basic situation for the gay community had not altered in any respect. The law continued to drive gays into double lives, into insecurity and desperation. Those readers with recent experience of the countries which persisted longest with anti-gay legislation – among them Austria, Ireland and Finland – do not need to be reminded of the consequences.

It can be easily understood that there was widespread disquiet at the end of the 1950s when it became clear that officials in the justice ministry were drawing up extensive plans for a conservative reform of the legislation referring to sexuality. In response, an important collection of essays was published in February 1963, edited by two lawyers (one of whom, Fritz Bauer, was about to become well-known through the Frankfurt Auschwitz trials) and two medical professionals. The blurb to this volume explained that the book had been put together 'out of a great anxiety about developments in the reform of penal law relating to sexuality, an approach which owes nothing to knowledge and to the idea of tolerance, but is driven largely by black and white personal prejudices'. Some contributions critiqued the authorities' proposals to criminalize adultery and sex before marriage, but the main weight of the volume lay with §§ 175 and 218. It's quite a comment on the state of the Federal Republic in the 1950s that this was the first significant statement of opposition to the legal instruments under discussion.

For reasons we have already mentioned – different life priorities, the threat of blackmail and the complete lack of openness – few intellectual arguments had been publicly advanced against these paragraphs. More striking perhaps was that even the most fashionable sociologist of the 1950s, Helmut Schelsky, often regarded as being responsible for the modernization of post-war German sociology and in particular for helping to introduce sociological reflection into German jurisprudence,[10] had published a book outlining conservative, not to say reactionary views about homosexuality and abortion.[11] If even sociologists behaved conservatively, it was hard to know where the opposition might come from. The unanimity changed with *Sexuality and Crime* (1963).[12]

This was a substantial volume, with over twenty contributors. Most striking in its honesty was the way in which Adorno opened his essay. A celebrated and original thinker on a wide range of social and moral issues, Adorno began: 'It's a sobering thought for a theoretician that the only contribution he can make to a practical controversy of his day has already been articulated long ago, and

10 On the (belated) introduction of sociology into German jurisprudence by René König, Schelsky and Ralf Dahrendorf, see: Requate (2008, p. 119 f).

11 Schelksy (1912–1984) belonged to his generation, in that his early works appeared in the NS years and contained significant concessions to their ideas. His *Soziologie der Sexualität* (1955) strongly attacked Kinsey's approach to sexuality and put forward familiar arguments against homosexuality. See: Herzog (2011, p. 122).

12 Fritz Bauer et al. (1963). It should be noted that Bauer found himself in strange company with his fellow contributors to the volume. Especially Giese and Bürger-Prinz had close links to NS eugenic and sexual theories (see: Steinbacher, 2011, p. 216f). Bauer was a pragmatist in his campaigns.

invariably better than he can manage.' His remark appears to be true of the whole volume. The many arguments against §§ 175 and 218 are well made, but anything but new. When the authors reflect on cultural relativity and the huge variety of activities which different people regard as 'normal', then Pascal had got there first, some three hundred years before. The illogicality of the law and the fact that it was based more on habit than logic, had been themes of Tacitus and Seneca – let alone Magnus Hirschfeld or Kurt Hiller before 1914. On the absurd assumption of the middle-classes that they and their prejudices represent the whole of society; on the Canute-like efforts of the law to lay down fixed criteria when the tide of relativism, pluralism, multiculturalism and of course medical science was sweeping in – with all these insights the authors are convincing, but in no way original. Everyone knew the arguments, no-one had listened.

Leaving aside Adorno's discussion of the authoritarian personality and its links to fascism, only two reasons for the justice ministry's threatened initiative are suggested by the authors: first that the Federal Republic's commitment to rearmament had revived arguments about population growth; and secondly, that parliament had fundamentally misread its function in a democracy. As Herbert Jäger, a lawyer specializing in ethical issues, wrote: 'It cannot be the job of parliament to shout out its gut feelings and to react to issues merely by parading received opinions and prejudices: instead it must control the workings of a highly complex mass society in a planned and sober fashion'.[13]

Perhaps this and other expressions of opposition prevented the draft legislation being enacted. Perhaps it lost its drive as Adenauer went out of office, the Auschwitz trial may also have briefly shaken the self-confidence of the officials in the justice ministry. Perhaps even in the ministry some knowledge about the Wolfenden Report in Britain had seeped through (although the day-to-day experiences of homosexuals had changed less radically than the Report had recommended). At all events, by 1969 Heinemann's reforms decriminalized homosexual activity between consenting adults, leaving in place only the provisions protecting vulnerable people and minors from exploitation by homosexuals. After 1969 the word *schwul* ('gay') gradually shed its inverted commas. We should not think of this as in any way the automatic, culminating point of an unstoppable tide of historical change. Not only did this reform take courage and commitment on Heinemann's part, but – as Dagmar Herzog points out – the campaigners continued to need an extraordinary amount of hard work,

13 Jäger (1963, p. 277).

patience and vigilance.[14] The debate was not ended, nor the struggle for tolerance and equality, but one goal at least had been achieved.

5.4 § 218 in the Federal Republic

We have seen that it took twenty years before the Federal Republic did away with the more questionable aspects of § 175 and the Frankfurt cases had showed something of the cost of uncertainty in that field. The malign influence of NS legislation was still present in more than one regard. In common with some – but by no means a majority of – other European countries, the Federal Republic inflicted on itself a still longer period of uncertainty in respect of § 218. The three cases I wish to present in this section illustrate some features of that situation, though they have little directly to say about the real problems of this area: the shame of back-street abortions, and the health risks women took in order to end an unwanted pregnancy. What is articulated in all these trials is the clearly inferior status of women before the law. Two of the trials concern women helped by doctors who were sympathetic to their position and less than punctilious in their interpretations of the law. The third shows how the BVerfG, in one of its most controversial judgments, threw out a compromise laboriously worked out by the *Bundestag*, demonstrating that the court was not so much responding to political pressure, as itself acting politically. The trials cover the early 1960s, the late 1970s and the end of the 1980s. Taken together they show the difficulties which the law had in handling this matter sensitively, let alone rationally.

The first case concerned Dr Axel Dohrn, a surgeon at a hospital near Hannover.[15] He was dismissed from his post in 1959, charged with performing over a thousand operations to sterilize women. These were the days before reliable or safe contraception, and the operations had been conducted at the request of the women concerned; the operations had been entered openly in the hospital's register and were explicitly included in the training schedule for the hospital's nurses, while the patients had been fully counselled, knew the finality of the operation and – together with their marital partners – had given their formal consent. The medical indications for the operation were vague (although patients wishing to end a pregnancy on the grounds of threatened genetic illnesses always got accepted), and the social indications

14 Herzog (2011, p. 152).

15 On the Dohrn trial see the *Spiegel* articles listed under Dohrn in the Bibliography. Also Sieghart Ott (1964), and Requate (2008, p. 113 f).

straightforward: the women had to have the number of children which they wished, and to request the operation. Dr Dohrn was highly respected by his patients, but he was himself a man of strong principle, who defended his actions both individually and within an overall ethical framework, which he repeatedly articulated to the court. Although he believed that it was good for doctors to help their patients achieve what they wished for themselves, Dr Dohrn was perfectly capable of refusing an abortion even to those women whose application had been approved by the official channels. He certainly did not perform operations simply to do his patients favours.

In 1963 Dohrn was sentenced to six months imprisonment by the *Landgericht* in Hannover. The difficulty with the sentence – and the reason why it was revoked on appeal by the BGH – was that Dohrn had committed no offence.

5.5 'It's Not You, Doctor, Who Have Offended Me, but the Judges'[16]

As I mentioned earlier in the chapter, NS legislation had had no qualms about sterilization. The fact that the patients were often forced into such procedures – Jews, Sinta, homosexuals and anyone carrying a genetically transmitted disease or disability – caused no problem for the doctors, who were legally covered by RGB § 14, the 'Law for the Prevention of Hereditarily Diseased Offspring', an early landmark in NS legislation which had come into force on January 1 1934. In effect, however, apart from the eugenic and racist provisions just referred to, NS law criminalized sterilization and abortions in all other cases save the clearest medical indication, and StGB § 226b laid down harsh penalties for doctors infringing those provisions.

§ 14 therefore combined two separate elements. It contained an eugenic element such as could be found in the legislation of several democratic countries before and after the war: this element was mixed with explicitly NS ideas about using sterilization to deal with undesirable social groups. Perhaps because of this ambiguity, the law was not repealed after 1945 in all the federal states, along with other explicitly NS legislation, as laid down in the Control Council's Law No. 1. In Lower Saxony, where Dr Dohrn had the ill-fortune to practise – as in other states in the British Zone of Occupation – the law had remained on the books, prostrate. This was in marked contrast to Bavaria, Hessen and Baden-Württemberg and the whole of the GDR. At a federal level it was not removed from the book until August 1998. As a result of the Control Council Law,

16 The title is the remark of a patient giving evidence to the examining judge, quoted in Ott (1964, p. 195).

however, StGB § 226b (in which the criminalization of sterilization had been enacted) had been annulled. A NS law implied that sterilization was criminal, but the code no longer contained its penalization. In terms of legal provision a gaping hole was left, and Dr Dohrn fell into it.

Gaps of this kind require the legislators to restore order, but this did not happen, either in state or federal parliament. The reasons for this omission say much about the situation of the mid-1950s. Even though sterilization does not destroy life – and Dr Dohrn repeatedly stated his preference for the operation over abortion on these precise grounds –, attitudes to the issue were far from clear. The Protestant churches, for instance, while still proclaiming the blessings of a large family, as they had in the NS state, had no post-war position at all on sterilization, and only the Catholic church maintained a principled opposition, on that question as well as on abortion and birth-control. As a result, the political parties of the Federal Republic were frightened of possible reactions if they embarked on legislation, and so let the matter rest. To have failed to remove the legal sanctioning of compulsory sterilizations contained in § 14 was probably unimportant – other sections of the criminal code and of the Basic Law would have been more than sufficient to prevent such procedures being carried out. What was left unfinished was the de-criminalization of the practices of Dr Dohrn. To start his prosecution took no more than the readiness of a jealous rival in his hospital to denounce him, followed by local political intriguing and, most significantly, a public opinion in which morality (*any* morality, as the BVerfG's judgment on § 175 suggested) was not only a sacred cow but one of the principal links to the NS system.

Furthermore, Dohrn's case – for all that it highlighted an alternative to abortion – revealed the central importance of one element of the defence of § 218: namely the state's interest in women's fertility. The view of his patients was that the charges brought against Dr Dohrn denied them the right to decide on whether or not they wished to remain fertile, and for this reason, as well as out of respect for him, they hastened to Dr Dohrn's support, both in and outside the court. They would not accept that their fertility was something which the state had the right to force them to maintain. Quite clearly, however, the Federal Attorney General at the time was entirely in favour of exercising this right, for he commented to the press in connection with the Dohrn case on 'the low birth-rate and serious shortages in the Federal Republic's work-force, gaps which we can hardly fill'.[17] Was this any different to the NS state legislating so

17 Attorney General Dr Wagner quoted in: Der Lückenbüßer. *Der Spiegel* 45/1964, p. 71. A detailed account of Catholic theology and statements by leading Protestant theologians on the subject of sterilization is given in Ott (1964, pp. 78–113).

as to have more soldiers at its disposal? No wonder the proponents of a reform of § 218 were convinced that the state's objection to abortion came from its continued concern about the size of the population – whether for the workforce or for the army seemed less important.

The focus of the argument against § 218 had therefore shifted to where it has stayed since: women's right to self-determination. Even the expert witnesses who lined up to criticize Dr Dohrn's clinical practices admitted to their own uncertainty when asked directly by the defence: 'Is a woman unconditionally obliged to remain fertile?' Unlike Dr Dohrn they had tried to close their mind to the wider issues of principle, and the women knew it. One is reminded of Albert Ramsbottom's mother, after Wallace the lion had eaten her son, being consoled by the magistrate with the suggestion that she could have more children. Mrs Ramsbottom got 'proper blazing' and rounded on the magistrate: 'Wot, spend all our lives raising children / To feed ruddy lions? Not me!'[18] She and her whole gender had a point.

In terms of historical relevance, the crucial feature of this trial was the claim of the penal system to judge citizens' private actions according to moral criteria on which they had not been consulted. The text of § 226a defined grievous bodily harm – into which category, as we shall see, *faute de mieux*, the court grotesquely placed Dohrn's actions – as an offence regardless of the victim's consent in all circumstances when it 'offends against morality (*gute Sitten*)'. So the law gave immediate priority to 'morality' and blatantly ignored the wishes of the patients.

At one level at least the court had an explicit understanding of morality: it suspected Dr Dohrn of conducting sterilizations in order to allow his patients to indulge in adultery and prostitution free from the risk of unwanted pregnancy. This suspicion meant that the patients too were also on trial in this case, even though they supposedly appeared as defence witnesses. With this idea in mind the prosecution had breached all medical confidentiality and trawled through thirteen hundred case notes looking for evidence of prostitution and adultery: evidence which in no case had been forthcoming before their search. No concrete evidence of these activities was subsequently produced in court. The prosecution's actions were therefore of questionable legality, though the patients who took legal action against the prosecution service

18 Albert Ramsbottom was the hero of the dialect monologues famously performed by Stanley Holloway from the 1930s. They combined great humour with much populist, common sense. The full text of 'Albert and the Lion' can be found in www.lyricsfreak.com/s/stanley+holloway/albert+and+the+lion_20606126.html. König contended the real issue in § 218 was class, not abstract morality (1963).

on these grounds got nowhere.[19] Even worse – and here we hear the echoes of aspects of the Hetzel case – the court suspected that sterilizations had been carried out in order to enable the patients to enjoy what the judges referred to as 'uncontrolled sensual pleasure'. If the law helped women to lose their fear of becoming pregnant, so the prosecution appeared to believe, they might enjoy sex. Such enjoyment was an offence against morality.

At this level the prosecution's behaviour was shameful. Perhaps, however, one should give the judges credit for at least reflecting on how they could generate the moral rigour which a guilty verdict required. It must be remembered throughout this case that Dr Dohrn – since he was married to a 'half Jewish' woman and was in consequence for many years excluded from practising as a doctor in the NS state – had to listen to moral critiques of his work from fellow doctors who had obediently administered NS medical policies and, among other things, presumably conducted forced sterilizations. The court did not articulate that problem, but it was at least aware of the vulnerability of some of its medical witnesses on this point, and as a result devoted long passages of the judgment to establishing a morality which could be used to sentence Dr Dohrn.

The animus against Dr Dohrn was personal, and it was logical that the prosecution's original decision to proceed with the case turned to § 14 and the ethos which that NS law had evoked. Nevertheless, the judges had little choice but to admit, somewhat regretfully, that § 14 could not in itself establish the immorality of the defendant's actions in post-war Germany. They had to seek out another source of authority. Not only, as we saw, was there no accepted single view on sterilization, but – rather than concede that the moral vacuum in which they had to work had made § 226a inapplicable[20] – the judges argued that the court's view of morality did not require any form of validation. They rejected any reference to what the population at large actually thought, or to the real moral sentiments of the time – the unpopularity of Kinsey's demographically based study in conservative circles was too great for them to refer to popular opinion. In any case, they had heard the attitudes of a number of

19 The patients were unsuccessful when they took the prosecution service to law for its gross interference in their privacy. They lost their case first because the hospital passed on the case-notes and described this as an action of the administration, not as a breach of confidence on behalf of the doctors, and secondly because, in the mind of the prosecution, the patients 'were so strongly associated with Dr Dohrn's criminal action that their behaviour is to be condemned on moral grounds' (Ott, 1964, pp. 178 f, 199).

20 The text of § 226a is given in Ott (1964, p. 114). Also in: https://dejure.org/gesetze/StGB/226a.html. The explicit suspicion of prostitution, adultery and gross sensual pleasure (Ott 1964, pp. 148, 168, 199).

'ordinary people' in the persons of Dr Dohrn's patients appearing as witnesses. There could be little doubt what these women thought, and the judges did not agree with them.

The judges further claimed to be uninfluenced by expert opinion (though they had exposed the court to nearly a whole day of medical experts giving their opinions), but instead claimed that their approach was solely 'directed to the moral order which is basic to communal life in our state' – a clumsy circumlocution for the 'moral law' to which the BVerfG had also claimed allegiance in 1957 in dealing with § 175, without attempting to define it.[21] Yet the decisive fact, the judgment explicitly claimed – in a way reminiscent of Orwell's *1984* –, was not 'what the public actually thinks but what correct moral sentiment requires the public to think'. In other words – and we shall find another example of this absurd logic in Chapter Nine as the judges struggled to find a common-sense attitude to another contentious question – even in the absence of clear moral positions from the protestant church and from publicly acknowledged authorities, the only people who were fit to represent the moral law of the day were the judges themselves.

It had been easy during the NS period to define the moral law, and the difficulty with the formulation of § 226a was that it assumed the post-war moral sentiment to be as unambiguous and inflexible as during the NS years. The judges were well aware of the historical nature of judgments based on morality, but they were so determined to 'nail' Dr Dohrn that they produced another toxic piece of casuistry to advance their decision: 'Provided the legislator has not pronounced,' they wrote, 'and provided no manifest change in the understanding of morality has taken place, then prosecutors and courts are *obliged* to follow the laws and to regard as offensive to morality what has always been regarded as offensive to morality.' It would be hard to find a clearer example of the legal system not only leaving the abolition of NS legislation to the Allies but regarding the difference in moral climate between the Federal Republic and NS Germany as unimportant (showing, as they wrote, 'no manifest change in the understanding of morality' – did that mean, for instance, that no shift in the public view of antisemitism or of total war had taken place since 1945?). What's worse: the judgment not only reinforces Stolleis' theory that judges were misled by their blind adherence to the letter of the law: it suggests that the judges were perfectly happy to stay with the morality of the Nazis because they still agreed with it.

Extraordinary as it sounds, Dohrn was charged with grievous bodily harm further citing StGB §§ 224 and 225, and the length of his sentence was

21 Ott (1964, p. 260). The judges' historical understanding (pp. 202–03).

determined according to a scale designed in the nineteenth century – as *Der Spiegel* pointed out incredulously to its readers – to deal with the outcome of public house brawls.[22] The sentencing depended on the organs lost or irreversibly damaged in such fights (these included noses, ears and eyes, but hardly the tying of a ligature in an internal organ). Unfortunately for the court, however, that scale would have produced a minimum of two years hard labour, which the judges feared would have been regarded by the public as inappropriately severe. Instead, in its search for a way to penalize Dr Dohrn, the court settled on StGB § 216, which covered the case of a doctor involved in an assisted suicide, for which a minimum sentence of six months was possible. Sterilization therefore was passed off as self-harm, certainly not as a legitimate medical procedure. Dr Dohrn's counsel protested at the judges' approach: 'You can't just flick through the law books until you find a bit that suits you'. But that is just what they had done.[23]

It's reassuring to see how unambiguously Dr Dohrn's sentence was quashed on appeal. All legal systems are potentially able to produce cases in which a court cuts loose with the normal rules and sets out to 'get its man', at whatever price to legal correctness. Dr Dohrn was just one innocent victim of such small-mindedness. For our understanding of the history of the Federal Republic, however, we can see two features of the times reflected in this extraordinary case. First, the eagerness of the state to involve itself in the private life-decisions of its citizens, and to do so on the basis of a morality continued from the NS years and impervious to change or challenge. Dohrn's case reflected the same spirit which wished to put adultery and pre-marital sex on the criminal code – as if the only way the state could envisage 'protecting the family' was to criminalize something. Indeed, the legal authorities elevated morality to a sinister 'moral law' which only they defined, as if personal choice by its citizens was not part of a democracy. Secondly, the Dohrn case was a direct product of the legislators' fear of broaching matters of sexual and reproductive behaviour, even where a severe problem had arisen and fresh legislation was urgently required. Legislators were scared either to re-define a moral code suitable for a pluralistic democracy or to show any form of leadership in sensitive matters. As Jäger had complained in the context of § 175, politicians seemed more than ready to go on 'parading received opinions and prejudices'. The Dohrn case revealed how unnatural natural sentiments could be, and what bad law they make.

---

22 See: *Der Spiegel*: Der Lückenbüßer (p. 71).

23 Quoted in: Ott (1964, p. 287).

5.6 The Campaign against § 218 Moves Forward

As we saw, by the end of the 1960s Heinemann had got a significant reform of § 175 through parliament, and that did nothing to reduce the demand for reform of § 218. Protests and demonstrations continued to put pressure on the government. Among the more effective of these protests was an article in the magazine *Stern* in June 1971, imitating a still larger action conducted in France earlier that year, in which 343 prominent women had confessed to having committed the crime of abortion and being 'sluts' (*salopes*). Under the heading 'I have had an abortion' German women too challenged the legal authorities to punish them and showed their contempt for § 218.[24]

After the electoral triumph of Willy Brandt in 1972, followed by his unexpected resignation in 1974, Helmut Schmidt was left with a majority and the determination to restore § 218 to the government's agenda. By then the parliament divided roughly on the following lines: the FDP favoured the term solution (i.e. permitting abortions in the first three months); the CDU wanted the so-called 'indications solution' (i.e. requiring medical indications) and the SPD divided between the two, although the protest in *Stern* did something to move the Party to the more radical position. In June 1974, by a narrow majority, the term solution was passed by the *Bundestag* but was immediately appealed to the BVerfG by CDU and CSU members, as well as a number of CDU-controlled state legislatures.

In 1975 the court decided in favour of the appeal, concluding that the solution passed by the *Bundestag* was unconstitutional.[25] The judgment explicitly gave priority to the life of the unborn over women's right to self-determination. The court further bound the *Bundestag* to criminalize abortion – it clearly usurped parliamentary powers by issuing the instruction that abortion should be made 'not only illegal, but criminal'. In consequence, near open warfare broke out between the court and the government, and certainly between the court and the opponents of § 218. At no other time in the Court's history did it appear more strongly to be setting itself up as an alternative legislator. The fact that there were two minority dissenting opinions, one put forward with great force by Judge Rupp-von-Brünneck (as we shall see, this was not the last time

24 On the French women's declaration and the *Stern* article see: Herzog (2011, p.156 f) and Schlemmer (2012, p. 238 f). Also: Gante (1993, p. 186).

25 The judgment is in *BVerfG E* 36, p. 1 f. It is discussed extensively, among other sources, in Collings (2015, pp. 148–58). A detailed critique of the judgment can be found in: Sigurd Graf von Pfeil (1979, pp. 15–46). Also: Wesel (2004, pp. 247–58).

she would upset her fellow judges in the cause of liberty), did little to reassure public or parliamentary opinion.

The *Bundestag* did in fact find a solution in 1976, fundamentally decriminalizing first-term abortions, conceding only that abortion should take place after mandatory counselling, during which the so-called 'social indication' (i.e. non-medical factors such as the economic and social circumstances of the individual case) could be taken into consideration. This certainly was far from pleasing everyone, but for the time being appeared to have ended the debate. Nevertheless, the judgment left significant issues burning in the public mind. There was, first, a strong objection to the high moral tone adopted in the BVerfG judgment (which was rightly blamed for the reinforcement of the prohibition). It was as if the authorities wished not only to criminalize abortion, but to present it as a personal moral failing. Many people also objected to the use of language such as 'man's place in Creation' when discussing the morality of abortion. Whether they were another attempt to re-introduce theocratic legislation, or an empty phrase in a post-Christian culture, the words were felt to be meaningless in a scientific age. This view was reinforced when the judgment argued that the moral law was independent of the demands of public opinion, and that, however much public opinion might change on this issue in future, the moral imperative of the ban on abortion would remain unaltered. In other words, the law was claiming to be greater than the society which made it, and the law was here to stay. Some historians have explained this stance by pointing out that, in comparison to the US Constitution, the Basic Law is more focused on communitarian perspectives than on individual rights and that therefore general societal issues tend to be highlighted.[26] That may be so, but there seems no reason why in a pluralistic society a communitarian approach needs to be clothed in elitist and moralistic language.

Secondly, there were widespread complaints about the illogicality of the decision: a case in point being the 'morning after' pill. Did women need counselling before using that pill, campaigners wished to know, since that pill aborted prenatal life, and the court had insisted that from the moment of conception prenatal life stood under the protection of the Basic Law. The law seemed inconsistent. In similar fashion the inconsistencies of § 175 legislation (even after its relaxation) had left significant questions unanswered. Why, for instance, had it excluded any reference to Lesbian behaviour, campaigners asked: why did it focus exclusively on penetrative sex acts, when it was claimed to be the morally questionable nature of homosexuality which was under fire? None of

26 The arguments concerning the individualism and collectivism of the two constitutional courts are summarized by: Nanette Funk (1996, here p. 233).

the uncertainties increased confidence in the logic of the law. It was felt that, instead of preaching abstract morality and offensively slurring the procedure of abortion by comparing it to NS practices, the Court should have tackled and offered solutions to real problems.[27]

Finally, the medical profession was unhappy that medical decisions on abortion had been taken out its hands. Individual doctors needed to be protected against prosecution – that was understandable –, but they wanted to have control in their area of activity, even when the profession was far from united on the question.

5.7 The Last Razzia

The final trial in this chapter was rightly described as the 'most spectacular abortion trial in German legal history'. It opened in September 1988 in the historic town of Memmingen, Bavaria, and concerned the activities of a local doctor, Horst Theissen.[28] Dr Theissen had conducted abortions in his own clinic (rather than a hospital), without following to the letter the process of mandatory counselling laid down by the *Bundestag*. Not only the doctor, but no less than one hundred and fifty-six of his patients were named on the charge sheet and summoned to appear in court. As in Dr Dohrn's trial, the confidentiality of medical records was ignored; once again private histories were laid open to general scrutiny in open court. The events and tensions of the late 1970s were immediately re-mobilized and Memmingen became the centre for heated protests and demonstrations. Theissen was sentenced to two and a half years imprisonment (eventually in 1994 reduced on appeal), and almost without exception the women were fined a not inconsiderable sum of money. The law had taken its course.

Whatever the Bavarian prosecuting authorities had achieved, they had made no contribution whatsoever to solving a national problem. Just as Irish women travelled across to England for abortions, so in fact women who required an abortion in Bavaria and Baden-Würtemberg could and did travel to another federal state where the law was more liberally interpreted. Theissen's crime was to do openly what everyone else did covertly. As usual, there were

27 Pfeil draws attention to the NS slurs in the judgment (1979, p. 37).

28 I have drawn my information on the Memmingen trial from the retrospective account given by the newspaper *Augsburger Allgemeine*, available on: http://augsburger-allgemeine.de/politik/Abtreibungsprozess-in-Memmingen-Frauen-am-Pranger-id26881786.html. See also: Gisela Friedrichsen (1999).

no new arguments put forward here; in their dogged determination to proceed with the trial regardless of its cost to individuals the authorities seemed to have learned nothing from the past. All too familiar was the gross hypocrisy of the individuals involved in bringing the case to court. Towards the end of the trial, for instance, it became known that one of the three judges had recently sent his girl-friend to Hessen for an abortion. Need one add that this particular judge had been notable for the intrusive manner in which he cross-examined the women and (on occasion) their partners?

It would be good to report that the blatantly aggressive conduct of this trial would have had the same effect as the Dohrn trial nearly thirty years previously. Certainly there have not been any comparable trials since then, but in fact the far more significant feature of this story, the one responsible for moving the question forward, came from a quite different source. Following the fall of the Berlin Wall and the subsequent unification of the two German states, the women of the former German Democratic Republic complained that their rights to abortion had been unreasonably diminished when the GDR constitution was dissolved. (They referred in particular to the absence of mandatory counselling in the GDR.) This was accepted and the legislation was reformulated.[29] The modification introduced in 1995 left significant uncertainties in the law (in particular with regard to foetal disability). In the wake of what Herzog calls 'the new sexual conservatism at the end of the millennium' (for instance, Bavaria introduced stricter state legislation in 1996) the legislation was back before the *Bundestag* in 2009 – this time with a strong emphasis on criminalizing the doctors. The issue is still active and the problems await a solution.

One final point should be mentioned. A particular significance attaches to the fact that the European Court of Justice was slow to pick up the two legal issues which have been the subject of this chapter. This is also true of the European Court of Human Rights. Unfortunately the cause of their reticence was not the sense that personal behaviour should as far as possible be kept out of the court. In general the courts' influence has been towards reinforcing liberalization of that kind, even if the court has been conscious of the need for a margin of appreciation in applying its judgments. This has had the effect of obliging member-states to move away from punitive legislation or repressive practices. Experience in Ireland in the field of the de-criminalizing of homosexual activity, for instance, has shown the real importance of the European court's rulings to the practices in a particular member-state, which finds it

29 On these issues in the German Democratic Republic see: Funk (1996). Observations on the European courts in Herzog (2011, p. 213 f).

difficult to hold a repressive line when the European court has ruled in the opposite direction. In recent years the Union has even come to regard applicant states' attitudes to homosexuality as a norm of membership. Whether this is reflected in present member-states' approach to homosexuals in their own country is the subject of more substantial doubts.

As to the timing of these judgments, it is not for this book to determine whether the European Court of Justice (despite the views of its British detractors) is too subservient to the wishes of member-state governments, and whether 'popular opinion' would have been more effective in altering its position. As a fresh wave of conservatism and populism sweeps western Europe, all courts may in future be more busy ensuring that the basis of the freedoms won is not compromised. On the other hand the result of the recent Irish referendum (May 2018) gives hope that, at least in Europe (the future of *Roe v. Wade* being at present less certain), legislation hostile to women may be losing ground.

CHAPTER 6

The *Spiegel* Affair

During the years of the Cold War a number of events took place across the world which could easily have triggered the hot war. Among these provocations were the repeated military actions of the Soviet Union in crushing protest movements in their satellite states, from East Berlin in 1953 to Prague in 1968. There were the moments of extreme tension, such as the Soviet shooting down of the American U2 spy plane in 1960 or the building of the Berlin Wall in the following year. But we should not forget two pairs of events in which major international threats shared the surprising feature of being overshadowed by events in national politics.

The first took place in the autumn of 1956. As the Soviet troops moved in to crush the Hungarian uprising on November 4, a number of responses were possible: among them a co-ordinated NATO retaliation and concerted pressure through the UN. Unfortunately these actions were made impossible because of significant disagreements among the Western allies, disagreements which were caused by the Anglo-French invasion of the Suez Canal Zone a single day after the Soviet army went into action in Budapest. Of all actions – and whatever its potential justification –, the invasion of Suez happened at the wrong moment. Other matters were more important, and the misjudgment and imperial arrogance of Britain and France could hardly have been worse timed or more disruptive of a larger issue.

German politicians were all too aware of the need for timing in international affairs. Helmut Kohl often remarked how lucky it was that the Berlin Wall opened before Saddam Hussein invaded Kuwait in the summer of 1990. He feared that the Bush administration would not have managed to handle two events of that magnitude at the same time. Who knows which might have been neglected.[1]

In a less elevated manner the greatest crisis of the whole of the Cold War, the Cuban missile crisis – ten days engraved deeply on the memory of several generations throughout much of the world – threatened to be overshadowed by a domestic problem. It was played out while the German public had its eye on the biggest, yet most unnecessary crisis to date in the history of the Federal Republic: the so-called *Spiegel*-Affair, which for a month or so pushed Cuba to the side of the German headlines. Although the matter was of little

1 See: Marie Elise Sarotte (2005, p. 179).

importance to the US government of the time, and fortunately did not distract from the management of the larger crisis, as had been the case with the Suez invasion, the *Spiegel*-Affair did more to discredit the Federal Republic in the eyes of Western Europe and of the Americans than any other post-war event. It shook Adenauer's regime to its foundations.

In the autumn of 1962 *Der Spiegel* became involved in issues of military security – not for the first time in its history, but never before on such a public scale. The problem arose less from the revealing of details of new equipment or secret weapons, for the German army possessed no such weapons and those which it aspired to possess – such as atomic grenade launchers – had long since been fully discussed in the international technical press. The problem arose within the context of the defence minister's long-running disagreement with the NATO allies and with the USA in particular concerning the Federal Republic's access to nuclear weapons. Defence Minister Franz Josef Strauss insisted that the German forces should be equipped with these weapons, within both the artillery and the air-force. His insistence was based on the belief that, in the case of a rapid – and in view of their numerical superiority – successful advance by Soviet forces stationed in East Germany, NATO would not risk all-out nuclear war merely to 'save' Hamburg or Berlin, but would leave the Soviet troops at the point which they would have reached: on the Rhine. The fact that the nuclear option was cheaper, in that it required, in Strauss' opinion, a smaller German army than NATO plans envisaged, reinforced Strauss' determination.

In the major NATO autumn manoeuvres of 1962, known as Fallex, these claims were put to the test. With US secretary for Defence McNamara in attendance (surprisingly Strauss himself was absent), these manoeuvres and associated war-games made clear that the arming of the German army with nuclear artillery would not have the effect which Strauss had promised, Indeed, so many technical problems with the German forces emerged during the exercise that it was no longer possible for Strauss to claim either for his personal strategy or for the forces for which he was responsible that they were adequate to the defence of the country.

This outcome was the basis for an 8000 word article in *Der Spiegel* on October 8 1962, under the title: 'The *Bundeswehr* – only a qualified ability to defend'. As it turned out subsequently, the article's author, Conrad Ahlers, had not only restricted the article to information which had been published elsewhere (in subsequent months *Der Spiegel*'s archive staff demonstrated this fact after trawling through 35 000 previously published articles on defence questions, and 8 000 other published sources), but prior to publishing the article Ahlers had used his contacts with the secret service (the *Bundesnachrichtendienst*,

BND) to confirm that his article was not handling any secret material. In fact, as we shall see, such a judgment had been only an opinion and lacked all legal status, but at least it was a fairly authoritative opinion, and, whatever its status, no-one but the German authorities disagreed with its findings.

Indeed, a striking feature of the whole affair was the inward-looking nature of the administration's thinking. Despite Strauss' habit of pressurizing witnesses by emphasizing NATO's impatience with security leaks such as the *Spiegel* article, there was no evidence at all that the article had caused problems for the allies. The other NATO countries, and especially the USA, had a more relaxed attitude to reporting on military issues, and when the NATO Supreme Commander (Europe) declared in November 1964 that the *Spiegel* article had contained nothing secret at all, no-one could have been surprised. Nevertheless, the German authorities instituted their own judicial enquiries into breaches of security in the report. This isolation has to be seen as a product of German history: trusted allies were not something Germany had ever had in the twentieth century, and there was little experience in dealing with them – indeed, the only allies Germany had had were unreliable and anything but trusted.

Strauss however was so outraged that the outcome of the manoeuvres had been made public and his grand strategy thereby shown to have been misguided, that his ministry began to prepare a major action against *Der Spiegel*, spearheaded by the accusation of high treason against the magazine's editor Rudolf Augstein and the reporter Conrad Ahlers for betraying military secrets. In order to give his team more legal leeway and to force witnesses to testify, the charge of bribery of public officials was added to the accusation – without supporting evidence. The action of Strauss' ministry revealed itself first by the improperly conducted quasi-extradition of Ahlers from Spain in the night of October 26 and by the simultaneous occupation of the *Spiegel* building in Hamburg. These events would become the core of the *Spiegel*-Affair.

6.1 The Dimensions of the Affair

The *Spiegel*-Affair was played out on many different levels. Adenauer's government, in the person of Franz Josef Strauss, closed down the offices of *Der Spiegel* news magazine for a number of weeks. Government officials thus censored the contents of the magazine, which – thanks to the practical support of (rival) publications (there were plenty of newspapers convinced of *Der Spiegel*'s guilt: solidarity was the exception rather than the rule) – continued to appear. The authorities held the chief editor Rudolf Augstein and other journalists in custody for up to three months, without charges being preferred, and misused international treaties to effect the arrest of Conrad Ahlers. It is more than likely that the majority of the government's actions was illegal according to German law: others were perhaps legitimate – it's there that the obfuscations of individuals and whole departments of state have muddied the picture. At all events, press freedom and the rule of law were seriously challenged.

The repercussions of the Affair affected most aspects of the Federal Republic's political and cultural life. It had a clear effect on long-term political attitudes within society, in particular on those of the student generation and university professors, leading to a significant increase in their political awareness and a new sense of responsibility for their state. In that sense it both marked the end of the Adenauer period and can also be seen as preparing the way for the German student movement of 1967 onwards. It also contributed to a sense, widely shared in the general public until the beginning of the 1970s, that the students were fundamentally right in their critiques of the establishment.

The Affair had a damaging and long-lasting effect on German coalition politics, and challenged the SPD and the FDP in their understanding of their role in the political establishment. The FDP lost its faith in Adenauer while the SPD, despite the conciliatory tones of its reformist Godesberg programme, rediscovered some (but not much) civil courage. By contrast, Strauss' CSU party learned nothing from events, and although Strauss was forced out of Adenauer's government, his popularity in right-wing circles was enhanced by the Affair.

Events round *Der Spiegel* were for many days excluded from any parliamentary discussion, but, when they were finally addressed in a twice extended question-time, the *Bundestag* witnessed the unedifying but repeated spectacle of a senior minister blatantly lying to parliament. Strauss' lies were not aimed to protect military secrets or to preserve national security, but merely to save his own skin by concealing his personal involvement in events. The Chancellor himself hardly behaved better, making extreme statements to parliament, on the basis of his own anger and arrogance, rather than of actual evidence. Among other things Adenauer accused Augstein of committing high treason for personal profit. Tensions between first ministers and the media are not a new phenomenon. (It will be recalled that at about the same time British Prime Minister Wilson felt and expressed to parliament a similar loathing of the Beaverbrook newspapers, in hardly more measured language.[2])

Finally, a number of legal authorities were shown up in a poor light and revealed to be anything but independent of political influence. The president of

2 Wilkinson (2007, p. 283 f).

the third division of the BGH (into whose remit national security and therefore the crime of treason fell) was reduced to putting forward his views on the Affair via an article published anonymously in *Der Spiegel* itself. His views were concealed in a historical tribute to the journalist Carl von Ossietzky, who had been sentenced in 1929 for revealing the activities of the secret *Reichswehr* (which at the time was conducting military training in the Soviet Union in defiance of the conditions of the treaty of Versailles). The article criticized the secrecy of the action being taken against Ahlers and Augstein, and, while pointing out the inadequacies of StGB § 100, insisted on the legitimacy of journalistic investigations of military affairs.[3]

Eventually, the Affair cast the BVerfG too in an ambiguous light – although characteristically the case was not heard until January 1966. Following earlier unsuccessful requests to the court for an injunction, Augstein and others addressed a formal petition to the constitutional court, only for half the judges to reject the petition and the case itself therefore not to be heard. In fact, however, the divisions among the judges were so serious that, for the first time, the dissenting judges published their opinion – a practice initially called for by the SPD when the court was set up, but at the time of the Affair still explicitly excluded from the court's procedures. Subsequent to this judgment, minority reports became a standard practice of the court. Despite these shock-waves, however, the most striking feature of the *Spiegel*-Affair was the trial that never was: the trial of the editor of the magazine on a charge of high treason.

6.2 Old Antagonisms

The geographical distance between Munich in Bavaria, the power-base for Strauss and the CSU party of which he was the leader, and Hamburg, where *Der Spiegel* had been published since 1953 (it began publication in 1947 in Hannover) is some eight hundred kilometres, but the atmospheric and ideological distance between the two cities is infinitely greater. Hamburg, once a free city of the Hanseatic League, is a separate and proud federal state, with elaborate forms of democratic self-government; Protestant, and open to the influence and attraction of America and the North European democracies – at the time of the Affair its Senator for Internal Affairs was Helmut Schmidt, later to become a distinguished Federal German chancellor and, incidentally, a personal friend of Ahlers. Throughout the Affair Hamburg vigorously defended its

3 The *Spiegel* article on Ossietzky: Judex, Droht ein neuer Ossietzsky-Fall? *Der Spiegel* 41–1962, pp. 34–6. Details of Ossietzky and the Reichswehr trial in: *Die Zeit* Online – 10. November 1995.

autonomy against the Federal capital, Bonn, and still more so against Strauss. The large circulation of *Der Spiegel* – half a million at the beginning of the 1960s, three quarters of a million by the end of the decade – was made up of well-educated readers, taken from across the generations, with a largely urban background. Buying the magazine on a Monday was an essential ritual for a wide section of the new Germany – a readership determined to avoid the mistakes of the recent past and to modernize their country. At the time of the Affair, however, one should not think of *Der Spiegel* as being in any sense left-wing. Its only party-political sympathies were towards the Liberals, at that time members of the coalition with Adenauer. *Der Spiegel* never really 'spoke for the nation', but it asked questions about the past and the present to which many people wanted answers.

Munich: predominantly Catholic, until 1918 seat of an eccentric royal family, suspicious of outsiders and fiercely loyal to its own customs, especially to those over which other parts of Germany wrinkled their nose in disapproval. Theodor Eschenburg – doyen of political scientists of the period cited as a fact that at the height of the Cuban missile crisis Defence Minister Strauss was drunk at a reception in the President's residence. Even sober, there would be no love lost between Augstein and Strauss, especially since in Franz Josef Strauss the party had produced an intellectually brilliant figure, with a passionate relationship to power on the national as well as regional stage. Strauss was determined to be Adenauer's successor, although he was given to that kind of suspicion of central government and of democratic legal forms which had led Bavaria in 1950 to vote on principle against the introduction of the Basic Law.[4] Strauss' characteristic folksy dress, his drinking habits and his carefully calculated practice of spontaneously 'speaking his mind' to Bavarian newspapers appeared to ensure his popularity with the CSU and his consequent usefulness to the coalition partner, Adenauer's CDU. Nevertheless, to a magazine such as *Der Spiegel* – originally founded in the days of the British occupation zone and modelling itself on the best journalistic traditions of Western Europe and the USA (its appearance was consciously modelled on *Time*) – Strauss represented both a personal target and an example of the erosion of democratic government by what was alleged to be populism, a form of political life of which events following 1933 should have made all Germans suspicious.

It had certainly been more than personal vindictiveness on behalf of *Der Spiegel* which had already caused the magazine to be involved in reporting a

4 Another example of Bavaria's different legislative arrangements is the fact that Bavarian law does not protect the confidentiality of journalists' sources. See Schoenbaum (1966, p. 183).

number of scandals around Strauss' activities as minister.[5] Strauss' personal ministerial style had made him a natural target of investigative journalism on a whole series of issues, from the trivial (for instance his small-minded persecution of a traffic policeman who had once delayed his ministerial car, or the Barth affair) to more major matters. A scandal had been running since 1958 concerning the Lockheed Starfighter F104G (G for Germany) – a plane which Strauss had imposed on the Federal Republic's air-force as an all-weather combat fighter-bomber, but which had not only proved itself incapable of delivering the required performance (combating supersonic Soviet bombers and delivering nuclear weapons deep into the Soviet *bloc*) but constantly showed itself less than airworthy. Before it was finally withdrawn from service, the Starfighter had killed nearly 120 pilots. The global Lockheed bribery scandal – which showed that everywhere else in the world where Lockheed military hardware had been ordered bribes had been paid to government officials and ministers – made inevitable that similar suspicions should be raised in Germany. Strauss' unexpected and abrupt shift of support to Lockheed's plane from the French Mirage III had directly brought such suspicions onto his own person.

More recently, *Der Spiegel* had published a story according to which Strauss had directed the US defence secretary (then Thomas S. Gates) towards a particular holding company, Fibag by name, for the building of thousands of living quarters for US service personnel in Germany – his recommendation concealing the fact that the company was one in which Strauss had a personal financial interest. Few people were persuaded by the parliamentary commission which, by the narrowest of margins, exonerated Strauss in the Fibag scandal, or by the failure to uncover evidence of Strauss personally profiting from his decision in favour of Lockheed. Such evidence in the case of Lockheed would have been no more than the icing on the cake for Strauss' opponents: the appalling performance of the plane and the subsequent casualty figures were the real issue. But on the grounds of these and other investigations of his behaviour in office Strauss was hardly well disposed towards the magazine. He was on record as calling *Der Spiegel* 'Germany's modern-day Gestapo'.[6] Once the *Spiegel* Affair was in full flow, Strauss of course repeatedly assured a sceptical public that he was not exacting personal revenge on the paper, but few believed him, and when the Affair was over, the antagonism had been set in concrete.

5 For the Barth- and Fibag-Affairs see *Spiegel*-Online; for Starfighter see Wikipedia.

6 Strauss' description of the *Spiegel* as a modern Gestapo quoted by Schoeps (1983, p. 141). The FAZ quotation (p. 34).

The story of the *Spiegel*-Affair is not easy to tell. The further one gets into the events, the more one is caught up in the tissue of lies, evasions and 'lapses of memory' with which top civil servants, primarily but not exclusively in Strauss' own ministry, obscured the real course of events. The truth emerged only slowly and belatedly. Also, the focus of the Affair shifted constantly. It showed how slowly the law moves, although much of its length was directly caused by inter-departmental disputes, for instance concerning the right of one minister to set in train arrest-warrants and to deal with foreign police forces. While there were significant legal and constitutional issues behind these disputes, the real forces appear to have been largely personal: Strauss' self-assertion and contempt for due process, the hesitations of fellow-ministers (coming from a different party in the coalition) to expose Strauss and risk endangering the coalition, and the plain, old-fashioned power-politics of the mandarin civil servants. One need hardly add that incompetence and bungling as well as personal intrigue played a significant part in shaping the Affair. It makes the events unedifying – as the conservative newspaper *Frankfurter Allgemeine Zeitung* commented with its own form of arrogance, 'Strauss seemed not to know the difference between Germany and the Balkans'. Generally, it is hard to establish an objective narrative, and all but impossible to narrate briefly. Some important legal issues were raised, but for the most part the Affair showed the authorities' widespread casual indifference to procedure and a worrying ability to bend the law.

6.3 The Principal Legal Issue: Military Secrecy

Throughout the *Spiegel*-Affair one significant legal issue remained unresolved, the extent of military secrecy which is feasible within a democracy. The issue is certainly not one to which other democratic states have found easy answers, as the 'Lohan affair' in Britain showed in the mid-1960s and more recently on a global scale the Snowdon affair. What relationship should exist between the kind of secrecy which governments find convenient and which they present as being essential for national security and that democratic discussion of a state's security and defence policy of which a free press is the guarantor? If the *Lüth* judgment had elevated freedom of expression above other aspects of the legal code, then its relationship to military secrecy threatened to become problematic.

A charitable view of the Adenauer government's handling of the Affair would be that the Federal Republic had had little chance to gain experience in this field. It's certainly true that, at the time of the *Spiegel*-Affair, recent history was hardly on the side of openness on behalf of the state. From the Dreyfus affair to the execution in 1951 of Ethel and Julius Rosenberg for betraying nuclear secrets to the Soviet Union, it seemed as if high treason were the only category which counted in matters of security – in that respect the draconian measures of the NS state seemed in harmony with the wider spirit of the age.

There had of course also been historical and technical reasons for this approach. For as long as it seemed possible for the great powers to gain exclusive use of a particular technology – atomic fission, a strategic plan to invade a neighbouring country, or a new weapon design – an absolute view of secrecy could be understood. It wasn't possible either in 1890 or in 1945 to buy popular magazines explaining the key military technologies on which military supremacy was based, and as a result absolute secrecy appeared to be a realizable dream for the state. Hence draconian punishment was meted out to the offenders. Defenders of *Der Spiegel* have pointed, however, to important counter-examples from these years: notably to Hanson W. Baldwin's unfavourable comparison of the US Sherman with the German Tiger tanks, a report published in the midst of war in 1945. Far more important than any possible betrayal of military secrets was the fact that Baldwin's article and the ensuing publicity actually led to the immediate and successful upgrade of the Sherman.[7] How different from today's situation, in which arms manufacturers are anxious to circulate knowledge of their technical advances both for the purposes of deterrence (North Korean H-bombs and British 'super-accurate' bombs) and as an advertising strategy aimed at enhanced sales.

Openings for investigative journalism concerning the military had hardly been available in Hitler's Germany, while even in the Weimar Republic Ossietzky's trial had ended with his imprisonment as a traitor. So one could say that the *Spiegel*-Affair took place at a time before the Federal Republic had got used to the administrative procedures, still less come to understand the advantages of a more democratic approach to military secrets. These failures were identified, but hardly rectified. Theodor Eschenburg, no friend of *Der Spiegel*, was appalled not only by the government's flouting of the law, but by its incompetence in implementing legal procedures. He even suggested by way of explanation that the police had made so many legal errors in conducting the search of the *Spiegel* offices because they were out of practice at house-searches! So inexperience in wielding power – seventeen years after the NS state had ceased to exist – was part of an explanation.

The fact remains, however, that military secrets are a sensitive issue in all democratic societies. In the aftermath of the Affair a number of shortcomings

7 Hanson W. Baldwin wrote his article on January 5 1945 in the *New York Times*, following the negative experiences of US armoured divisions in the Battle of the Bulge.

in the relevant legislation became clear. StGB §§ 99 and 100 were widely recognized as being imprecise and confused. In particular the law failed to accommodate itself to the fact that what is or is not secret can change at short notice, since the government of the day requires the power from one moment to the next to declare that something is secret, and at the time of the Affair there were no established procedures to challenge such a decision. The concept of Freedom of Information was largely unknown in the 1960s, and even in the USA, where the idea was most loudly championed by the press, the administration's newly formed Office for Strategic Information had done nothing to bridge the gap between secrecy and openness. The arbitrariness of secrecy practice had already been highlighted in 1959 when Strauss had placed in a regional newspaper a long article on the NATO plan MC70 which contained far more confidential material than Ahlers was to include in his article.[8] In a similar incident, the British Air Minister had outraged the press in 1954 when he addressed an audience on the subject of a new vertical-take-off plane while it was still on the secret list and the press had therefore been prevented from even mentioning the existence of the plane.

In the months after the Affair circles sympathetic to *Der Spiegel* expressed admiration for the system adopted in Britain from the time of the 1914–18 war, the so-called D-notice (since 1993 more properly the DA-notice.) This system seemed ideal to the German press, since (although such notices were invariably followed) it was not legally binding on the press to obey a D-notice, and the procedure made explicit provision for negotiation and discussion on the particular question through the Service Press and Broadcasting Committee (SPBC), whose membership was made up of representatives of the media and of senior civil servants from the relevant ministries.[9]

Reverting to the discussion contained in Chapter Four, it's worth pointing out that – although British newspapers are not allowed to refer to specific D-notices (since to do so would have the effect of making public what the state wishes to keep secret) – the general public does in fact know about D-notices. Not only are they mentioned occasionally in parliament (in general terms at least: the first occasion was in 1961), but thanks to the work of Le Carré, Len Deighton and other writers of spy fiction the general public has gained some idea of the situation in which such notices are issued. Once again the efficient

8 Strauss' leaking of the MC 70 plan in: Schoenbaum (1963, p.53).

9 The admiration for D-Notices is expressed i.a. by Schoeps (1983, p. 109). We note that Max Weber diagnosed the way the German administrators were attracted to the English system, without doing much to change their own (Weber, 1982, p. 71).

operation of a legal system depends in part on the wide and unprofessional mediation of legal knowledge.

The UK's system does not cope well with major breaches, like Snowdon. What is identified officially as a 'gentlemen's agreement' is not always robust enough to withstand pressure, and the concept of 'gentleman' is increasingly seldom applied to the world of newspapers. There are also many opinions to the effect that a government's ability to silence the press on particular issues has been counterproductive, for instance in some sex scandals involving figures from the establishment. Nevertheless, at the beginning of the 1960s the system seemed far more assured than the circumstances which the *Spiegel* case revealed.

The German situation was further complicated by the defence ministry basing its accusations against *Der Spiegel* on the so-called 'mosaic' theory of secret information. According to this – a standard theory in the world of espionage –, it can be deemed a breach of secrecy for a journalist to put together in one place previously separate pieces of information in themselves not secret. Bringing together known facts can, it is argued, be instrumental in betraying a secret. Given that in any case speculation, rather than hard facts, dominates much military intelligence work (starting with the assumption that foreign intelligence services know most of the secrets anyway), mosaic theory – as Christina Wells has written recently – strengthens justifications for all types of government secrecy and because of the abstract nature of intelligence work 'creates a vacuum of knowledge that effectively paralyzes judicial assessment of the government's claims'.[10]

The problems of the 'mosaic theory' underline a further fundamental difference between the idea of secrecy in the Federal Republic and in the United Kingdom. For all its apparent informality, the D-notice system operates according to a formal definition of secrecy. By agreed procedures the state determines what is secret, and by that determination the matter *becomes* secret. This is in marked contrast to German understandings. The German system – referred to as a 'material' definition of secrecy – leaves it to a court (in fact the 3rd Division of the BGH) to determine, from the nature of the actual material, whether or not the material was to be regarded as secret. The *Spiegel*-Affair highlighted the practical problems caused by this approach. Ahlers and Augstein were initially arrested on suspicion of betraying military secrets; on the basis of that *suspicion* Adenauer made his outrageous statements to parliament about Augstein making his living from high treason, but on both these occasions the central

10 Mosaic theory is discussed by: Wells (2006). See also: Basten, who explains the legal reforms after 1968 which made this issue irrelevant: (1983, p. 48 f).

question as to whether the material which had appeared in *Der Spiegel* was secret or not had yet to be resolved. Not only had Ahlers and Augstein not been found guilty: it had not been proven that anything secret had been revealed.

Consequently, not until *after* the BGH had pronounced on the matter could it be established whether or not an offence had been committed and whether there had to be an answer to the charge. The first *formal* charges were delivered on Augstein and Ahlers in October 1964, two years after the scandal had broken and the BGH's decision was not given before May 13 1965. Indeed, one of the reasons why the BGH refused to open a trial against Ahlers and Augstein (thus making it the trial that never was) was that the court judged it impossible for the two journalists to have known *at the time of their alleged offence* whether the material they were publishing was secret or not. Their ignorance was both actual and technical. Indeed the legal construct in itself involved the potential contradiction that, if the facts in an article were not secret at the time of publication, and became secret only later after the court had reached a decision, then in effect Ahlers and Augstein – and any other defendant under this legislation – were liable to be found guilty only retroactively. At the time they published, there could have been no offence. *Nulla poena sine lege.*

This had hardly been a problem before 1945. In the NS period the word 'traitor' in the mouth of a minister was enough to ensure a death sentence. But once this legislation had been taken over into the law of the Federal Republic in 1951, it was a disaster waiting to happen. It's small wonder that the BVerfG – in justifying its refusal to allow Augstein and Ahlers' petition – avoided any confrontation with the complexities of the secrets legislation and made a fundamental distinction between spies and journalists in the handling of confidential material and thus attempted to take the heat out of the situation.

There's a considerable irony in the fact that this, Federal Germany's biggest scandal, was military in nature. For, despite national stereotypes which are slow to die out, the Federal Republic itself was not (and, I suggest, still is not) militaristic in any sense of the word. Indeed, most people wanted to forget the war, never again did they wish to arrive in a situation where dangerous buffoons in uniform led the country to disaster. This was the clear message of the massive demonstrations in 1955 against the remilitarization of Germany, and of the unbroken protests against the stationing of nuclear weapons on German soil. Militarism was the goose-stepping parades in East Germany and shooting to kill at the German-German border. For the Federal Republic enough was enough. As a result there was a remarkable lack of interest in military affairs. The major national newspapers had only a single military correspondent among them, and the Fallex report was never going to have raised much interest. This of course contrasted sharply with the situation in Britain, where each of the national newspapers had a specialist military correspondent and competed strongly against one another to get their hands on military stories. Chapman Pincher (of Beaverbrook's *Express*), for instance, was a widely acknowledged expert in military questions, but his position had no equivalent in the German media. Even Augstein had only skimmed the article when Ahlers had submitted it, since he – in common with the majority of his readers – found the topic little more than boring. Whatever else the *Spiegel*-Affair provoked, it was surprise that anyone took these matters seriously. Yet, despite media indifference, the plain fact was that the next war in Europe was certainly going to be fought on German territory, and that the Federal Republic's basic survival was entirely dependent on military alliances. Whatever else the defeats of 1918 and 1945 had brought to Germany, it was not military security. Yet for all the importance of these issues, neither the German public nor, it seemed, the German legal system was interested in getting a handle on military matters.

6.4 A Brief Consideration of the BVerfG Judgment

The judgment of the BVerfG – published on August 5 1966 (in fact, of course, it was not a judgment but an explanation of its rejection of Augstein and Ahlers' petition) – is a disappointing document.[11] It was reached in response not to any complaint against the decisions of a lower court (though the judgment of the BGH in November 22 1962 was challenged), but to Ahlers' and Augstein's personal complaint as a *Verfassungsbeschwerde*, focusing on the occupation of the *Spiegel* offices. The court made clear that the constitutional complaint covered only specific features of the affair, and that the court was formally unable to look beyond those issues explicitly mentioned in the submission. It was clear too that the court was relieved not to have to pass a wider judgment.

The judgment itself was marked by a series of rather trivial balancing acts. It critiqued points of detail – for instance that the Defence Ministry had not bothered to check how many of the facts in Ahlers' article had been published elsewhere and that the addition of the bribery charge had been inappropriate,

11 The judgment of the BVerfG is found in *BVerfG E*, 20, pp. 162–230. Its remarks on press-freedom in the judgment, pp. 171 f, 176. The court's comment about public access to technical issues (p. 214). Collings (2015, pp. 80–90) suggests shifts in the court's personnel as the reason for the unexpected outcome. He suggests that the court made up for its decision by simultaneously annulling an archaic rule (dating back to 1934 and renewed in 1941) allowing the police to attend any public meeting held in the state. Reaction to the decision included, Collings remarks further, a certain relief that even the BVerfG had become unpredictable.

since there was no likelihood of incriminating material on that point being found. The court pointed out that the action had been poorly planned, and that the practical issues of searching offices on seven floors of the building, consisting of 117 rooms and 77 separate editorial offices had hardly been considered. Nevertheless, the court felt unable to see the overall picture behind these facts. It critiqued the notion of secrecy which over-complicated the authorities' actions, when 'in the long term the revelation of significant weaknesses in defence capability – despite any short-term military disadvantages – is more important to the well-being of the Federal Republic than keeping those weaknesses secret'. That was common sense, but hardly a point of law.

Despite these reservations, the judgment had nothing to say about the distinction between formal and material understandings of secrecy, although this legal uncertainty had reduced elements of the Affair to farce. In a rather bizarre piece of argumentation, the court instead merely differentiated between 'journalistic and common high treason' (*publizistischer und gemeiner Landesverrat*) – an argument taken directly from the *Spiegel* article on Ossietzky. It left open what the law should do if a journalist were also a spy.

Similarly, the court accepted that it was essential for the press to preserve the confidentiality of its sources, while at the same time pointing out that the *Grundgesetz* contained no explicit privileges for the press (the Hetzel case showed something of the background to this) and followed this surprising assertion with the stern remark that 'it cannot be assumed *a priori* that the press is incapable of committing criminal acts'. The court did nothing to suggest the general need for freedom of information. On the contrary it commented on the relationship between openness and secrecy in the following terms:

> If the press concerns itself with individual technical issues of the military, then the balance shifts. The public's need for information becomes less important, on the one hand because the readers do not possess specialist knowledge sufficient to form an independent opinion; on the other hand, it is not necessary for readers to be in possession of this specialist knowledge for them to form their own political judgments.

We can see here clear traces of the particular type of argument which *Lüth* had brought out. The court was asserting that the law should be interpreted in keeping with the highest political goals of a democracy (hence the court's focus on people being in a position to form 'their own political judgments'), but the logic seemed flawed. Today certainly, and no less in 1962, a number of major political judgments are recognized to depend centrally on the general public's assessment of governments' competence and honesty in their approach to specialist and technical military matters. Above all, for instance, military procurement has been revealed as an area most susceptible not only to excessive secrecy, but to financial incompetence by the ministries and to corruption at a number of levels – something by no means confined to the Federal Republic. (One needs only think of the German Starfighter affair, or the anxieties raised by the one-time inability of British Army military personnel carriers to survive IED attack.) The particular approach which had been used by the BVerfG amounted to a mixture of shying away from controversial issues and seeing the case in the milky light of high-minded principle. This second feature seems to have been what led the judgment away from reaching clear conclusions. In short: its conclusion – that the occupation of the *Spiegel* offices had not been in breach of individuals' constitutional rights – was as unimpressive as its individual arguments.

I've suggested a positive reason why this judgment seems out of focus. It would also certainly be possible to place this case on those balancing scales which other historians have described, of cases showing the court's independence of and yet closeness to the aims of the government of the day and to understand the court as endeavouring not to ruffle government feathers. I prefer to see two other lessons in the BVerfG's entanglement with the *Spiegel* Affair. Not for the first time, the problems of the Federal Republic and its awkward relationship to its own legal institutions, did not come down to issues of major legislation. The lawlessness of the authorities in bending proper procedure clearly took place at a level well below what the BVerfG was used to dealing with. Manipulation by senior civil servants, misleading statements by ministers, personal animosities and careerism – none of it unique to the Affair, but all of it hard to identify and for courts (and still less a constitutional court) to correct. Secondly, if that is so, then we are reminded of Galay's cool assessment of the questionable value of giving excessive prominence to human rights in the *Grundgesetz*: Human rights – whether the protection of individual citizens against arbitrary arrest, or the protection of press freedom – are best guaranteed, Galay commented, not in absolute declarations on paper, but in the actual workings of the society and its legal-administrative instruments and institutions.[12] And the Affair showed these off in a most unfavourable light.

Anyone wishing to understand the 1960s and 1970s cannot ignore the Affair. So many elements which lay behind the accelerating tensions of those years had their origin in the spectacle of politicians' apparent contempt for the law, and of the law's apparent compliance with political convenience. Public reactions to the proposed emergency legislation would certainly have been less

12 Galay (1964, p. 160).

hostile if the Affair had not taken place. That neither Strauss himself nor his top ministerial civil servants suffered any legal consequences for their actions – though the hearings both clearly established that offences had been committed and revealed that the legal authorities were determined to take no further action – would look increasingly outrageous in the 1970s, as the state insisted on ordinary people (teachers, postmen and train-drivers) being sacked if they could not *at all times* demonstrate their loyalty to 'the basic democratic order'. In terms of the history of the Federal Republic's legal system, the Affair once again showed up the problems associated with taking over chunks of legislation from other, undemocratic systems, during the anti-Communist fervour of the early years. It was not just under the pressures of the struggle to contain urban guerrilla movements that the legal system's vulnerability would be shown up. The cracks were visible some years before.

Worse still, one might argue, was the erosion of confidence which the events of the Affair brought about among those who should have been the champions of the Republic.[13] These people are the subjects of later chapters.

---

13 A final note on the Affair. It was the first time that the name of Siegfried Buback – who led the public prosecution of the *Der Spiegel* during the Affair – first became widely known. (See Chapter 9.)

CHAPTER 7

The Frankfurt Auschwitz Trial

We started our accounts of significant post-war trials with the Nuremberg Tribunal in 1946–47. However, this choice was dictated by more than chronology, for the Nuremberg Trials not only attempted to mark the end of a particularly appalling period in German and European history: they marked the beginning of a new process, namely the international community's recognition of the need for legal mechanisms capable of handling crimes on the largest scale, crimes committed by entire regimes and against entire peoples. What had begun as a day of reckoning with the crimes of the NS past, all too soon came to be understood in the context of atrocities still to be committed.

The 'great' war of 1914 had never lived up to its title of the 'war to end all wars'. Somehow, in that it pulled back the curtain on the incompetence of the generals, the blindness of nationalism and the brute indifference of the European nations to the slaughter of their young men, that war might have been hoped to mark the outer limit of one form of inhumanity and unreason and to have issued an unmistakable warning of what must never be allowed to happen again. But, as everyone knows, it did not have that effect, and killing of which even the Great War had not proved capable came to be little more than a technical challenge which the next war would easily solve. In a similar tragic way, the NS murder of the European Jews did not act to mark any outer limit, never to be surpassed. Instead, over the next half century it came to be emulated in a number of countries across the world. In consequence, Nuremberg came to be seen as the model for the international community in its determination to punish and ideally to deter the perpetrators of other genocides. Janus-like, the Trials looked in both directions, to a shameful past and to a shameful future.

We shall indicate at various points in the course of this chapter something of the development of international law and of the international courts which took place after Nuremberg and which made possible the legal actions following the Yugoslav Wars, the Rwandan genocide and other such crimes against humanity. At the same time, it is to be expected that the Nuremberg Trials should have had an internal effect within Germany itself, and its most significant, if rather belated, consequence was the Auschwitz trial which took place in Frankfurt am Main between 1963 and 1965. It is to this trial that we turn in this chapter.

7.1 At Last the Silence Is Broken

At various points in this book we have referred to the failure of the Federal German legal system to deal adequately with the crimes committed during the Third Reich. Within the judiciary itself the refusal to confront its own involvement in the NS state was striking and understandable only in terms of an unimaginatively defined self-interest, but it unfortunately belonged to its time. More widely in the federal states and in Konrad Adenauer's government there was an absence of political will to tackle the problem. Despite an ostensibly stronger stance against Nazism than the other main parties, the SPD was also more concerned to pursue immediate economic and political goals than to confront the crimes of the recent past. They too had skeletons in the cupboard. As we've suggested, the problems the country faced were real enough, but their magnitude did little to explain the reluctance to engage in prosecutions of NS criminals. Adenauer's claim that 'a relatively small percentage' of Germans had been Nazis was at best ambiguous – more importantly, it allowed the real problem to be ignored.[1]

In defiance of Adenauer's statistics, National Socialism had swallowed into its brutal state not only the Party and its more extreme organs such as the SS, but every aspect of Germany's life and social structure. That's what totalitarianism means. The churches, the public service, police and judiciary, teaching, medicine, agriculture and industrial planning, the national bank (which melted down the gold looted from the Auschwitz prisoners) – none of these areas had represented a field of activity uncontaminated by Nazism, and while the armed forces held out longest with their self-image as a professional, non-ideological cadre, untouched by Nazism, by the 1990s even that image had crumbled as it became known to a wider public how deeply the army had been involved in atrocities against the civilian populations in the occupied territories (not just in the East, but also, for instance, in Yugoslavia). Where could one start with prosecutions, and which section of the establishment had an interest in opening up the horrors of the past? For, as Hannah Arendt wrote, 'the truth of the matter is that there existed not a single organization or public institution in Germany, at least during the war years, that did not become involved in criminal actions and transactions'.[2]

1 Adenauer quoted in Hannah Arendt (1978, p. 18).

2 Arendt (1978, p. 159). A critique of her thesis of the banality of evil in: Yaacov Lozowick (2000). Further details of Hans Oberländer (Minister for Displaced Persons) and of Hans Globke (Adenauer's assistant) and Globke eagerness to become more involved with the

Unfortunately, official short-sightedness also reflected wide-scale public attitudes. It is clear from the popular literature and culture of the Federal Republic in the 1950s that people's memories of the Third Reich consisted above all of feelings of helplessness, which had increased still further as they were sucked as cogs into the machinery of total war, being made part of actions for which, criminal or not, ordinary people felt no responsibility whatsoever. Together with its increasing consumerism, the Federal Republic offered identity and allowed people to wipe out the unpleasant memories of the past, and for the first time to take some responsibility for their lives, for instance in the rebuilding of their country. It's true that something of their identification with the NS period continued in the form of anti-Communism and a patriotic, but strongly anti-militarist, support of the West in the Cold War, but otherwise it was felt that sleeping dogs should continue to slumber. The past was mercifully over. Virtually no-one seemed interested in digging around in the ashes of the Third Reich and uncovering its crimes. There were few votes to be had in fighting against these attitudes.

Gradually, however, under the pressure of three elements these attitudes started to change. The first change was a generational shift. It would not be until the 1980s that a radical student generation began seriously to challenge not just their professors and politicians, but also their parents and grandparents about what they had done under Hitler. Nevertheless, by the end of the 1950s a generation was emerging with greater distance from the NS state which had robbed them of their childhood and their untroubled conscience. Secondly, in the wake of a growing dissatisfaction with the Adenauer regime – augmented by the scandal of Adenauer continuing to employ Hans Globke as his *chef de cabinet* (in 1938 Globke had written an authoritative commentary in support of the Nuremberg race laws) and compounded by the appointment of Theodor Oberländer as a minister in his early cabinets – people began to reflect on the continuities between the Federal Republic and the Third Reich. After all, under the Hallstein Doctrine the Federal Republic had declared itself, for better or worse, to be the sole legitimate representative of the German people and hence the follow-on state of previous German states, including the Nazis. This questioning is clearly reflected in the literature of the late 1950s and early 1960s. Henrich Böll's *Billiards at half-past Nine* and Günter Grass' *The Tin Drum* are perhaps the best-known examples.

'Jewish question' in: Arendt (1978, pp. 72, 128f). Otherwise see *Spiegel*-OnLine. The highly controversial army exhibition under the title: *Scorched Earth* (*Vernichtungskrieg*) – *the crimes of the Wehrmacht 1941–1945* opened in 1995 and was shown in various German cities.

If these were gradual processes of change, a final impulse came in 1960 with the arrest, trial and subsequent execution of Adolf Eichmann.

7.2 The Implications of the Eichmann Trial

Eichmann had been an 'expert' on 'the Jewish question' at the RSHA, and although he worked within rather than initiated the Nazis' overall policy towards the Jews of Germany and the countries which Germany occupied after 1939, he was a key figure in the Final Solution, being responsible for the collecting of the Jews living in the occupied territories and for their subsequent transport to death-camps such as Auschwitz. After escaping from Germany at the end of the war, Eichmann had settled with his family in Buenos Aires until in 1960 he was snatched by Israeli government agents, and in April 1961 put on trial in the District Court of Jerusalem on fifteen counts, including crimes against the Jewish people, crimes against humanity and war-crimes. After a trial which held the attention of the world, Eichmann was found guilty, and immediately following the rejection of his appeal and his plea for clemency he was executed at the end of May 1962. Nothing since the Nuremberg trials themselves did more to remind – or indeed, in the case of the younger generation, to reveal to – German citizens and the world the deeds of the NS state.

The Eichmann trial focused on two, seemingly contradictory elements of the holocaust: the first of these was, in Hannah Arendt's celebrated phrase, the essential 'banality of evil'. By this Arendt meant that Eichmann himself had seemed to possess few characteristics which corresponded to the enormity of his crimes. The attempts which had been made to demonize a small number of the NS war criminals had been unsuccessful – even though this approach was widely popular in the Federal Republic, since it well served to shuffle off any general responsibility for the past. As Hannah Arendt pointed out, the Jerusalem prosecutor too endeavoured to make Eichmann out to be a demon, yet he failed, for in sentencing Eichmann the judges focused dispassionately on what he had done, rather than who he was. For all the prosecution's efforts to make him interesting in his evil, the truth remained less exciting: to the watching world Eichmann was a nothing, a faceless cipher.

The trial showed that one of the worst of the NS organizers of mass-murder was a person who could perfectly easily fit into everyday suburban life in the Federal Republic (or anywhere else in the world, for that matter) without drawing attention to himself, and whose most characteristic feature was not burning hatred or sadism but the ambition to do well in his career. Under their uniforms such criminals turned out to be the most ordinary of people; when the régime passed, they reverted to the everyday. The type of perverse, demonic antisemite of the war-comic and horror film had in no way actually carried out the genocide. Indeed, the holocaust was planned bureaucratically so as not to need that type of person. The actual murderers were unremarkable, banal people: they were (in the title of a successful post-war German film) 'in our midst' and did not stand out from the crowd.[3]

In short: an ambiguous situation had emerged in the early 1960s. On one hand, it became harder to separate the ordinary people of Germany from Nazism and from the Final Solution. If such people as Eichmann were capable of carrying out inhuman crimes, then it seemed plausible to spread the responsibility for such crimes more widely. By the same token, however, the Eichmann trial showed that genocide was an impersonal, technical process. Its implementation had depended on an apparatus of interlocking 'technical services' and these had been run by faceless people, who appeared to have no greater personal or *inner* link to the murder machine than might be found in any routine job in industry. At his trial Eichmann maintained that he quite liked Jews.

The Nuremberg trials had eliminated some of the most prominent Nazis. It would have been possible to believe that the past had been adequately dealt with. Yet the Eichmann trial showed that, as one went one step further down the hierarchy, there were plenty of criminals still unpunished. It was the small people who had been no less essential to the Final Solution, yet the legal process had passed them by.

7.3 Auschwitz-Birkenau[4]

The Eichmann trial made one final contribution to public awareness in Germany. Although Eichmann had himself only infrequently been to the place to which he had sent so many, his trial focused attention on a particular institution within the murderous apparatus: the death-camp of Auschwitz-Birkenau.

Auschwitz was of course known about before the Eichmann trial, both among the Allies and (if only in its outlines) to the German public. But in

3 The German film: *Die Mörder sind unter uns* was one of the earliest post-war German films, directed by Wolfgang Staude in Babelsberg. Note Heinrich Böll's comments during the Frankfurt trial itself: 'Too many murderers are running round scot free in this country. Many of them will never be found guilty of their murders. Guilt, remorse, repentance or any understanding of the past have never become categories of social behaviour, let alone factors in our political life' (quoted Vogt, 2014, p. 1).

4 Details of the construction of Auschwitz in: Steinbacher (2013, pp. 17–54).

contrast to camps such as Dachau or Buchenwald, which had been opened in the early years of the Third Reich and were situated close to large German centres of population, Auschwitz did not take its first prisoners before June 1940 and was much further away. It was not 'liberated' in the sense that the Allied armies had found some concentration camps more or less intact as they moved into Germany in the closing weeks of the war. When the Red Army arrived at Auschwitz, there was little left to see.

Things had hardly changed after the war. Before the collapse of the Soviet bloc in 1989 there were few if any Western tourists going to Krakau and Auschwitz. Auschwitz and its pendant Birkenau (the site of the intensive killing facilities) were in all senses 'off the map' in the minds of West Germans and West Europeans alike. There had been little mention of Auschwitz in Nuremberg, partly because the Gestapo had destroyed so many of its files relevant to the death-camps and Himmler had ordered the destruction of all the incriminating parts of the camp itself; and partly because the victims of the Holocaust had had little or nothing to do with the preparation of the trials. Hans Frank denied that it was part of his area of responsibility. Before the arrest of the *Kommandant* of Auschwitz, Rudolf Höss, in April 1946 (and therefore too late to fit into the Nuremberg schedules) there had been little attempt to investigate further.

In Poland there had been major trials of the Auschwitz personnel as early as 1947, when, understandably, the Polish authorities had conducted Höss' trial themselves (he was tried in Warsaw in the same year and executed in Auschwitz), and a more general Auschwitz trial had taken place in Krakow later in the same year, again resulting in a number of executions – but those who had been tried represented, in the limited perception of the immediate post-war German public, only a tiny proportion of the numbers of Germans missing in the East. They did not stand out from the crowd. The passing years helped people to forget, and did nothing to disturb the impression that Auschwitz had already been dealt with as a problem.

Similar trials to those in Poland did take place in others of the states in eastern Europe from where Jewish people had been transported to their death in Auschwitz, but these trials too had hardly impinged on the German public. A very small number of trials had also taken place in West Germany in the 1950s, but these had been small-scale events which usually resulted in inappropriately lenient outcomes for the accused, and once again none of this had had any significant impact on the public.

In this search for justice, more than anywhere else, we see the effects of the amnesty laws which the Justice Ministry had constantly been introducing throughout the 1950s. From 1960 all crimes were amnestied which carried a sentence of less than fifteen years (this included all manslaughter charges) – it left the few courts anxious to pursue NS crimes with no choice save the charge of premeditated murder. This silence was broken finally in 1963, when a trial opened in the state court (*Landgericht*) in Frankfurt am Main which attempted to deal with the Auschwitz-complex and which was conducted by the federal state of Hesse against 'Mulka and others'. (Mulka had been the deputy commandant of Auschwitz.) This promised to be something different: the Eichmann trial had, at the very least, raised expectations, and Frankfurt seemed destined to fulfil them.

7.4 Preparing for the Trial

It will seem self-understood that such a trial should be conducted in Germany. Few mass crimes cried out more loudly for justice, and few failures to prosecute could have been more shameful for the Federal Republic. Not to have acted after the Eichmann trial would have exposed the repeated efforts to declare a statute of limitation for NS crimes as a conscious attempt at whitewash. After the attempts to achieve a complete amnesty for NS crimes had finally been abandoned, the Frankfurt trials produced their effect. Similarly, the failure of the prosecution of the RSHA[5] would have been unmasked as a deliberate cover-up. It was here that the generational shift in attitude was important, as too was a sense – even within government circles – that the Republic needed a more coherent approach to the issues of the NS past and should at least investigate, if not actually prosecute, its crimes.

Nationally and internationally it was time to challenge what has been called 'the culture of impunity' among the perpetrators of these crimes.[6] Adenauer had worried about Germany's loss of face internationally if trials of prominent ex-Nazis took place and the horrors of the past were once more paraded in public, but he could not ignore the fact that any failure by the Federal Republic to take legal action on Auschwitz would have damaged the state infinitely more. Paying substantial financial compensation to Israel was no substitute

5 The RSHA, comfortably ensconced in Berlin, was the organization behind the camps and staffed with the classic 'desk-top murderers'. Trials of its leaders had failed in 1958 and 1969. The Ulm trial of 1958 (see p. 158) saw no chance of moving beyond the actual murderers to those who issued the orders. Two factors militated against decisive action: BGH opposition, in part due to that court's determination to defend the NS civil service, and the superior orders defence, which the BGH had made unchallengeable in the post-IMT years. See background notes to this chapter.

6 The phrase is from James Crawford (2003, p. 109).

for national self-examination and for the prosecutions which should properly be its result. The rich cultural life of the Federal Republic, with its increasing commitment to facing the NS past, could be nothing other than a lie without such action. The problems with bringing the matter to court, however, were considerable and went beyond political reluctance and foot-dragging, for they were not only bound up with public mind-sets but involved significant technical and – predictably – intrinsically legal obstacles.

The central difficulty was the complex and systematic nature of the crimes round which a death-camp such as Auschwitz was built. Initially this presented itself to the Frankfurt prosecutors as a problem of scale. In the trial no fewer than fifteen hundred witnesses were identified, of whom three hundred and sixty were called to Frankfurt in order to prosecute twenty-one defendants, while in addition fifty witness statements were tabled from people either unable or unwilling to travel to Germany to attend the court. Five judges and nine lay judges served. The case took five and half years to prepare and lasted over eighteen months.

No less problematic was the question of the representativeness of the figures brought to trial. The twenty-one accused were the only ones to appear in court out of the seven thousand personnel who had kept the institution of Auschwitz-Birkenau running. The accused therefore represented only a fraction of the functionaries within the camp. In terms of the wider organization, this number merely underlines the statistical insignificance of those brought to trial in Frankfurt. Administrative staff in Berlin, primarily in the RSHA, were not summoned to court. Nor did the trial manage to include those middle-ranking functionaries responsible for collecting the victims of Auschwitz-Birkenau from their homes in various countries, nor those who organized their transport. Those tasks were not carried out by Eichmann single-handed, but by a whole staff of local transport managers, as well as by the various army commanders whose permission was needed to release trains for a purpose of which they were aware. The Frankfurt trial did not include those who produced and constructed the physical apparatus of killing. In all areas of Auschwitz the few who were charged were outnumbered by those not in court. A famous poem by Bertolt Brecht from the 1930s contains the lines: 'As a young man Alexander the Great conquered India. All on his own? Caesar defeated the Gauls. Did he not even take his cook with him?'. Brecht meant the lines to debunk heroic historical writing and individuals' claims to greatness, but the Auschwitz trial raised the same question in another, still more telling direction: that of responsibility.

The accused themselves represented, albeit thinly, a certain cross-section of the work in Auschwitz-Birkenau. They came from Section III, the political section – responsible for the 'enhanced interrogation techniques' used for internal 'security' –, from the 'medical' services and from among the guards, although the general administration (Section 1) was hardly represented. The massive technical apparatus of which Auschwitz was the centre was imperfectly reflected in the definition of the defendants as: 'Mulka and others'. Richard Baer, Höss' successor as *Kommandant* at Auschwitz, had originally been among the accused (having been tracked down by the Frankfurt authorities), but had died before the trial began, and his adjutant, Robert Mulka, took his place as the most senior SS-officer in court. This was unfortunate, since it was clear that a deputy would find it much easier to shuffle off personal responsibility than the actual *Kommandant* himself, but there was little the prosecution could do about that. They had to run the trial with the defendants they had.

Nevertheless, scale in itself was not the real problem in preparing the trial. Issues of evidence and other legal questions were more significant. In particular the question of individual responsibility for the killings remained intractable. Atrocities committed by particular individuals tended to present less of a difficulty to the court – that is, provided they had been witnessed by people who had not only survived, but twenty years later were able to identify the perpetrators and willing to testify. It was not clear, however, how conventional justice could follow its normal procedures when the significance of the crimes in question lay in their systematic rather than their individual features. It was impossible to understand Auschwitz without grasping the organizational, supra-individual nature of the crimes. The millions of killings were clearly not a series of individual atrocities. It was not merely a problem of scale, but of proving responsibility. To respond to this awareness meant that effectively it was Auschwitz itself which was meant to be on trial, and Auschwitz itself which was the massive blot on Germany's past with which the law had to deal. Yet the available law was designed to deal only with individual offences.

Even at the time, this mismatch between legal thinking and the crimes of Auschwitz surprised no-one. Throughout his trial it had been Eichmann's proud insistence that he had personally killed no-one, and no witnesses had been produced in Jerusalem who could reliably refute his claim. This is where the problem started, no less in Jerusalem than in Frankfurt. After the Eichmann trial many people felt that a desk-top murderer was more responsible than those who actually carried out the practical work of large-scale extermination, but tangible proof and legal precedents were more elusive. In fact, in Auschwitz the mechanical operations of the murder machine, the actual killings, were carried out by common criminals, the so-called 'Greens', who were transferred from other prisons precisely in order to carry out that role. Their title was 'prisoners with a function' – *Funktionshäftlinge*. They were themselves obviously prisoners too, and no less obviously under the direct control of the SS. Within the environment of mechanized death, it was paradoxical (and somehow hardly the point) to establish their responsibility for their actions. It was the SS staff who needed to be nailed by the prosecution.

One simple way of demonstrating the problem is to examine the extent to which existing definitions of murder failed to cover this asymmetric relationship between action and responsibility. The criminal code contained in RGStGB § 211 the following definition:

> A person commits murder who out of pleasure in killing, in order to satisfy sexual drives, out of greed or other base motives, maliciously or cruelly, using methods dangerous to the community at large, or in order to make possible or to conceal another crime, kills a human being.

The Frankfurt trial would show the problems which arose when a legal code which, for a killing to qualify as murder, stated that 'base motives' had to be behind actions, was applied to mass murder. It had already helped the defendants at the abortive RSHA trial – the danger was that it would be brought into play in Frankfurt too. Absurdly a readiness to destroy millions of people did not qualify as a base motive. In Auschwitz the killing was driven by characteristics which could, in other contexts, be quite positive: such as 'efficiency', 'obedience' and 'integration': these were what kept the killing machinery in motion. This was a world where 'base' personal motives were not intended to play any part and where the organizers of murder seldom carried out the murders.

In short: The murder-machine of Auschwitz-Birkenau was set up in such a way as to operate without the need for individual acts of homicide. Although cases of individual brutality were widespread, not only the work-organization but the very language of the camp turned mass-murder into an automatic process. Nevertheless, as official inspections of the camp revealed, the SS-workforce enjoyed a high degree of independence and autonomy and could shape their activities as they wished.[7] Morally, few would disagree that all those who took part in Auschwitz-Birkenau were responsible for their actions, but it is seldom the case in law that a moral indictment can be transferred into a legally punishable offence. The dream of such a moral law is hard to realize. (We saw how Flick's ruthless expropriation of the Jewish-Czech steel concern was explicitly identified by the Nuremberg court as morally reprehensible, but not an offence at law.) The most effective murderers were those who merely

7 Evidence on the inspections' finding that SS staff had considerable autonomy in Auschwitz was given at the trial and is discussed by Pendas (2006, p. 158).

signed pieces of paper or organized a work-rota, yet the law seemed incapable of recognizing that, still less of punishing it as a formal crime.

Again this cannot have been much of a surprise in 1963. Nuremberg had not really been an orthodox court of law at all, with the result that the judges had found it much easier to skate round difficulties of this kind. They succeeded more easily than would have been possible in any conventional court. It's instructive to note a recent summary of the legal deficiencies in 1947: 'Nuremberg crimes were not actually formulated as crimes', Andrew Clapham writes, 'with the specificity we would expect of a criminal trial'.[8] The difficulty was that little had been learned between the two trials: the Federal German legal code had not been modified to cope with the situation of Auschwitz, and Frankfurt was determined to be a proper criminal trial, with all the limiting factors which that implied.

In addition to the problems of sentencing Auschwitz, one specific issue – which had been particularly important at Nuremberg and, as Arendt made clear in her discussion of the Eichmann trial, had remained unsatisfactory after Eichmann's execution – still lacked national or international consensus as to its resolution: namely, under what laws charges were to be brought against the criminals of a now defunct state. This uncertainty was partly an issue of political will on behalf of the legislature, but it also had to do with conflicting interpretations of the legal status of the Third Reich. It could not even be agreed by historians and lawyers whether there had been a formal legal basis at all in the Third Reich. While the Nuremberg laws of 1938, for instance, had clearly taken the form of written laws (and no less clearly made possible the Final Solution by radically diminishing the formal citizenship rights of the Jewish citizens of Germany), they were something of an exception. The subsequent crucial decisions in pursuit of the Final Solution were not written down as laws: perhaps these particular decisions were not written down at all but had been taken simply on the basis of Hitler's spoken words. The so-called *Führer*-principle – on which the whole NS state was run – meant just that, and eminent legal authorities of the time (notably its principal legal apologist, Carl Schmitt) were not slow to recognize that the word of the *Führer* was the only centre of the legal system. The legal framework of the state was therefore not its laws.

This caused a severe problem for post-war judges. Since German criminal law requires that the accused have knowledge of the illegality of their act, judges had therefore to decide whether a person could be found to have acted illegally if there had been no framework of law which defined the actions on

8 Clapham (2003, p. 40).

which the person was indicted.[9] This wasn't a parlour game in legal sophistries, for if there had been no laws, then any subsequent legal approach to crimes committed in that state would inevitably have had the effect of introducing an element not present in the NS state itself and arguably therefore invalid *post hoc*. Amid such uncertainties about the 'discontinuity principle', almost any formal legal approach in 1963 risked being dismissed as retroactive legislation – the common complaint unsuccessfully put forward by all the defendants at Nuremberg, and one much harder for a conventionally constituted German court to ignore.

Alongside problems of jurisdiction, the classification of the crimes themselves had remained problematic. As we saw, the court at Nuremberg had centred its cases on the charge of starting a war of aggression. Crimes against humanity had been mentioned as a category in Control Council law no. 10, but the phrase had remained too little defined for it to play a significant part in the prosecution case, although the sentencing clearly showed that the judges had in effect been swayed by the concept. (The execution of Julius Streicher is explicable only in terms of the judges' general sense that his actions were part and parcel of crimes against humanity: but that decision had hardly based on foundations other than the laws of the Control Council.) Furthermore, the Nuremberg court had been careful in their use of any catch-all phrase such as 'war-crime', lest the term should have been used against the Allies themselves, both in their domestic activities and in their conduct of the war. It had worried the Allies that the old tag *Tu quoque* should not be used against them. In any case, many of the outrages of the Third Reich had been committed during peace time, and yet the Nuremberg tribunal had been predicated on Germany being a defeated belligerent nation.

In consequence of such difficulties, we recall that the Nuremberg Charter and its prosecutions had proceeded on the legal basis of a UN resolution reflected also in § 10 of the Allied Control Commission, and that no attempt whatsoever had been made at the time to bring charges under German law or, for that matter, under German court procedure. While the trials had been able to operate, for instance, on the basis that simple membership of the SS was in itself criminal (which did not mean, of course, that every member of the SS was punished – it was merely an additional charge for those who got arrested), by 1963 such a blanket approach was unlikely to have found much public support, and was in any case more than inadequate to deal with the enormity of the crimes of Auschwitz-Birkenau. Being in the SS was a qualification for working there, but that was no longer the point.

9 See Wittmann (2006, p. 212).

Partly because of reasons of state prestige, it was determined that the trial would be conducted on the basis of the German penal law as defined in the penal code in force at the time of the offences, the *Reichsstrafgesetzbuch* of 1871. The desirability of the Federal Republic enacting retrospective legislation to deal specifically with NS crimes had been publicly debated, but the Frankfurt prosecutors' decision in favour of the 1871 legislation meant at least that none of the defendants could claim to have been ignorant of the law under which they were tried. The time-honoured principle of *nulla poena sine lege* seemed to the authorities in Frankfurt a more realistic guiding principle than any new legislation, even assuming that the political will had existed to set up such new legislation in the first place.

7.5 Gathering Momentum

The case started, however, on a level more mundane than abstract legal debates of this kind. A petty criminal, himself once a detainee in Auschwitz, living in the Stuttgart area, recognized a neighbour of his, Wilhelm Boger, as having worked in the political section of the administration in Auschwitz-Birkenau, and denounced him to the authorities. (Ever since the Nuremberg trials, during which, among many other such instances, Hans Globke had roundly denounced his friend and co-author Stuckart, denunciations had been a common element in trials concerning the NS past: usually, although not in the Boger case, for the purpose of the denouncer exonerating himself.) Despite the fact that the denunciation had come from a notoriously unreliable source – indeed the man had already been found guilty of perjury in a previous denunciation – a series of factors led to the matter being taken further.

In April 1958 public attention had focused on the trial in Ulm of members of one of the notorious death-squads (*Einsatzgruppen*). The accused were charged with the murders of five and a half thousand Jewish men, women and children in Lithuania in 1941. It suddenly became news that murderers of this kind were still at liberty. The trial suffered, as the Auschwitz trial was to suffer, from the failure of the criminal code to include crimes such as that which came to light in Ulm – none of the accused was found guilty of a more serious offence than being an accessory to murder. However, a significant response to the trial was the creation in 1958 of a supra-regional research centre in Ludwigsburg (ZSL) with the brief of 'investigating NS crimes of violence'. This served to focus a shift in the activities of German historians examining the NS period: after 1958 the Eastern Front would be a major topic of research. The ZSL became a mechanism which could reliably verify denunciations and in addition move from the individual case to a more complete historical picture. It was to be an important element in the preparation of the Auschwitz trial.[10]

Another figure played a crucial role at this point. Fritz Bauer – a long forgotten but highly significant 'founding father of the Federal Republic' (Jochen Vogt) and an admirer of the reforming minister of the Weimar Republic, Gustav Radbruch – was the Attorney General of Hesse. A judge before 1933, Bauer had returned from exile in Sweden (where he had been associated with the future German chancellor Willy Brandt) to pursue his legal career. He had been outraged at the way in which the Nuremberg Trials had ignored the Holocaust, and in the 1950s had been involved in the formal rehabilitation of the conspirators of July 20 1944 – in itself a highly significant political act on his part, for many people continued to regard the conspirators as traitors and common criminals. By a strange chance, Bauer had come into possession of extensive documentation on the administration of Auschwitz-Birkenau. It was Bauer who had brought the individual circumstances of the Boger case to the attention of the International Auschwitz Committee (IAK, an organization made up of former detainees). Working with Ludwigsburg, this agency was in a position to verify the accusation against Boger. Still more importantly, the IAK had the international clout to support Bauer in creating the momentum for a wider trial.

The involvement of the IAK and from 1959 of Ludwigsburg, combined with the horrors revealed in the Eichmann trial, gave a necessary impetus to the Frankfurt Auschwitz trial. The prosecution authorities in Stuttgart – certainly in the opinion of the IAK – had shown little enthusiasm for unravelling the implications of the initial denunciation. Even in the unlikely case that a prosecution had been run from Stuttgart, any subsequent legal action was liable to have been conducted as an individual trial, and in all likelihood such a trial would have led to Boger's acquittal, as so many had done in the past, on the grounds of the shortage of individual witnesses. It was easy to find no witnesses if one did not really want to look.

10 The best source on the ZSL is Annette Weinke (2008. On the Ulm trial p. 10 f; on the shift of historians' focus p. 15 f). Ten years later, with the student movement, this shift was strengthened, though challenged in the *Historikerstreit* in the 1980s and by Chancellor Kohl's actions and President Reagan's visit to the SS-cemetery at Bitburg.

When the BGH formally transferred the Boger case to Frankfurt's jurisdiction, however, a combination of Fritz Bauer's idealism, the IAK and the systematic foundation offered by a proper historical archive not only gave the Frankfurt prosecution access to witnesses, but lent the trial a strong push in the direction opposite to an individual hearing. Their initiative was towards putting Auschwitz-Birkenau on trial as an institution, through a coordination of individual indictments, and above all through a proper understanding of the bureaucratic structures inside and surrounding Auschwitz.

The legal case depended on the work of academic historians. Without that historical understanding, for instance, it would have been all but impossible to identify many of the blatant untruths in the defence offered by the accused. (This had been illustrated during the Eichmann trial, when the accused himself had ended up producing multi-coloured flow-charts to make clear to the court what role he had played in the apparatus of murder. Eichmann was the *only* person in court to understand the structures.) Such a thing could not happen again. Once again, justice depended on proper historical research.

7.6 A New Type of Trial

There were huge implications in the decision to broaden the action in this way, in terms both of the conduct of the trial and of its likely outcome. The historical precedents were of great importance.

Bauer's approach echoed the wish of the prosecutors at Nuremberg to have a representative trial, and his motives were the same: the education of the people of Germany and of the world. This ambition had been visible in the determination of the prosecutors to put German heavy industry on trial as an institution, rather than merely to punish its most notorious members, such as Krupp. In Bauer's hands the trial came to resemble a kind of class action against Auschwitz as an organization. Bauer and the IAK hoped to show the collective responsibility for Auschwitz, albeit at a low level of the hierarchy. For obvious reasons they had little possibility of follow-up action at a higher level of responsibility. No CEO or share-holder could be put on the stand, either because they were already dead or because they could not be identified more precisely.

However, there was an ambiguity in Bauer's attitude. For all its desire to broaden the trial, the prosecution did not subscribe to the idea of communal guilt: it wanted to find and to punish individual perpetrators. It wanted the *scale* and systematic nature of the crime to be clear, but did not attempt to cast any blanket guilt onto the German people at large. Collective guilt was not on the prosecution's agenda, yet much of the evidence and, indeed its whole approach, pointed precisely in that direction. This apparent contradiction was resolved in the fact that Bauer's overriding ambition had been to achieve a public trial in Germany. Its educational and moral purpose had been more important to him than assuring long sentences for the accused. He set up the trial as if he knew it was bound to fail at one level, and in fact, as his biographer stresses, Bauer was explicitly prepared to swap large-scale educational effect for retributive individual punishment.

A characteristic approach taken by the Frankfurt court in handling this dilemma was to copy a feature of the Eichmann trial and consciously to give a voice to the victims. It was a consequence of this decision that civil counsels were added to the prosecution team, gaining their accreditation to the court on the basis of representing small groups of victims, even though it was not the victims who were bringing the case, but the state of Hesse. The witnesses therefore took on representative function, no less than the accused: the groups defining themselves roughly on ethnicity – Jewish, Polish, Russian, Czech and others.

In view of the tensions reflected in the Cold War division of Europe, the ethnicity of the victims meant that they became identified with distinctive ideological critiques and analyses of the nature of National Socialism. Inevitably such analyses involved some view of Nazism's relationship to the Federal Republic. (It should be noted that these were the days when the standard catchphrase used about the Federal Republic in the Soviet Bloc was that it was a 'fascist state'.[11]) Many witnesses needed explicit authority from their own government to travel to Germany to give evidence – a circumstance which frequently led the defence to challenge the genuine nature of the witnesses' evidence. It was easy to claim that they had been allowed to travel merely in order to defame the Federal Republic. At the time of the trial, for instance, the Federal Republic did not have diplomatic relations with Poland – it took Willy Brandt kneeling ten years later in contrition in the Warsaw ghetto to make these relations possible: the trial broke diplomatic as well as legal new ground. The variety of prosecution voices had the further consequence that some of the energy of the court was taken up with preventing certain of the co-prosecutors – especially Friedrich Kaul from the GDR – from delivering denunciations of the

---

11 Apart from the general designation of the Federal Republic as 'fascist', authorities in the Soviet Union and the GDR never moved on from Stalin's labelling of the SPD as 'social fascists' throughout the early 1930s.

Federal Republic in keeping with an orthodox Communist reading of recent history, and in particular accusing sections of its capitalist industry of making possible the rise of NS state and by extension Auschwitz. The theory may or may not be persuasive, but had little to do with the circumstances of the trial.

Despite their negative effects, these tensions had a significant positive effect. They introduced into the proceedings an adversarial element which so many German trials lack and of which the dull and 'banal' defendants were by themselves hardly capable: this in turn produced those unforgettable courtroom-exchanges which more than anything else forced themselves onto the memories of the younger generation. In short: this was not a trial that would be easily forgotten, still less swept under the carpet. It was meant to be, in Robert Hariman's phrase, 'a common forum [...] performing the laws', thus 'turning the material of the trial into social knowledge'.[12]

The 'class action' nature of the proceeding had three further if narrower effects. First the establishment of evidence involved not merely individual eye-witnesses, but academic historians, who were themselves still at an early stage of their understanding the workings of the NS state. Their contribution was essential to the process of establishing the importance of individual actions within the larger system. Secondly, each defendant and their defence-team could continually re-open the issue of the relationship between individual responsibility and a technical system of which the individual accused were the instruments. Indeed, it was the obvious defence, one which the prosecution's approach explicitly opened to them. This defence surfaced as an acute form of the familiar superior orders defence (*Befehlsnotstand*) – a later version of Wharton's 'irresistible physical constraint' to which we referred in the first chapter.

Thirdly: not only were by definition the vast majority of victims dead, but the few witnesses had, again by definition, virtually no overview of the system in which they had assumed they would themselves be killed, nor was it probable that any of even four hundred witnesses would have observed all the accused in the actual performance of individual acts of violence and murder in a multi-purpose and geographically extensive camp. (Auschwitz-Birkenau covered a total area of no less than forty square kilometres.) It transpired for instance that only four of the witnesses had ever seen Mulka on the Ramp, that notorious place by the railway lines at which the deportees arrived, the place at which the separation took place between those (never more than about twenty-five percent) who could be used in the factories at Auschwitz

12 Hariman (1993, p. 21).

and those destined for immediate killing. It took massive commitment on Fritz Bauer's behalf, and a great conviction that justice had to be seen to be done not to despair or to wish that the Allies had followed their early plans and summarily executed the entire staff of Auschwitz-Birkenau at the end of the war. As in other cases Bauer had to watch the failure to secure convictions against participants in the various NS euthanasia programmes, his confidence cannot have been high. By the time of the trial he was under attack not merely as a man who had 'betrayed' his country during the war – an accusation scandalously made against Willy Brandt by Franz Josef Strauss (as if more honourable things were done inside Hitler's Germany than outside) – but, as a Jew, for being *parti pris* in the Auschwitz case and therefore unsuited to be director the case. It took genuine courage for Bauer to continue with the case.

7.7 Individual Moments from the Proceedings

The general issues discussed so far crystallize when we turn to the actual transcripts of the trial. In this section we give just two samples. We stay with the two defendants who have already been introduced into the narrative.

The following scene is concerned with evidence given against Wilhelm Boger, who had worked in the 'political section' of Auschwitz. It was the denunciation of this man which had triggered the whole trial, since Boger had escaped from a transport of Allied prisoners extradited to Poland in 1946 for a trial which would undoubtedly have led to his execution and – after a perfunctory case against him as a *Hauptschuldiger* (principal offender) was dropped in 1951 in the Federal Republic – had been living under his true identity in the Stuttgart area.

In the first scene a witness describes an episode in which he had attempted to barter a bottle of schnapps against some medicines which a friend and fellow prisoner had needed. When caught he had been sentenced to twenty five lashes and eight days in the *Stehbunker* (a cell in which prisoners were compelled to spend the night standing up: torture by sleep deprivation therefore). He had to undergo interrogation by the political section, which wished to discover where he had obtained the schnapps. On his first visit, as he was passing Boger's office, he saw Boger throw a prisoner out of the window. Boger subsequently had seen the witness bring water to the prisoner as he lay outside, and had immediately left his office and had beaten up the witness. The badly injured prisoner had subsequently died, while Boger had taken over the subsequent interrogation of the witness.

WITNESS: I said I'd found [the bottle] under a pile of cement. Boger put me on the swing[13] and beat me until I lost consciousness.

PRESIDING JUDGE: Are you sure it was Boger who beat you up when you brought water to the injured man? What did he say at the time?

WITNESS: Nothing. He beat me up and kicked me. When I got out of the swing Jakob in the bunker helped patch me up.

PRESIDING JUDGE: Defendant Boger, what have you to say to what the witness has just said?

BOGER: Some of it is true, some invented. I never threw a prisoner out of the window, and I've never beaten anyone so badly that he died.

PRESIDING JUDGE: So the witness was not beaten unconscious because of a bottle of schnapps?

BOGER: That's certainly possible. The instruction to conduct an enhanced interrogation always came from the head of the section.

PRESIDING JUDGE: That's to say from Grabner, who's deceased.

BOGER: Yes, but I still doubt that the witness knew me.

PRESIDING JUDGE: He says you fixed him in the swing.

BOGER: Could be.

DEFENCE COUNSEL DR ASCHENAUER: I request that an instruction be read to the court which makes clear which groups of prisoners could be subjected to enhanced interrogation without permission from Berlin.

PROSECUTOR VOGEL: Does any instruction permit prisoners to be beaten to death?

BOGER: Neither I nor any other member of the political section ever beat a prisoner to death.

ORMOND: (*counsel representing the civil plaintiffs*) You said that some of the witness's statement was true. What parts of his statement did you mean?

13 A notorious torture instrument in the camp, also known as 'the speaking machine'. A similar device is clearly described in accounts of Guantanamo Bay as permitting 'beating, binding in contorted stress positions'.

BOGER:	Enhanced interrogation.
ORMOND: (*to the witness*)	Has your health suffered permanent damage from your time in the concentration camp?
WITNESS:	I twice had a basal fracture of the skull, my nervous system suffered permanent damage. I lost the toes off my left foot to frostbite and I caught typhus. I am only forty percent fit for work.

We see here both the prosecution's insistence on the individual case and the defendant's simultaneous determination to deny the facts of individual situations, and his indifference to admitting the general circumstance. We presume that no further witnesses to this episode could be found, and that in sentencing Boger the judgment would have to be reached according to whether the judges believed the particular witness. For this incident there's no attempt to establish the exact date and time: the court had heard enough of the monotony of killing and brutality in Auschwitz no longer to believe that accuracies of that kind could be achieved.

Boger's defence counsel tried to imply the existence of higher order which might serve to exonerate his client, but it's not clear that he adequately knew the background to decision-making in Auschwitz or could therefore have had a particular document in mind. This was a symptom of a general problem. Defence counsels suffered from a lack of preparation time, as well as from the low prestige of their job in this trial, and the absence of detailed background knowledge (though Aschenauer had served in the IG-Farben trial) – all this damaged their effectiveness in the cases.[14] We recall Eichmann drawing flowcharts for the court so that someone might finally understand how the Third Reich actually functioned; his own counsel obviously did not understand. Boger himself hid behind denial, in other cross-examinations disguised as memory lapse, as well as behind the jargon by which torture and its instruments were known, and blamed anyone who was already dead. (Grabner had been executed in Krakau in 1947.)

In this scene the counsel for the civil plaintiffs offered the witness the chance to put his wider personal experiences to the court, even though the evidence was not strictly relevant to the incident under discussion. (His reference to frost-bite, for instance, had no relevance at all to the punishment which had just been described to the court.) It is also noticeable that, in contrast to other

14 On the defence counsels Aschenauer and Stolting see Pendas (2006, pp. 153f & 222–24 resp.).

court-systems, the witnesses were confronted directly by the defendants, and not only during their actual court-appearance. Indeed, few of the defendants – not even those facing charges which, if proven, would have brought immediate life-imprisonment – were physically in custody at the time of the trial, and in consequence the witnesses ran the daily risk of bumping into men who twenty years ago had tortured them and killed their friends. To face such people in the witness-box was one thing (and this scene shows the advantages of the court's flexible attitude); to meet them as they drank coffee or washed their hands in the men's room put still further psychological pressure on the witnesses.

We return briefly to Robert Mulka. Mulka's first statement to the court, as he pointed to the plan of the camp which hung permanently in the court-room, was the claim that he had never gone into the camp itself, but had stayed outside the perimeter fence. (At this, other defendants present in court made clear that they found his claim absurd.) More significantly, Mulka denied ever having been on the ramp. Not only did the court refuse to believe him on either count and produced witnesses to refute both claims: their purpose was dictated by the need to include in their judgment the *number* of deaths for which the accused could be held personally responsible. Only by proving that Mulka had been on the ramp and taken part in the 'selecting' could the court properly substantiate the magnitude of Mulka's responsibility. We offer one snatch from a subsequent questioning:

PRESIDING JUDGE:	Defendant Mulka, did you issue the instructions for journeys to Dessau?
MULKA:	I only know of one such procedure. Glücks signed the instruction and I put my signature on the bottom left. It was to fetch disinfectant.
PRESIDING JUDGE:	On the document it says: 'For Jewish resettlement' and 'Signature certified by Mulka'. You knew what 'Jewish resettlement' meant, didn't you?
MULKA:	Yes, I knew that.
PRESIDING JUDGE:	And what were the materials for Jewish resettlement?
MULKA: (*barely audibly*)	Yes, raw materials.
PRESIDING JUDGE:	Well, they were Zyklon-B.
MULKA: (*still more quietly*)	Yes, Zyklon-B.

PRESIDING JUDGE: Mr Mulka, you've always maintained that you had nothing to do with the gassing of the Jews. But you did, didn't you.

MULKA: Yes, Mr President, I signed an instruction for a journey to Dessau.

DEFENCE COUNSEL DR STOLTING II: I'd like to ask for the conversation to be repeated. It was very hard to follow, since Mr Mulka was not speaking into the microphone.

The Presiding Judge repeats Mulka's statements.

DEFENCE COUNSEL DR STOLTING II: Mr President, let's get this in proportion. I ask you: fetching Zyklon-B with a five-tonner – that was enough gas to kill tens of millions of Jews.

ORMOND: That's just what they did.

Few moments sum up the case more precisely. Mulka wished to argue that 'all' he did was to countersign a requisition for transport. While he continued to deny having been on the ramp (he had subsequently to admit that he had entered the compound – although he alleged that it had been for the purpose of his own medical treatment), his denials of having any involvement in the mass-murder of Jewish prisoners broke down at this point. Strikingly this did not happen because of the uncovering of some past violent, sadistic or 'base' action by Mulka or on account of any psychological break-down in the present. Instead Mulka's admission came more banally, on account of his having countersigned one document. Compared to the work of the criminal inmates at Auschwitz, who were forced to carry out the gassings and remove corpses to the crematorium, Mulka's action might seem to have been unremarkable. Certainly on his evidence here it would have been hard for the prosecution to establish those 'base motives' which the *Reichsstrafgesetz* of 1871 required in order to make a murder charge stick: it was understandable that the less serious charge of being an accessory to murder became the goal both of the defence (once they realized that an acquittal was not going to be possible) and eventually of the prosecution too. But the difference between signing a transport chit and dropping gas crystals through the shutters of the bunker needed far more careful handling than it was afforded by the defence, and a different set of legal instruments for the prosecution.

Incidentally, once again here, defence counsel came off badly, both in terms of his skill in argument and – shockingly – in his failure to comprehend the magnitude of the crimes committed in Auschwitz. While the court's visit to the crime-scene in the Auschwitz camp in December 1964 certainly appears to have sobered up some of the defence teams, one of the principal defence counsels – Dr Hans Laternser (whose experience of such trials went back to the Nuremberg Tribunal, where he had defended the military High Command[15]) – maintained his profound suspicions of the prosecution case throughout the trial, as his subsequent memoirs made clear. Mulka was not well represented by his defence, but the court's scrupulousness protected him from the worst consequences of that failure.

7.8 Sentencing and Final Considerations

Unlike the Eichmann trial, in which the sentence was entirely predictable even before the trial had begun, it was not clear how the Frankfurt trial would conclude. The involvement of the IAK (and to a lesser extent of the institute in Ludwigsburg) ensured that the court possessed both a determination to prove the case against the guilty and the experience needed to uncover the fullest possible truth about the workings of Auschwitz. There was no doubt too about the commitment of the judges and prosecution to see justice for the victims. Fritz Bauer's spirit was very much alive in the court, even though he personally stayed away from the hearings. But the difficulties in fact-finding on individual actions and the necessity under § 211 of the *Reichsstrafgesetz* to establish 'base motives' for the killing – when added to the scrupulous application of the principle that the accused were to have the benefit of doubt – meant that the sentencing was far from a foregone conclusion. In other ways too, complex issues of motivation needed to be clarified before sentencing could take place.

Just as in the Eichmann case, there was a conflict in the court's focus between drawing attention to the suffering of the victims and establishing what the individual accused had actually done. This conflict of interest made elements of the one hundred and eighty-three days on which the court had sat less streamlined than might have been desirable, but, as we saw, that had been Bauer's original intention.

Apart from the difficulties of evidence which we have already discussed, the court had to deal with the principal argument on which the defence was to base its case and the subsequent appeals. The defence was based on the superior orders defence, to which the coercion argument was added: the claim that the defendant had only acted on orders, which it would have been dangerous to him to have disobeyed. Without that element of 'free responsibility' which

15 Laternser's account of the trial in Laternser (1966).

the legislation obliged the prosecution to establish, murder charges were not accepted.

Since the Nuremberg Tribunal there had been a major intensification of discussion concerning the responsibility of subordinates not to carry out criminal orders. The various editions of Oppenheim's *International Law* record the consensus on the matter since the First World War, and Hannah Arendt herself felt that the 1947 revisions of this matter by Lauterpacht could be seen as a definitive statement which was more than adequate to cope with the issues arising in the Eichmann trial.[16] The so-called Nuremberg Principle had been to deny automatic immunity to those using the 'superior orders defence', although Satō's recent study of *The Execution of Illegal Orders* has shown the Principle in fact to have been less than absolute, and in any case gradually weakened in the succession trials at Nuremberg. As we saw, Flick explicitly benefitted from a relaxation of the Principle when his plea of obeying superior orders was accepted.

Strikingly, neither Oppenheim nor the Principle was used in Frankfurt. Instead, the court was obliged to operate within two rulings of the BGH which had had the effect of causing the same understandings to be applied to the Waffen SS as to other service branches.[17] This instrument – apart from effectively decriminalizing the SS – consisted in the ruling that no subordinate could be held responsible for carrying out an order: only the superior issuing the order was responsible. This ruling flew in the face of the Principle. Furthermore, on the basis that all major orders had come from people who were by then dead, even surviving superior officers in fact had few grounds for anxiety. Once Hitler was dead no-one could be found guilty.

The BGH ruling applied to all the defendants in Frankfurt, with the exception of Bednarek, who was himself a prisoner in Auschwitz rather than a member of the SS. This ruling produced a situation in which the law appeared to side with the real perpetrators, for it could not be denied that they occupied positions within a formal, if criminal, hierarchy. In order to ensure that this disadvantaging should not happen too blatantly, and that the SS-criminals should not get off scot free, the court tried to develop more suitable local procedures – some of which were invariably overturned on appeal. It remains incontrovertible that the BGH had selected from a varied international debate

16 Arendt's discussion of Oppenheim-Lauterpracht reflecting 'the general sentiment of humanity' (1978, p. 148). For this discussion see also Satō (2011). Lauterpacht is one of the principal protagonists of Sands' *East West Street* (2016).

17 The relevant BGH cases are: BGHSt 2 (1950), 251; in the second judgment BGHSt 18 (1963), 89.

on these matters the one (internationally outdated) line which most protected German war criminals. Frankfurt had to live with the consequences of the ruling of the highest appellate court.

Debates on individual responsibility within genocide have continued in Europe and the United Nations. As everyone knows, genocide did not stop in 1945, and the Federal Republic has not been the only country slow to deal with the criminals of its recent past. Four elements have become associated with the debate.

The first was the notion (tried out by the defence at Eichmann's trial) that crimes against humanity originated in what is called a 'state function': that is, that the crimes were inseparable from the whole rationale of the state, rather than originating with the power of individuals within the state. For that reason it was argued that individuals could not be held responsible for those crimes. (This was a variant on the earlier idea that international treaties bound states, but could not bind individuals.) This idea was firmly rejected by the international community, having already been rejected in Nuremberg. Jackson pointed out that the doctrine of the immunity of a head of state, when combined with the 'superior orders defence', meant 'that nobody is responsible',[18] and Nuremberg would not admit either defence, nor would the international community.

In Britain, for instance, in a landmark judgment concerning the right of the Chilean dictator Pinochet to immunity from prosecution (e.g. when visiting Europe), the House of Lords ruled in 2000 that the torture which was widespread in Chile during Pinochet's years in power could not be regarded as a 'state function' – thus overturning a conventional ruling which would not have held Pinochet personally responsible for the torture which took place during his rule.[19] Pinochet was declared to be not immune from prosecution, since the orders leading to torture and murder were ruled to have emanated from him in his individual capacity, rather than from an impersonal entity, 'the state'. The Frankfurt trial could not debate this argument (in part because the defendants were much further down the hierarchy), but instead, in trying to overcome the restrictions imposed by the BGH ruling, it was obliged to focus on differentiating between merely carrying out orders and going beyond those orders. Under that ruling, obeying an order could not be the basis of a charge: this concession gave the court still greater reason to pursue vigorously those of the accused who went even the smallest step beyond the terms of their orders.

A further strand of the debate had approached the illegality of obeying illegal orders from a different angle. It was suggested that orders should not be

18 Jackson quoted by: Satō (2011, p. 54).

19 The Pinochet case is discussed by Philippe Sands (2003, esp. pp. 82 f, 93 f).

obeyed when they were recognizably out of keeping with the 'normal' tenor and content of orders otherwise received from a defendant's superiors. It was hoped that the idea of the 'normal' would filter out ambiguities about an order's criminality, by making the decision of the subordinate more straightforward. This approach was tried out in the Eichmann trial, but without success since it became clear that Eichmann found his orders out of keeping with his 'normal' orders only in late 1944, when for once he had been dumbfounded by these orders and found them 'abnormal'. However, this happened for the grotesque reason that, with the war clearly lost, Himmler had unexpectedly decided to keep Jewish detainees alive to be used as a bargaining counter with the Allies, and in consequence reversed his policy and changed his orders. In Eichmann's orders, crimes against humanity had been the 'norm'; a deviation from the norm could not be taken therefore as an indication of anything criminal – instead it represented a diminution of criminality. So no shift in orders could have given a clue that the orders were illegal. Hardly surprisingly this argument was not used in the Auschwitz trial. Nor did the defence try to argue – as had been put forward in Kaltenbrunner's defence at Nuremberg – that the defendants had been deprived of responsibility by the 'hypnotic power' of the 'devilish atmosphere' of the Final Solution. More mundanely, the killing and murder had become so institutionalized that they continued even when the camp was evacuated as the Red Army came closer and no orders ever deviated from that norm.

Thirdly, rather than operating with the concept of murder as defined in the criminal code, the concept of genocide had increasingly formed part of international law, being first formulated in the Genocide Convention of December 1948 and for which Lembach had fought. There would be little disagreement with the point made by Hannah Arendt in reflecting on the Eichmann trial: that genocide is qualitatively, and not merely quantitatively, different from murder, and that the charge of being an accessory to genocide is to be differently founded than that of being an accessory to murder.

As Johannes Schmidt points out in his commentary on the judgments in Frankfurt, the use of the concept of genocide would have spared the court the elaborate and somehow profoundly inappropriate business of ascribing the responsibility for specific numbers of deaths to individual defendants and evolving formulae to differentiate between one 'unified action' (*Handlungseinheit*) – for instance the gassing of two hundred people – and two hundred separate individual murders, each of which was one 'unified action' on its own.[20] The trial order laid down in 1963 (and only subsequently overhauled) demanded that in a preliminary examination of the facts the

20 On the 'Tateinheit' and other legal issues, see: Schmidt (2013) & Pendas' discussion of 'ideal and real concurrence' of disparate elements of a crime (2006, p. 197f).

individual 'unified actions' on which the defendants were charged should be clearly identified. This practice made impossible the prosecution's original hope to present the whole of Auschwitz as one 'unified action', an interpretation which would have simplified the prosecution and effectively focused all charges on the single charge of genocide. This strategy failed no less comprehensively than the 'criminal conspiracy' charges by which Jackson and the UK prosecutors at the Nuremberg Tribunal had hoped to tie together in one charge the disparate criminal actions which had made up the NS movement and to establish responsibility for crimes jointly on all the accused. A further consequence of the trial order in Frankfurt was that when, at various points in the proceedings, the court uncovered more punishable actions by the defendants than were originally in the charge (witnesses remembered new things, other testimonies brought different actions to their mind than those on which the original indictments had been based), the court had no power to act on these. This was only one of the difficulties of trying the case without the category of genocide being recognized as a crime, and Frankfurt undoubtedly suffered from the Federal Republic wilfully failing to keep up with developments in international legal thinking.

Finally, it became established in the years since 1947 that it can be in the interests of international justice for crimes against humanity to be tried in countries other than the countries of the perpetrators or of the victims. This was once more not an issue discussed in the Frankfurt trials: not only were acknowledgements made of the rights of Poland to try the crimes committed by Germans on Polish soil, but other countries – including the GDR – were given the right to represent the interests of those of their nationals who were among the victims of Auschwitz. Whatever reasons of prestige and/or of self-interest had prevented the Federal Republic from requesting the extradition of Eichmann for trial in Germany (Fritz Bauer, who had passed on the information concerning Eichmann's whereabouts to the Israeli authorities, had applied for such an extradition request to be issued), such questions were increasingly separate from the central issues of justice on which the international legal scene was focused. In this respect it would be possible to regard both the Eichmann and the Frankfurt trials as being archaic. Considerable tension arose between Bauer's determination to educate the Germans and non-German nationals' feeling that their sufferings should be at the centre of attention. It seemed that crimes against humanity should be tried internationally.

Although they could not adopt international practice, the judges in Frankfurt handled the legal difficulties presented by the BGH ruling in a more pragmatic fashion, and tried to keep legal debate to a minimum. For instance, the court established that the coercion element of the superior orders defence was simply untrue in the case of the defendants. The court examined a number of cases in which individuals (above a certain level in the Auschwitz hierarchy) had asked for a transfer, either from Auschwitz itself or from particular duties inside the camp. In none of these cases had the individuals suffered any negative consequences for having made their request. It had been possible to avoid carrying out orders without one's life being threatened. *Befehlsnotstand* was therefore shown up as no more than an excuse, and it proved itself to be incapable of sustaining the pressure which the defence put upon it. Without challenging the BGH decision of 1962 directly, the Frankfurt judges therefore managed not to be blocked by it, and their success indicated that the BGH decision needed further reflection if it were to be successful in future prosecutions.

Nevertheless, of course, the court was obliged to find many of the defendants guilty on the lesser charge of being an accessory to murder. On appeal other defendants were reclassified to the lesser charge. Not only the BGH ruling, but also the lack of concrete evidence of personal killing or of 'base motives' as detailed in RGStGB § 211 brought about this revision. Furthermore, the judges tended to prefer that charge for those defendants 'who could not be shown to have killed on their personal initiative, beyond the orders they had received'.

For all these reasons the sentences on the two figures on whom this chapter has concentrated came out as follows. The deputy *Kommandant* Mulka was found guilty of being an accessory to murder and being one of a number of accessories to jointly committed murders. Four cases rated at seven hundred and fifty murders each were put on his slate for the appearances he had been observed to make on the *Rampe*. No evidence was found, however, of any particular zeal in carrying out more than what his orders had contained. He was therefore sentenced to fourteen years hard labour. Mulka, perhaps more than the other defendants, had done everything he could to impede the work of the court. His testimony had begun with the claim that he had not participated in the machine which he had helped run. As the Presiding Judge remarked in his summing-up: 'The defendants essentially did little more than keep silent and to tell lies. They refused to help uncover the truth by themselves telling the truth.' It was admirable, if perhaps naïve, to imagine that defendants would be keen to participate in any general educative purpose by telling the whole truth, but the judge's remark underlined the educative basis on which the whole case had been established from the start.

Boger on the other hand was found to have been involved in numerous individual killings. He had also worked on the *Rampe* and, perhaps most significantly of all, he had been shown to hold a violent personal dislike of Polish people, and in the eyes of the court that dislike qualified as a 'base motive' for his actions. The law seems to imply that killing out of indifference was qualitatively superior. Boger was therefore found guilty of one hundred and fourteen murders, and (according to the bizarre arithmetic I mentioned earlier) was sentenced to life imprisonment one hundred and fourteen times over.

So the man second in command during the time that the killing machine was working at full capacity received fourteen years (perhaps at his age – he was born in 1895 – this was effectively a life-sentence). Boger, working in a smaller and more immediate environment but much lower in the hierarchy, not really in a situation to give anyone orders, but perhaps less able to assess the orders which he received, got one hundred and fourteen life sentences.

7.9 Final Comments

The consequences of the Frankfurt trial were various, and I sketch two points briefly at the end of what is already a long chapter.

Even Hermann Langbein had to concede that German public opinion was less than galvanized by the trial and that it took some effort on his part to believe that anything more lasting than a few individual convictions had been achieved.[21] Repeatedly the proceedings uncovered fresh criminals and fresh crimes, which the court could not touch. Yet Langbein remained positive, and in that he was a representative of the feelings of the victims.

The effects of the trial proved to be more long-lasting than the trial itself. Leading writers of the time took up its themes, less through the work of the press (the *BILD*-Zeitung and serious legal journals remained surprisingly silent on the trials[22]) and much more through the efforts of public intellectuals and writers. Rolf Hochhuth raised the theme of responsibility to a particularly high level in his play *The Representative* (1963), which examined Pope Pius XII's attitude to the Final Solution and his failure to act more decisively against it. Although it bypassed many of the issues of the trial, Hochhuth's play became a focus of debate and controversy across the world. More specifically, Peter Weiss turned various scenes from the Frankfurt trial into his 'oratorio' *Die Ermittlung* (The Investigation, 1965) and as his work established itself as an indisputable canonical masterpiece of post-war German literature it reached many young

---

21 Langbein (1965, pp. 9–20).

22 On the silence of academic journals and the Springer press see: Pendas (2006, pp. 265, 270). Weinke gives an illuminating account of official efforts to discredit Simon Wiesenthal, who specialized in bring NS criminals to justice (2008, 78f).

people in schools and universities across Germany and the world, its premiere taking place simultaneously on four stages in the Federal Republic and in East Berlin, before being staged in London by Peter Brook and in Stockholm by Ingmar Bergman. Strikingly it was revived in November 2007 at the Young Vic in London by a company from Rwanda, implying that its message was still felt to be relevant to a country which had to face up to its own genocide. Not only in Germany, Jochen Vogt commented, 'the curtain of silence had been torn away'.[23]

For reasons which we have discussed, the trial's conduct under § 211 of the *Strafgesetzbuch* was archaic and the prosecution appeared to have had no opportunity to take cognisance of the moves in the UN and in various states of Europe and the world to create explicit international legislation dealing with genocide and crimes against humanity. Some reasons for this deliberate filtering out of international opinion may have been purely subjective: among them *tu quoque* and other still less positive factors – such as Adenauer's contemptuous dismissal of those trying to discredit his compromised *chef de cabinet*. In fairness though it must be remembered that in 1963 Rwanda, Yugoslavia, Cambodia, or Abu Ghraib had not yet begun to dominate the world's headlines (the Vietnam War was only just starting to be a matter of world concern), and as a result the court tended to look backwards rather than forwards when trying to come to terms with torture and genocide.

But no less important perhaps was the fact that the insistence on a German court trying the Auschwitz criminals – admirable though it may have been in so many respects – not only made improbable the use of the concept of genocide (in any case, not until the state of Israel came into existence was it clear that the Jews were a *nation*), but overly insisted on the national characteristics of Auschwitz. The extra-territoriality of Auschwitz was known and recognized. But these were not just German crimes: they were crimes against humanity and perhaps it was humanity, rather than the Frankfurt court, which should have been trying them. And as far as German justice was concerned, Bauer's failure with the so-called euthanasia trial of 1967 showed once more, even after the Auschwitz trial, the severe limitations on legal routes to justice in NS crimes.[24]

23 On Peter Weiss' close involvement with the Auschwitz trial, and his writing of the drama *The Investigation* in such a way as to share in Fritz Bauer's overall educational ideals see: Vogt (2016).

24 Loewy & Winter (1996). See also Arnau (1967, p. 60 f). It's disturbing to notice how strongly Arnau agrees with Heinrich Hannover in his view of German justice (p. 97).

Nevertheless, the trial represented a genuine attempt to involve German justice in sorting out the worst criminality in Germany's history. It would be grotesque to imply that the lost honour of German justice could possibly have been restored by this trial, for the more important perspective was that of the victims. There were many flaws in the way Frankfurt gave these people a voice and took away the impunity of some of their torturers, but at least that voice spoke, and as it did so it wrote a major chapter into the history of the Federal Republic and its legal system.

CHAPTER 8

The 1970s: the Campaign against Radicals – Ideology Becomes the Crime

8.1 Prologue

I suggested in the Introduction that my approach to the subject could be compared to a review of the history of my generation (born during the Second World War). The trials and the issues which stood behind these cases would amount to a central part of the experience of this generation. Seen in this way, the history of the Federal Republic should not become abstract, but be understood as a chunk of people's everyday lives. To review these trials combines various types of history, not only legal history, but personal and political.

Nowhere is this more true than of the events and cases detailed in this chapter. I recall vividly the uneasy sense with which people like myself, living outside the Federal Republic, recognized that the political opinions which we held cost us nothing, while the lives of many like-minded contemporaries in Germany were blighted by the procedures which this chapter describes. To this day one can glimpse the divisions which arose forty years ago between the victims of these processes and those friends and colleagues who, by compromising with the system or by simple good fortune, ensured themselves a future within it. It is not fanciful to include these personal rifts among the various 'divisions' of Germany. Within this chapter and the chapter on the terrorism trials, names are mentioned from 'the generation of 1968' whom today hardly anyone remembers, while other names from that generation have adorned ministers of state and filled the newspapers for more than twenty years. Often the differences lie in chance alone. It is a generation whose obituaries will need careful reading.[1]

Despite these personal elements, I wish to preface this chapter with a different type of reflection, one rooted in nineteenth-century history. It points to an issue in law which is particularly emphasized within societies, such as the Federal Republic for at least its first fifty years, which are in transition. It

1 What happens to radical lawyers as they join the establishment (and start wearing ties) is discussed in an amusing article by Uwe Wesel (1998). The shift of Daniel Cohn-Bendit is no less striking: from revolutionary student leader to Green and then to being friend and adviser to President Macron.

highlights also a characteristic of the Federal Republic in the 1970s: the sense that history is always in danger of repeating itself and that negative structures and negative outcomes of change have long been endemic to German politics and culture and represent an understandable and ever-present fear within those societies.

The historical illustration needs only brief details.[2] In the revolution of 1848 Gustav Adolf Schöffel, a nineteen-year old student of philosophy in Heidelberg, took part in the first phase of the uprising in Baden and as a result was dismissed from the university. He moved to Berlin, where – partly because the university would not allow him to matriculate in order to continue his studies – he began to edit a newspaper, touchingly called *Der Volksfreund* (The People's Friend), which appeared irregularly but was significant enough for a colleague of Karl Marx to draw it to his attention. Schöffel's interests in politics were varied, for in Berlin, alongside his journalistic work as part of the movement for change, he organized delegations to the local parliament in order to represent the city's day-labourers. When, on April 19 1848, he published an article criticizing first minister Camphausen's plans to restrict suffrage (the promise of an elected parliament had been one of the early achievements of the revolution in Prussia), Schöffel was arrested, and his trial opened very few weeks later, attracting considerable attention in the city.

The court was reluctant to charge Schöffel directly with putting forward the case for universal suffrage, since a majority of the population of Berlin wholeheartedly agreed with him on that. Consequently, the prosecution preferred a double incitement: in the first place that of threatening the personal well-being of Camphausen himself (by criticizing his policy) and, secondly, incitement to riot. Schöffel's defence was straightforward: the freedom of the press had been promulgated not only in the wake of the *Bundesversammlung* (Federal Assembly) in Mainz, but the King of Prussia, Friedrich Wilhelm IV, had passed a Press Law on March 17 1848 abolishing censorship and granting amnesty to those who had fallen foul of the previous laws. Both in its opinions and in its existence, therefore, Schöffel's *Volksfreund* appeared to be in keeping with the progressive spirit of those laws.

The prosecutors got round the difficulty posed by the Press Law by having recourse to a whole gamut of legislation which predated the legislation of 1848 by some fifty years, and which neither the revolution nor the King of Prussia

2 More details on Schöffel in: Ridley (1979). Marx's account of press censorship in Prussia in *Rheinische Zeitung*, July 14 1842 and *Neue Rheinische Zeitung*, March 22 1849.

had thought to annul. The first general codification of the law in Prussia, the *Allgemeines Landrecht für die preußischen Staaten* of 1794, had at the time represented a progressive step. But, hardly surprisingly, since it was drawn up as the French Revolution was turning into the Terror, it took a very different view of newspapers like Schöffel's. It was easy for the prosecution to prove, according to those old statutes, incitement to riot (ALR §§ 166, 167) and to revive the idea of someone being 'intellectually responsible' for a crime (ALR §§ 67 and 76) and hence being punishable, even if that crime (i.e. injury to the person of Camphausen) had not taken place. To add insult to the injury of its verdict, the court referred to the Press Law of March 1848, but used it merely to justify the destruction of all copies of *Der Volksfreund* which had been confiscated at the time of his arrest. The repressive laws had not been removed by the reform movement, while the progressive laws were used merely to sanction a further repressive administrative measure.

Gustav Adolf Schöffel served his term and went on to lose his life fighting in the final phase of the revolution in Baden. He remains a sympathetic and generous-spirited figure, who refused to compromise his ideals for the sake of a quiet life. As a footnote on history, however, Schöffel points to two uncomfortable truths: first, that history does not proceed along a straight line, but goes forward in one place and backward at another. The modern always co-exists, often for a prolonged period, with what it displaces. Even a major historical upheaval such as the 1848 revolution mixed progressive and regressive tendencies. What's more, a relatively progressive king, trying to respond positively to the situation of the moment, managed to open the door to further repression. Clearly these outcomes were not automatic effects of the legislation, but depended on a legal system which, at best, was obsessed with the paragraphs rather than the spirit of the law, and at worst was staffed by judges ideologically opposed to the progressive movements of their day, including those endorsed by the king.

Secondly, Schöffel's case shows that the law moves more slowly than other elements in society, and that, as we suggested in the Introduction, the citizen needs to be conscious not simply of what is new in the law, but of the old laws whose teeth have yet to be pulled. Both lessons – and many figures who, in part at least, shared Schöffel's misfortune at the hands of the courts – are writ large in the cases with which this chapter is concerned. These truths showed themselves unmistakably, as we saw, in the Frankfurt homosexuality trials of 1950, but while it might be argued that those trials stood in the shadow of Nazis and of the years most clearly marked as Adenauer's 'restoration', this chapter is concerned with the 1970s and with the actions of a social-democrat government.

8.2 Background to the 1970s

The late 1960s saw the Federal Republic drifting into crisis. Some of its difficulties were shared with other western countries: there was, for instance, yet another oil crisis and a sense that economic growth was coming to an end, a general frustration with many features of the Cold War, in particular with its effects in Vietnam and Africa, and an incipient anxiety about the future of the planet's resources. Nevertheless, a great deal of the German crisis was home-grown.

The stranglehold of the CDU party on German politics had begun to slip with the death of Adenauer. His successor Ludwig Erhard, father of the 'economic miracle' in the 1950s, found it difficult to project the image of invincible prosperity which had once been his trade-mark. As a result the CDU was significantly weakened. Following major internal reforms in the Bad Godesberg programme of 1959, the SPD was beginning to look more electable and its leader, Willy Brandt, the Mayor of West Berlin, was increasingly identified with the hope of a new way in politics. The dynamics of the times appeared to have shifted, but the foundation of the Grand Coalition in November 1966 – in which the SPD joined forces with the CSU and the CDU to form a government, thus compromising with just those forces which the party had been formed to overcome – disappointed these hopes.

Rather than representing a stabilizing and consolidating moment in German politics, the Grand Coalition marked a significant turn for the worse. A country which was only slowly starting to assume democratic respectability was too deeply scarred by the memory of massive governmental majorities in the NS years for this Coalition not to cause anxiety. The pretence of a parliament from 1933, in which all members agreed with Hitler's government, had not made unanimity popular with the thinking electorate. From 1966 the FDP formed the only, relatively insignificant, parliamentary opposition. This unbalanced and worrying situation led to a characteristic response from particular social groups outside parliament: namely the determination to take upon themselves the function which the parliamentary system appeared no longer able to perform – that of providing an effective opposition. It was understandable that a heady rhetoric became established in these groups: they proudly announced that they were 'rescuing democracy' and 'fighting the return of fascism in Germany'. The steady growth of the neo-Nazi NDP party during these years added resonance to the sense of crisis, as did revelations about the NS past of the then Chancellor and leader of the CDU, Kurt Georg Kiesinger (needless to say, Kiesinger was a lawyer and his NS past had never stood in the way of his career). The groups most identified with the movement against the Grand

Coalition, the trades-unions and the students, found the perfect acronym to describe themselves and to contribute to their sense of identity and mission: they called themselves the APO, the extra-parliamentary opposition.

The Grand Coalition itself further increased social tension in 1967 by proceeding with the last of a series of attempts to pass emergency laws. These would lay down the exceptional measures by which the state could protect itself in times of national emergency. This legislation, the *Notstandsgesetze*, inevitably awakened memories of the fact that Hitler had managed to destroy the democracy of Weimar by means of emergency laws, although the emergency legislation of 1967 did not propose to confer exceptional powers on the President, as Article 48 of the Weimar constitution had done.

The economic crisis of the late 1960s awoke further parallels with Weimar, for in it people detected another example of the inability of dysfunctional parliamentary democracy to solve major economic problems. None of this guaranteed the Grand Coalition widespread backing for its legislation and in any case for many people the *Spiegel*-Affair had shown the lying, press-censorship and indifference to the law with which governments were likely to respond to a perceived emergency. In consequence, the APO could rely on popular support in its anxiety that the foundations of German democracy were under serious threat. This support is not to be equated with a swing of popular opinion to the political far left – after all, neither the practices of 'real socialism' in the GDR, nor the behaviour of the Soviet Union in crushing the Prague Spring of 1968, nor the historical precedents of the attitude of the German Communist Party to the rise of the NSDAP in the 1930s made any convincing or popular argument for the left – but it was evidence of a general unease with the institutions of the Federal Republic.

Into this situation one further element got mixed, with explosive results. In June 1967 the Shah of Persia (present-day Iran) paid a state visit to the Federal Republic, and in the course of his visit, as was expected of all leaders of the 'free world', he spent time in Berlin and looked contemptuously over the Wall. The Shah was far from a stranger to western media. He had sat on the Peacock Throne of a thousand-year dynasty, while his wife's luxurious life-style filled the fashion pages of glossy magazines. The Shah's authoritarian régime was propped up by American foreign policy (which, elsewhere too, was having problems with puppet governments), and internal opposition was crushed by a brutal secret police. By coming to Berlin the Shah offered an easy cause around which many shades of student opinion could crystallize.

Street demonstrations against the Shah proceeded in ways which were to become standard European practice, but the most significant event took place away from the action. A theology student, walking without provocation down a side-street far from any demonstration, was shot and killed by an off-duty policeman. The name of this student, Benno Ohnesorg, became a talisman for the whole student movement which was to follow, and the date of his murder, June 2, took on iconic significance throughout the 1970s. Meanwhile the fate of the policeman himself, Karl-Heinz Kurras – in a subsequent mockery of justice he was exonerated for the shooting (much more recently he was shown to have worked for the East German *Stasi*) – reinforced parallels between the polarization and violence which swamped the Weimar Republic and the events of 1967.[3]

In particular the students made the reasonable assumption that the shooting had been a reaction to the anti-student feeling whipped up by the Springer media empire (which had a near monopoly over the press in Berlin), and they launched a campaign against Springer, not only in Berlin, but throughout the Federal Republic, aiming to prevent the distribution of his newspapers. These actions in turn led to major demonstrations, numerous arrests, trials and to the conviction of many demonstrators, as well as to further attacks on students in the Springer press. This was the beginning of a sustained hostility between Springer's press, especially the *BILD-Zeitung*, and German intellectuals.

It is a considerable understatement to say that the international wave of the student protest movement associated with events in Paris in May 1968 found ready acceptance in the Federal Republic.[4] Indeed, events in Paris further inflamed the situation by giving it a pan-European dimension. Yet the student movement was anything but monolithic. Hundreds of splinter groups emerged across a wide ideological spectrum, from socialist to green and Christian, taking up a range of disparate issues, both domestically (including reforms inside the universities) and in global politics, where imperialism and oppression were their targets and Vietnam the universal cause. The wide spectrum covered by the student movements was further shown in the division between the violent and non-violent elements at the time.

The diversity of the student movement was shown finally in the endless debates which it provoked and in which it spent much of its energies: how students were to change the world and whether the answer was to reform or to revolutionize society. It remains an open question as to whether it was

3 On the strange juxtaposition of the trials of the radical lawyer Fritz Teufel and Kurras see: Hermann (1967). In his memoirs, the head of the Stasi, Marcus Wolf, plays down GDR hospitality to Baader-Meinhof members, but makes no mention of Kurras (1997, p. 277).

4 A sharply focused account of 1968 in Germany is found in: Ingrid Gilcher-Holtey (2001). On the situation in other countries: Arthur Marwick (1998).

disillusionment with the politics of the streets, and thus an acceptance of their own failure, or a new tactic of a continuing revolution when the influential student leader Rudi Dutschke (who had narrowly survived an assassination attempt in 1968) announced that the way forward for the student movement lay in what, borrowing a phrase of Mao's, he called 'the long march through the institutions'. By this Dutschke appeared to mean that students should continue their fight to change society not on the streets, but from within the institutions of the state in which they would find employment after graduation. When in 1970 the SDS was dissolved and the state declared an amnesty for offences committed during the mass demonstrations, there did therefore finally seem to be a chance that violence and protest were coming to an end.

By then a new element had entered the politics of the Federal Republic. In the elections of 1969 – ending the Grand Coalition and putting the CDU into opposition for the first time in twenty years – the SPD in coalition with the Liberals won an overall majority and Willy Brandt (who had been Foreign Minister in the Coalition) became Chancellor. Not only did Brandt's rise to power represent a completely fresh wind blowing through the political establishment: his impeccable anti-Nazi qualifications seemed to mark the end of the shabby compromises with the past which Adenauer had begun and which were finally represented by Kiesinger's Chancellorship.

Some people thought that Brandt's election took away the *raison d'être* of the APO, but opinions soon changed on this point. While the election slogan which marked his arrival in office could not have been more appealing to the student generation – 'Risk more democracy!' –, Brandt's important success was in the continuation of his foreign policy towards the countries of the eastern bloc. Within very few years, Brandt, famously photographed on his knees in the Warsaw ghetto, acknowledging NS crimes, had initiated *détente* with Poland, with the Soviet Union and, in the Basic Treaty, finally signed in 1975, with the German Democratic Republic itself: the other half of a divided Germany.

Despite this quite extraordinary readiness to deal with the Communist *bloc*, at home it was left-wing (sometimes formally Communist) people against whom Brandt's government directed its energies. Since the Bad Godesberg reforms, the SPD was anxious not to be associated with any radical views, so in internal matters the party conformed to the views of the conservative establishment. In the early 1970s Dutschke's remark had given the establishment an unrealistic fear of the wholesale subversion of the state by former members of the student movement, and this in turn led to the administrative and legal measures whose details form the remainder of this chapter: the so-called *Berufsverbot*, the attempt to exclude from the public service anyone with a radical past. These draconian measures divided and unsettled the Federal Republic for the whole of the 1970s, and severely undermined the younger generation's support for the SPD – a loss of support which would have been inconceivable in the 1960s.

When one adds to this the gradual emergence of organized if small-scale urban guerrilla movements associated with Andreas Baader, the journalist Ulrike Meinhof and the so-called Red Army Faction (RAF), it becomes clear that by the early 1970s the country was in serious turmoil. What made the situation worse was the fact that, in their conflict with the state, sympathy for the students was potentially more general than is sometimes the case. The crisis was thus not simply one of law and order, or of anarchy and violence for their own sake, but of the identity and self-confidence of the Federal Republic and in particular its relation to the post-war generation. This problem was highlighted in that generation's ambiguous view of urban terrorism and forms the central feature of the trial discussed in Chapter Nine.

Rather than internal stability and *détente*, therefore, the 1970s saw a great increase in the dynamism of historical events. External and international events came into flux. With the PLO murder of Israeli athletes at the Munich Olympics in the summer of 1972, public anxiety about international terrorism and hijacking escalated. Student discontent increased considerably, driven also by uncertainty about the job-market. The response of the government was also itself profoundly radicalized. Its focus shifted towards ideology and policing, while the law showed that it was not just a static set of regulations, but an active force mobilized by the state to criminalize left-wing ideology and to create a security network so tight that terrorism could be rooted out. Things moved faster, as if careering downhill, and historians of the decade struggle to get the narrative into neutral, in order not to follow that headlong rush.

As we pass the talismanic milestone of the year 1968 – a year of particular significance in the history of most West European countries, and of the United States – we move towards a type of trial which so far we have encountered only in the banning of the SRP and the KPD in the 1950s, one based on a particular reading of the constitution, rather than on the criminal law. These were not really political trials (although the wishes of the government were clear enough) and certainly not show trials: they were too far from effective publicity for that, but they were intended as warnings against sympathy with the Soviet *bloc* and with the GDR in particular. However, the state showed no concerns about the rise of a revanchist neo-Nazi movement, and this omission was something the Federal Republic would come to regret bitterly.

8.3 The Legal Basis of the *Berufsverbot*

The starting-point for the cases in this field was given by the so-called *Radikalen-Erlass* (Decree on Radicals), which was passed by the *Bundestag* on January 28 1972.[5] This Decree did not in fact amount to new legislation and was not included in the criminal or civil codes: instead its function was to encourage the public authorities to be more active in using existing legislation to combat extremism. Three principles were enshrined in this decree, and we quote them in full:

> 1. In accordance with both the Federal public service laws and those of the *Länder* only those persons may be recruited into the public service who offer the guarantee that they at all times support the free democratic basic order as defined by the Basic Law. Public servants[6] are duty bound both in and outside their work to be actively committed to the preservation of this basic order.
>
> The carrying out of this principle is mandatory.
>
> 1. Every case must be considered and determined individually. The following principles are to be applied.
>
> *Applicants*: no-one engaged in activities inimical to the constitution is to be appointed to the public service.
>
> If an applicant is a member of an organization which pursues activities inimical to the constitution, then his membership of that organization justifies doubts as to whether the applicant would at all times support the free democratic basic order. Such doubts will normally justify the applicant's rejection for a post in the public service.
>
> *Public servants*: should a public servant, either through his actions or through his membership of an organization which pursues activities inimical to the constitution, fail to fulfil the demands of § 35 of the framework Public Service Law – this Law obliges the public servant to show in all aspects of his person loyalty to the free democratic basic order as defined by the Basic Law and to be committed to preserving

5 An easily available source of the text of the Decree on Radicals in: www.lexexakt.de/index.php/glossar/radikalenerlass.php.

6 The first two paragraphs of the Decree refer to *Beamte*, i.e. tenured civil servants of a certain status. This rank of the public service was much more widely occupied in the Federal Republic than in many western societies, and could be found in services such as post and railways, as well as in the profession from which our first two cases are drawn: secondary school teachers.

that order at all times – then his superiors are obliged to draw consequences from the situation of that individual and to examine closely whether he should be removed from the service.

2. *Manual workers and other employees of the public service*: such workers are constrained by the same principle.

There were three levels on which these measures were carried out. The first, as we shall see, took the form of individual hearings, when an applicant or a civil servant in post was summoned to a hearing of an appointments board which informed the person about the doubts which had arisen about her or his loyalty to the state. The second level was provided when the applicant appealed against the decision of the hearing and these appeals came to the administrative court in the particular federal state. Further appeals remained within higher levels of the administrative courts on a state basis. Occasionally an applicant could get an appeal hearing at the labour court. The third level was provided by judgments of the BVerfG – always remembering that this was not an appellate court. The court expressed its opinion both within the context of other judgments and then in one individual case in 1975. In these cases we shall see that, quite apart from arguments advanced by the victims of this measure, there were often significant conflicts between the courts and the administration, which frequently proved more than reluctant to accept, let alone to implement court decisions.

Out of the court cases to which the Decree on Radicals gave rise – invariably, of course, on appeal, since the hearings themselves were conducted according to a purely administrative procedure which often lacked judicial forms and safeguards – I shall present three in the following section. They are all taken from the years between 1972 and 1976. I have chosen celebrated cases and used material mostly published in book or pamphlet form at the time, since these were the cases which caught the imagination of the German (and international) public. But their personal elements should not disguise the fact that the impact of the *Berufsverbot* was a collective one and the sheer regularity of such cases was part of the effect which they exercised on the generation of ex-students. The shock lay primarily in blighted careers, but in part also in the recognition that the SPD, precisely at a time when it was breaking new ground in its foreign policy, could be so repressive at home. A further shock was that measures allegedly designed to combat extremism could so palpably increase the divisions in Federal German society. Added to these shocks was genuine shame at the behaviour of the legal and administrative systems of the Federal Republic, recently so proud of having overcome its totalitarian past.

8.4 Three Individual Cases

One straightforward but eloquent case was that of Silvia Gingold.[7] Ms Gingold was a probationary teacher in Hessen, well liked and well integrated in her school and with every expectation of her appointment being made permanent. On July 31 1974 she was informed that 'information' had been provided about her by the state security service (the so-called *Bundesamt fur Verfassungsschutz*) concerning her activities over an eleven year period – that is, from her seventeenth birthday on. (Incidentally, the admissibility of hearsay evidence of this kind, untested by the defence, had been accepted at the time of the emergency legislation and was a constant feature of hearings and trials alike.) Among the accusations against her were: attending a youth rally in East Berlin, taking part in a rally to mark twenty years of the GDR, membership of a socialist youth group and membership of the German Communist party, the DKP. In the phrase which was to resonate through the whole decade, she was asked to confirm her loyalty to the 'free democratic basic order'. When she did confirm it, she was not believed.

For less than a year her case rested with the ministry and she continued her work on the basis of short-term contracts. In June 1975, however, she was dismissed from her position on the grounds of her membership of the DKP. Her appeal against this decision came to trial before the administrative court in Kassel (May 12 1976). The court heard the full story of Ms Gingold's family and its involvement with communism, and it determined that, in itself, her membership of the DKP gave insufficient grounds for dismissal. The court therefore demanded that the decision be reversed. Ms Gingold was permitted to resume her work temporarily, in the same low status as before, until July 1977 when the state of Hessen's appeal against the judgment of the administrative court was heard. The administrative high court of Hessen confirmed Ms Gingold's ineligibility for a tenured position as teacher. 'It is generally known and recognized', she was informed in her final letter of dismissal, 'that the aims of the DKP are inimical to the constitution'. She was refused any right of appeal, and although she worked until her retirement in 2011 in the inferior status of contract teacher, she lost out on the pay, privileges and status of a civil servant and went through her life labelled an enemy of the constitution.

Our second case took place in Bavaria.[8] The case was less tidy than that of Ms Gingold, in part because of the habit of both the school principal and

7 Basic material on Silvia Gingold in: Kahl (1978). See also Wolfgang Bittner, Der Fall *Silvia Gingold*. WDR/ NDR, 20.11.1977.

8 For the Offergeld story see: Franz von Auer (1974).

the Bavarian ministry of education of fabricating evidence against the accused and denying him access to documents central to the case against him. These tricks had the intention of obscuring the profoundly political reasons for the teacher's dismissal and presenting it as a disciplinary case. Since the security forces were less involved than in the first case – after all, the defendant was an active member of the SPD, the government party (albeit on a federal rather than state level) – the state was reduced to relying on misleading denunciations and fabricated complaints from parents about the teacher's work. The state authorities had realized that they could use the Decree on Radicals to discipline and intimidate critical or non-conformist teachers. Anti-communism was a flag of convenience in their plans, and the case reminds us of the Catholic establishment's profound dislike of the SPD throughout the first twenty years of the Federal Republic.

Rüdiger Offergeld taught religion and German in a Munich high-school. He was, like Ms Gingold, on the edge of being made permanent, when he was elected to the section of the teachers' union national executive concerned with the situation of probationary and young teachers such as himself. Evidently, membership of this union served as a red rag to a generation of Bavarian administrators nostalgic for the days when Hitler had abolished all unions and made labour relations so much simpler. Hardly surprisingly, the national union was in the habit of making comments critical of aspects of the state's education system, and both the school principal and the state ministry defined such criticism as active disloyalty.[9] The ministry interpreted loyalty to the state as meaning an unquestioning obedience to superiors.

Having tried to get the Catholic Church to do their dirty work for them (the teaching of religion in Bavaria is regulated jointly with the Church, and had the Church taken away Mr Offergeld's licence to teach the Catholic faith he could not have kept his job), the ministry dismissed Mr Offergeld on April 11 1974, quoting § 42,1 (2) of the Bavarian code. A further charge was added of influencing pupils' religious opinions. Subsequently the Cardinal responsible, Joseph Ratzinger, later to be known on a different stage as Pope Benedict, did take away Offergeld's *missio canonica* and put the final nail in Offergeld's career, as well – presumably – as furthering his own. Often in the many trials which he conducted in order to right the injustice committed against him, Offergeld must have felt no less betrayed by his own party, for it was that party – the

9 The union in question was the GEW – certainly the specialized and more traditional of the unions which teachers were eligible to join and the most comparable to a 'professional association'. Later generations of teachers tended to head for the more general (and hence more powerful) public service union, the ÖTV.

SPD – which had created the climate in which such dismissals could take place, than by his church.

The third case concerns Charlotte Nieß-Mache, and also took place in Bavaria.[10] Ms Nieß-Mache completed the first part of her law degree and applied to the Bavarian authorities for a position as *Referendarin* (the second part of German legal training, which is completed within the context of work experience). Her application was rejected, on the grounds that, alongside her membership of the ÖTV and the SPD, Ms Nieß-Mache had been a member of the 'Association of Democratic Lawyers'. In 1974 the security services had decided that this association supported the DKP 'in its efforts to achieve a Popular Front', and despite the decision of the administrative court that membership of the Association did not, *in itself*, amount to sufficient grounds to exclude a candidate from the final part of her qualification, the authorities refused to alter their verdict, and Ms Nieß-Mache was unable to take up a position in Bavaria.

These three cases were substantially typical of the *Berufsverbot*. A more complete list would involve employees of the administrative civil service, such as secretaries and administrative assistants, engine drivers and postmen (at the time these services were in state ownership and their employees therefore civil servants). Particularly distasteful was the variety of organizations to which the accused had once belonged and for the membership of which they were punished. (There was never any serious effort made to see if they were *still* members of these organizations.) Protesting against nuclear weapons, against the Vietnam war, supporting the African National Congress – any of those activities was sufficient to make the security services inform employers of a person's unreliability and to lead to dismissal or rejection. The disappointing of career hopes, the stress of lengthy hearings with obstructive administrators, seldom with appropriate legal assistance, were exacerbated by the fact that during the long periods in which their cases were under consideration many of the victims were out of work, but could not be described as 'available for work' and therefore were ineligible for unemployment benefit. As one postman discovered, the fact that he had a faultless work-record did not help his case: his professional reliability was taken by the hearing as evidence of 'the Communists' excellent propaganda for their allegedly "legal" aims'.[11]

10 Material on Charlotte Nieß-Mache: Frankenberg (1978). Also: Aha, der Sumpf, in: *Der Spiegel* 48/1975. Here details of the authorities' smearing of these people by associating them with terrorism. Also Requate (2008, p. 351).

11 The state's view that communists work hard only for tactical reasons quoted in: *Ohne Zweifel für den Staat* (p. 111).

The publicity for these cases had three sources. First: the local press and media, varying with the 'public interest' of each case. (Unusually, *Der Spiegel* reported on the Gingold and Offergeld cases from 1974.) The national newspapers were slow to make the reporting of *Berufsverbot* cases a regular feature. Only after the weekly newspaper *Die Zeit* ran a series of feature articles on the *Berufsverbot* from July 1978 did the reporting of these cases by the national press become more established. Secondly pressure groups, including the unions, public intellectuals and writers and student organizations, were active – although the intimidating effect of the measure was particularly pronounced among students. But the legislation also threatened members of university staff sympathetic to the cause of the students: political scientists, sociologists, law-professors and theologians in particular. Thirdly, there grew up a significant network of groups campaigning against the *Berufsverbot*. The Committee for Basic Rights and Democracy devoted much attention to the *Berufsverbot*. In the spring of 1978 a sub-group of the Russell-Tribunal (originating from the philosopher and political activist Bertrand Russell) was set up to report generally on the condition of human rights in the Federal Republic. This group had a clearly international base, but it is doubtful whether its reports reached a significantly wider public than other forms of information.

Furthermore, national committees were set up to protest against the *Berufsverbot* in a number of European countries, notably in Italy, the Netherlands, France, Denmark and the United Kingdom – in other words, countries which had every reason to recall fascist Germany with distaste. Meanwhile, paradoxically, exiles from Hitler's Germany in Britain had little sympathy with the new generation of victims, regarding them as extremists and lumping them together with the Stalinist Communism which many of them blamed for the rise of Hitler. Sympathy for the them was indeed a rare commodity. Interestingly, as Harrington and Carter (2014) point out, the USA, having given the radicals a convenient word for the *Berufsverbot* – 'McCarthyism' –, operated its employment policy more transparently and more fairly.[12]

While answering two million requests for information for *Berufsverbot* proceedings, the Federal German security services totally failed to identify a real spy at the highest level of the state – as the Guillaume affair showed in May 1974.

---

12 We notice the readiness of legislators in the USA to modify their similar legislation. The intransigence of the German authorities was an essential part of the polarized situation. Harrington and Carter (2014, p. 389f) highlight the exclusive use of the US labour courts, the courts' loyalty to the First Amendment, and the introduction in the Civil Service Reform Act of 1978 of a strengthening of employees' rights.

Ms Gingold's case gained particular resonance because of three additional circumstances. Ms Gingold was the second generation of her family to have been the target of discriminatory legislation in Germany. At the end of the 1930s her parents had had their German citizenship taken away under the Nuremberg laws, and they had been forced into exile in France. (It had not been easy for Ms Gingold to regain her German citizenship, for exile and a change of nationality never went down well with the German authorities.) Her parents had – as members of the Communist Party – been active in the French resistance to the German occupation of 1940–1944, an activity for which the French government had subsequently decorated them. Their involvement drew the attention of President Mittérand to their daughter's situation, and he added his support to the campaign, although with little discernible effect. Thirdly, hardly as a coincidence (for these circumstances were normal in German courts), not only had the three judges trying her appeal been themselves explicitly involved in the NS court system, but one of them – Edmund Chapeaurouge – had been involved in the judgments which had deprived Ms Gingold's parents of their German citizenship in 1938. If any case seemed to argue that the real opponents of the free democratic basic order – the Nazis – had nothing to fear from the *Berufsverbot*, then it was this one, for they were administering it.

8.5 The Legal Issues

The general legal issues with which these trials were concerned could hardly have been clearer. Article 3.3 of the Basic Law guaranteed that an individual should not be discriminated against on the basis of her/his race, gender, religious or political opinions. Other articles stressed the freedom of every citizen to choose her/his profession without interference from the state. This position was in clear conflict with the state's determination to control the student movement through discrimination. A controversial issue was therefore the exact meaning of a civil servant's loyalty to the state, and this became a hotly debated historical issue.

One justification was to place the *Berufsverbot* positively in the context of the attitudes discussed in Chapter One. It was argued that the *Berufsverbot* was an attempt to ensure the *active* loyalty of public servants to a positive enactment of democracy and humanity. To the extent that the commitment to the 'free democratic basic order' meant anything, it could be presented as a much needed re-enforcement of democratic structures. No more should civil servants operate within the system passively as technocrats, merely paid by the state for their expertise, but not co-operating with its most fundamental aims.

Just as in the Flick trial, this view was guided by contemporary historical understandings of fascism's rise to power. It was part of the standard interpretation of the collapse of the Weimar Republic in 1933 that an excessive liberalism in practice and in the constitution had bestowed on influential public servants the freedom to follow their personal ideologies in carrying out their public duties, with no reference to the declared aims of the state. During Weimar examples of anti-democratic agitation within the state apparatus could be found most obviously in the judiciary and in the military, but also in the teaching profession.[13] The anti-republican bias shown by the *Reichsgericht* in Leipzig throughout the years of the Republic, for instance, or the leniency shown to Adolf Hitler after the failure of his *Putsch* in 1923 both offer strong proof of this judicial bias.[14] Similarly, the anti-democratic intriguing of important sections of the army (notably the circles round General Schleicher) manifestly contributed to the final collapse of the democratic state. Bracher's phrase was that the rise of Hitler depended on 'the self-destruction of liberalism'.[15] The *Berufsverbot*, it was argued, was designed to save the Federal Republic from similar self-destruction.

One of the fullest rejoinders to these arguments on the obligations of the public service was made by Rüdiger Offergeld's legal team. There was no difficulty for them in establishing that the Basic Law was ostensibly protective of workers' rights to belong to and to organize trade-unions, or to identify that the Basic Law made an absolute distinction between an individual's membership of the appropriate union and that individual's relationship to his/her actual employer. Citing authoritative commentaries on the Basic Law, Offergeld's team drew attention to standard commentaries on the *Grundgesetz*, which state that:

13 Andersch's haunting story *Der Vater eines Mörders* (1980) describes the lessons taught by the schoolmaster father of Heinrich Himmler – hardly a friend of the Republic which employed him.

14 Strikingly, Hitler and his fellow insurgents were not sentenced under the Law for the Protection of the Republic. Bavaria had taken that law out of its legislation. That was one reason why the trial was heard locally and the defendants leniently sentenced – not that the *Reichsgericht* would have been sterner. Cf. Blasius (1983, pp. 87–8).

15 Bracher (1955). See also: Duve & Kopitzsch (1976). Alfred Grosser (1976) states strongly the claim that 'Bonn is not Weimar'.

> The duty of loyalty does not impose on the public servant a particular loyalty to his/her professional class and status, a loyalty which should swallow up his whole personality. Loyalty can relate to nothing other than the norms of a democratic constitution, within the framework of which the public servant is committed to the political aim of the public service: that of carrying out the law (*Gesetz und Recht*).[16]

The claim therefore that Offergeld had 'insulted' members of his profession by belonging to a union which was critical of some of the general practices of the education system was absurd. No less absurd was the suggestion that the public service was some kind of secret society, tied in any different way than other sections of society to the upholding of the law. As the text of the Decree on Radicals itself had made clear, the law was formulated in terms which related primarily to the professional *caste* of the *Beamten* and only by extension to employees who just happened to be paid by the state. Nevertheless, their special status did not – so Offergeld's defence team argued – require any special relationship to the law.

It is seldom convincing for a state to critique its own liberalism, as those who defended the *Berufsverbot* from the historical perspective of Weimar were obliged to do. Certainly, against the climate which we described at the start of this chapter, official arguments did not persuade many people of anything except the state's authoritarian attitudes. A particularly forceful reason, however, why the state's arguments in the 1970s remained unconvincing was that the instruments used to 'correct' the tendency of liberalism towards social chaos were not new ones formulated in any democratic spirit, but were invariably archaic pieces of legislation going back to the times of the *Kaiser* and obviously refreshed during the Third Reich (when under the Law to Restore the Professional Civil Service of 1933 civil servants swore an oath of loyalty to Hitler 'until death'). This paragraph (and its equivalents in the codes of the various *Länder*), was formulated at various times between 1933 and 1939. (Had anyone been so minded, that paragraph could properly have been mobilized against the officials of the RSHA, and used as conclusive evidence that Hitler's civil service had not been characterized by neutrality, but by unquestioning loyalty to the murderous objectives of the state: the failure of that trial showed that all this legislation was directed only against the left.) Since the legislation

16 The defence team's reference to the GG in: Auer (1974, p. 125). Other authorities quoted include: Maunz & Dürig (1958 f); and Hamann, Hamann jr. & Lenz (1970^3).

of 1938 had also had the explicit function of excluding the Jewish citizens from the public service – and ultimately from citizenship – its mobilization in the practice of the *Berufsverbot* awakened the worst of associations with all the consequences of that measure.

This was far from the first time that legislative instruments from the problematic past had been used by courts, always inappropriately, in order to get a grip on the social disorder of the 1970s.[17] Another example was given by the charges brought against the demonstrators arrested in various protests against both the Shah and subsequently the Springer press. Charges were brought on a range of measures dating back to the *Kaiserreich* and sharpened up in Weimar and under Hitler. It was not that these measures had not been modernized as the years had passed: they had simply been lifted into an inappropriate context. The nineteenth-century mind-set which had caused these laws to be formulated was, of course, totally out of keeping with the mind-set and situation of the 1970s, but the laws were still there, and prosecutors felt free to use them.

The *Berufsverbot* repeated what, in the case of Dr Axel Dohrn, had been an opportunistic use of outdated legislation, against which only the Basic Law appeared to offer any protection. In all cases of this kind, the defence referred to the Basic Law, with greater or lesser effect. As the *Berufsverbot* procedure became more common, the pattern of legal debate was established: a conflict between the progressive Basic Law and the old obscurantism still inherent in laws which the present had yet to annul, to say nothing of the dubious practices revealed in the administrative system. The government had committed itself against the liberal promises of the *Grundgesetz* and given a free hand to state administrators to explore further obscurantist elements in the statutes.

The *Berufsverbot* cases provide an important illustration of the dilemma raised in the Introduction: the relationship between the development of the legal system and the social and political events of the time. They also represent a significant judicial backlash against the late 1960s. Requate (2008) has identified a series of ways in which the judicial system responded initially to the democratic euphoria of 1968. Judges for the first time had joined trade-unions, rather than staying in their professional associations; occasionally they extended their understanding of what constituted democratic debate, moving from the *Lüth* judgment's acceptance of calls to boycott to the right to demonstrate and (rarely) to blockade the delivery of Springer's newspapers. In a number of ways judges were constrained into adopting the language of

17 For further examples of the state resuscitating archaic laws on riot and public disorder see: Requate (2008, p. 178 f). These included StGB § 113 (resisting arrest), § 115 (rebellion), § 116 (riot), § 125 (breach of the peace) and § 240 (intimidation).

reform. But after 1972 the judicial system became visibly more reactionary. Judges were increasingly happy to comb the penal code to find harsh measures against radical students. Radical judges found their promotions blocked by conservative colleagues in the judiciary. As we shall see in Chapter Nine the rights of defending counsels were curtailed, and – as Ms Gingold's experiences showed clearly – the decriminalization of contacts with the GDR which had been achieved in the late 1960s was simply ignored. The reformist Justice Minister Gustav Heinemann was elevated to the office of Federal President in 1969, but rather than being a victory for reform, it was a political action, and judicial thinking went in the opposite direction. In the name of defending 'the free democratic basic order' the judicial system was ready to move against democracy.

8.6 The BVerfG Judgment[18]

The *Berufsverbot* cases raise an important question: why the victims did not repeatedly appeal to the BVerfG. While the cases were fundamentally similar, as was the authorities' indifference to proper legal procedure, the particular circumstances varied greatly. Although the BVerfG clearly dealt with its one case in as general a way as possible, it could well have been argued that there were different circumstances and therefore different grounds for various constitutional appeals. Nevertheless, the route to the court was always open, and few victims attempted to take it.

One reason is that many of them were reluctant to involve the BVerfG out of their loyalty to the DKP, lest their action caused the court to ban the party itself. Their reluctance was ill-founded, for major actions of that kind started with the government, rather than with individual cases, or with the electorally insignificant party, which in fact *ordered* its members to avoid that route. Another complicating factor was the large number of different courts which were involved, from administrative to labour courts. (By and large, the labour courts – used to handling matters of employment law and to practising impartiality between employer and employee – sided with the individual defendants, sometimes in very explicit terms, but the employers, being the state, had few reservations about simply ignoring the judgments of the labour courts,

18 Details of the BVerfG judgment in 1975: *BVerfG E* 39, pp. 334–75. Dissenting opinions: Judge Walter Seuffert, pp. 375–8; Judge Rupp-von-Brünneck, pp. 378–85; Judge Wand, pp. 386–91.

automatically appealing them, and in the meantime stone-walling demands that the victims be reinstated.[19])

Less obscure were the state's reasons for not simply banning the DKP. Not only was the administrative route easier and less controversial, for it spared the state the embarrassment of conducting its programme of *détente* with the communist states while banning communist organizations at home. In fact there was also a clear effort by all authorities to keep the existence of the *Berufsverbot* as secret as possible. It was a regular addition to the charges against the accused that they had informed the media about the details of their case. Participating in marches or protests against the *Berufsverbot* was often cited as a reason for distrusting an applicant's loyalty to the state (often with the justification that 'only communists cared about the issue') – indeed the authorities consistently denied that the *Berufsverbot* existed, even to those on whom it was being inflicted. The very use of the word itself was suspect. No wonder references to Orwell's *1984* were so common at this time.

The situation described in the third of our cases took the bolder route to the BVerfG – not Ms Nieß-Mache herself, but the object of an all but identical accusation. (Another case was sent to the BVerfG not on petition, but for clarification by the administrative court of Schleswig-Holstein.) The appellant in this case had been active in an organization for law-students in Kiel, the 'Red Cell Legal Studies' (*Rote Zelle Jura*), and his complaint concerned the discrimination which meant that he was not only refused entry to the second part of the legal qualification – the verdict brought with it effectively not only exclusion from the numerous branches of the profession which were in the gift of the state, but also the more general exclusion from an essential part of legal training.[20] Without completing his time as *Referendar* the appellant could not qualify as a lawyer.

In considering this case, the Second Senate of the BVerfG paid more attention to historical issues, such as those touched upon earlier in this section, than it appeared to devote to the individual circumstances of the case. The ostensible purpose of the court in considering these historical parallels was to define its approach to two central issues. The first was that the loyalty of the public

---

19 An instance of a labour court defending proper procedure in an exemplary fashion is offered by the state labour court in Düsseldorf. See: *Ohne Zweifel*, (1982), p. 149 f. Requate argues that the labour courts had from an early stage – through their President, Hans Carl Nipperdey – asserted the freedom to *make* labour law. This was possible because of the ambiguity of the GG on economic structures: this openness allowed autonomy to remain with the labour courts (2008, p. 64 f).

20 Requate (2008, p. 347 f).

servant to the state had been formulated in historical terms in the legislation which was relevant to the *Berufsverbot* cases, both at a state and at the Federal level. Although the BVerfG judgment was at pains to point out that there was no quasi-sacramental or 'special' relationship between the state and the public servant (such as had existed during the centuries in which kings and emperors were defined as ruling by divine right), it did recognize both the general legitimacy of and the need for the state's expectation of loyalty from civil servants. What was particularly significant was that not only did the BVerfG accept the traditional nature of the expectation of loyalty, but that the *Grundgesetz* itself had used traditional terminology in its references to the civil service. This was hardly surprising, since there were many senior civil servants attached to the Parliamentary Council and involved in drafting the *Grundgesetz* – nevertheless, GG § 33,5 was formulated as yet another deliberate anachronism. It read: 'The law relating to public service is to be organized by reference to the traditional principles of the professional civil service'.[21] Did 'traditional' mean in the time of the *Kaiser*, of the Weimar Republic, or of Hitler? Why was this void left in a document aiming at a democratic fresh start?

In its decision the court was essentially following through the decision it had taken in highly controversial circumstances in 1953. Defying the BGH and the government – both of which were convinced that the Federal Republic had to take over all the pension and employment rights which civil servants had been expecting in the NS state – the BVerfG decided that the civil servants working for the Nazis had worked for a state which no longer existed and whose obligations the Federal Republic could not be expected to take over. This was an implied critique of the Basic Law's reference to the 'traditional principles of the professional civil service'. These people were in fact 'the civil servants of Adolf Hitler'.[22] By extension: applicants were properly subject to the political constraints of working in a democracy.

Secondly, there was no doubt that historical arguments had established a new concept – not present in the Basic Law – at the very centre of constitutional thinking in the Federal Republic and therefore within the BVerfG: the idea of the 'militant democracy' (*wehrhafte Demokratie*). The *Lüth* case had argued a positive interpretation of this concept, when it stressed that democracy depended on the active *conflict* between opinions and therefore allowed Lüth full rights in putting forward his opinions actively. In the *Berufsverbot* case the

21 The text of GG § 33,5 reads: 'Das Recht des öffentlichen Dienstes ist unter Berücksichtigung der hergebrachten Grundsätze des Berufsbeamtentums zu regeln'.

22 *BVerfG E* 3.58, p. 140 f.

idea had a restrictive meaning: a militant democracy was one in which democracy actively, rather than re-actively, stood up for itself and took preventative measures to keep its potential enemies at bay. If it made mistakes about who its enemies actually were, then so much the worse for them.

It was also clear that the BVerfG had learnt much from its experiences with the ban on the KPD. This shift in attitude was shown in two elements of the judgment – elements which certainly were the most unacceptable to those whose sympathies lay with the victims. The first was a differentiation between an unconstitutional political party and an unconstitutional political group or more informal organization. Part of the appellant's defence to the BVerfG had been that the organization in question (the *Rote Zelle Jura*) was under no kind of ban or proscription and that membership of the group could not therefore be adduced as evidence of unconstitutional attitudes. The court dismissed this argument, although it accepted that the lower (administrative) court – which had used the appellant's membership to find him unsuitable for the public service – had not possessed 'complete proof of the unconstitutionality of the *Rote Zelle Jura*'. (Once again we see how seldom the evidence given against the accused was tested by the courts – not even by the highest court of the land: the issue of whether or not the *Rote Zelle Jura* was unconstitutional or not did not even get discussed.) However, in the court's view, the insufficiency of the evidence used by the lower court did nothing to support the appellant's case to the BVerfG; indeed 'his objection would be relevant only if his membership of a political party were to be under discussion'. The BVerfG was here rather petty in its clinging to its own exclusive right to proscribe a political party. Simultaneously, however, the court made clear that *no* guarantee of the loyalty of an official to the state could be assumed simply on the grounds that, in the case of the political party to which he or she belonged, 'no decision of the BVerfG concerning the unconstitutionality of that party had yet been taken'. In other words: the absence of a ban on a party did not mean that membership of that party was constitutional. The DKP, therefore, had not been banned by the BVerfG, but that court saw no objection to other courts regarding membership of the DKP as unconstitutional, and on that basis proceeding against individual members.

If that was bad news, worse was to follow. For the BVerfG formally accepted the right of lower courts and administrative boards to determine which groups and organizations under the level of a political party were unconstitutional – using the authority of GG § 9. This meant in effect that, since the unconstitutionality of an organization was declared only at the moment when an individual had been deprived of his/her livelihood, all the offences projected by the hearings into membership of a particular organization were *post hoc* decisions.[23] In effect, the defendants were found guilty on the basis of *retrospective* legislation – or at least retrospective administrative *fiat* –, for it was only the decision of the hearing or trial which made the organization unconstitutional. This retrospective punishment was not only generally encouraged by the Decree on Radicals, but it became the standard practice of an unassailable combination of state administration and the security services, from whom in the vast majority of cases the information concerning membership in an 'unconstitutional' organization had come. And whenever victims complained about this manifest injustice, still more when they argued that their particular organization had pursued aims which were compatible with the constitution, they were told that their level of political naivety was such as to make it doubtful whether they ought to be in the public service in the first place.[24] Adenauer's original order of 1950 had at least listed individual organizations which it regarded as incompatible with membership of the public service: the *Berufsverbot* did not give that clarity, except retrospectively.

Taken together therefore these judgments presented a bleak picture. Not only was it dangerous to belong to any group with any kind of politically 'radical' agenda, for it was open for any individual committee or assessment board to determine, without proper evidence, that the group was unconstitutional. At the same time, membership of any political party was liable, at any point in the future, to be interpreted by the BVerfG as unconstitutional, and the fact that it had not been banned at an earlier juncture did not make past membership legal. As Offergeld's experiences showed, in Bavaria – where the norms of democratic behaviour seemed often to have relaxed their grip on the state – not even membership of the SPD offered the victims of the *Berufsverbot* any guarantee that their political behaviour would be judged as constitutional. This amounted to nothing less than continuous intimidation.

8.7 Dissenting Judges

These decisions could have gone the other way – indeed, it emerged from three dissenting opinions that not all the judges were comfortable with the

23 We note the practice – common to many countries, of course, but problematic in some – of applicants using their war-record as proof of good character. It seems unlikely that much energy went into checking details of that record. See: Requate (2008, p. 98).

24 The catch-22 ending up with the defendants being accused of naivety, if they tried to explain how the organization they had belonged to was not unconstitutional, is discussed in: *Ohne Zweifel* (1982, p. 114).

judgment. Judge Wiltraut Rupp-von-Brünneck went to the crux of the issue when she wrote: 'A party must be free to have members and to recruit new members [...] for a party exists only in its members.' Judge Walter Rudi Wand added his voice to the criticism of the danger of a government criminalizing a party 'which it cannot show to be unconstitutional, but which for other reasons it does not care for and which makes life uncomfortable for the government'. He also identified a danger of intolerable 'snooping' and of 'continuous spying' on ordinary citizens.

At the heart of the court's written justification of its decision, however, less surprisingly perhaps, was the court's acceptance that a public authority had the absolute right to reach its own evaluation of the suitability of a candidate for a particular post, and that as part of that evaluation it was entirely legitimate to raise the general question of the candidate's ability 'to identify himself [...] with the idea of the state'. In any case, the evaluation of an individual candidate was not one which the BVerfG could change, or even comment on. When the BVerfG ruled that these decisions lay outside its jurisdiction, the appellants' case was lost before it had begun. Once more, administrative practice was more effective than major legislation for the state to achieve its aims.

One further comment from Judge Rupp-von-Brünneck throws an interesting light on the *Lüth* judgment. This judge challenged the constitutionality of the government's decision of September 1950, in which, among other things, the right of the state was established to institute an investigation against state employees whose political opinions were unwelcome to the state. The grounds for Rupp-von-Brünneck's challenge were exactly those which had been so admired in the *Lüth* judgment. Because neither the Basic Law nor the BVerfG had been properly established at the time of that legislation, Rupp-von-Brünneck argued, the central principle of *Lüth* – namely that existing legislation should be re-interpreted in the light of the basic rights paragraphs – had not been applied, and that the legislation itself (as well as the judgments based on it) was therefore flawed. In the light of the judge's remarks it's hard to escape the view that the idealism of the *Lüth* judgment had been little more than a product of a period of optimism within society as some of the worst features of the 'restoration' showed signs of easing, and the first indications of the end of the Adenauer period were observed. As soon as that general optimism waned, and the internal problems of the Federal Republic became more visible, this idealism was abandoned and the human rights paragraphs relapsed into mere phrases, much as John Ford Galay had predicted ten years before.

8.8 Final Thoughts

Does it all matter? There are solid and respectable histories of the Federal Republic which fail even to mention the *Berufsverbot*, or which dismiss its mention as a left-wing fantasy. Indeed, it might be argued that it is our focus on legal matters which gives prominence to this aspect of the 1970s.[25] Clearly the Federal Republic's 'victory' in 1989 gives impetus to this view. In that year the democratic system – a tender plant transplanted into the unpromising soil of 1949 – showed itself victorious over a collectivist authoritarian state. It may seem churlish not to acknowledge that victory by insisting on the passing problems of a group of unrealistic and marginalized radicals.

The truth is, however, that from Ohnesorg's murder in 1967 social, intellectual and political life were energized as never before and passionate feelings unleashed which left their mark on the country. It was not just the younger generation which was radicalized. The law itself changed and was differently interpreted in these years. And those changes themselves became hardly less passionate and ideological than the attitudes of the students themselves. The authorities and the judiciary too were caught in the accelerating dynamism of the time, and their outburst of energy is a crucial element of the history. If we cut out the passion from either side of the 1970s, it would be like attempting, in Nietzsche's metaphor, to transpose the *Eroica* Symphony for a tin whistle. What we wrote would not be the history and would miss the truth of these years.

It's not a question of choosing between a partisan and an objective historical judgment. The truth concerned less the raw passion of these years, the dead certainties of sharing (vicariously perhaps) in some of the radical ideas and actions of the generation of 1968 or, on the opposite side, of gaining the passionate conviction that long-haired students wanted to destroy the Republic. Rather the truth is to be found in the presence of doubt within the conflicting passions. This is particularly true, as Chapter Nine graphically illustrates, of generational attitudes to the actions of the urban terrorists – 'sympathy' with Baader-Meinhof was anything but unconditional on the left –, and also

25 A standard history – Wolfrum (2005, p. 109) – puts the *Radikalenerlass* in inverted commas and speaks disparagingly of the way in which the clichés about the perennially anti-democratic character of German governments are still being 'served up'. I would claim that the 1970s – and, as Chapter 11 strongly suggests, the period after 2000 – do not make sense without an awareness of how the Degree on Radicals was handled. This was a matter of more than one generation.

of the uncertainty with which that generation clung to its sweeping views of the world.

So were the victims a danger to the state? We should, I believe, see the vast majority of the DKP membership as being ideologically and temperamentally out of sympathy with terrorism. At worst perhaps they did not identify fully with the state as it tried to combat Baader-Meinhof, since they identified that state with the measures which had deprived them of their own careers. But while they were not 'militant' defenders of the Republic, they were certainly not planning its downfall.

If there was one element of German society threatened by many of the victims (and by the student generation at large) it was the education system and the universities in particular. All too few universities had attempted to come to terms with the appalling compromises they had made with Nazism. Like judges and other legal officials, university professors had managed to stay in office after 1945 despite their enthusiastic support for Hitler and readiness to pervert their academic subject in order to serve him. Their unchallenged authority in the universities of the 1950s and 1960s and the arbitrariness of their exercise of power was in some cases little short of scandalous, as the behaviour of Professor Ponsold demonstrated. Yet education was an area – marked in the third case in this chapter by the *Rote Zelle Jura* (the group of 'critical' law students) – where the collective effort of victims did pose a threat to institutions. Subsequent events, however, notably the success of the Reform Universities, made clear that that threat had been justified, and that the universities were much the better for the revolution which had been fought through in these years.[26]

A final revolutionary change could be seen in the general shift of perspective which many of the victims brought with them. They were members of the first generation to look beyond the narrowly defined integration of the Federal Republic into the West (equated with NATO and the European Economic Community) and to respond to global issues, such as South Africa, Vietnam and the Middle East. No-one could claim that their concerns were not legitimate, or that the governments of the world were on the way to tackling these global issues without prompting from the younger generation. In this field the victims and the student generation from which they came were well ahead of their political masters.

---

26 In the cultural field there were countless examples of professors (e.g. of German, or history) continuing in office after 1945. Perhaps the case of the eminent literary theoretician Hans Robert Jauß (ex-SS officer) is the most striking. See the reviews of recent biographies in the *FAZ* of 16.06.2016.

The authorities invariably failed in their 'hearings' to establish whether the candidates still held to the views of the organization to which they had once belonged.[27] Silvia Gingold, as the administrative court in Hesse commented, was debarred from the civil service on account of her behaviour as a seventeen-year old. For most of these people the slogans and the political fashions had fallen away, but the revolutionary broadening of the world-view of a generation remained, and in the long run – although student activism on these issues was explicitly described by the authorities as being 'inimical to the constitution' – the Federal Republic has had reason to be grateful for the generation's positive engagement with these causes, for they have become the focus of the civilized world.

27 The word *Jugendsünden* (the sins of one's youth) has too often been applied to the actions of prominent figures in order to trivialize what they did during the NS period. Reasonable judges often (and I suspect rightly) used it to characterize the organizations students joined and the positions they held. But the word seems to have been unknown to the practitioners of the *Berufsverbot*. Wesel's summing-up of the KPD ban applies equally to many of the victims of the 1970s: the party was, he writes, banned for 'a theory it no longer held to' (2004, p. 92).

CHAPTER 9

Chasing after Sympathizers – Threats to the Rule of Law

During the years of urban terrorism the 'snooping' and 'continuous spying' on ordinary citizens which Judge Wand had feared became a reality. This was less a product of the *Berufsverbot* than of terrorism, local home-grown terrorism. Nevertheless, it was, to put it mildly, an unfortunate state of affairs that, as the state confronted violent and armed threats to its institutions and its citizens, the *Berufsverbot* and its endorsement by the BVerfG had ensured the continued existence of a significant group of highly educated citizens profoundly alienated both from the institutions of the state and from the traditional party of democratic opposition. If the state does not enjoy the confidence of its citizens, successful security measures are harder to achieve.

The overlap between the *Berufsverbot* and terrorism was far less direct than the state's actions might have presumed. Certainly, the principal victims of the *Radikalenerlass* were anything but sympathetic to terrorism. The DKP – in Wesel's words 'a bourgeois party with a touch of pink'[1] – showed as little enthusiasm for the RAF as did the leaders of the GDR, who at worst were glad to encourage any group which made trouble for the Federal Republic. But an overlap did exist at the level of ideology or slogan, as the two movements answered the question which the 1970s posed – the same question which confronts modern historians, as it had the APO in the late 1960s: did the state, in its belief in 'militant democracy', cross a line and leave democratic process behind? This is a classic case of what Richard Ashby Wilson calls the 'Hobbesian dilemma – how do we defend liberty without compromising our hard-won freedoms?'.[2]

We earlier encountered – in the context of defence minister Dreher's impatience with due legal process in the 1950s – the suggestion that democracy has to break its own rules in order to defend itself. It is no secret that this is a potential weak point of democracy, for once that point has been crossed – as Chancellor Heinrich Brüning discovered in 1930, when he suspended parliament and ruled by presidential decrees –, it seems impossible to go back. If the authorities really believed that people like Gingold or Offergeld threatened

1 Wesel (2002, p. 166.)

2 Wilson (2005, p. 13) Later quotation: p. 14.

the state, they seemed extraordinarily insensitive to the damage which their own actions caused to democratic procedure. The *Berufsverbot* victims had no desire to attack the state: they merely wished to use democratic means to change some of its policies.

Terrorism, however, issues its most direct challenge at this point. Ulrike Meinhof described the tactic of escalation on which the Baader-Meinhof group engaged in terms of forcing the state to show that, when seriously challenged, it was in fact not democratic, but, in the language of the day, 'fascist' – a crude terminology which goes back to Stalin. Meinhof stated: 'that's the dialectic in the strategy of the anti-imperialist struggle: that resistance leads to the system reacting, it leads to the escalation of the counter-revolution and it changes the political crisis into a military emergency situation: the enemy then shows its true face'.[3] If the RAF managed to provoke the state into abandoning democratic procedure, then the state would have effectively unmasked itself. We need to ask how far this tactic was successful.

On the *Berufsverbot* itself, however questionable one may find the BVerfG's approval of the measure, the fact remains that the process was constantly in the courts and that the party responsible for it was subject to electoral judgment, locally and nationally. It would be naïve to imagine that it was only in response to public pressure that eventually (by the mid- to late-1980s) the state relaxed its measure, for unemployment, especially in the teaching profession and the intimidation of students and staff at university had played a significant part in pushing the students away from political radicalism. But gradually the state did move away from a procedure which so obviously contravened the Basic Law. The real issues arise in terms of the state's response to terrorism.

As we noted, the majority of the *Berufsverbot* victims were passive in their approach to the law. They routinely appealed their first hearing, but with monotonous regularity the state appealed any court decision in favour of the victims, and at that point when the state won its appeal most victims gave up. Facing endless legal actions, they accepted a non-tenured position or went somewhere else. There was little other choice they could make.

Other sectors of the radical student movement posed a more serious challenge to the legal system, starting – as the example of the *Rote Zelle Jura* showed – with university law departments and their links with the NS past. Their first targets outside the university were archaic court procedures and the continued activity of ex-Nazis in the judiciary.

The late 1960s saw a sustained critique of the institutions and rituals of the German courts. This was highlighted at a moment when the radical young

3 Meinhof speech in court on September 13 1974 in: Blasius (1983, p. 142).

lawyer Fritz Teufel, while on trial for stone-throwing during a demonstration, was ordered to stand up in the court-room. He agreed to this pointless formality, adding the celebrated comment: 'if that helps the truth to come out' – thus, incidentally, showing the difference between an inquisitorial and an adversarial court system. The laughter which greeted his remark was misleading. On one hand it aimed to expose – just as Tergit and Sling had forty years earlier – the gap between respect for the law and the law's arrogance. Teufel and his generation of radical lawyers wished to deflate the sense of the law's superiority over ordinary citizens. At least in the early 1970s German courts showed some tolerance of this tactic, for many sections of the judiciary accepted the need for more democratic procedures and for a separation of legal formalities from obsequious attitudes towards those who administered them – after all, that had been a hope of legal reformers for at least half a century. The fundamental liberalization of the post-war period had finally begun to penetrate the bastions of the law. Official reforms of court procedure had been promised for years, but no official changes were introduced until 1965. Teufel's generation of lawyers was taking reform into their own hands and they could count on some support, though such sympathy was soon exhausted.

The Baader-Meinhof group, of course, offered a far more serious challenge to the law. The short spiral of violence – which began with the arson attack on the Frankfurt Department store and culminated in the dramatic events of 1977 – does not need rehearsing in detail here. The challenge was obvious: the preference for violence over consensus and argument, and that challenge failed. As the ideologues trivialized the group's violence and casually justified the murder of public servants, such as policemen and security guards, they increasingly separated themselves from the broad mass of the population. Their hope of provoking popular revolution became more absurd with each of their violent actions. As they murdered, they successfully prevented any analysis of the social and economic structures which they wished to unmask, and they lost any significant support from a broader base.

These were real losses, for in fact the Federal Republic had previously shown that it was susceptible to change when facing peaceful direct action, especially when its relationship to Nazism, or – as we examine in Chapter Ten – serious environmental issues were at stake. For instance, in the 1960s Beate Klarsfeld took direct action to draw attention to the role of prominent ex-Nazis in the FRG. Her actions were non-violent but hardly legal, for they involved an attempted kidnap and in its most celebrated expression giving Chancellor Kiesinger a public slap in the face (the German courts sent her to jail for a year for that slap). Following Klarsfeld's attempt at kidnap the authorities actually got round to prosecuting the people her action had exposed and restarted the trial of the notorious SIPO chief of Lyon, Klaus Barbie – this after years of deliberate inaction. After the Auschwitz trial the state certainly felt vulnerable to the charge of NS sympathies, and change was possible. Violence and murder were the most effective way to lose public sympathy for that cause.[4]

Terrorism's other assault on the legal system was the attempt to turn the trials, which members of the RAF eventually faced, into an ideological attack on the state. The defendants and their counsels saw the courts, rather than themselves, as being on trial. Here, far from showing flexibility, the state took a hard line, and the effects of this response were devastating. Wilson echoed many German commentators when he pointed out in 2006 that such escalations invariably result in the 'delegitimation of counter-terror policies' and cause 'damage to the reputation of the state and an increase in support for its opponents'. Few situations illustrate that more clearly than the legal system's response, epitomized in Stammheim, the custom-built prison and court-house outside Stuttgart in which the trials took place.

The first casualty was a fair trial. The celebrated international lawyer Geoffrey Robertson comments that by definition 'terrorists' cannot have a fair trial, since the defendants' presumption of innocence has been taken away from the start.[5] Of course, after their arrest the defendants did everything possible to use their trials for an ideological attack on the state, but the state found no way to counter this tactic without making the situation worse. In fact, the state failed in almost all respects: its attitude to less prominent figures of the RAF who wanted to leave the terrorist movement entirely failed to persuade such people to come out of illegality (the mishandling of the Boock case in 1976 was the classic example of that failure[6]); it failed to negotiate via the prisoners and thus to save the life of prominent kidnap victims, and it failed, as all studies could have predicted, to preserve the reputation of Federal German justice both internally and internationally. Indeed, the claim that the state had murdered the three Stammheim prisoners is an unfortunate but characteristic example of the self-inflicted wounds of counter-terrorism in the FRG.

4 Teufel's moment in court see: Wesel (2002, p. 64 f). On Klarsfeld see: *Spiegel* On-Line, War das die Klarsfeld?; also: Requate (2008, p. 11). See also: Brunner (2002).

5 See: Robertson (2006, p. 169). Robertson gives a convincing account of the 'cathartic effect' of a fair trial in 'demystifying defendants who have appeared heroic to their followers'. See also: Hogan & Walker on the false dichotomy of security and rights' (1989, pp. 36, 91).

6 On the friend-foe mentality and its effects on discouraging defection from the RAF see: Hannover (1991, pp. 109–28). See also: *Der Prozess* (1985). Boock's case was a prominent example of an RAF member who had challenged the leadership and wanted to get out of terrorism. Wesel strongly agrees with the claim that the state missed important opportunities to defuse terrorism (2002, pp. 264–7).

A second response was a series of smaller administrative counter-measures, rescinding the procedural reforms of the late 1960s. These measures included the reduction of the formal level of suspicion needed to justify the issuing of an arrest warrant, and all-too often the replacement of a judge's authorization of such a warrant by an operational police decision. In this, as in all the counter-terrorist procedures, independent jurists saw the long hand of the emergency legislation, from which so many of the Republic's initial problems had stemmed. As Hitler's lawyer, Carl Schmitt, had commented: 'Real sovereignty lies with the person who determines the state of emergency'.[7] Critics note a real shift of power from parliament to the executive, with the result that a state of emergency became the everyday way of doing business.

It was in the treatment of the defence counsels that the state came most clearly to erode proper democratic safeguards. While the Baader-Meinhof prisoners exercised free choice in selecting the lawyers to represent them, their relationship to the counsels prior to and during trial was placed under extreme pressure. Restrictions were placed on the number of defence counsels permitted to the defendants, while the confidentiality of the lawyer-client relationship came under direct threat. In their extensive memoirs and analyses of these years all the prominent counsels insist that the authorities regarded them with hardly less suspicion than the defendants. Some of the measures were petty: temporarily withholding documents, or subjecting counsels to humiliating security checks. Most important were three factors: the absolute hostility of the lawyers' professional associations to any lawyer prepared to defend 'terrorists' – this had the result that the defence counsels could not rely on their professional body to help them stand up for their rights, and those of their clients. Secondly, an atmosphere of fear pervaded Stammheim so strongly that all deliberations were taken under severe psychological pressure. Finally and above all, the approach of the courts and judges divided defendants and counsels into sharply separated categories of 'friend' and 'foe': only judges and prosecutors were 'friends', everyone else was an enemy of the Republic.

Most serious of all was the infamous law preventing all contact between the prisoners themselves, the *Kontaktsperrgesetz*; in which counsels saw a major infringement of the defendants' rights.[8] Other national systems certainly gave prisoners awaiting trial less well equipped accommodation than the Stammheim prison had, but generous accommodation and equipment should

7 Carl Schmitt, quoted in Henne, (2010, p. 176). See: Mehring (2010, p. 5).

8 The *Kontaktsperrgesetz* was commonly justified by reference to StGB § 34 – which invokes the 'justification on the grounds of an emergency'. See: Krüger (2012).

not be equated with good conditions, nor the importance of the isolation regime be underestimated.

What does this all amount to: a fascist system co-ordinated across the various institutions of the state? Yes, the BVerfG had a bad day when the issues of Stammheim or terrorism came before it,[9] but it's also true that shortly after that case the court took a strong line – one uncomfortable to government – on surveillance measures and the right to privacy. Was this just an attempt to claw back its libertarian tradition, having sacrificed it when the pressure was on? What Alfred Andersch's notorious 1976 poem claimed (see below) – that the state was reproducing the totalitarian system of Nazism – was a widely discussed scenario (otherwise the conservative *Frankfurter Allgemeine Zeitung* would hardly have given it space), but it was not really true, and it lacked a plausible cast.

The SPD was forced into a corner, which they had partially constructed for themselves, but when the immediate crisis had passed (and they were out of government) the party endeavoured to regain its traditional libertarian position. The failure to purge the NS judicial system had created among prosecution services and judges a climate of opinion less likely to produce justice for outsiders and non-conformists. Nevertheless the system continuously opened itself to European courts, made no attempt to return to a *Sonderweg*, a special German approach to law and order. The antisemitism and militarism intimately associated with fascism were never part of the Federal Republic governments, not even during the 1970s. We must take seriously, however, Wesel's argument that the 1970s had seen a final end to the separation between the police and the security services, thus restoring the circumstances which made NS oppression possible,[10] but it would be hard to find any European state in which that separation was maintained, with or without an emergency.

In the NSU case (the subject of Chapter Eleven) this link re-emerged as a major problem, just as the case itself became acute because of the absurd conviction of law-enforcers in the 1960s and 1970s that the only danger to the state came from the left. We are left with a general climate of threat, a 'German autumn' of fear and hopelessness, of significant failures in the state and justice systems – however, a situation from which the Republic *could* emerge, even if it as yet has been slow to do so in all respects. Our next case illustrates both the threat and the positive fact that they judicial system possessed the ability to overcome the threat. But, as we shall see, it was a close-run thing.

9 See Collings (2015, p. 172).

10 Wesel (2004, pp. 330, 370).

9.1 Reactions to an Act of Terror

On April 7 1977 the Chief Federal Prosecutor, Siegfried Buback, was travelling to work in his official car when a motor-cycle pulled up next to the car. The pillion passenger took out a sub-machine gun and killed Buback, his driver and the accompanying policeman. The next day the press received letters on behalf of the 'Kommando Ulrike Meinhof', claiming that the killings were in revenge for the 'state murders' of Ulrike Meinhof, who had hanged herself in Stammheim in May of the previous year, and of Siegfried Hauser, who had died in the course of the siege of the Federal German embassy in Stockholm in 1975.

The murder of Siegfried Buback and his companions in the car was not the last action of the 'Baader-Meinhof group' and its successor organizations. The murder of the CEO of the Dresdener Bank, Jürgen Ponto, followed in June 1977, and in September the head of the Federal German employers' association, Hanns-Martin Schleyer, was kidnapped and some weeks later found murdered, while, in another action aimed at forcing the authorities to release the principal members of the group, a Lufthansa plane was hijacked and flown to Uganda, where it was subsequently stormed by German special forces and all the passengers released unharmed. It was these actions which prompted the suicides in Stammheim. While they did not mark the end of the group's activities, they did mark the beginning of the end of a period of ten years in which 'Baader-Meinhof' dominated the headlines.

To a generation which recalls the 1970s the memories are not good. The attempts to arrest (and in the case of Baader to re-arrest) the Baader-Meinhof group took on the dimensions of a military operation, which transformed the look and the feel of the whole country. Add to that the expanding international activities of the Palestine Liberation Organization (marked in Germany by the killing of Israeli athletes during the 1972 Olympic games in Munich), the activities of the IRA around the British Army bases in the north of the Federal Republic, and the urgent need for the airline industry to tighten security at airports – in such a situation the changes in daily life in the Federal Republic were palpable and potentially alarming. Heavily armed police stood around on street corners, the cities felt threatening, and travel less than free. Polarization characterized much of personal and social relationships. When this period came to an end, there was little place for public rejoicing. The world had changed in those years, and it was hard to think that things could ever get back to normal.

In such situations the dividing line between 'society' and its 'enemies' is never as clear cut as the authorities would like, and in all societies there is a tendency for alienated groups to radicalize and for anxious majorities to exclude. All societies appear to contain an uncomfortable percentage of citizens who are not only discontent with the actions of a particular government but are alienated from the whole rationale of the state and who therefore lead their lives without reference to the values which the state professes to promote. The cases with which this chapter deals concern such people and those who tried to build bridges to them.

9.2 An Unwanted Requiem

Nearly three weeks after the murder of Siegfried Buback – following a period of national mourning decreed by the Federal government – an article appeared in a student union Info-sheet at the University of Göttingen. Its title was: *Buback – an obituary*. It was in two parts, the second of which was hardly ever reprinted or even mentioned in the storm of protests which followed the initial publication. It was the first paragraph which launched the whole affair. It read:

> I can easily describe my immediate reaction to the gunning-down of Buback – how it 'affected' me. I could not, did not wish to (and do not wish to) conceal my sneaking pleasure. I've often heard that fellow winding up public opinion. I know that he played a central role in the persecution, criminalizing and torturing of left-wingers.

The author signed himself Mescalero (it turned out that this was the name of a branch of the Native American Apaches). He claimed to be a member of a group: *Movement of the undogmatic spring*. Perhaps today the title seems bizarre: within the student movement of those days, with its cliques and ideologically defined splinter groups and its all-night debates on the finer points of Marxist theory, Mescalero was making clear that he was a 'Sponti', rejecting the dogmatism of Marxism and contemptuous of the discipline of conventional political parties. The spring which his group undogmatically invoked – like the Arab spring of recent years – was an ill-defined utopian hope of a different and better world. It reminded people of the famous slogan of the student movement in Paris: *l'imagination au pouvoir*.

In particular the word 'sneaking' (*klammheimlich*) took on considerable overtones for students and academics. When, a few weeks after Mescalero's article, the police shot and killed a terrorist suspect, Willi Peter Stoll, a chat show host raised a storm by admitting to his 'sneaking' pleasure that Stoll was dead (no evidence had been presented against Stoll: he was merely a suspect, but no less dead for that). The student response was to accuse the TV audience who cheered the host's remark that forty years previously people like them had formed the large section of the population which had felt a 'sneaking pleasure' at the Nazis' elimination of the Jews. These were high stakes, and neither 'side' hesitated to make political capital out of the murder.

It is not surprising that, for all the author's anonymity and the obscurity of the publication, the article caused a national furore. Across the political spectrum the press condemned it – the Springer Press hardly less vehemently than the less right-wing *Frankfurter Rundschau*. Politicians condemned it, once more across the spectrum. We need to recall that the 1970s were the years of what in the 1950s and 1960s had seemed like an impossible dream: single party federal government by the SPD, after 1976 with Liberal support, although many of the individual federal states had a CDU administration. Willy Brandt – since the Guillaume-Affair no longer Chancellor, but still a figure of great authority in the SPD – said of the Buback murder that people like Mescalero were 'perhaps to an incomparably higher degree [responsible] than those fanatics who pulled the trigger on their automatic weapons'. Among those serving politicians routinely condemning Mescalero and expressing their revulsion that a student should express pleasure at a murder were the heads of federal states and their justice ministers, who would have found inadequate any response which did not follow up public condemnation of the author with legal action. And it was here, as we shall see, that the problems occurred. But first we should identify the climate of opinion to which these actions were a response, and which turned the Mescalero affair into a significant part of the history of the Federal Republic.

9.3 Sympathizing with Terror?[11]

In the language of that period we need to focus on one of its key-words: *Sympathisant*. The origin of the word appears to be in the 1930s when the idea

11 *Der Spiegel* ran a title-article on sympathizers, 'Mord beginnt beim bösen Wort', in: 41/1977, pp. 28–47. Here the Brandt quotation (p. 28) and the attacks on 'bed-wetters' etc. Groenewold describes the attack on sympathizers as the key element of the state's campaign against radicalization. For Böll's involvement see: Grützbach & Böll (1984). Böll's remark about only B-M knowing he did not agree with them: in *Der Spiegel* 41/1977, p. 42. His argument concerning the lack of proportion in the measures of the state against a small group of active terrorists is echoed by Blasius, who points to: 'the disparity between the narrow base of terrorism in the Federal Republic and the broad and permanent reactions of the state' (1983, p. 10).

of a Communist (or Fascist) sympathizer featured prominently in Europe and the USA, always with a hostile overtone. The word clearly meant something slightly different from merely 'feeling sympathy with' a person or a cause, but equally it did not mean identification with that person or cause. A fascist sympathizer was someone attracted to elements of fascism (perhaps because they thought fascism made the trains run on time), but certainly not a person arguing for dictatorship. (People who argued for that were simply called Fascists.) A communist sympathizer might admire the achievements of the Red Army, or, out of indignation at the plight of the working-classes during the Depression, see a need for a radical change of economic system, or simply despair that anyone other than Stalin would have the determination to stop Hitler. (That's why Hitler liquidated communist sympathizers.) When the war broke out, fascist sympathizers outside Germany got interned. After the war McCarthyism tried to criminalize every aspect of the 'sympathy' with communism, while the British took a more tolerant view, with mixed results, but all systems had difficulty separating supporters from sympathizers, and in fact few bothered to try.

The problem was anything but new in the Federal Republic. In 1972 the novelist Heinrich Böll had responded to a report in the *BILD* newspaper on the 'Baader-Meinhof gang' with an article attacking *BILD* for whipping up hatred and hysteria. He asked – since Baader-Meinhof seemed to be getting increasingly forced into a corner and their actions were becoming correspondingly more desperate – whether Ulrike Meinhof wanted 'a judicial pardon or safe passage', and proposed that the state should offer her safe passage (that is to say: a guarantee that she would not simply be gunned down like Stoll if she gave herself up) and promise her a fair trial. Immediately he was savagely attacked in the Springer Press as a 'sympathizer' with terrorism. *BILD* summarized the situation in words which made liberals of the time shiver: 'In a few years the Baader-Meinhof terror will be over, but the much greater threat to our democracy comes from people like Böll'. In the efforts to overcome the legacy of Hitler's state, people tended to identify critical intellectuals like Böll with democracy, rather than to see him as its enemy. The *BILD* was not going to change this opinion.

In response to these attacks, Böll wrote the brilliant short novel *The Lost Honour of Katharina Blum* (1974), the whole point of which lay in its subtitle: 'How violence arises and where it can lead'. By 'violence' Böll meant not only the one action in the novel – the murder of a *BILD* journalist – which had (loose) affinities to the actions of the terrorists, but a whole series of actions carried out by the 'forces of law' and other organs of 'the basic democratic order'. We should count as violence, Böll argued, the way women are routinely treated in society, the way powerful corporations buy influence over newspaper opinion or reporting, or, we might add, the way asset-strippers clean out the pension funds of the companies they buy and sell and thus destroy thousands of lives by perfectly 'legal' means. Clearly, as the next chapter shows, the destruction of the environment is also violence. If we wish to root out violence, we must understand it to be something more than urban terrorism. It has causes which the community must deal with, rather than merely attacking one of its symptoms. Böll's novel provoked still more fury in the usual circles, and its reception indicated that a sympathizer was anyone who attempted to understand a particular unpopular phenomenon, rather than merely condemning it.

What happened to Böll was repeated over these years, as not only the radical intelligentsia fell out of favour – variously labelled 'the real murderers' and 'Marxist-Leninist bed-wetters' by the 'popular' press – but established figures too, often theologians and churchmen. These included Bishop Scharf of Berlin – labelled 'Baader-Meinhof bishop' after he had visited Ulrike Meinhof in prison in 1974 and tried to persuade her to come off her hunger-strike – and Helmut Gollwitzer (veteran member of the confessing church during the Third Reich and professor of theology in Berlin), who never ceased to call for moderation on both 'sides'. Any politician who failed to join the hysterical condemnation of Baader-Meinhof suffered at the hands of a concerted effort by the right to smear the SPD and Liberal parties by associating them with terrorism. When a senior official of the North-Rhine-Westphalian Ministry of Justice paid a routine inspection visit to Baader-Meinhof prisoners in Düsseldorf he was made the subject of a campaign of vilification which subsided only in 1974 when urban terrorists narrowly failed to kill him in a bomb attack. In fact, Böll commented drily, 'the only people in the Federal Republic who know that I have never sympathized with the political ideas of the Baader-Meinhof people are the Baader-Meinhof people themselves'.

Böll's novel had touched the neuralgic point of the state with his discussion of what constituted violence. The idea of counter-violence (*Gegengewalt*) had featured prominently in the philosophical-political writings which had inspired the student movement. We encountered it earlier in Baader-Meinhof's justification for their initial action, the burning of a Frankfurt department store. Industry 'terrorized' the public into excessive consumption (*Konsumterror*), so the argument went, and burning down the store was therefore counter-violence. The idea took on still greater importance in the efforts by the students to counter the violence of the Springer Press, which they believed had led to the death of Benno Ohnesorg. Trying physically to prevent the distribution of the Springer newspapers was 'counter-violence' and therefore justified. Gollwitzer expressed a view similar to Böll's, if more global, when he said that 'anyone who gets upset about bombs at home in Germany but has nothing to say about the years of US carpet-bombing in Vietnam is not being honest'. There's no need to underline the international appeal of this argument.

It was state violence too, the distinguished writer Alfred Andersch argued in a provocative poem published in 1976 in the *FAZ* when the state does everything in its power to stop people it disagrees with getting jobs as teachers. His poem *Article 3* (3) contrasted the human rights paragraph of the Basic Law with the realities of the victims of the *Berufsverbot*. Like Mescalero, Andersch – one of the senior and most admired fathers of post-war German literature – described the state's treatment of these victims as 'torture' and ended his poem with a gruesome and extreme image that epitomized the depression and demoralization of the Federal Republic in the mid-1970s. His poem made clear how completely the enthusiasm and elan of the early student movement had been wiped out. This was the 'German autumn':

> We've seen it all before:
> A smell is going round –
> the smell of a machine which produces gas.[12]

Such was the climate in which the Mescalero letter appeared. Being thought a sympathizer was not recommended for Nobel Prize winners, Social Democrat politicians or bishops. By writing frankly of his response to Siegfried Buback's murder, some anonymous student was about to get it in the neck.

9.4 The Knives Come Out

There are many moral issues in the Mescalero letter and there was no shortage of people eager to point them out. Casually identifying the human being and family man with his office, failing to differentiate between the 'target' and the two men killed with Siegfried Buback – these were matters which the author himself would later regret. But they were typical of the period – perhaps too of other periods and countries. Typical also was the treatment of urban terrorism (as Mescalero's description of himself as an urban 'Red Indian' implied) as if it were some kind of 'Cowboys and Indians' game. We might remember that these were the days when films such as *Butch Cassidy* and *Bonnie and Clyde* were major box-office successes. No-one could deny that sympathy with the criminal heroes was a central part of these films' appeal, or that this attitude easily leaked over into real life – not just in Germany. Little doubt either that

12 Andersch's poem *Artikel 3* (3) appeared in the *FAZ* on February 2 1976.

members of the Baader-Meinhof group sometimes thought of themselves in that way too, as if they were starring in an action-packed political thriller. It was not surprising that such attitudes spread, or that their consequences were often questionable. In Britain, for instance, covert admiration for the Great Train Robbers was allowed to obscure the fact that the gang had permanently ruined the health of the security guard whom they had attacked. Somehow the 'audacious' crime was more glamorous than the reality of its violence. Was it altogether surprising that, when the IRA landed a mortar bomb in the garden of the British Prime Minister's residence, a 'sneaking' admiration, as if for a sporting achievement, could be observed in circles otherwise opposed to murder and violence? In the Federal Republic in 1977 there were two difficulties with identifying these factors and adequately responding to them.

First: the Mescalero letter had a disconcerting ability to speak for a large section of the student population, and to express the widespread alienation of that generation from its state. Estimates by the authorities in Berlin put at 15–20% of the whole student population the number of people who would have shared Mescalero's sentiments. While the authorities were worried that students like Mescalero were precisely those people who were offering members of the Baader-Meinhof group safe houses, identity papers or money and thus making the apprehension of the group particularly difficult, a more balanced view might have been that people like Mescalero would never have posed any threat to the state. Dreaming and words were more their style than action.

In any case Mescalero disapproved of violence and the second half of his article made clear his principled opposition to it – while defining violence in the broader sense which we mentioned above. Here he criticized those who whipped up hatred against other sections of society, and in that condemnation he included not just Siegfried Buback and the 'killers' in his department, but also those who killed with guns and bullets. Hatred was out of place, Mescalero argued. The 'sympathy' with romanticized screen idols was never more than skin-deep, a sign of frustration rather than a model which he intended to imitate. His article outlined its author's wish for his generation: a society without violence or terror, and it expressed that aim 'in the name of socialism, or – if you like – anarchy'. Like nearly all idealists of the left, Mescalero called for measures to bridge the gap between the students and 'the masses' – a gap constantly experienced in reality (the hostility of the police to student demonstrations being one of many symptoms) and therefore annoying to the ideology of student revolution, and frustrating because it prevented student revolt turning into widespread social change.[13]

13 For an examination of student ideology in search for the new vanguard of revolution, see: Gilcher-Holtey (2001, pp. 11–24).

In all these opinions Mescalero spoke for a wide spectrum of student opinion, and what infuriated the authorities and the newspapers and all 'right-minded' people was his brutal honesty in stating his feelings so openly.

The second problem was that these opinions hardly broke any law. That did not stop the authorities trying to bring Mescalero himself to court together with – in a fatal but almost inevitable escalation – anyone who sympathized with him. Proportionality went overboard. Within a very few days the Göttingen student union faced criminal charges for being responsible for publishing the info-sheet in which the article appeared (eventually the union was fined 1800 Marks) and action was taken against a number of other student union publications which reproduced the original article. A school newspaper was also prosecuted. As the police tried to discover Mescalero's identity, a number of Göttingen students were treated as dangerous criminals, strip-searched and handcuffed while their rooms were searched. In no less than twenty-one cities across the Federal Republic charges were brought against the student unions and against academics who had expressed any kind of solidarity with Mescalero – even though the principal concern of these academics had been with the erosion of free speech by the intimidation of Mescalero and his 'sympathizers' and solidarity with colleagues facing prosecution. In Augsburg, in a federal state whose first minister had proposed to close down the entire student union permanently in the wake of the Mescalero affair, a court imposed a suspended sentence of six months on union officials. (The sentence was subsequently annulled.)

While all that activity gives the impression of a co-ordinated action, the measures taken could hardly have been more disparate. In an important development, forty-seven academics joined forces to issue a volume documenting the Mescalero letter (which they reproduced in full) and the early reactions to it. Quickly they found themselves facing various threats from the different states in which they worked, ranging from suspension and dismissal to fines. But since the professors came from various federal states, there was no unity in the charges, and the outcome of their cases seemed to depend entirely on local political considerations, not on established law. Peter Brückner in Hannover, for instance, was immediately suspended from his university chair by the university authorities (it would be another three years before his suspension was rescinded); at other universities staff were merely threatened with dismissal unless they signed public statements condemning the murder. It was not that there existed any spectrum of opinion about terrorism – the uncertainty was about the best way for the law to respond to it.

The Senator in Berlin responsible for science and universities, Peter Glotz, hesitated to follow his colleagues in other federal states in the frantic attempt to discipline those university staff and students who had become involved in the Mescalero affair.[14] In fact, he roundly condemned those ministers who both initiated formal legal proceedings against their employees and at the same time rushed to the media with personal denunciations of those employees. Glotz found it 'scandalous' that ministers of justice should be so little concerned to ensure a fair trial, and should try simply to gather popularity by following the media hysteria. He publicly expressed the same hope as Böll and Gollwitzer: namely 'to bring some movement into the entrenched positions taken up in our society and to introduce some differentiation into the debate'. In doing that he would have frustrated the deliberate aim of the Baader-Meinhof group to force the state into extremism. Glotz' wishes did nothing to defuse the situation, or to prevent prosecutions taking place in Berlin, and he had to recognize his own desperation, admitting that his party, the SPD, had completely forfeited the influence it had once enjoyed within the student body. The party leaders' policies had so radicalized the party's natural supporters that it could no longer communicate with them. The law seemed the only route of communication.

Because of the variety of response, as well as for the easy availability of material, we shall choose just one of the trials for detailed consideration and discuss the legal issues of the Mescalero case on the basis of a trial before the *Landgericht* Berlin from October 30 1977. Fourteen academics from Berlin who had, as part of the collective of forty-seven, been responsible for publishing a documentation of the case and reprinting the Mescalero article in its entirety were the defendants.

9.5 A Chequered History of Controlling Free Speech

The principal instrument at this trial was StGB § 90a, which establishes the crime of insulting of the state and its symbols. It states

> Anyone who publicly, in a meeting or through distributing written material (1) insults the Federal Republic of Germany or one of the federal states, or maliciously makes them appear worthy of contempt or (2) treats disrespectfully the national colours, flag, coat of arms or national anthem of the Federal Republic of Germany or of one of the federal states shall be punished with imprisonment of up to three years, or with a fine.

14 Interview with Glotz in *Der Spiegel*: Jeder fünfte denke etwa so wie Mescalero, 41/1977, pp. 49–63.

The language here is anything but precise. I've rendered it rather colourlessly in the translation, but some of the individual words and distinctions – for instance, between *beschimpfen* and *verunglimpfen* – seem designed for philologists rather than lawyers. The difficulty for courts would clearly consist in determining what amounted to what kind of insult. Discussion of this kind was not helped by the widespread cheapening of political language which the tense atmosphere of the 1970s had brought about. It was an atmosphere in which the words 'sneaking pleasure' had – as we saw earlier – gone viral. It was no easier to establish the criminality of Mescalero's remarks when Franz Josef Strauss openly referred to the federal parliament as 'a pig sty'. The mayor of Frankfurt said that the squatters who were moving into empty buildings in the city were 'worse than the SA and the SS'[15] – the normal language of politics had been swept aside, and when it came to insulting the state it was hard to see at what point any law could identify a boundary between the legally acceptable and the actionable. So the basic terms of § 90a were not helpful in establishing clarity.

Almost inevitably, a particular problem of the paragraph was its age. (During its history it had experienced different numbers as the criminal code changed around it, but for clarity we shall stay with the number 90a.) Its most prominent use had been during the NS period, when any lack of clarity in the text could easily be resolved by the fists and cudgels of the SA thugs. Together with compliant judges, the NS paramilitaries cut through all unnecessary complications and determined instantly what words or actions were an insult to the Hitler state. The paragraph helped to break the bodies and lives of Hitler's opponents, and when under the Potsdam Agreement of 1945 (Section III,4 – subsequently reinforced in the Control Council Law number 1) all laws which had 'provided the foundation for the Hitler regime' were formally abrogated, § 90a might have been expected to vanish into history.[16]

However – in a way similar to Schöffel's disappointment in 1848 – the effect of this abrogation turned out rather differently. For in 1951, as we have already mentioned, Adenauer was looking to strengthen the legislative armoury of the new republic and re-introduced a range of measures. The effect of Control

---

15 Strauss' view and that of the mayor of Frankfurt quoted in: Agnoli (1977, pp. 78, 103).

16 On the Control Council: In fact it was only the element which penalized disrespect for national symbols which got explicitly repealed by the Control Commission. Clearly the repealed section referred to the swastika, even though it was not mentioned as such. It just shows how arbitrary the process of sifting out NS laws had been, for the protection of the state (used in the Mescalero charges) was of far more assistance to the Nazis than any specific legislation of their own on this point. Violence rather than law could deal with lack of respect of party symbols.

Council 1 was to oblige Adenauer's lawyers, rather than abandon the measure entirely, because of its contamination by the Nazis, to go back still further in time and to revive the 1923 version of § 90a. 1923 was of course not just the year of Hitler's fatuous and failed *Putsch*, but was right in the middle of a whole series of rather more serious attempted Communist uprisings against the republic – actions which the Law to Protect the Republic was designed to ward off. So, regardless of whether the law had come from 1923 or 1933 the effect of the paragraph remained the same.

The defence at the Berlin trial in 1977 argued that § 90a should not have been put into post-war legislation at all. The parliament which had approved the *Strafrechtsänderungsgesetz* had spent no more than six hours debating the measure, even though, as we have already seen in the BVerfG minority judgment of 1975, the package contained a number of further instruments which were to be influential in the legal events of the Federal Republic. Like so many other legislative instruments, the adoption of § 90a was justified as 'defence of the republic', and its vigorous implementation in this and many other trials of the 1970s was further justified in terms of the 'militant democracy' endorsed by the BVerfG. But it was obvious that – both in 1951 (just before the formal effort to ban the KPD) and in 1977 – the paragraph served to advance the same virulent anti-Communism which had marked its use after 1933. No-one could have been more strongly opposed to Communism than Adenauer and the first leader of the post-war SPD Kurt Schumacher, so the rejection of the Nazi version of § 90a and the adoption of the Weimar version were little more than tokenism: a piece of denazification window-dressing which in no way amounted to any real commitment to pluralistic democracy. The idea that in 1951 any German politician would have had the courage to invoke Control Law No. 1 and strike the law off the statute-book was absurd, no less so than that the western Allies – at the time deeply involved in the Korean War – would have had any interest at all in preventing the return of repressive legislation aimed at eliminating the Communist 'threat'. So once again the old became the new, and the defence of democracy appeared to lie in the hands of those prepared to destroy democracy in order to defend it. For, as the poet Erich Fried commented: 'A country in which you're not allowed to say that it's not a real democracy, is not a real democracy.'[17]

A particularly interesting debate developed round the implementation of § 90a, a debate which brings us back to the issue of the role of the concept of natural justice in the post-war years. To the thugs of the SA it was perfectly

17 Erich Fried quoted in Agnoli (1977, p. 97).

obvious that this paragraph identified enemies of the state and highlighted the way in which evils such as pacifism, trade-unionism, belief in parliamentary authority and freedom of expression insulted and defamed the NS state. In just the same way it was no less obvious to people that § 175 properly allowed for the criminal prosecution of homosexuals, just as § 218 brought morality into human reproductive behaviour – such forms of justice seemed absolutely natural. While it would be unfair to claim that pieces of legislation such as §§ 175 or 218 came into existence *because of* popular opinions, these opinions made it unlikely that legislators would be in any hurry to rescind the legislation. Judges – of the more civilized variety – are in any case less anxious than legislators to echo *vox pop* in justification of their verdicts, and hence in the Berlin trial and elsewhere there was explicit reference to a different, allegedly more objective criterion for judging whether or not a particular utterance or article was actionable as forming 'an insult' to the state. This criterion was to evoke the opinion of an 'unprejudiced and fair-minded reader' of Mescalero's article – in other words an idealized form of *vox pop*, and one which assumed that the reader had not been exposed to the popular press. In other court systems the function of the jury is to provide such an opinion, but no jury sat in the Berlin trial, and the judges had therefore to have recourse to other ways of ascertaining the view of that 'fair-minded and unprejudiced' person. In effect, they and the precedents to which they turned fell back on their own reading of the text. After all, who could be more fair-minded and less prejudiced than a judge? They found two precedents for this approach. In Chapter Five's account of Dr Dohrn's case we identified a third.

In October 1952, for instance, the BGH had dismissed a writer's appeal against his sentencing under § 90a. The writer had printed a pamphlet railing in colourful language against the Federal Republic. He had compared the republic to 'a freshly painted Cola Cola stall standing next to the huge, burnt-out but indestructible edifice of twelve hundred years of the German Reich'. The 'unprejudiced and fair-minded reader' was conjured up by the BGH to reinforce the lower court's view that the article in question did in fact turn the Federal Republic into an object of contempt. Referring to the 1930 version of § 90a – the so-called Law for the Protection of the Republic' (ironically the very year in which Chancellor Brüning had destroyed the functioning of the Weimar democracy by governing under the notorious emergency legislation) – the court went on, rather frighteningly, to explain that the offence was constituted even when there was no question of the state actually being endangered. The relevant fact for the court was that the remark in question had attacked the Federal Republic in the manner denoted by § 90a: it was 'in the attack itself that the law sees a danger'. It is hard not to see this as a significant restriction of free speech.[18]

More recently the OLG in Cologne had reached a similarly significant conclusion. An anti-draft group had condemned the state – referred to disparagingly as (among other things) 'the remover of study grants, the Springer Press and the state which gave us the emergency decree' – for compulsorily training draftees to 'murder their fellow human-beings'. On appeal the sentence against the group was upheld, once again in the name of the mythical average reader. The court insisted that while 'on their own political criticisms can never amount to an offence [...] the borderline to an offence is crossed when that criticism is offensive, derogatory or insulting' (the court did not seem disturbed by the tautological nature of its reasoning). The moment is reminiscent of the occasion when the BVerfG suddenly had had its fill of the KPD's angry campaign slogans and declared them anti-constitutional. A modern view might be that the boundary which was crossed was the boundary of patience, not necessarily the boundary established by any law.

The Berlin case ended abruptly. By the third day, the prosecution threw in the towel, and the judge summarized what was just about the only reasonable view of the original article when he said in his judgment that in fact 'the author [Mescalero] – although he declares his spontaneous pleasure [at the murder] – immediately subjects his feeling to critical analysis and for political-strategic and moral reasons arrives at a condemnation of the assassination'. It was hard to escape the conclusion that the whole trial had been unnecessary and that, had the prosecution service taken the trouble to read the entire article, rather than responding to the indignation of their ministers and the press, a great deal of public money (and further polarization of society) might have been saved.

Otherwise, one might have felt, this was a highly satisfactory outcome. The case showed the resilience of the judicial system, which had initially been led by the populist and party-politically motivated wave of hostility to the original article, but had subsequently come to its senses. In this and a few subsequent judgments the courts did gain some distance from these pressures and they reached a reasonable conclusion. Other courts too conceded that Mescalero when read in full did not approve of Siegfried Buback's murder. The juvenile court in Düsseldorf went so far as to describe the article as a political manifesto

18 BGH decision in: *Entscheidung des Bundesgerichtshofes in Strafsachen*. Vol. 3. Berlin & Köln: Heymann, 1953, pp. 346–8. (Number 92). OLG Köln judgment of June 8 1971, in: *GA* 1972, pp. 214–6.

'intended to draw students back who were at risk of sympathizing with terrorism'. In today's language we call that de-radicalization.

Yet the Berlin judgment remained unsatisfactory. While the fourteen accused were, naturally enough, relieved at the court's decision, their reflections raise less comfortable issues. First, they pointed out the unusual spirit of collegiality in the court. After the opening of the trial, when the authorities had attempted to turn the courtroom into a maximum security area, with body searches for the public (the accused refused to submit to such a search), a far more civilized atmosphere had become established in court. Of course that wasn't particularly surprising. Academically highly trained judges and prosecutors faced a dock in which highly trained educationalists, sociologists and academic lawyers were sitting, and fairly soon a thoroughly academic discussion took place. Like and like discussed some legally sensitive issues and agreement was reached, in the form of an acquittal. It was all very cosy.

On the defence side, however, these factors were seen as anything but positive. When the power relationships were different, they argued, when individual students or less articulate defendants appeared in court, then the judges were less open to discuss broad legal issues; the atmosphere was far from cosy and the outcome invariably different. The defence pointed to the trial simultaneously being conducted against the type-setters of the AGIT press which had published the documentation. Under different paragraphs they were found guilty in 1979 and sentenced to a jail-term.[19] This sentence shows that the reaction of the legal establishment against the liberal reforms of the late 1960s was well under way. Considerable unease was also felt at the fact that one of the co-editors, Peter Brückner, was still suspended from his post by the university authorities. Civilized behaviour in one court did not alter far less civilized behaviour in other courts, nor did it extend across the whole of the judicial system. While the LG Berlin mended one plank on the legal system, other courts and other jurisdictions had no problem in driving the ship of law further on to the rocks, and finding the accused guilty as charged, siding with power rather than with reason or a less compromised form of justice.

19 On the AGIT-printers see: Wikipedia, also: *Der Spiegel* 1978/45, p. 92 f.

CHAPTER 10

The Rub of the Green – a Range of Environmental Cases

10.1 Historical Prologue

'The further we went upstream from my father's mill,' we read in a novel of 1884 telling the story of the desecration of a local beauty-spot,

> the more contaminated the water became. Dead fish floated downstream as, holding our noses against the stench, we filled our sample bottles with water, taking care to write on each bottle the exact spot where we had taken the sample.
>
> Two and a half kilometres from Dr Lippolde's house we arrived, with a sense of awful inevitability, at what we had expected: the source of the sufferings of the mill, the starting-point of all my father's misery. Looking across at where a tiny tributary flowed into the stream and pointing to a disgusting pool of sticky, stagnant water flooding a water-meadow, Dr Asche spoke for the first time. 'There you are', he remarked, with a certain hearty satisfaction.
>
> On the other bank, overshadowing the meadow, grey and gigantic in the mist, loomed Krickerode, with its battlements and its turret-like chimneys. Krickerode – the great industrial achievement of the modern age, puffing out clouds of black smoke and jets of white steam, working at full power, even on Christmas Day itself. Krickerode!
>
> 'Sugar', said Asche sarcastically. 'The idiots go on about the bitterness of life, but they can never have enough sugar – and that's what you get.'[1]

Wilhelm Raabe's novel *Pfister's Mill* is one of the earliest novels to give a reflected account of the destruction of nature by industry. It's fairly unique in nineteenth century literature, since a central character – Dr Adam Asche, whom we meet in the above extract – is an industrial chemist, able to analyze the water samples and to prove the link between the pollution of the stream and the giant sugar factory. It is still more unique in that the action culminates in a trial at which, with Asche's help, Herr Pfister successfully sues the factory owner for

1 Raabe (1980, pp. 102–03).

damaging his business and his home. The novel's irony is that, worn out with the effort of bringing his case to court, Herr Pfister dies prematurely, and his business is closed, as his son moves to the big city and himself participates in the modern life of which Krickerode was such a potent symbol.

Raabe was well informed about the state of the environment and about the inadequacies of environmental law in the second half of the nineteenth century.[2] No educated European could fail to be aware of the observations of Alexander von Humboldt on the negative effects of man's damage to the natural landscape, and industrialization had simply made the problems more acute. Although Raabe uses the food industry as his example – that was suggested by his personal sources for the novel –, he knew the huge importance of the chemical industry, in which Germany rapidly came to assume a leading role in these years. Raabe identified the dilemma of a country, only recently emerged into nationhood and some way behind the industrialization levels of other European countries. Germany was simultaneously caught up in sentimentality about its nature, especially about its virgin forests as a symbol of its vigour as a nation, and yet determined to assume its place in the sun, among the other 'great powers'. Even the reception of his novel illustrated this problem, since potential publishers argued that readers would be put off the novel because, as one of them wrote, 'there's too much of a stink there'. People wanted industrial expansion, but did not wish to confront its negative consequences.

Raabe saw too the transformation of the cities, the social isolation and unhealthiness of life there, marked by the great epidemics which devastated Berlin (cholera, 1834), Hamburg (cholera, 1892) and Gelsenkirchen (typhoid, 1901). Raabe recognized the inadequacy of the legal protection of the environment, how the ancient laws which promoted freedom of trade remained indifferent to protecting nature. Only in a few parts of Germany which had retained elements of French law did nature itself enjoy any legal protection. Industry demanded unlimited clean water for its production processes, but neither nature nor urban society had any protection against the waters which – as in Pfister's experience – industry released back into the environment. The reader of Raabe's novel notes that it was not environmental legislation which Pfister could use against Krickerode, just simple tort, like BGB § 826 under which Veit Harlan initially secured Lüth's silence (see Chapter Three).

The relative unimportance of environmental issues in the statute-books did not change significantly for at least fifty years after Raabe had published his

2 For a general account of the legislative background of this period see: Kloepfer (1994). Humboldt's account of the effect of deforestation on water-supply goes back to his travels in South America. See: Angela Wulf (2015, pp. 5, 57 f, 60).

novel. What little legislation did exist remained within regional law: national law made no reference to the subject. In Germany the environment remained a matter for the individual states. Legislators were concerned with public safety in the neighbourhood of ever larger and more hazardous factories, but it was explosions, rather than pollution which were seen as a threat to the public. In fact, not until the *Reichsnaturgesetz* (*Reich* Nature Law) which the Nazis introduced in 1935 did the idea of legislating to protect nature receive any national attention. The *Kaiserreich* and the Weimar Republic had begun to develop garden cities, together with what we now call green-belt spaces, but nature and landscape were not considered appropriate objects of law until 1935. Strikingly much of the environmental legislation of the Federal Republic goes back to that law – an irony which has caused occasional soul-searching among historically aware environmentalists.

10.2 Environmental Protection in the Federal Republic

Following 1949 the Federal Republic repeated the errors of the years after 1871, setting aside environmental concerns in pursuit of the 'Economic Miracle'. With Raabe's novel in mind, we note that water legislation remained especially fragmented and ineffectual, although sooner or later a country rightly proud of the legal protection of the purity of its beer would have to tackle the growing impurity of its water. How slowly the issue was grasped can be gauged by the fact that the pollution of the Rhine was not addressed by national law or by multi-national convention before 1963.[3] Importantly the *Grundgesetz* contained no reference at all to the natural environment, and it was not until the end of the century that § 20a was inserted, to cover protection for animal and plant species and for their habitat, as well as a responsibility for passing on the natural world to future generations. The paragraph applies to the 'basic natural conditions of life': water, soil, air, climate, bio-diversity, the protection of endangered plant and animal species, together with 'landscape in its various interdependencies'.[4] We note that the duty of protection is imposed on all agencies of the state, but the paragraph does not give local communities the right to assume responsibility for certain environmental issues, which remain the proper concern of specific federal or state agencies. The cases which we

3 See Sands & Peel (2012, p. 151 f). See also their account of the failures of regulatory control shown up in the aftermath of the Sandoz accident in 1986 (p. 155).

4 See the commentary on the GG: Hönig & Wolff (2016, pp. 291–95). Sands & Peel discuss definitional problems at the international level (2012, p. 13 f).

cover in this chapter would not have been materially affected had GG § 20a been applicable at the time.

In the GDR the situation was not fundamentally different. For a number of ideological reasons, connected with Marxism's glorification of human labour in making nature subservient to man (the Christian churches had a similar problem with the Bible's instruction to man to subjugate nature), as well as economic necessity, environmental protection was not an issue before the 1970s. Where environmental concerns were expressed – as in Monika Maron's celebrated novel on pollution in the massive industrial complex in Bitterfeld, near Leipzig – the writers' focus was essentially political. It is the suppression of the problem by the Party rather than the nature of the problem itself to which Maron devotes most attention. (For that reason *Flugasche* (1981) was published in West rather than in East Germany.)

On both sides of the wall, the major impulses to promote environmental legislation initially came from outside Germany, not just in the steady onmarch of international law, but in the development of science on a global scale. Neither impulse is without its ambiguity. International law will not necessarily influence environmental developments within the nation state and science does not always speak with one voice. But more accessible pressures were created: for instance by Rachel Carson's world-wide bestseller *The Silent Spring* (1962). When ten years later the Club of Rome began to question the concept of unlimited economic development – following the Meadows' 1972 provocative collection of essays, *The Limits of Growth* –, these voices found a ready response from the student generation, although positive responses were muted by fears that the environmental protection called for in these studies might prejudice full employment. Ultimately of course it was international events which spoke the loudest: the potential catastrophe at Three Mile Island (1979), followed by Chernobyl (April 1986) and Fukushima (2011). On another front, public opinion was shaken by the effects of the dioxin explosion at Soveso (1976) and of the chemical accident at Bhopal (1984). These events had a considerable impact on German environmental policy, right up to the decision to abandon nuclear power, which was motivated almost entirely with reference to Fukushima.

Nevertheless, the most important factor in German environmental law has been the role of EU legislation. Here is it less appropriate to see political motives behind the adoption of these laws by successive German governments: much rather it is a basic fact about the environment which has promoted the growth of supra-national legislation. The framework of the nation state is manifestly too small to tackle significant environmental problems. Krickerode was built upstream on a small German river, its smoke and discharges ruined a water-meadow and a length of stream. How else than through supra-national legislation could nations tackle pollution issues on rivers such as the Rhine and Danube, which flow through half a dozen European countries, or control one of the first international pollutants, the acid rain, produced in the UK and other west European countries and destroying the forests of Germany and Scandinavia? The move to Europe was only logical.

The wider pictures can be seen only outside the framework of specifically German law. Of all the trials discussed in this book only the Flick case is based more strongly on international law than the events detailed in this chapter. It is European legislation which has come to dominate environmental matters, less out of the indifference of individual member states (though this continues to be a problem), or the unsuitability of German courts: most evidently, developments are a result of the awareness that environmental issues transcend national jurisdictions, and that only continental and global solutions are in any way appropriate. While the policing and monitoring of environmental crime remain initially at least in the hands of national governments, its legislative framework is European, and its mechanisms transcend national boundaries.

It could sound, therefore, as if a German chapter on this topic were irrelevant, and indeed, if this book were simply a history of jurisprudence in the Federal Republic, environmental topics would occupy a modest and highly technical place in the story. There is a simple reason why this is not so. If there is one feature of the Federal Republic which has struck non-Germans for the last fifty years, it has been the obvious, everyday and at one time distinctively German concern about the environment. From the 1950s on, generations of Irish and British students visiting Germany had to learn the importance of separating their daily rubbish and of claiming the deposit back on drink bottles and cans. By now recycling has made much progress, yet, while not even the sixteen million plastic bottles dumped each day in the UK have influenced government policy, the Germans have always taken a far more rational approach to environmental issues.

This was not just an urban matter. British and Irish students were obliged, while strolling through the German countryside, to understand the importance of protecting the *Grundwasser* – this at a time when they did not even know how to translate the word into English – and from the mid-1970s on they have had to find their way through German culture in the face of almost continuous protests and demonstrations relating to the environment.

For the last forty years the teaching materials with which students are trained in the German language have reflected the concerns of the German press about environmental issues. In a striking marriage of environmentalism with international politics, the fervour with which students opposed American missiles being set up in the German countryside was more than matched by the messianic zeal with which all ages campaigned against peaceful atomic power and its threat to the environment. The list of causes, as we shall see, has an almost liturgical quality: Wackersdorf, Brokdorf, Kalkar, Gorleben – these names became as familiar as Pershing, Baader or Bayern München. Certainly anyone wishing to understand Federal German history needs to get a grasp of this element, and if all this chapter achieves is to show the rather marginal function of German courts in these processes, the point will have been made.

Quite apart from any other repercussions, it is only this background which makes explicable the emergence of the first genuinely new political party in the FRG, the Greens. Their first electoral success was in Bremen in the state elections of autumn 1979. Shortly after the party was formally constituted – earlier and more effectively than in other European states –, and within a short period the party found its way into state and federal governments.[5] It also shows the emergence of a form of political direct action far wider than Baader-Meinhof and far more effective, since it chose to play the game according to and enriching the rule of law: the so-called citizens' initiatives, the *Bürgerinitiativen*. Protecting the natural environment has transformed the political environment, both nationally and – as Sands and Peel show – internationally. The Rio conference in the environmental field explicitly recognized 'the right of individual citizens to participate in decision-making process' and – as we shall see, this was of crucial important in the anti-nuclear movement – to have access to information'.[6]

For reasons of this kind this chapter needs to tread especially carefully. Not only are environmental issues hardly less acute now than at other stages of human history, but it is of the very nature of the topic that present-day concerns reflect and are usually a product of concerted political campaigns, in which not only ideologically driven pressure-groups but investigative, sometimes sensationalist journalism continue to play a significant part. Because of the highly technical questions thrown up by environmental issues, a non-specialist may be tempted to regard as scientifically correct what are in fact simply political decisions or journalistic scoops. The ban on the production of DDT or dioxin (in the Stockholm Convention of 2001), just as the abandonment of nuclear power generation, has involved broad public opinion as well as that disinterested scientific expertise by which international environmental law likes to see itself being driven. While my narrative makes no pretence at neutrality in its preference for nature reserves over industrial waste-dumps,

5 A text close in time and spirit to the emergence of the Greens is: Elim Papadakis (1984). See also: Conradt (2001, p. 126 f).

6 Quoted Sands & Peel (2012, p. 91).

telling the story of other campaigns involves the risk of siding with the political victors or successful journalistic scoops, rather than with scientific objectivity. I hope my readers will be on their guard against me.

10.3 Violence among the Trees

One of the causes most beloved by environmental activists in the Federal Republic concerned an issue which would have been close to old Pfister's heart: the building of the west runway at Frankfurt airport. The time-scale of this project overlapped more or less exactly both with the state's adoption of the *Berufsverbot* and with the activities of Baader-Meinhof. Some authorities understood the response to the proposed runway as further proof of the link between radicalism and violent hostility to the state, yet as we look back from the present day the issue itself seems rather archaic, like the defence of Pfister's mill. With the planned expansion of London's Heathrow airport and after decades when former Soviet and US military air-strips, following heavy canvassing by local authorities, have been taken over by budget airlines rather than returned to the landscape, the issue at Frankfurt seems in retrospect idealistic and principled. It concerned the preservation of about three hundred acres of the forests which stretch out to the south-east of the city. The question was the conservation of nature in its pure form, the conflict between economic modernization and the natural environment.

When the funding for the new runway was approved in November 1967, forty-four formal complaints were registered: when the plans for the terminal were published a hundred objections were raised. These were duly rejected by the administrative court of Hessen, which concerned itself with the checking of the formal aspects of the authorities' decision-making rather than with any environmental issue. After this judgment the occupations of the site began in earnest, involving at times over a hundred thousand protesters. Since the demonstrators – when expelled from the site – spilled out onto the nearby major motorway and closed it, police methods in clearing the sites became more robust, with injuries on both sides. One of the principal organizers of the protests, Alexander Schubart, was dismissed from the public service (defending the environment clearly did not come under the heading of upholding the 'basic democratic order' to which civil servants were committed) and given a suspended sentence. The state government (SPD) rejected the call for a referendum on the issue, and gradually the demonstrations diminished in size, as the democratic possibilities were exhausted. After the runway was taken into use, a small protest presence was established at the edge of the site, but when in November 1987 the authorities attempted to clear that camp, two demonstrators opened fire on the police (using stolen police weapons) and killed two policemen. Two demonstrators were subsequently sentenced, one for manslaughter. The violence of the urban terror movement had crossed over into ecological protest: what was to become the perennial dilemma of the ecological movement had declared itself dramatically in one of its first test-cases.

The opposition to the extended runway in Frankfurt anticipated what was perhaps the principal ecological concern of the mid-years of the Federal Republic: the death of the forests caused by acid rain. More than any other, this issue touched the essence of traditional German views of nature, for the huge forests of Germany have, at least since the Romantic period, represented a core value of both local environmental concerns and national identity. Over the years massive sums of money has been put into measures to reduce SO2 emissions. The matter has remained consensus politics for all parties, and much national and European policy-making has been driven by the strength of German public feeling on this point.

The issue implies a need to reflect on the enthusiasms of the nineteenth century. Raabe's account of industry polluting nature was far-seeing and for its time far from naïve. By distancing his text from the sentimentalizing of nature (we noted that his principal character joins up with the industrial world which has destroyed his father's mill) Raabe exposed an issue raised by the positive aspects of the NS law of 1935: the link between nationalism and environmental thinking in the cult of *local* nature (expressed most disagreeably in the doctrine of Blood and Soil) – a dimension from which, one might suggest, only the international dimension of environmental planning can rescue it. Even today we can see links between anthropocentric 'green thinking' and not always reasonable forms of dogmatic local patriotism. Such tendencies caused Mark Halsey in a recent essay to search for ways of defining environmental offences in less emotive terms than as 'a crime against nature' (2009). In previous chapters we have seen that 'natural feelings' were a poor guide to justice: environmental issues are another area, Halsey argues, where we need to be careful of natural feeling. The remainder of this chapter, however, will show that it is neither easy nor always desirable to hold back natural feeling.

10.4 Chemical Pollution – 'Everyone the Loser'

If we are looking for reasons why environmental issues so seldom come to court, then we might start with the chemical, dioxin.[7] Dioxin was at one time

7 Details of the dioxin scandals, in Ludwigsburg, Vietnam, USA and Hamburg are taken from Degler & Uentzelmann (1984).

present in an alarmingly wide range of industrial and domestic products, from cosmetics, wood-preservatives and hydraulic oils to herbicides. More widely known, of course, was the use of dioxin in Agent Orange, the defoliant produced by Dow Chemicals, with which the US forces tried to flush out the Viet Cong from the protective jungle. The Vietnamese people continues to suffer from the after-effects of that form of chemical warfare, and even domestically the US government has had to pay $180m to compensate its own veterans whose health was wrecked by their contact with Agent Orange.

As if this Agent had not been warning enough to the Federal Republic of dioxin's toxicity, there had been a serious accident at the BASF factory in Ludwigshafen in 1953, one which the company did everything possible to keep secret, insisting that the workers contaminated by dioxin were treated only by the BASF's own medical team. These were the years when the economic miracle seemed more important than regard for the work-force's health, but even in the 1960s and 1970s society was slow to recognize the danger. The experiences of Love Canal and Times Beach – both of these sites in the USA had had to be evacuated because of dioxin contamination – should have been warning enough. But after July 1976, when scores of people were killed and injured by the dioxin explosion in the la Roche plant in Seveso, north of Milan, public awareness was finally aroused. The question was whether it was already too late.

Dioxin unfortunately damages the health of the community in less spectacular ways than explosions. When various types of waste are incinerated, for instance, significant quantities of dioxin are released into the atmosphere. In addition, dioxin can seep into the ground-water from industrial plants and industrial waste-storage areas. This was shown by the dioxin scandal which broke in Hamburg in the early 1980s.

Following a TV documentary drawing attention to an unusually high level of birth defects in a suburb of Hamburg close to a huge, privately run industrial waste-tip, the SPD Senator with responsibility for the environment, Wolfgang Curilla, started his own investigation. He soon discovered that unacceptable quantities of dioxin were getting into the atmosphere via incineration, and that even larger quantities were seeping into the water system. Contrary to the managing company's claims, the tip was not properly sealed off, and seepage was taking place both into the ground itself and directly into the water-system. Hamburg was sitting on a huge poison-store.

The obvious place to start the search for the source of the dioxin was the chemical company C. H. Boehringer Sohn – a company which had had acted as one of the suppliers to Dow Chemicals. Typically for these years, the company had been anything but scrupulous in handling its own chemicals. Examination of the company's records showed that forty-one barrels of contaminated material could not be accounted for. The assumption was that they were buried, and leaking, somewhere on the dump. Curilla, using the local administrative court, managed to pressurize the company into stopping their dioxin production (it has been doubted whether the chlorophenols with whose production the company continued are significantly less toxic than dioxin) and – apart from keeping his investigations confidential – Curilla himself appears to have acted quickly and responsibly. This view was not shared by the electorate, however, and at the local elections following the documentary the newly formed Green Party made dramatic progress at the polls. The political lesson was clear: absolute transparency was essential in environmental politics. Already too much had been concealed, and the people of Hamburg would not accept what looked like collusion between state and industry. However, neither the next legal steps nor the required environmental remedies were remotely clear.

On the environmental side Curilla's office suffered from a significant lack of technical know-how. Characteristically for such situations the regulatory authorities were overly dependent on the offending industry both for the environmental testing and for any technical solutions to the problem once it had been identified. It clearly was not feasible, as in Love Canal or Time Beach, simply to relocate the entire population of the Hamburg suburb. The cost of removing the whole dump and the contaminated topsoil was estimated at between 20 and 40 billion DM. Against this background, the company persuaded the city authorities that any attempt at legal action would – in the words of Hamburg's First Minister – 'leave everyone the loser'.[8] But whichever way round, a solution was hard to find. While there was no suggestion of improper pressure being exerted by the company, it had not escaped the attention of the media that a future president of the FRG, Richard von Weizsäcker, was on the board of Boehringer at the time. At all events, no trial took place. The scale of the pollution seems to have defeated both the political and the legal processes. Sands and Peel, discussing questions of liability for pollution, observe 'an unwillingness to establish rules of international law that might impose excessive costs'.[9] The Hamburg case makes clear that it is not just international law which is informed by that reluctance.

We can find cases in which dioxin pollution actually came to trial from the intervening years, but these actions took place on a quite different scale: they both were and involved chicken-feed. For instance in 2016, after a long

8 The Hamburg government chief's comment in: Dioxin: Ruhigstellung veranlaßt, in: *Der Spiegel*, 1/1985, pp. 54–6, here 55.

9 Sands & Peel (2012, p. 701).

procession through the various courts, a small animal-foodstuffs manufacturer in Schleswig-Holstein lost his appeal against a fine for producing and distributing in a number of federal states animal-feeds contaminated with dioxin. The case had set off widespread public alarm, for it demonstrated how easily dioxin could enter the human food-chain through contaminated meat, eggs and fruit. The *Oberlandesgericht* confirmed fines totalling less than five thousand euro.

If we ask why the fines were so low, two explanations offer themselves. First, clearly, environmental legislation is aimed at preventing crime, rather than punishing it. It has always been in the official mind that the greatest financial punishment a company can suffer is to lose the confidence of its customers, and that this sanction from the market will represent a more realistic deterrent than any set tariff of fines imposed by the courts. Regulatory authorities, comments Rob White in his discussion of 'environmental criminology and ecological justice' (2008), will therefore always be more interested in strategic alliances with industry rather than criminal prosecutions. Not simply because of the sheer scale of environmental problems, but on account of the difficulty of establishing true liability within a large corporation. That's the reason why the small chicken-feed companies, rather than major companies, end up in court. '*Mens rea* required for felony convictions is easier to prove in a small, or closed corporation setting'.[10]

But there is a further reason for the lack of energetic legal action against polluters, one buried deep in the sad logic of the world's present economic order. The presence of dioxin in the human food-chain is a part of the 'boomerang' effect, similar in structure to the effect which Hannah Arendt observed in political ideas.[11] Because much of the agricultural support to the Third World takes the form of agricultural chemicals to increase local food-production, many companies have used the Third World to dispose of products no longer found acceptable to the European market. They appeared to copy the strategy of the tobacco companies, which – as the enthusiasm for high-tar cigarettes diminished in Europe – marketed these products more intensively in the Third World, with the difference that in the case of agricultural chemicals the problem came back to haunt Europe. The crops contaminated in the Third World by, in this case, dioxin in pesticides formed part of the ingredients of the animal

10 White (2008, pp. 194–5).

11 The 'boomerang' effect is described in: Degler & Uentzelmann (1984, p. 18). The early cases of dioxin in animal foodstuffs are described in: Christoph Peck (1984). The later, less innocent case, in: *Der Spiegel*-Online, January 5 2011. The end of the case in: https://www.topagrar.com/news/Home-top-News-Dioxin-Skandal-Urteil-rechtskraeftig-4414984.html.

food-stuffs manufactured in the First World from imported ingredients. This process is well known to manufacturers, since – as a *Spiegel*-documentation at the time cheerfully informed its readers – they cannot actually remove the contamination before using these imported ingredients: they merely dilute them until a level of contamination has been reached which lies under prevailing European norms. Whatever this may say about the ethics of the food-industry, the practice implies a strong reason why fines are small and individually applied. The only alternative – as it had appeared to be in Hamburg – is a solution of such radicalism (i.e. overturning aid programmes, banning the export of toxic materials, compensating third world producers, etc.) and expense that, in the First Minister's words, 'everyone would be a loser'.

For the experts in technical regulation both the above scenarios – Boehringer and the chicken-feed – are all too familiar. It is agreed that there was a huge deficit in enforcement in the 1970s and 1980s, which was only gradually replaced on the regulation side by a range of EU directives, most notably on incineration (November 1988), initially concerned with SO_2, and subsequently widened to include general air pollution. The process did not stop there, and there are now some four hundred regulations concerning water-quality. Although the EU standards were not as rigorous as the original German values and despite the general assumption that the system is working well, the level of unknown offences is estimated variously at between 25 and 90% of the known cases. The paradox is that the principal accomplishment of the years since the early 1980s is felt to be the EMAS (the Eco-Management and Audit Scheme) initiative. While we would have to concede that state regulatory bodies have acquired far greater technical competence than was available to the authorities in Ludwigsburg or Hamburg, this increased competence has not been accompanied by a commensurate increase in their readiness to intervene. In particular, the EMAS specifically leaves to the incineration plants the responsibility for monitoring their own emissions infringements and for reporting. While there is a specialist national regulatory service, voluntary compliance is the aim and the reality of this initiative.[12]

The more serious drawback with this system is a financial one. Up to now the electricity-generating companies and the waste-incineration plants have had no difficulty in implementing the scheme and even in tightening their own standards, for the simple reason that they have been able to pass on directly to the consumer the additional costs involved in this monitoring and reporting. The arrangement, however, entirely depends on the existence of monopolistic

12 My account of the implementation of European environmental directives, including EMAS, is taken from: Bültmann & Wätzold (2002).

suppliers of services. With the liberalization of the energy market, for instance, where end-price has clearly become the primary factor in consumer choice, producers are given a big disincentive to accept supplementary costs for monitoring. This would be likely to become another area in which, from the citizens' point of view – in the words of ministers in the UK looking recently at the pricing of energy – 'the market is just not working'. The temptation under a weak regulatory regime to skimp or cheat on figures would be strong. In the Federal Republic the situation has already brought various citizens' initiatives into direct conflict with the state, for they strongly favour the greater involvement of the regulatory authorities. They have resented the 'cosy' agreements between the state and energy suppliers and incineration companies and have demanded to be represented in these negotiations. They have on occasion been successful in their actions to prevent new incineration plants being opened, but that has not solved the potential problem with existing plants.

In short, the openness and universality of EU directives on the environment have both created the possibility of acting against public authorities or private companies to prevent infringements, for instance of clean air provisions, but it has also created a situation of diminished transparency, throwing into question not just the complacency with which environmental issues were handled by the political establishment, but the likelihood of effective enforcement.

10.5 Reflections on a Small Victory for the Environment

There is another important dimension to these kinds of planning decisions. I have so far risked portraying the Hamburg situation, or the contaminated chicken-feed, simplistically, as if the problem arose between two parties: a more or less scrupulous private industry sector (in the case of Hamburg, both Boehringer and the owners of the waste dump) and the affected public. On this model the state of Hamburg, its Senate and the Senate's environmental office-holder placed themselves between the two parties in a number of roles, ranging from investigation, with the purpose of allaying public fears aroused by the TV documentary, to protective action, halting Boehringer's dioxin production, an action supported by the administrative court.

This model is true up to a point, but it leaves out the whole process by which the state itself was complicit in the problem and involved in both sides of the case. (It was this complicity which was partly responsible for the governing party's subsequent punishment by the Hamburg electorate.) It was, after all, the state which had enacted the planning laws which had permitted the dump to be created in the first place. While it may have been impracticable physically to remove the dump, any attempt to oblige the owners or the beneficiaries of the dump to remove it or clean up the site would undoubtedly have involved a legal case based on the conditions under which planning permission for the dump had originally been granted. It's more than possible that the original permission would be found to have come from a previous jurisdiction when, for instance, regulations for water-purity had not been established, or when the NS régime was more concerned with industrial production than with urban environmental policy.

There's a second, no less important time-lag. Science is always evolving, and what is good science at one time quickly becomes overhauled. In consequence the law, and with it the state authorities, will – as Sendler (2003) points out[13] – always be some way behind in monitoring and legislating for technological advances, just as, in the majority of cases, industry itself would have proceeded differently in the past had it possessed the knowledge available in the present. With or without historical and scientific change, in most environmental issues except the most crassly criminal, the state will inevitably be on both sides of environmental legal disputes. That's where the complexity starts.

To illustrate the complexity of environmental cases within the compass of this single chapter is not easy, for the complexity is not only caused by the state authorities being, as I suggested, involved on both sides of the dispute and by rapid technical changes: it is also caused by overlapping legal provisions, by possible conflicts between federal and regional authority and by a mind-blowing miasma of administrative detail – Papadakis speaks tellingly of the 'circularity' of political communication in this field, while a later observer compared the multiple complexity of environmental issues to a kaleidoscope, not just multiplicity therefore, but constant change.[14] Environmental cases of this kind are further clouded by the fact that they often run over a number of years, if not decades, invariably under governments of different political complexion. Thanks to the generous assistance of the legal firm responsible for the successful conduct of the case, I wish to give here a sample outline of such complexities, in a case which was heard by the Hesse state administrative court, which reached its judgment on November 23 1988, and which was decided on appeal at the Federal Administrative Court on November 26 1991.[15]

13 Sendler (2003, p. 72).

14 Papadakis (1996, p. 54). The kaleidoscope comparison comes from Edith Brown Weiss, quoted in Sands & Peel (2012, p. 92).

15 My profound gratitude goes to Herr Matthias Möller-Meinecke of the Rechtsanwaltskanzlei EDIFICIA in Frankfurt for drawing this case to my attention and subsequently generously supplying the documentation. Details: Hessischer Verwaltungsgerichtshof 5. Senat. Date of decision: 23.11.88. File: 5 UE 1040/84. The appeal: Bundesverwaltungsgericht 7. Senat. Date of decision: 26.11.1991. File: 7 C 16/89.

The case concerns a disused mine-pit known as Grube Messel, situated in the south-east of the state of Hesse, between Frankfurt and Offenbach. The pit had been worked from the mid-nineteenth century for the extraction of iron-ore, subsequently for anthracite and clay and finally for the oil contained in the extensive shale layer. In this layer a few interesting fossils were discovered in the early 1900s, and these discoveries were accompanied by a brief academic interest. Only after 1971, when the industrial exploitation of the shale layer stopped, did fossil collectors make a series of discoveries at the site – discoveries of global importance, which led in 1995 to the recognition of Grube Messel by UNESCO as a world heritage site. Extraordinary discoveries have continued to be made there, and the area is now both a protected area for wild-life and a site of special scientific interest, where – to quote the environment minister for the state of Hesse speaking in 2002 – one can observe 'a successful example of contractual nature protection' (he was referring to the management agreement entered into by the state, the local authority and the local community) and 'a modern and effective form of conservation'.[16] He was able to point to the flourishing population of black-throated divers now settled on the lake and to the adoption of Grube Messel by the EU programme of networked protected reserves, 'Natura 2000'. The site's importance in palaeontology, in particular for early mammal fossils, has been compared to that of Pompeii for human archaeology. Behind this gratifying success-story, however, lie twenty years of legal and administrative conflict.

In 1974 private interests founded an association to establish the use of Grube Messel as a major industrial waste-disposal site – a purpose to which its central location in an area with a wide range of chemical and other industries made the pit particularly suited. At the time, scientific interests appeared to have been satisfied by First Minister Holger Börner (SPD) promising twenty years of access to the western part of the site, which had previously proved especially rich in fossils. However, this harmony between development and science not only excluded environmental considerations, but proved to be temporary. Over the next years the state government came into the hands of different coalitions: for a while SPD – FDP; after 1984 a minority SPD government was kept in power with Green support. From 1985 the Greens entered the ruling coalition, only for both to be replaced in 1987 by the CDU. These shifts in government brought different general approaches to the environment, notably when at one stage the Greens announced the specific policy of abandoning the plan for the industrial waste-disposal unit. This policy was in turn reversed by the

16 Press release of the Hesse Ministry of the Environment, August 12 2002.

CDU. But the significant actions took place on the level of the law rather than in politics.

In 1977 the state had issued a regional plan, in which no particular use had been specified for Grube Messel. Representations were made by the consortium of regional industries seeking planning permission for industrial waste-disposal on the site. In 1981 the establishment of the industrial waste-disposal unit was officially approved and the regional plan altered accordingly. That approval was upheld by the local administrative court when the consortium took legal action against the Green environment minister's policy decision to refuse permission for the industrial waste-disposal unit. The administrative court in Darmstadt delivered its judgment in favour of the state planning authority – and thereby also of the consortium – on January 20 1984. Though a similar motion was put through the coalition in 1985 it was withdrawn in 1987 when the CDU state government was formed. The future for industrial waste-disposal seemed assured.

At this point a small citizens' initiative (*Bürgerinitiative*), which had been formed in Messel with the explicit intention of opposing the building of the waste-disposal unit, lodged a fresh objection to the project, even though by this time ninety per cent of the work to prepare the site for waste disposal, including the erection of permanent buildings, had been carried out. At the basis of this late objection was the claim that the community's own planning for Grube Messel had foreseen an entirely different use for the area, based on its scientific importance, as had now been certified by the renowned Senckenberg natural history museum in Frankfurt. This time the objection was heard by the administrative court in Kassel.

As we read the documents of the court's deliberations, it is striking to note what a small role specific environmental issues actually played. Instead, attention was primarily focused on regulations relating to the planning process itself and on the conditions under which the planning authorities could legitimately change the original planning document, in which, as we saw, no reference had been made to any industrial use for the pit. When finding against the industry, the court based its judgment on the fact that the revisions made to the area plan in 1981 had not included complete technical details of waste-water and solid waste management on the site. Although the 1981 planning decision had been taken on the clear understanding that the authorities would be presented with complete technical details of these matters at a later date – thus routinely ensuring that the site was in conformity with the requirements of environmental and building-regulations – the legal team engaged by the *Bürgerinitiative* identified in this a breach of the planning process, namely the requirement for 'completeness' in the 1981 application. Completeness was meant here less in the sense of what today is called transparency: it referred much rather to the level of technical detail entered on an application. The court agreed with this submission, and the case was won.

Since it might have been felt that the industry had lost its case on a technicality, and since the basic right of the planning authorities to modify their own regional plan and to grant permission for the location of an industrial waste-disposal unit at Messel pit was in no way challenged – any more than the right of the state to introduce legislation varying the conditions of its own planning decisions – it caused little surprise when the industry, in conjunction with the state ministry for the environment, sought leave to appeal this judgment. The Federal Administrative Court granted leave to appeal and delivered its judgment in 1991.

The outcome of the appeal must have seriously frayed the nerves of the legal team and its clients, who had benefitted from the judgment and against whom the appeal was directed. The federal court explicitly stated that the outcome of the appeal was entirely open and questioned the decision of the lower court on at least three substantive points. In the first place it expressed itself not entirely convinced that the requirement of completeness had been appropriately applied to the circumstances of the case. There was no dispute over the requirement for the planning permission for the industrial waste-disposal unit to have taken explicit regard to the environmental consequences, especially for the ground-water (that had been the substance of an expert opinion tabled by counsel for the local community). In fact, however, the court pointed out the likelihood that such provisions would in fact have been adopted in accordance with sections of the planning regulations which had not been specified in the actual text of the decision, on which the lower court had based its verdict. It implied the possibility that these sections were included in other relevant documentation, which the lower court had not examined. It seemed possible to the appeal court that the requirement of completeness might not have had to be met in every separate section of the planning decision.

The federal court further questioned whether the lower court had been right to see this alleged shortcoming in the planning decision as sufficient reason to oblige the state authorities to cancel their plan for the industrial waste-disposal unit. It was possible, the federal court said, that the Kassel court could simply have contented itself with requiring the shortcomings to be made good in the documentation and on this basis could have allowed the development to go ahead.

No less significant was the third area of doubt raised by the appellate court. The court pointed out that it had *not* examined the question of the validity of the community's own plan for the pit. This remark was important on two levels: first in considering the overall relationship between a local and a regional plan – a question which the Darmstadt court appeared to have settled in its judgment of 1984, when it gave clear priority to the state's planning activity over local opinion. The federal court went on, however, to suggest that – even if one left that question out of consideration – the issue might not have been simply an abstract conflict between the planning 'sovereignty' of the state and that of the local community, but something much more tangible: the court required further examination of both the provenance and, no less importantly, the date of that community planning document. Was the local community's plan sufficiently concrete, and did it have any binding quality? It was, after all, a *post hoc* objection based on a local planning decision which might itself have been constructed subsequently to the time-frame of the state's planning decision, and therefore invalid.

Fortunately for the community of Messel and for the black-throated divers which adorn its waters, all these considerations were expressed by the court in the subjunctive, a form of the verb which is known in German as the 'unreal'. The court had no reason to turn into reality its speculations about possible revisions of the lower court's findings, for the reason that on June 25 1991 – while the appeal was still being considered – the authorities in Hesse announced that they did not intend to implement the planning decision permitting the establishment of the industrial waste-disposal unit. They explained this move to the court by reference to the fact that since February 1990 the state government no longer regarded Grube Messel as a site for industrial waste disposal. At that point all parties to the appeal agreed that there was no further substance to the court action, and the federal court needed little prompting to award costs against the state of Hesse, which had, as the court pointed out, 'itself brought about this decisive event [i.e. the change of policy] and thus of its own free will assumed the part of loser in the action'. It went on to underline that 'the motive for the state's action lay entirely outside the sphere of the court'. This was a discreet reference to the fact that, following the announcement of the appeal against the Kassel decision, no fewer than 12,000 objections to the dump had been received.

The third phase of the action concerned the demolition of the buildings.[17] For the local community the action which it brought and which was heard by the Hesse Administrative Court in November 1993 did not bring success.

17 The third action was heard before the Hessischer Verwaltungsgerichtshof 5. Senat. Date of decision: 11.11.93. File: 5 UE 441/88.

At various points in the court's deliberation the precarious nature of the whole legal position was made clear. Central to this was the insistence of the court that the original planning decision of 1977, including the 1981 amendment permitting the locating of the dump in Grube Messel, was still valid. Neither the 1988 court decision, still less the 1991 decision of the federal court, altered that legality. It would require fresh legislation to alter the status of the plan, not the political decision of the state government not to proceed with one aspect of it. It was incorrect to suggest that the purpose-built buildings on the site had been built contrary to the law and therefore should be removed, despite the fact that they were entirely unsuitable both to the general character of the area and to the particular future use of the site. At a future date a change of state policy could re-establish the buildings' absolute legality, for the legality of the plan had not been diminished by the previous court-cases. In any case, in accordance with the principle of proportionality, the legal situation in no way justified imposing on the industry the high costs of demolition. So the buildings could stand.

What then does this case show? First, it makes clear that within the complexity of regulation controlling local authority actions and the added complexity of environmental law, it is possible for a far-seeing legal team to win unlikely victories; or at least to postpone the final victory of the state long enough for the political dimension of the case to be fully appreciated by the state's politicians. Perhaps it shows too that courts may tend to lay particular emphasis on the local dimension of the planning process, even if the local dimension is not articulated with the formal rigour expected of state agencies and has not been given full legal authority for its planning activities.

It would be mere speculation to ask to what extent the possibility that the state government was influenced in abandoning support for the waste-disposal project by the thought that Grube Messel might one day be recognized as scientifically important by UNESCO and subsequently by the European Commission. It's likely that the Hesse state authorities and the governing parties looked back over a series of situations in which environmental issues had become a liability for the party in power. If that were so, their response implied that environmental law – though it was little discussed during the Kassel trial and in the federal court – compensates in its political force for the ambiguities under which it suffers in administrative practice. While, as we saw, Halsey argued against the undercurrents of 'natural' sentiment which he detected in much ecological thinking, the Grube Messel case demonstrates that ecological thinking has managed to assume more progressive political overtones, although these weightings too are of course – as for instance in the case of European Commission support – themselves subject to radical political change. In particular, encouragement from Brussels can easily be portrayed as interference by Brussels.

At all events, the decisive step in this case was political rather than legal in character. In the light of some of the speculations of the federal court, it seems possible that, on their own, the legal instruments might not have managed finally to shift a state determined at all costs to implement its planning decisions, even when they so seriously threatened the environment.

10.6 Problems of Atomic Power: Atomkraft? Nein Danke

The complex issues behind the enforcement of environmental law become clearer as we discuss the subject of the last section of this chapter: the industrial development of another silent killer, radioactivity. So too do the political implications of the topic, for the extent of public disquiet and protest far outweighed any protests which had gone before. No-one could have lived through the 1980s without having seen – and possibly worn – the small, round and highly iconic badge carrying the slogan: *Atomic power? No thank you!*. In nuclear energy the gap in information and understanding between the public and government and industry has proved to be still wider than in the problems of chemical waste. The technology was much newer and unproven, and, perhaps most problematically, it has proved extraordinarily difficult to find reliable professional opinions on policy options produced by experts who were themselves not identified either with the nuclear industry itself or with the public opposition to it. Once again the shining impartiality of science was hard to achieve. As a result, the state agencies are invariably suspected of being complicit with state policy when they assure the public of the safety of a particular scheme. This emerged starkly in the Gorleben hearing, by the end of which the evidence supplied by the two state commissions concerned with reactor and radiation safety was publicly discredited and finally withdrawn altogether.

The development of nuclear power is similar to the problems of chemical waste in that it hardly offers our narrative many significant trials. Developments were conditioned from the outset, for obvious reasons, by Allied attitudes towards the Federal Republic possessing any form of nuclear capability – much as similar concerns have affected US-Iranian relations over the last decades. In the mid-1950s, with the integration of German forces into NATO, the way was clear for the Federal Republic to enter EURATOM, and the Federal Republic was able to embark on the more than thorny path to nuclear energy, a policy change marked by the passing of the Atom Law in 1960 – a piece of legislation quite distinct from other environmental law.[18] Since nuclear technology itself was in a state of continuous development, there were frequent changes of policy, both by the industry itself and by the government, but not every change of plan had a technical origin. Some were caused by local circumstances, others by global considerations (most notably by the escalation of the oil-price in the second half of the 1960s); increasingly, however, political pressures have played the major part. And in the celebrated case of the atomic physicist Klaus Traube the security forces – planting listening devices in his home because they suspected him of passing over nuclear secrets to the RAF – not only further embarrassed the government but discredited the pro-nuclear lobby. (Traube had changed his opinions and become an opponent of nuclear power: an inconvenient conversion and one which had to make him a potential traitor in the eyes of the authorities.[19])

As one would expect, quite apart from protecting the public against the dangers inherent in operating nuclear plants, the focus of most of the debate has from the start been what to do with the still radioactive spent uranium which the commercial power-stations were going to produce. An early proposal – not just in the Federal Republic: the policy reflected a global consensus – was to store the nuclear waste in a geophysically stable environment underground. The extensive salt-mines in central Germany seemed to offer an ideal site. As soon as the federal government announced that no new reactors would be approved without adequate arrangements being made for nuclear waste management, it purchased the salt-mine workings at Asse in Lower Saxony, some ten miles south-east of Wolfenbüttel, and started experimental work on the site, which ran until 2007, when the site was closed. In February 1977 the government of Lower Saxony declared its readiness to test the area of Gorleben, an obscure hamlet in the east of the state situated above the salt layer, as the site for a re-processing plant, and a month later the DWK (a consortium of industries interested in the reprocessing of nuclear fuel) made formal application to

---

18 An outline of contemporary international approaches to nuclear regulation can be found in Sands & Peel (2012, p. 78 f).

19 On Traube see Wikipedia. The case brought about the resignation of Werner Maihofer, minister of the interior, in 1978: two whistle-blowers were accused of betraying state secrets, and in 2004 the BVerfG finally passed a scathing judgment on the behaviour of the BfV. Trust in government had not been increased when the First Minister of Baden-Württemberg, Filbinger, was found to be granting nuclear contracts to a company in which he had an undeclared interest. The protesters' sense that nuclear development was a conspiracy seemed well founded. See: Papadakis (1984, p. 65).

establish a plant at Gorleben. With this application the question of the acceptability of such a facility to the local population shifted above ground.

The story of the following years has been repeated in many countries and in more than one region of the Federal Republic. In all these places it has followed a pattern similar to that of the fracking controversy which continues to divide western countries. A rural area, chosen partly for its distance from population centres and partly because of its ability to handle the initial requirements for water supply and dispersal, has been encouraged to put itself forward for consideration. Local politicians and regional assemblies have tended initially to encourage such projects. On the one hand their support has come from party loyalty, in that they represented the same parties which had reached decisions on the federal level. On the other hand, regional authorities have had in mind the in-flow of capital investment and jobs to their otherwise underdeveloped region. In any case, politicians have assumed that where nobody much lives nobody much will care.

For reasons of this kind the woods near Gorleben became the chosen destination for storage and re-processing, agreed by federal and state authorities at the highest level. From this moment on the DWK started to provide itself with the legal instruments certifying its processes as safe. (This was the first stage of federal complicity.) The next stage was that the consortium started to buy up land on which to store spent reactor elements – an action which immediately destabilized land-prices and drew protesters to the region. As soon as the name of Gorleben was known, 15,000 demonstrators turned up on the planned site. At this point conflicts between land-owners, small and large, in the area became public: loyalty to the region and profitability were hotly debated.

The next years saw a series of test-drillings, bitter manoeuvring among political parties, and heated debates about the transport of the spent fuel-rods. At this time the acronym CASTOR became known to the public for the first time: these were the round containers in which radioactive material was to be transported by rail from the nuclear power stations from within Germany and from further afield.

Doubts about nuclear re-processing were greatly increased by the so-called Gorleben-Hearing, a week-long public debate in Hannover in March/April 1979, at which international experts and interested parties discussed the advisability and in particular the security of re-processing. The Hearing opened at a dramatic moment in the history of nuclear power, in that the failure of the cooling system at Harrisburg (Three Mile Island) had just launched what threatened to be a catastrophic nuclear accident. International experts immediately projected on to the map of Germany and Northern Europe the potential consequences of a similar accident at Gorleben. At one level the state of Lower Saxony co-operated fully with this conference and at the time was ready to accept its conclusion: namely that there was no case for embarking on re-processing. When other countries were pulling out of re-processing, the conference agreed that it was illogical for the Federal Republic to press ahead with it. First Minister Albrecht formally announced in May 1979 that the state would not grant permission for re-processing at Gorleben. At the same time, however, he announced an extensive programme of research, test-boring and the establishment of a storage facility on the site. In short, while he ruled out re-processing, for the time being, Gorleben remained a centre for a range of activities which were sufficient to cause activists to renew their protests.

It was striking that Albrecht, while stressing the absolute need for safety in all nuclear projects, took a very different line to that of the experts. The experts had debated the meaning of safety in the nuclear industry. Should safety be defined to mean that the specific dangers of a project had been clearly identified and removed, or should dangers be presumed until absolute safety had been finally proven? This was an absorbing scientific debate. However, Albrecht's view was that re-processing should not proceed until the general public was persuaded that safety was guaranteed – a truly political answer to a technical question and one which left the door open for a campaign to persuade the population that storage, rather than re-processing, was safe. Albrecht's difficulty would be to carry through that persuasion effectively.

An important element in the argument in favour of nuclear re-processing was the imminent development of a new type of reactor, the so-called fast breeder. Both the representatives of DWK and Albrecht himself made clear that this development could offer the financial and technical justification for reprocessing. (Technical experts at the Hearing disputed this opinion.) It was therefore a highly sensitive matter when in 1979 – in response to an individual constitutional complaint, demanding that the absolute priority of human life guaranteed in the *Grundgesetz* should logically lead to the prohibition of the development of more nuclear reactors – the BVerfG gave judgment on the fast breeder at Kalkar (on the lower Rhine). In certain respects the BVerfG was called on to make its most important judgment in the environmental sector.

The court's judgment was unremarkable, partly at least because of its recognition of its own absolute lack of technical knowledge.[20] It criticized the

---

20 The Kalkar judgment of the BVerfG in *BVerfG E* 49, 89 ff. In an important article on risk as a legal problem, printed shortly after the judgment and drawing on the situation of the atom industry, an attempt was made to draw out the significance of the court's judgment. Dr Hellmut Wagner speaks of an element of risk which lies beyond the understanding of the court and which is comprehended only by what he calls 'a philosophy of safety shaped by scientific-technical knowledge'. Wagner goes on: 'this philosophy is something

legislature for leaving too much latitude in nuclear matters with the executive, pointing out that in effect the executive was constantly being invited to react to its own proposals – for instance, it was left to the executive to approve those security arrangements which it had itself set up. Nevertheless the judgment stated: 'It's not the job of the court, to assess this situation [i.e. safety] – that's the job of the elected political institutions. In this area there is a shortage of legal standards'. Beyond this the court concentrated its attention on the question as to whether § 7 of the Atom Law (relating to 'the peaceful production of atomic energy and protection against its dangers') was in accordance with the constitution or not. This was the precise issue appealed to the BVerfG by the administrative court concerning Kalkar. The court decided fairly quickly that the paragraph was in accord with the constitution and accepted that a certain generality of phrasing – such as the 'adjusting of safety provisions to the current state of science and technology' – was inevitable in legislation of this kind. The court's decision was strikingly open, but such phrases were felt essential to provide 'a dynamic [i.e. historically evolving] protection of human rights'. To those anxious about the run-away development of highly risky nuclear technology, these seemed hardly reassuring comments.

In view of Albrecht's ambivalent position and after the BVerfG's judgment on Kalkar had been given, demonstrations and protests grew in proportion. The Easter March (a significant event in the calendar of the socially aware – the institution began as a mass protest against the stationing of US missiles on German soil) took Gorleben as its subject in 1980. No sooner did the local administration approve the construction of rail links to Gorleben, than fresh demonstrations of up to 10,000 were held. As other names came up in other parts of the country similar waves of protest moved round the map, disrupting building work and unsettling the political structures of the area. To simplify the position: for nuclear re-processing the name of Wackersdorf became the focus (this is in Bavaria, close to the Czech border), for advanced fast-breeder nuclear reactors Kalkar and for storage Gorleben. (Gorleben was additionally attractive to the authorities for its proximity to the German-German border. This was not just a policing decision based on the fact that demonstrators would be travelling to Gorleben from one less direction than would be the case in a more central site. The choice of Gorleben also involved international

which the law – despite its scepticism about such philosophy – must accept, without sacrificing its original task of forming judgments on the basis of a critical assessment of the situation as a whole' (1980). The Kalkar judgment was only one among many judgments reached by the BVerfG on matters of atomic energy, starting with its ban on a national referendum on the subject (Collings 2015, p. 4). See also the court's response to a personal complaint at the reactor in Mülheim-Kärlich, in: *NJW*, 1980,14, pp. 759–69.

relations, for Albrecht explicitly saw it as a kind of retaliation against the GDR authorities for their own nuclear dump at Morsleben, just over the border from Gorleben.) When the federal government encouraged the speeding up of test work in Gorleben, 11,000 protesters formed a human chain in the area.

The first radioactive material arrived for storage in Gorleben in October 1984 and in February 1985 50,000 demonstrated in Wackersdorf and again in October of the same year the same number.

With this measure of popular opposition, it was predictable that political positions would start to change. In 1984, for instance, the Lower Saxony SPD come out categorically against any future nuclear re-processing in the state. In 1992 a new local coalition of SPD, UWG and Greens decided to oppose the whole Gorleben project – in this case they were explicitly supported by the local Protestant churches, which opposed the CASTOR transports. Behind the various local rivalries, and the all but inevitable fact that people after a certain length of time became tired of campaigning on the same issue, the anti-nuclear protest managed to find imaginative ways to mobilize support. They used the tried US techniques of sit-in and stay, and set up their own local radio station as part of their occupations: radio stations which showed themselves to be better informed on technical matters than the established radio media. Most importantly, they linked in their work with society's wider concerns about environmental issues. This was shown in their second most effective slogan: *Gorleben is everywhere.*

The federal government too was starting to re-think. In the so-called Article-Law – finally passed in May 1994 – it decided finally in favour of storage rather than re-processing. Meanwhile the CASTOR transports to Gorleben continued. After the first delivery in April 1995 – which gave protestors their first experience of blocking the railway transport at various points through the Federal Republic – the costs of transport escalated significantly. The next transport cost 90 million DM and the one after that, in 1997, 111 million. Even in June 1980 just under six and half thousand police had been required to control a demonstration at Gorleben. None of this amounted to a strong incentive for federal or state authorities to continue with nuclear power. In the autumn of 1998 the SPD, in coalition with Bündnis 90/die Grünen agreed to pull out of nuclear recycling as part of the commercial production of electricity. Since the newly elected Chancellor, Gerhard Schröder (SPD), in his capacity as leader of the Ju-Sos (the SPD youth movement), had been active at many of the anti-nuclear demonstrations, this change of policy was hardly surprising, but with Three Mile Island and Tschernobl (1986) the international approach to nuclear had undergone significant change too. The last consignment of radioactive material left France in April 2002. The final end of re-processing took place in July 2005.

It's striking that across this controversial period – apart from the token judgments of the BVerfG – only two issues found their way into court. The first occasion was in February 1985, when the Lüneburg upper administrative court prevented the transport of radioactive material through its jurisdiction. The court found that § 6 of the *Atomgesetz* allowed for the storage of fuel elements, but not of spent core elements, which were to have been in the first CASTOR transport. The court demanded that the legislature rectify what it saw as a legal anomaly, and until the law was changed the court prevented the material from travelling to Gorleben.[21] Local politicians were indignant when the DWK – which had insisted on the absolute urgency of the transport in question – merely sent the used core-elements elsewhere for storage. Not for the first time the local officials felt trapped between mass protests and an unreasonable industry. For various reasons the court's ban discouraged transports for nearly ten years, but, once resumed, the transports were interrupted on only one occasion, when the CASTOR containers from a French reactor were discovered to be leaking radioactive material.[22]

The second legal issue in the atomic power controversies had nothing whatsoever to do with environmental law – it was the old problem, familiar from the late 1960s: the rights of demonstrators.

In fact, the question was as old as the Federal Republic itself. The issue had first surfaced in the strong-arm police measures taken against the students demonstrating against Harlan's film. With the emergence of political demonstrations as a basic life-form of the movements of the late 1960s younger lawyers exposed the inadequacy of the legal instruments used by the authorities to prosecute street protesters. Not just the archaic sources and understanding of many of these measures, going back to the time of the *Kaiser*, but their incompatibility with the right to demonstrate enshrined in § 8 of the *Grundgesetz*.

The issue arose initially with regard to the protests at Brokdorf (a nuclear power station, some thirty miles down the Elbe from Hamburg).[23] Initially – in a re-run of the ethos of the *Lüth* judgment – on May 14 1985 the BVerfG

21 Decision of 22.03.85. Reference: AE: 3VGD 7/85. On the transports see Poggendorf (2008, p. 125 f).

22 We note that – even after the report (1996) on the Soveso accident – international regulation did not cover either cross-border transport of hazardous or nuclear materials.

23 The principal judgment on demonstrations was expressed in the Brokdorf verdict of 1985 (*BVerfG E* 69, 315 f). For a discussion of this judgment see Collings (2015, pp. 208–11, 259) and Wesel (2004, pp. 288–91). See also: Müller-Heidelberg, Finckh, Narr & Pelzer (1998).

annulled the administrative court's ban on the Brokdorf demonstration at the end of February 1981. Over 50,000 people had already ignored the ban. The decision greatly annoyed the government of Helmut Kohl, since the BVerfG judges declared that demonstrations legitimately enshrined 'the possibility of public influence in the political process' – as if the conventional apparatus of political representation no longer exercised that function. This view was seen as another high-point in the 'arrogance' of Karlsruhe vis à vis Bonn. In addition, the court had to rule on the particular issue of whether a sit-down protest was a legitimate form of non-violent demonstration or whether it was a form of duress and hence violent. This problem had occupied many levels of the courts on and off for many years and caused the BVerfG serious difficulties. Many constitutional complaints had resulted from the fact that, while the infringement of a ban on demonstrations involved the offender in nothing more than a fine, participation in sit-down protests resulted in offenders getting a criminal record. On this matter the BVerfG initially sided with the authorities, but after nine years, during which demonstrators were criminalized and other demonstrations banned by the lower courts, the BVerfG declared in favour of the demonstrators' rights, even the right to sit down.

The considerable size of the demonstrations and the geographical extent of the areas which were to be kept free almost inevitably led to police overreaction. The CASTOR transports, for instance, were judged by the police to require the policing of a fifty-metre exclusion zone down the entire length of the railway tracks from the German border to Gorleben. In direct contravention of the *Grundgesetz* guarantees of freedom of movement (§ 11) public spaces thereby became no-go areas, not just for an hour or two as the transports passed through, but – as the authorities vainly attempted to keep the timetable for the transports secret – for periods of up to five or even nine days at a stretch. Large numbers of citizens were physically man-handled and charged with breaches of the peace when they entered these areas. Particularly violent treatment was meted out to those participating in a tractor blockade of the site and in March 1997 at a protest at the unloading station in Gorleben.

The great gain of these years was political. If the dioxin issue saw a major upsurge in the fortunes of the Greens, the nuclear issue gave all but unstoppable momentum to a whole new form of political organization: the so-called citizens' initiatives, the *Bürgerinitiativen*. Not only did these groups develop a representative power which left behind the effectiveness of traditional regional political structures. Their insistence on providing themselves with high-level technical expertise and their freedom from party labels meant that, in the spirit of Rio, central government and national agencies tended to offer to these groups better access to technical information than that enjoyed by regional government representatives – something greatly resented by the latter. The so-called K-Gruppen (activist left-wing remnants from the student movement: the popular press would regard them as a politically motivated 'rent-a-crowd') tried repeatedly to seize control of the citizens' initiatives (most markedly on the question of the use of violence) but it remained an achievement of these initiatives that they not only achieved their goals in closing down nuclear power, but managed to do so by following their own chosen methods, and without violence on their part. The lesson of Frankfurt Airport had been learnt. Furthermore – despite a perennial tendency of rural populations to resent the 'intruders' from the cities who get involved with local issues – the initiatives were largely successful in holding on to local support. As we suggested, the contrast to the situation of Baader-Meinhof in their form of ideological protest could hardly have been greater.

It would be misleading to see in these movements a forerunner to the 'populist' movements of the present. In the eyes of much of the popular press the protesters were merely trouble-makers, and, while the anti-nuclear-movement mobilized large numbers of people and strengthened minority political parties, it never outgrew the dimensions of a protest movement. In comparison with the populism associated, for instance, with British or French anti-Europeanism, the citizens' initiatives took care to remain better informed on the core technical issues than the traditional political parties; they practised full transparency and maintained a reasoned and intelligent participation in the technical discussions in the field of energy generation. In addition, part of the environmentalists' success lay in their ability to communicate, outside the immediate terms of their campaign, the vision of a positive lifestyle in an environmentally better world. Looking at this history of the Federal Republic one sees a sustained shift among the student generation away from the 'materialism' of the post-war years: the non-materialist values which the protesters shared were more comfortable when embedded in environmental thinking than when presented in the initially more ideological and political context of the student generation. While the authorities saw the environmentalists as dangerous radicals, today's society has been persuaded by many of their ideas, and the legacy of their thinking remains active – perhaps even occasionally effective.

CHAPTER 11

Danger from the Right

11.1 Post-heroic Law

There are many trials suitable for this concluding chapter, expressing the characteristic features of the present historical moment and illustrating the central argument of this book: that trials are a sensitive guide to society and its historical development. The Federal Republic is not in a heroic age any more. Re-unification, for generations presented as the great hope of the Federal Republic, happened in an unlikely way, in a coincidence of statesmanship by Helmut Kohl and Mikhail Gorbatchev and a GDR leadership which paid the price for not keeping up to date. But whether the pictures of the joyful crowds in Berlin in November 1989 have kept their excitement and whether the long-awaited encounter of East and West Germany lived up to the promised euphoria – opinions may well remain divided on these matters. In consequence there is a strong temptation to end this book not with a bang, such as made by the *Spiegel* Affair, or the Auschwitz trial, but with a whimper – not because, as the poet predicted, the world will end like that, but because things have declined in Germany since the stunning events of 1989. The whimper is as historic as the fall of the Berlin Wall, and it too should be registered in this chronicle.[1]

The age, with its increasing populism and its obsession with commercialized sport, is well expressed in the football trials. The case of Uli Hoeness, for instance, – one-time flying winger of the world-cup winning German team and subsequently president of Bayern München – is all too typical of the age. Although his crime was overshadowed by the behaviour of top FIFA officials, Hoeness has just finished a period of comfortable imprisonment for a sizeable tax fraud. Such is the prestige of Bayern München that the jail conditions appear to have been arranged round Hoeness' convenience and his compassionate leaves scheduled in remarkable harmony with the team's fixtures: the only rules which this privileged group follow are those of football and the only reality is money.

1 T. S. Eliot's poem 'The Hollow Men' was often quoted in the 1950s, for it seemed to summarize the sense of disillusionment of the time. As the hero of John Osborne's play *Look Back in Anger* (1956) remarks: there are no more Causes – by extension: after re-unification in 1990 nothing left to work for. On the demise of the GDR see i.a.: Byrnes, Conacher, & Holfter (2018).

The disconnect between Hoeness' treatment and ordinary citizens' experience of the law could hardly be greater, or more typical of this age. It is part of history. There has been no red card for class justice. While in Britain retail magnates seem able, without legal hindrance, to grab hundreds of millions from the pension fund of their employees, in the USA successful political careers are built on the readiness to foreclose on people whose accounts are overdrawn by a few cents. Why should the Federal Republic be any different? Brecht's famous question – 'What's breaking into a bank compared with founding a bank?' – still awaits an answer, and Hoeness' case adds to these sad truths the extra element of media glitz.[2] The problems raised in Chapters 2 and 8 remain alive.

Characteristic of the present – and not just in Germany – is the dilemma of the law facing the power of the social media. It is illustrated in the sad and widely circulated story of the television weatherman – another of the newly charismatic social roles of the present – accused of sexual misdemeanour and therefore suspended from his work. In court it was found that the weatherman had no case to answer, and yet he discovered following the trial that he could not resume his job among the isobars. The brittleness of position, the power of rumour within today's litigious society and the inability of the law to grant restitution in the face of the blogosphere are cruelly exposed in Jörg Kachelmann's experiences. Ratings – not to mention the judgment of the social media – count more than the sober verdict of courts. In such an age it is pointless for a judge to ask 'Who are the Beatles?' – the law has not yet learned to keep up with other agencies.[3]

We opened our account with the historic tribunals judging the criminal leaders of the Third Reich, and it would be appropriate to end with the trials of the leaders of the GDR after the Wall had fallen. The trial of the century – that of Head of State Erich Honecker, extradited in 1992 from Moscow to face justice – did not take place, but the lesser cases against the GDR offer an opportunity to explore the way in which the Federal Republic has come to terms with the criminal actions of a regime which had collapsed on its own doorstep. No genocide was alleged and no international tribunal was planned, for the offences of the leadership belonged in different categories to those applied at Nuremberg. Instead, trials have focused on the various killings at the German-German border. For once not only the little people who physically

2 For the Hoeness case see on-line sources. On his comfortable imprisonment: Oliver Stöwing, Uli Hoeneß ist fast ein freier Mann, in: *Berliner Morgenpost*, 23.02.2016. Brecht's remark is from *Threepenny Opera* (1929), widely available in English. Erstwhile BHS-boss Philip Green dominated the British media for much of 2016: Mr Mnuchin – nominated by President Trump as Treasury Secretary – was described as 'foreclosure king' in the *Guardian*, 30.11.16.

3 On Jörg Kachelmann see Wikipedia.

carried out the various fatal shootings were sentenced, but the desk-top murderers too – Defence Minister Heinz Kessler, his Deputy Fritz Streletz and SED-man Hans Albrecht. For the lesser figures the BVerfG ingeniously found in the legislation of the GDR (rather than in its practice) a respect for life which the GDR's political leaders had not always detected, and accordingly found the border guards guilty according to the laws of the system they had unthinkingly served. This saved the court having to invoke the *post hoc* legislation of the Federal Republic. Unprotected by the financial power of a Friedrich Flick these men and their bosses experienced a different type of justice and were made to pay for the inhumanity of the fallen regime. (Incidentally, this was a case where the failure to have the Basic Law approved by the population of the new federal states had consequences.) James McAdams (2001) has written these trials up fully, in English, and I refer to his book, rather than re-tell the story here.

It seems premature, finally, to write much about the legal cases and on-going complexity arising in the context of the increasing prominence of refugees and asylum-seekers recently settled in Germany. Important judgments concerning religious tolerance have been reached on questions such as the burka and hijab, and an uneasy compromise has been found with the Bavarian schools' insistence on hanging a crucifix in every state classroom. Nevertheless, the political dimensions within which legal and security forces operate and the legal terms on which recent immigration has happened appear so fluid at the moment that it would be unlikely that anything written now could be relevant a year from hence. Looking back at the 1992 reform of asylum legislation, in which public opinion played so prominent a role,[4] it is hard to believe that significant change is not likely in this field.

Regrettably, few trials more fully epitomize that link between history and the law which is our concern than the recent so-called NSU trial. Its actors offer a banal and uninspiring expression of old prejudice and old violence, perpetrated not against recent immigrants but against members of established, once-immigrant communities, many of whose members – thanks to the legislation introduced by Chancellor Schröder in coalition with the Greens after 1999 – have a dual citizenship. The crimes were committed some ten years ago, but at the time of writing the trial has only just finished and the written judgment has not yet been made available.[5] While we cannot claim that this trial

4 Headscarves and crucifix decision of the BVerwG see: *NJW*, 2003, 3111, p. 342; also Wesel (2004, p. 315 f). Also Corinna Sicko (2008). On the reform of the asylum law in 1992 see Stuart Parkes (1997, pp. 57 f, 103 f). On the shift in SPD attitudes at the time see: Downs (2012, pp. 163–6).

5 Judges are allowed time to prepare their written judgments according to the length of the trial in question. In the NSU-trial the judge has 91 weeks to produce the judgment. Only when it has been published can defence or prosecution appeal the verdicts to the BGH. Since Judge

has dominated European headlines, the circumstances surrounding it continue to colour international views of Germany and its legal system.

The outcome of this trial is less important than these general circumstances and the questions of justice which they raise. These questions do not involve – like *Lüth*, or § 175 or Mescalero – subtle legal differentiations, but more basic questions. The case displays two features typical of united Germany: both the spread of extreme views among sections of the public and the direction from which future threats to democracy and the rule of law are likely to come. In this case, not just the united Federal Republic, but the separate development of the two former states come into question. This book began with Nietzsche looking for a critical 'moving on' in history: we end with the opposite of his hope – neo-Nazism and the law's ineffectual encounter with it.

In the context of united Germany these movements form – to use Cas Mudde's term – the 'third wave' of extremism, following the SRP in the early 1950s (see above, Chapter Two) and the NPD in the 1960s and its further development in the Republicans and the DVU.[6] The third wave – not just in the former GDR but in many other former Soviet bloc countries – has presented the West with an unexpected legacy of Communist rule. In fact, however, in the whole world right-wing extremism and violence are no longer the prerogative of unstable and immature states. For that reason the lessons of this trial reverberate more widely than merely offering insight into a special German situation. It is usual for commentators, in writing of right-wing extremism in a number of European countries, to hope for the gradual political defeat of extremist groups and for the victory of a liberal political consensus, but even the optimists pray fervently that no significant economic crisis takes place to increase the discontent which is at extremism's heart. Not only politics: the instruments and institutions of the law also have a central role to play in these developments. It follows that the errors which the institutions of law and order have made so publicly in this case contain lessons for a wider world than Germany.

For these reasons we will deal with the ten murders – nine of them against members of ethnic minorities living in Germany – which led to the trial of Beate Zschäpe in Munich. This trial opened in May 2013 and closed on July 10 2018 and is embedded in the public mind as the NSU-trial: the exposure of the

Götzl is said to be hoping to retire in June 2019, it is assumed that the judgment will be ready before the full period has elapsed. Even at that stage no re-trial is on offer: merely an opportunity to challenge the verdict (no new evidence is admissible). See: Wie es jetzt im NSU-Prozess weiteregeht, in: *FAZ* 12.07.2018.

6 Mudde (2000, pp. 3, 18).

National Socialist Underground – the name of the self-appointed terrorist trio of Zschäpe, Uwe Böhnhardt and Uwe Mundlos (the latter two violently deceased in November 2011). For a large number of families the story is one of great personal tragedy, and it is this tragedy which must be worked through by the Federal Republic in the coming years. For reasons which we examine here in detail, the outcome of the marathon trial has been variously described as a triumph for the neo-Nazi movement, as a bitter disappointment for the families of the victims and as a low point in the Federal government's policies on migration.[7] All this happens at a time when Frau Merkel's government faces hardly less significant problems in this field from other forces.

11.2 Ten Murders

On September 4 2000 a florist, Enver Şimşek, was shot and killed in Nuremberg. Four months later a nail-bomb attack was carried out on an Iranian-German family in Cologne, injuring twenty people. In June 2001 Abdurrahim Özüdoğru, a shift worker and jobbing tailor, was shot dead in Nuremberg. Less than a week later Süleyman Taşköprü was shot dead in Hamburg. Six weeks later Habil Kiliç, joint owner of a food-store, was gunned down in Munich. In February 2004 Mehmet Turgut was shot dead in his snack-bar in a Rostock street. Another nail-bomb exploded in a part of Cologne with a high immigrant population, and exactly one year later Ismail Yaşar was shot in the face (a feature common to nine of these murders) and died in Nuremberg. Less than a week later a Greek immigrant, Theodoros Boulgarides, was killed with the same weapon in the key-bar he ran in Munich. The following April Mehmet Kubaşik was shot dead in Dortmund. Two days later Halit Yozgat was shot dead in his internet café in Kassel. Less than three weeks later a serving police officer, Michèle Kiesewetter, was shot dead during a coffee-break in her police-car in Heilbronn and her colleague Martin Arnold severely wounded.

Of course these were not the only unexplained violent deaths during this decade. Official government figures suggest that since 1990 48 murders have been the result of right-wing extremism. (The serious press put the figure

7 For the *Süddeutsche Zeitung* the trial has left the Neo-Nazis 'dancing for joy' (NSU-Prozess: Das Gericht hat eine historische Chance vertan', 13.07.2018); the disappointment of the families is the central point of *FAZ*: Nach dem Gefängnis ist vor dem Gefängnis, 12.07.2018; various media have argued about the blow to Frau Merkel's migration policies, see e.g. Ferda Ataman: NSU-Trauma: Nichts ist wider gut, *Der Spiegel* 14.07.2018.

at 138.)[8] But more significant was the unmistakable evidence of the link between some of these murders: in nine of these cases the same distinctive handgun was used; the dates chosen for some of the murders were indicative of links, as was a certain, if imprecise, geographical focus, let alone the obvious fact that all the victims, with the exception of the two police officers, came from well-established immigrant communities. Nevertheless, it took some time before these murders were linked into the series as which they are now generally seen, and in connection with which Ms Zschäpe was brought to trial.

It did not take these murders for the authorities to realise that the Federal Republic was facing a significant problem with anti-immigrant violence. Within the first ten years after unification there had been several major acts of violence against hostels in which recently arrived immigrants had been housed. This was collective violence, perpetrated by crowds of up to 3000 people rather than particular individuals, and in contrast to the murders listed above with no possible ambiguity about their motive. The names of Rostock and Hoyerswerda, Solingen, Lübeck and Mölln will remain as challenges to humanity on the pages of recent German history.[9] Academic observers around 2000 had confidently predicted that this violence would get worse, and politicians were well aware of the danger which these riots posed to the state. Manfred Stolpe, SPD first minister of Brandenburg, was particularly gloomy as he contemplated the arson attacks on refugee homes: 'This', he said, 'is how something began that ended in Auschwitz'.

11.3 The Origins of Racist Violence

There is no shortage of sophisticated explanation as to why this violence tended to be strong in the states which until 1990 made up the former German Democratic Republic. Sociologists have given convincing accounts

---

8 Statistics on right-wing extremist murders in: Gregor Gysi (2013), p. 218. Gysi is the leader of DIE LINKE in the *Bundestag*. It has been claimed that the security forces had to investigate more than ten times that number in order to establish a possible link to the NSU. Nach dem Urteil im NSU-Prozess. Der Vorhang zu, die Fragen offen. *Taz*, 13.07.2018.

9 The reference to previous arson attacks on migrant and immigrant accommodation is to: Rostock (Mecklenburg-Vorpommern, 1991), Hoyerswerda (Saxony, 1992), Lübeck (1996), Solingen (North-Rhine Westphalia, 1993) and Mölln (Schleswig-Holstein, 1992). The most serious of these attacks were Solingen, in which five Turkish people from three generations were killed, and Lübeck (ten deaths). In Solingen the attack was more of an individual initiative, and two neo-Nazis were sentenced. See i.a. Benedict (1998, p. 123 f). The prediction that things would get worse e.g. Zimmermann (2003, p. 222). Quotation from Stolpe in Fraser (2001, p. 65).

of the patterns of the escalation of discontent into mob violence. These explanations – here simplistically reproduced – include: the rapid collapse of the economic structures on which the GDR had built its relative economic success. As COMECON fell apart, so the markets in the Soviet *bloc* which the GDR had served ceased to exist, and much of the production capacity of the GDR lost all customers. Other elements of the economic collapse have been variously blamed on the behaviour of West German industry and commerce, anxious to extend their business empires into the newly available markets of the East, and therefore doing little to support East German enterprises, indeed deliberately preventing East German producers from offering serious competition. The real efforts of West German capital seem to have been directed towards re-acquiring property in the former GDR and consolidating its monopoly. In addition to the sense of loss felt in the East, the West German economy offered life-styles and jobs attractive to the mobile elements in the population of the GDR, especially younger women. All these factors caused a strong sense of resentment and abandonment among the disaffected youth who remained among the ruins of old industries and unwanted trades. Defeated economically by the Federal Republic, there was nowhere else for people in the East to direct their anger except downwards. Sociologists speak of these people as 'modernization losers'.[10] However, this should not disguise the fact that a number of prominent figures in the neo-Nazi movement came from stable and comfortable middle-class backgrounds, not adversely affected by the economic collapse. Not all racist violence is an automatic response to personal loss.

Social and economic dislocation formed one element of the problem. Politics played an important role in the build-up of violence. The considerable ideological resentment, which had been felt against the former GDR regime and for which the GDR itself had offered no kind of outlet, paradoxically contributed to difficulties after the *Wende*. These feelings were not softened by the fact that many of the former politicians of the East were participating in the new political structures of united Germany. The PDS (Party of Democratic Socialism: the follow-on Communist party) was only one example of this continuity. For Western politicians and observers looking for the integration of the two states, this was a positive development. For those who had engaged in extreme protest against the GDR regime, it was less good news. One might have thought that these bitter and often violent protest-movements – movements which the GDR authorities had proved incapable of understanding, let alone defusing – might have given the disaffected GDR youth good reason to welcome the West, where opposition to the SED and an unforgiving approach

10 The phrase 'modernization losers' e.g. in: Zimmermann (2003, p. 236).

to the former GDR police could always be counted on. Even when the Federal Republic, from the 1970s on, bought out a number of these youthful protesters from GDR prisons and settled them in the West, it earned no gratitude from the neo-Nazis. For them the FRG remained an enemy. These protest movements saw both East and West as part of one hated 'system' – an impression strengthened by the formation in 2005 of yet another 'grand coalition', which once again left less visible room for non-conformity.[11] But the political radicalization of punks and skinheads and the emergence of clandestine terrorist activity require more explanation. Two elements in particular showed their importance.

The first was the inexperience of the population of the former GDR in contacts with ethnic minorities. Unlike the Federal Republic, the GDR had no tradition of employing migrant workers. Since the state operated closed borders towards those countries from which traditionally large-scale migration had come, there were, apart from very small settlements of workers from North Vietnam, few ethnically identifiable groups in the country. This meant that the society had no actual experience of other ethnicities. Despite socialism's constant appeal to internationalism, multiculturalism did not feature in the socialist *bloc*. Ignorance and inexperience seem more important than the theory occasionally put forward to the effect that it was general failures in East German children's socialization which made them open to violent racism.[12] Everyone who knows contemporary Germany has to be suspicious of such generalizations: we know too many exceptions among former East German youth to be persuaded by such sweeping theories. Lack of experience offers a much more likely explanation of how racism could take root.

An often quoted remark in accounts of hostility to immigrants is that 'no-one is born a racist':[13] in other words, new-born babies arrive in the world with a whole series of individual likes and dislikes but none of them have problems with ethnicity. Babies are colour-blind. After that stage of life, however, culture and experience play a part and, as in other countries which remained for a long time outside multi ethnicity (Ireland is one example where emigration

11 Downs (2012) offers interesting reflections on the relationship between 'pariah parties' and a parliamentary system closed to accommodations – among such systems few are more exclusive than the Grand Coalition (p. 168). Gysi (2013) makes the point more polemically. On the anti-system thinking of the extreme right see: Zimmermann (2003, p. 226), and on the various strategies to capture extremist thinking within conventional political groupings see: Downs, *passim*.

12 Some of the most biting critiques of the socialization of young people in the GDR can be found in: Zimmermann (2003), esp. quoting Richard Stöß (2000).

13 'No-one is born a racist': see Funke (2015, p. 361).

rather than immigration was the trend before the economic boom[14]), the population of the GDR knew virtually nothing about new migrants. In the West both the immigrant communities – starting with the original so-called 'guest workers', the Turks – and the settled community had had time to adapt to the situation and, if imperfectly, to integrate and adjust. This did not happen in the East. German citizens there experienced an abrupt shift from an almost total absence of ethnic minorities to the enforced participation in a state open to large-scale immigration. This situation was brought about by the explicit policy of the Federal Government to 'share out' immigrants equally across the constituent federal states. This policy brought the old GDR quickly into the modern age.

Resentment at the allocation of immigrants to the individual federal states was by no means confined to the former East German states. The state of Bavaria, for instance, has a long history of resisting federal policy on immigration. Notwithstanding the touching scenes at the Munich railway station when refugees from the Syrian conflict were given a whole-hearted and emotional welcome by ordinary people, Bavarian politicians have sharply contested the Federal government's immigration policies, and some years back – during the Chancellorship of Gerhard Schröder (SPD) – they started the highly problematic practice of blaming the presence of immigrants on another party, in that case the Social Democrats. Over the years since 2015 the CSU, led by Horst Seehofer, has engaged in repeated public conflicts with Merkel's government. The CSU were not alone in this. 'Every immigrant', CDU General Secretary Volker Rühe had grumbled during the Schröder Chancellorship, 'is an SPD immigrant'.[15] The governing party has changed since then, but the resentment has remained. The party-political and ideological colouring of responses to immigration has not proved easy to reverse. It is unmistakable that the mobilization of anti-immigrant feeling for party-political ends has increased, and that the only party to profit from this trend has been the AfD, rather than the CSU or CDU.

11.4 The Role of the Extreme Right

Unfortunately, these were in no way the only or even the most important of the ideological currents working against multi-ethnicity. West German neo-Nazis played a significant role in encouraging and channelling the discontent and inexperience of East Germans into NS lines and into violence. It would be

14 For Irish comparisons see: Bryan Fanning (2011).

15 Rühe quotation in Funke (2015, p. 124).

easy to think that East German neo-Nazism was an over-reaction to the years of SED dominance: on the principle that 'my enemy's enemy is my friend', even Nazis could be made to seem preferable to Communists. However, the problem was also one for the Federal Republic, for its structures had allowed right-wing extremism to flourish long before the wall came down. Indeed, the failure to prevent the emergence of a disgruntled and violent neo-Nazi movement in the West can seem little short of a mockery of the state's countless, seemingly well-intentioned efforts at political education.

It is hard to imagine what more Hitler could have done to make himself an object of hatred to the German people: his total war had provoked the destruction of the rich fabric of historic German culture in the German cities; he had brought about an irreversible loss of national territory; he had discredited the German name across the world for several generations, and he had caused the unnecessary deaths of millions of German citizens – to say nothing of ordering the murder of millions of other Europeans. Surely with that list of achievements no-one could regard Hitler in a positive light. But they do. The neo-Nazis even hold meetings celebrating Nazism on the site of the former concentration camps. Helped by corrupt and self-seeking historians and by the intellectually and morally vacuous work of Holocaust deniers such as David Irving (despite the fact that he was banned from entering Germany in 1993, a regular visitor to neo-Nazi circles in Germany – the only audience in which he can count on agreement), enjoying the support and encouragement of racist groups in the UK (such as Combat 18) and the USA (German neo-Nazis admiringly taking over KluKluxKlan as the title of one of their splinter movements), an extensive neo-Nazi movement came into existence in the Federal Republic. It was this movement which deliberately exported its thinking and behaviour to the former GDR. Strikingly this has happened without there being significant personal family links among the present-day neo-Nazis to Hitler's servants and murderers in their parents' generation. The movement is driven by ideology, not family loyalty.

At present the organizations of the German extreme right are characterized by fluidity. One organization easily merges with another, on occasion changing its title and appearance, but not its convictions. Sometimes it morphs into a party standing in local elections; sometimes it takes the form of a concert-promoter, giving a platform to some of the viciously racist rock music bands of the UK and USA. Always there is a shooting-club in the background, usually with a conveniently lax enforcement of regulations.[16] Behind the violent rock

16 The murder of policewoman Michèle Kiesewetter is sometimes ascribed to the NSU's need for fresh weapons. It became clear in the course of the Munich trial, however, that the NSU had more than 20 firearms – pistols and rifles – in its possession. This paradox

and the military paraphernalia it seems to be the false clichés of NS comradeship and the offer of collective identity which recruit followers.

The hard core of neo-Nazism owes its fluidity to a cell-structure copied from Baader-Meinhof and other left-wing terrorist groups. In contrast to the extreme right parties of the second wave, whose parties, REP and DVU, had spent much time in bitter internecine warfare, the third wave movements appear to be able to work together, perhaps because they do not stand for election and are in less direct competition with one another. They are part of a wider pattern. After the collapse of the GDR, as old allegiances had to be revalued, the political landscape took on a general fluidity, as can be seen, for instance, in a shift from authoritarian 'left' (in the SED) to authoritarian right. Indeed, there were many SED people who ended up in the REP – ideology clearly playing no role in such moves. A few elements of the neo-Nazi movement have shifted in and out of the CDU (newly constituted in the new federal states after 1990 and looking to build its base there). Just as the SRP members moved over to the FDP when it was banned (the comparison of the early 1950s with the 1990s is not accidental: General Remer was a proclaimed hero of the later neo-Nazi movement too[17]), so neo-Nazis found it possible to make a home in a number of political contexts. On the occasions that individual neo-Nazi organizations have been banned – this happened, for instance, to *Kameradschaft* and to the group *Blood&Honour* (between 1992 and 2000 no less than fifteen neo-Nazi organizations were banned) – the effect on the movement has been minimal. Neither the NPD (the oldest of the formations to stand for election), nor the so-called 'Republicans' (REP) have ever been declared unconstitutional by the BVerfG. Even without electoral presence, however, the neo-Nazis are more than capable of sustaining their organizations and of continuing to recruit and to carry through elements of their programmes. Among the questions raised by the trial of Ms Zschäpe is the extent to which this general programme included the systematic murder of immigrant workers.

11.5 Institutional Failures

We will continue to focus on the background to these crimes before coming to discuss the trial itself. The lack of direction and focus of the trial has to do

draws attention to the need for further investigation of the links between the local police and the NSU (Nach dem Urteil ..., *Taz* 13.07.2018).

17 For Remer (the general who acted decisively against the July 20 1944 conspirators and thus became a hero of the neo-Nazis) see above, Chapter 2 and: Frei (1999, p. 327 f). On neo-Nazis and identity, see: Schedler & Häusler (2011, pp. 306, 315 f).

with the highly questionable methods by which the NSU was investigated and brought to trial. These methods have been a prime cause of the considerable disquiet felt at the trial's outcome.

We start with the police. Despite the unmistakable background of anti-immigrant violence against which this series of murders took place, the police – in more than one regional authority – was extremely slow to identify the actual milieu from which the murders were likely to have come. Instead, much police time and energy were spent investigating the possible involvement of the victims themselves in criminal activity. An early assumption was that the victims had got into conflict with the Turkish drugs mafia and that the murders were therefore the result of internal feuds within the Turkish community, or with the Kurdish PKK – both of these were assumptions for which there appears not to have been a scrap of evidence. The perpetrator of the nail-bomb attack in Cologne was caught on CCTV: the picture may have been indistinct, yet the man was obviously neither Turkish nor Kurdish – a fact which did not distract the police from following their own prejudices and thus significantly delaying the tracking-down of the actual murderers.

Police efforts went so far as to place the victims' families under intrusive surveillance and to conduct long cross-examinations of the next-of-kin with the intention of revealing the victim's criminal background. After months of unsuccessfully trying to establish that the victims had been criminals, and despite the families' explicit pleading that the neo-Nazi dimension of the murders should be explored, the only suggestion that the police profiling experts could come up with was of an *individual* with a pathological hatred of Turks. For a long time it never entered the police's reckoning that they were dealing with multiple murders organized by the extreme right. Their eyes were deliberately closed to the existence of the many groups in the immediate neighbourhood of the murders which were openly proclaiming their hatred of immigrants and their admiration for NS violence, even though the victims' families were familiar enough with right-wing hostility to their community and repeatedly drew police attention to it. The police did not take into consideration – at least for the first six murders – that the murderers might have come from that milieu. The only justification the police has offered of their approach was that they did not wish to panic the Turkish small-business community by exaggerating any external threat they might face. The Turkish community was at no point persuaded or comforted by this approach.

If these were errors of commission, they were compounded by the most extraordinary errors of omission. It has never been explained how the police failed to follow up their search of a garage rented by Zschäpe in Jena. In the garage a number of pipe-bombs were found, along with an extensive list of Uwe Mundlos' contacts in the neo-Nazi scene. To let Böhnhardt pack his bags and 'go underground' from his parents' house just round the corner from the garage and immediately after the search was an incredible lapse: when the police made no use of this contact list, dismissing it as 'not relevant to the enquiries' and failed to use it to trace the vanished trio, this set new standards for incompetence – or corruption.

To UK eyes all this looks like the behaviour of a police force riddled with 'institutional racism'. In study of these crimes a British observer of race-relations has described the German police in exactly these terms. The disrespectful treatment, indeed attempted criminalization of the victims' families had been a pronounced feature of the investigation into the racist murder of Stephen Lawrence in London in 1993, and the Macpherson report (1999) had identified these as endemic features of the Metropolitan police at the time.[18] In support of Fekete's theory we may adduce the fact that the murder squads gave names to their cases referring more or less offensively to the Turkish element of the crime (this although not all the victims were Turkish, all the victims were lumped together as 'Alis'), and the popular press followed this lead with headlines such as 'Döner murders'. To what extent the inexperience of the GDR police forces in democratic procedures played a role in their behaviour is hard to determine: it seems likely that the forces merely carried on with their traditional methods, changing only the stereotypical image of 'the enemy' – even though they were describing victims. Inexperience was possibly an ongoing feature of the police's excessive tolerance in giving permission for extreme right-wing marches, but none of these considerations alter the fact that the majority of the murders themselves took place in West Germany and the failures of attitude were part of police forces allegedly schooled in democracy.

Another difficulty is to establish whether the problem was that individual members of the police force were themselves members of extreme right organizations and therefore either consciously leading the investigation in the wrong direction, or merely indifferent to the killing of immigrant fellow-citizens: to such questions there are no sure answers. Certainly according to the various analyses of these events – for instance by the two parliamentary commissions established to examine the cases –, these negative features can be identified as having been prominent in police behaviour during the investigations. (Not for the first time it's clear that parliamentary commissions of enquiry are more rigorous in their pursuit of truth than the government. This can also be seen

18 Liz Fekete (2015). For a discussion of the use of phrases such as 'Döner-Murders' (a phrase sometimes initiated by the police, sometimes launched by the press) see (among other essays): Derya Gür-Şeker (2015). The outrage at the racist devaluation of the victims is conveyed by: Ferda Ataman, *Der Spiegel*, on-line: 14.07. 2018.

in recent reactions to the outcome of the trial.[19]) That at various points during the trial some of the investigating officers denied the claim of racist attitudes (e.g. 11.07.13) does not necessarily gainsay the facts.

There was another agency constantly involved in these cases, whose influence was more malign even than that of the police. The *Bundesamt für Verfassungsschutz* (BfV: the Federal Office for the Protection of the Constitution) – a branch of the security services, which we encountered in the 1970s as it sifted through two million cases looking for potentially disloyal servants of the state (see Chapter 8) – both directly and through its local offices in the federal states played a sinister role in the miscarriage of justice in these cases. Both its central and its local offices in the federal states had disturbingly close links to the neo-Nazi movement. The service had achieved this closeness primarily by recruiting leading members of the extreme right to act as informants.

The use of informants had, of course, been central to the tactics of the GDR *Stasi* (these were the so-called 'informal staff', the IM) as of many other security forces across the world in their attempt to counter internal subversive movements. The policy has proved problematic everywhere it was implemented. To be an informant for the BfV was clearly more popular than working for the *Stasi* had been – it was paid in cash, for a start – and there was no shortage of leading figures in the neo-Nazi movement ready to be recruited. Indeed, some estimates put the percentage of the neo-Nazi leadership on the BfV's payroll as high as 30%.[20] The advantages were obvious for these people, since the BfV offered its informants not only money but what looked like unconditional protection from prosecution. It allowed them to justify their own activities – often violent and usually illegal: including the purchase of arms and explosives and holding fire-arms drills – under the guise of ingratiating themselves with the 'hard core' of the movements in order better to inform the BfV. The practice, as we shall see, all but wrecked the NSU trial.

As the activities and identities of these informants have become known, commentators and politicians alike are agreed in condemning the whole system as catastrophic, amounting – in the words of the police – to official 'fire-raising': through the BfV the state had in effect been sponsoring the violent radicalization of the right. One of the important informants inside the *Thüringer Heimatschutz* (the neo-Nazi organization which supported the trio

19 On the various parliamentary commissions of enquiry see: Weigel (2013). Clemens Binninger (CDU), chair of the federal parliamentary commission, is quoted critiquing the inadequate outcome of the trial in: NSU-Prozess – das Urteil zeigt Härte gegen Zschäpe – und Skrupel. *Der Tagesspiegel*, 11.07.2018. A positive view of these commissions in: Ataman, *Der Spiegel*, 14.07.2018.

20 Percentage of agents in the THS see: Quent (2016, p. 208).

in their underground life), Tino Brandt, called the BfV's funding 'a zero-sum game'. Since Brandt received some 200,000 DM from the security forces, it is little wonder that informants were lining up to be recruited. Another neo-Nazi informer – recruited in 1995 just after being sentenced to eight years for a savage attack on a Nigerian asylum-seeker – could rely on a monthly subsidy of 1000 DM.[21]

No less fatal to the alleged intentions of the BfV – the defence of the state and its constitution – was the way in which the protection of informants led the BfV constantly to interfere with police investigation into the murders. The agency frequently warned informants of forthcoming police activity, so that they could be elsewhere when the raid happened, or conceal incriminating material. It repeatedly prevented the police from interviewing informants, even when these informants were important witnesses to the crimes the police were investigating. In the mid-1990s the agency destroyed a large quantity of personal records and documentation relating to the extreme right (this programme was referred to as 'Shredder') and again in 2011, by then, following the deaths of Mundlos and Böhnhardt, presumably with the intention of protecting the agency, rather than their informants. It has been known for over a decade that the behaviour of the BfV has allowed the series of murders to continue far beyond what might have been prevented. Whatever else the agency has to answer for, it has the blood of innocent victims on its hands. The only positive motivation which is suggested for the BfV's behaviour is its anxiety to keep the neo-Nazis in identifiable groups, thus avoiding the danger of the state being threatened by radicalized and unidentified loners. Nothing in the agency's record suggests that this policy was effective, and the hope that the BfV might learn from its own mistakes was dashed with the news that an internal report analysing these errors has been embargoed *inside* the agency for no less than 120 years.[22]

In searching for an explanation of these catastrophic failures – and by now the media's effort lies with explaining, rather than exposing them: the BfV, as

---

21 Brandt quoted in Quent (2016, p. 212). On the BfV blocking the proposed ban on the *Thüringer Heimatschutz* see: *ibid.*, p. 227. Details on Brandt's remuneration in: Gysi (2013), p. 216. On the destruction of documents see esp.: Funke (2015, pp. 241–340); and Aust & Laabs (2014, pp. 16–9). On comparisons with British approaches to the IRA through the 'supergrass' system see Porch (2013, p. 283 f). Two highly problematic cases raised in Ireland: Freddie Scappaticci ('Stakeknife') and the still unsolved murder of the Catholic lawyer Pat Finucane. Also see the McCormick case, described in: Boyd (1984, p. 34f). Notice Wesel's reference to German judges suddenly understanding the position of judges in Northern Ireland (2004, p. 318).

22 The claim is quoted in: Nach dem Urteil im NS-Prozess. Der Vorhang zu, die Fragen offen. *Taz*, 13.07.2018.

the *Frankfurter Rundschau* announced in a headline in February 2015, is by general consent 'in the pits'[23] – we run into a familiar range of possibilities. The BfV, as historians insist, was staffed (like other agencies of the Federal German secret services, from the Gehlen organization onwards) almost exclusively by former members of the NS secret services. This certainly remained the background to the leadership of the BfV until the 1970s. Its pedigree was important less for proving the continuation of direct NS ideology in the organization. Often the question of sensitivities to issues is more relevant than any active ideology: one would not, for instance, expect an organization with such traditions to be sensitive to matters of racial discrimination any more than former members of the RSHA would be expected to worry about just nine murders from the ethnic minorities. But it is surely stretching a point to see a *direct* connection, especially into the new millennium. It's more plausible to think of the distorting effect of the continuities in the agency's view of imagined enemies. Its traditional hostility to Communism (and Social Democracy) fully met Adenauer's expectations at the start of the Republic. It needed no encouragement to persist in the view that the danger to the state came exclusively from the left and to ignore any dangers from the neo-Nazis in the 1970s. No less significant was the climate of contemptuously anti-democratic sentiment, expressed in the agency's lack of any answerability to the parliamentary structures which had the constitutional task of controlling it.

There was also a rivalry between secret and normal police, a new development since the Baader-Meinhof days. Security services often feel superior to the police, since, as a senior officer from the BfV appearing anonymously before a parliamentary enquiry explained, 'the police are constrained in their contacts by the need to make an arrest'.[24] It seems that the BfV's refusal to share information often not only involved protecting their sources among criminals but also with preserving an advantage over the police by means of withholding information. In the intelligence services, information is power, and as the head of the Bavarian branch of the BfV lamely remarked trying to justify their silence during the murder series: 'if we gave away all our data, where would that leave us?' It was attitudes of this kind which led the Thüringen branch of the BfV to prevent the police from implementing a ban on the *Heimatschutz* – the organization from which Mundlos, Böhnhardt and Zschäpe and most of their support came.

---

23 Pitt v. Bebenburg, Verfassungsschutz im Abgrund, in: *Frankfurter Rundschau*, 23.02.15. Quoted in Funke (2015, p. 103). The reference to the desirability of keeping neo-Nazis within organized groups: René Heilig (2013, p. 96).

24 Quotations from BfV circles e.g. in: Funke (2015, pp. 282, 319).

There were two official enquiries into the NSU investigations by the federal parliament. The state parliament of Thüringen also conducted a full enquiry relating to the work of its police and security services. The information on which this chapter draws was confirmed in the course of these enquiries and the questions raised reinforced the critiques from other sources. The reasons why other federal states have not troubled to investigate the behaviour of their local agencies – a matter particularly relevant to Hessen, where, as we shall see, the case of Andreas Timme's recruitment cries out for investigation – are the subject of speculation highly unfavourable to the relevant authorities.[25] What is clear is that the promiscuous coalition politics of German federal states (where at various times not just mirror images of the Grand Coalition, but every kind of party-mix, have formed state governments) means that there is hardly a political party which was *not* in power sometime during the years that the worst mistakes were made in the NSU investigations. No party therefore has a particular interest in exploring errors in which it might itself have been closely involved.

Many commentators go on to relate the failures of the security services to the emergency legislation which set off the crisis at the time of the first Grand Coalition. Certainly the security force's default-setting was to justify their actions by suggesting that all their work was carried out on the edge of a national emergency.[26] Of course much of their work is on that edge, but the crisis of these murders was not, and in no way justified the security services keeping their activities under the radar of their parliamentary controllers and concealing information from the police. For whatever complex reason, the BfV made a mockery of the democratic process, and by so doing not only allowed a number of unremarkable and rather careless criminals to continue their murders for fully ten years but brought serious discredit onto politicians. On February 23 2012 Angela Merkel gave a solemn undertaking: 'As Chancellor of the Federal Republic of Germany I make a promise to you all: We are doing everything possible to find the truth behind these murders and to identify the accomplices and instigators of theses murderers. Our aim is to bring all those involved to justice. Every appropriate authority in the federal and state administration is

25 On the lack of a parliamentary enquiry in Hessen see Gabriel & Schau (2013). Here an explicit link is made between the NSU blunders and the period of office of Roland Koch (CDU), first Minister of Hessen (1999–2010), whose success in the election was alleged by some to have been due to anti-immigrant undertones in his campaigning and his use of illegal party funds (yet another echo of the Flick money).

26 Suggestions about the relevance of national emergency thinking come i.a. from Funke (2015, p. 300 f).

doing their utmost to achieve this end.'[27] Thanks to the security services the Chancellor's promise seems condemned to remain unfulfilled. It has been the new right which has profited from the loss of confidence this has unleashed.

11.6 Back to the Crimes

These general observations on the behaviour of police and security forces could hardly be more directly relevant to the particular crimes which concern us in this chapter. The series of murders was closely connected with the decision of three people with close links to various of the neo-Nazi organizations to move out of their normal circles in Chemnitz (where they were last seen in January 1998) and Zwickau (which they left in some haste in July 2000) on their way into the criminal underground. Indeed, even before that time they called themselves the National Socialist Underground. The three people were Uwe Mundlos, Uwe Böhnhardt and Beate Zschäpe. Despite having significant information about the trio's contacts, despite being in a position straightforwardly to arrest Mundlos while he was packing his bags at the parental home (they had just discovered bombs and bomb-making equipment in his garage),[28] despite having been supplied in 1995 by an informant with a whole CD of relevant information about the NSU, and despite evidence suggesting that various of their informants remained in contact with the trio during their ten years underground – neither the BKA nor the BfV did anything to stop the series of murders.

With truth so hard to come by and so many documentary records deliberately destroyed, the opportunity for the case to be fully presented was massively diminished. The situation was made still more impenetrable with the (at the time of writing) unsolved murder of a vital informant – 'Corelli' (Thomas Richter) – in March 2014, some ten months after the trial of Beate Zschäpe had opened in Munich. No less problematic is the fact that on November 4

27 Chancellor Merkel's promise reproduced (in sadness and indignation) by Funke (2015, p. 13).

28 Details of the raid on Zschäpes' garage Quendt (2016, p. 209); on the last bank raid and deaths in the caravan (with photographs) Aust & Laabs (2014, pp. 8–19). Somewhat surprisingly there has been a lack of conspiracy theories about the deaths of Mundlos and Böhnhardt. The comparison with the Stammheim deaths and the repeated suggestion that the two felt great resentment against the police and against those arguing for a ban on neo-Nazi organizations (a paranoia which may have been behind the murder of Michèle Kiesewetter) would have led one to expect counter arguments to the accepted view that the two simply killed themselves. See e.g. Quendt (2016, p. 259).

2011, in circumstances which have not been fully explained, the bodies of Uwe Böhnhardt and Uwe Mundlos were found in a burnt-out caravan in Eisenach. Both had been shot in the head. They had just carried out another bank raid (only at that point did the authorities identify a series of fifteen bank-robberies as having been carried out by these two men). Even in that investigation the authorities acted with striking incompetence: failing either to secure the crime-scene or to follow through on the discovery in the caravan of the police pistol, which turned out to have been taken off policewoman Michèle Kiesewetter at the time of her murder. It was immediately after the discovery of the two bodies that the BfV systematically began destroying some hundreds of files relative to its dealings with the neo-Nazi scene. The cover-up extended to the BfV's flat denial to parliamentary commissions of investigation that the BfV had set up programmes explicitly to establish contacts among neo-Nazis. Following these naïve attempts at deception, no fewer than four sectional heads from the BfV had to resign, together with the national President of the agency, Heinz Fromm. If the chickens were coming home to roost for the BfV, though only in the short term, the legal certainties for the forthcoming trial were still further eroded.

11.7 Problems with the Trial

We have already said that there had been little direct interest in the neo-Nazi movements on behalf of the courts. As early as 2003 the BVerfG had refused to continue with its enquiries into the possible banning of the NPD (the wing of neo-Nazism which was achieving limited success in local elections in the federal states in the East), even though the grounds for such a ban were far stronger than they had been for the KPD in 1956. In contrast to the Communists the neo-Nazis never made any pretence of conforming to the constitution or attempted to conceal their advocacy of violence. It may be debatable whether such a ban would have materially affected subsequent events: we noted earlier the considerable flexibility of neo-Nazi organizational structures and their ability to regroup. But a ban would have kept these people out of regional parliaments and it is more than possible that a constitutional banning of a party of the extreme right might have shifted official attitudes, perhaps in the way which *Brown vs. the Board of Education* changed attitudes to segregation. A ban would have been politically effective and internationally respected for giving a clear signal. However, the lesson behind the BVerfG's refusal to consider a ban on the NPD was in no way responded to by the security forces. For the judges concluded – by a majority – that it was impossible to determine which of the activities of the NPD had in fact been initiated and controlled by undercover agents of the security forces. They could not establish to what extent the NPD was alone responsible for its actions.[29]

In the earlier case of the NPD, the tactic of the BfV appeared to have depended less on informants and more on planting undercover agents into the party. Nevertheless, the same logic applied to the behaviour of such agents as would later apply to the informants in the neo-Nazi scene: they were all but obliged to escalate their own radicalism in order to establish their *bona fides* with the organization (and for that matter with the security forces). It was just for this reason that the court found it impossible to identify unambiguously those policies of the party which had *not* emanated from agents of the security services themselves. We suggested parallels to the policies of the British security forces in Northern Ireland during the Troubles. The two authorities shared a practice which was all but identical to that of the classic *agents provocateurs*, with the not unimportant difference that, rather than exposing the 'enemy' to apprehension and prosecution, the tactic made both apprehension and prosecution impossible. The problem had been clearly identified by the BVerfG in 2003, yet no lessons were drawn for the future policy of the security forces – again a clear hint of their general indifference to the law and contempt for the courts. The trial of Zschäpe would be the test-case for its effect on prosecution.

11.8 The Trial

The trial opened on May 6 2013 in Munich. There were five defendants. Zschäpe was charged with being an accomplice to nine murders, with arson, and with the founding and membership of a terrorist organization. Ralf Wohlleben and Carsten Schultze were charged with aiding and abetting nine murders by supplying the murder weapon. André Erminger was charged with aiding and abetting in setting off an explosive device, with theft, and on two counts of supporting a terrorist organization. Holger Gerlach was charged on three counts of supporting a terrorist organization.

Not until the trial had been proceeding for five years was a verdict reached. Many sittings of the court had to be adjourned because of Zschäpe's poor health. The defence counsels – nominated by the state –spent much time entering formal objections to the judge, Manfred Götzl and his two assessors. These objections were examined by another judge and dismissed. Equally Zschäpe spent much time arguing for the dismissal of her defence counsels,

29 See: Wesel (2004, p. 340 f) and *BVerfG E* 107, p. 339 f.

and in return the defence counsels spent much time asking to be relieved of their duties. Both (repeated) requests have been carefully examined and then dismissed. Similar requests were made at various times – and with a similar lack of success – by the defence counsels of the co-defendants. As is usual in German courts, the prosecution team included counsels representing the families of the victims.[30]

While this led – as it had in the Auschwitz trial – to a confrontation between members of victims' families and witnesses or perpetrators, the procedure seems to have been unproductive. The father of Halit Yozgat, for instance, had the opportunity to question one of the BfV's employees, Andreas Temme, who by his own account 'just happened' to be in Halit Yozgat's internet café (allegedly using a dating web-site) at the time of the murder and who had paid his bill at a counter splattered with the dead man's blood before – again on his own account – walking out of the café without noticing the victim's body lying on the floor of the café. Even when confronted in court by the dead man's father, Temme had nothing to add to this story, and this was one of many sessions which produced neither further information nor comfort to the bereaved. The court was not informed that Temme had been recruited by the local BfV despite (or was it because of?) strong neo-Nazi connections, reflected in his nickname of 'little Adolf'.

As if the time-consuming legal processes were not enough – inside the court-room too there were continuous other problems. At sensitive moments in the trial prominent neo-Nazis turned up to support (or on occasion to intimidate) witnesses. For the victims' families there was the disturbing sight of active neo-Nazis walking in and out of the court-room and on occasion giving evidence and then simply walking free – including NPD members of regional assemblies, for instance David Petereit from Mecklenburg-Vorpommern, editor of a neo-Nazi periodical which had expressed its explicit thanks to the NSU for its support (13.07.16).[31] To the victims' families that did not look like even-handed justice. The consul general of Turkey and various representatives of Turkish human rights organizations had claimed the right to be present at the

30 Comments on the conduct of the trial vary from those congratulating the judge on at least reaching a verdict and those more critical of the court's failure to disqualify more of the witnesses or focus the proceedings more strongly. See for instance the *FAZ*'s close analysis of the trial (NSU-Prozess: Der Preis der Gerechtigkeit, 10.07.2018) and: NSU-Prozess – das Urteil. *Tagesspiegel*, 11.07.2018.

31 The response of the prosecution counsels representing the victims' families to neo-Nazis walking freely in and out of the court in: Burschel (2015, p. 79). See also the interview with one of these prosecuting counsels, discussing the conduct of the trial: Fehler der Inlandsgeheimdienste (2013).

hearing, even though at the start it was one of the most eagerly awaited and therefore heavily visited trials of the time. (It can be imagined that the trial will have had some influence on the recently highly strained relations between the Federal Republic and Turkey. President Erdogan's accusation that Germany is a Nazi state will not have come simply from any personal knowledge of history.) Outside on the streets there have been neo-Nazi demonstrations and counter demonstrations by 'anti-fascist' organizations.

The conduct of the trial – and the approach taken by the trial judge – have been subject to continuous critical comment, both within the normal media and within various professional legal journals. Some commentators praise Götzl for having at least held things together. Others are critical of his tacit acceptance of the subversive actions of the police and BfV. Not all these critiques need concern us here, but it is striking that the Auschwitz trial – with a much higher number of witnesses and examining an organization of a complexity and an extent to which the small-minded activities of Mundlos, Böhnhardt and Zschäpe could not aspire – reached clear judgments within 183 days of sittings and some 21 accused. The comparison says something about the efficiency of the Munich court procedures, although it would be unreasonable to doubt the genuine desire of the prosecution for a result. Even if we ignore these issues, however, and ask about outcomes: the balance of four years of trial is far from encouraging.

Despite a psychologist's report describing her as possessing a robust and aggressive personality, Ms Zschäpe claimed to have been intimated by Mundlos and Böhnhardt, to have known nothing of the murders (which she claimed to regret) and – speaking in court for the first time: this on September 29 2016 (three and a half years into the trial!) – to have distanced herself from any neo-Nazi opinions which she had once held. Carsten Schultze – the prosecution's crown witness – further incriminated Wohlleben, while Wohlleben himself denied those allegations, claiming only a most tangential relation to the trio during their period in the criminal underground. Erminger and Gerlach admitted the bare facts of their support, but denied both that they knew anything of the purposes for which the trio were working and any personal involvement in criminal activities. Wohlleben, when questioned, has suffered a whole series of memory lapses on sensitive questions. This convenient amnesia has afflicted not only other witnesses from the neo-Nazi movement, but the few representatives of the security services who have appeared before the court.

It's almost banal in view of these issues to conclude our account of the trial by summarizing the verdicts. Beate Zschäpe was given a life sentence. Wohlleben was sentenced to ten years, but at the time of writing it is regarded as likely, since he has spent the years of the trial in custody, that the rest of his sentence will be commuted. Schultze was found guilty of being an accessory but he received three years of youth detention (relating to his age at the time of the crimes). A similar length of sentence was delivered on Gerlach, for supporting a terrorist organization. The court chose to believe André Erminger when he claimed to have been unaware of the purposes for which the gang were using the apartments and vehicles he had procured for them. His sentence was two and a half years. As the *Guardian* reported: 'it would be hard to believe that the defendants would have received such lenient sentences had they been working for a Jihadist terror cell.'[32] We emphasize that appeals may well be made against these sentences.

The court was forbidden to cross-examine Rolf Marschner, BfV informant in Zwickau (the town in which Mundlos, Böhnhardt and Zschäpe had lived towards the end of their murderous activities), thus no doubt sparing him the necessity for his own memory lapses. The court has heard unambiguous evidence that the BfV had blocked police investigation of the murder in Kassel (06.08.14). Furthermore, when one of the BfV's agents, Kai D., gave evidence, he explicitly referred to the strict limits which the agency had placed on the evidence he could give the court (19.11.14). So the BfV has blocked the court just as deliberately as it had blocked the police, but the judge has refrained from comment. The usefulness of such witnesses to the court was hardly greater than that of a BKA inspector who, while giving evidence, proved unable to identify Zschäpe in court, since he had left his spectacles at home (04.07.13). It seems reasonable to question whether justice is at all possible against the background of this security service behaviour. We are looking at a trial in which the procedures supposed to protect democracy threaten to undermine one of its surest foundations: the law.

A moralizing approach to this situation would stress the series of lessons which have not been learned in the course of the history of the Federal Republic. We mention only a few: the failure of both the courts and the parliamentary institutions to control the security forces (revealed by the *Spiegel*-Affair and by the *Berufsverbot*); the excessive freedom of action of federal and state ministers (see the *Spiegel*-Affair); the ambivalence of the state apparatus towards the legacy of Nazism. Emergency legislation has never ceased to be problematic, while the alienation of the police and security services (which was established as an explicit attempt to overcome the sinister collaboration of the two agencies in the *Gestapo*) has led to near anarchy. Such structural problems are in addition to the relentless recruitment of senior Nazi policemen into

32 Philip Ottermann: Neo-Nazi terrorist sentenced to life in jail for 10 murders, *Guardian*, 12.07.2018.

responsible positions.[33] The readiness of politicians to castigate the BVerfG, as if the function of a Supreme Court were merely to carry out government wishes, has weakened the respect for the law. It is far from clear that the court's unambiguous criticism of the security forces' use of phone-tapping (the judgment of 2004) has changed the practice of government agencies – they will always find justification from the terms of the next 'emergency'. In short: the *Lüth* judgment has not succeeded in persuading the state of the necessity of implementing the vision of democratic freedom enshrined in the *Grundgesetz*, not just with further paragraphs of law, but in the daily practices of government and administration.

These are some of the tasks which the Federal Republic has to face in its next seventy years. They are not its only problems, but they do seem to be among its most serious.

33 The background to the police in the Federal Republic – at least up to the 1970s – is unflatteringly examined by Wagner (2002) and Brunner (2002).

APPENDIX

Background Notes

Background Notes to the Introduction

I refer to more specialized *works of history* as the chapters pass through the various phases of the Federal Republic's development. A useful general English-language guide to the history of the Weimar Republic, Third Reich and both the Federal Republic and the German Democratic Republic, popular with readers and reasonably up to date with recent events, is: Mary Fulbrook (2009). Excellent as always A. J. Nicholls (1991). Institutional and political structures are emphasized in: David P. Conradt (2001[7]); Manfred G. Schmidt (2003); Arthur B. Gunlicks (ed.) (2003) and Werner J. Patzelt (2003). Also: Peter H. Merkel (1999). An earlier work: Carl Christoph Schweitzer, Detlev Karsten, et al. (1984). Particularly useful for its focus on transitions in the history of the Federal Republic: Ulrich Herbert (2002). The idea of the German *Sonderweg* (special history) outside West European norms was raised constantly during the so-called *Historikerstreit* in the 1970s. See: Kocka (1988).

For an excellent *history of jurisprudence* in the Federal Republic, with particular emphasis on the long-term processes of democratization, see: Jörg Requate (2008). A detailed study of this history during the 1970s: Thomas Basten (1983) and Osterholzer (2012). One of the very few relevant works in English is Michael Stolleis' essay (2001), which discusses the general shortage of historical writing in this field. For the earlier period: Stolleis (2004). Norbert Frei (1999) gives the fullest account of the problems caused by the NS traditions in the legal institutions immediately after 1949. Useful for the early years: Petra Gödecke (2008).

The *Stunde Null* was often debated by the younger generation of writers who formed the so-called *Gruppe 47*. Their focus was all but exclusively on the cultural devastation of Germany, but of course the group's writings dealt also with the social hardships and deprivations of the post-war years. See the classic anthology of Hans Werner Richter (1993[2]). In English see: Wolfgang Beutin (1993).

There is an extensive literature on the *origins of court-reporting*, both in sources like *Pitaval* and in the more modern media and fiction. Outstanding is: Jörg Schönert (1991). Here contributions on *Pitaval* and its German imitators (Joachim Linder: pp. 313–48); on court-reporting (Jörg Hennig: pp. 349–67 and Joachim Rückert: pp. 635–50). Also: Joachim Linder & Claus-Michael Ort (1995). In English and therefore concerned with US and UK: Leroz Panek (2006); Judith Rowbotham, Kim Stevenson and Samantha Pegg (2013); Roy Edward Lotz (1991); Thomas Cragin (2006). The importance of media to individual cases is well illustrated in the three case-studies included in Wetzell (2008): Sace Elder, Eva Bischoff & Daniel Siemens, and Todd Herzog.

Adenauer's constraints between his own desired internal policies and those imposed by the FRG's geo-political situation can be clearly seen in the detailed account given by Frei of the relationship between the first *Adenauer government and the NS past.* Frei's work (1999) offers a particularly useful account of the actual conditions under which the law was administered between 1949 and 1954, and he makes clear how the Allies – notably the British – constantly pushed Adenauer to act against NS sympathizers, both inside and outside his coalition partners, while expecting him to align the FRG firmly on the side of the West in its dealings with Communists, inside and outside the country. The sensational intervention of the British in arresting Werner Naumann (Goebbels' appointed successor) in 1951 shows the uneasy co-existence of the two systems of reference (Frei, 1999, p. 361f).

For *the justice system of the NS period*: Michael Stolleis (1998). A further excellent account is: Bernhard Diestelkamp & Michael Stolleis (1988). A particularly depressing element was the whole-hearted support which Nazism got from university law departments. On this topic see: Ingo Müller (1996). The most significant legal theorist during those years was Carl Schmitt (see his essay: Der Führer schützt das Recht (*The Führer protects the law*), in: *Deutsche Juristenzeitschrift*, 1934, col. 945–50). See also Dworkin (1986, p. 101 f) and: Mehring (2010).

Wolfgang Benz presents a sobering picture of the *de-nazification process involving judges*, in: Diestelkamp & Stolleis (1988, pp. 112–40). Still more hard-hitting Franz Arnau (1967, pp. 52–92). Also: Rebecca Wittmann (2006). With a particular focus on ZSL and official attempts to block its work: Annette Weinke (2008). An alternative view of de-nazification in: Otto Kirchheimer (1961, pp. 8–9).

Bias in judging NS criminals: The celebrated defence counsel Heinrich Hannover gives a telling account of the way in which SS men entirely eluded justice having murdered KPD chief Ernst Thälmann in a concentration camp at the end of the war: (1991, pp. 33–42). See also the Krumey-Hunsche case (these were associates of Eichmann, with the job of sending Hungarian Jews to Auschwitz): *Der Spiegel* 7/1965; hardly less scandalous the acquittal of Hans Joachim Rehse (who had sat with Freiser as an assistant judge in the notorious People's Court) on a charge of perverting the course of justice: *FAZ* 11.12.68, and Requate (2008, pp. 163, 231).

For attempts to subvert *Article 1 of the Control Council*, see Chapters 5 and 9. An important element in the discussion of a penal code's mutability under various régimes is the level of concreteness which a code adopts in defining offences and asserting its own goals. The Weimar Constitution was notorious for the abstraction of its formulations, and this meant that the text could easily be corrupted by being applied to different situations than those which its formulators had in mind – both by the Nazis and by Adenauer's judges.

Continuities with NS system: The situation of the Federal and state German *police* forces represents both the norm and a genuine blot on the post-war years. A particularly crass example of their attitudes was the concerted attempt by the post-war police to implement a policy of preventive detention against habitual criminals and potential 'enemies of the state'. See: Wagner (2002). Preventive detention had, of course, been the policy behind Himmler's concentration camps, whose passing the post-war police appeared to regret. These issues arise clearly in Chapter 11 below. See also Weinke (2008, pp. 40 f, 58 f).

A massive literature exists on *Marxist interpretations of the law*. The German post-war debate focuses – unsurprisingly – on the cases discussed in Chapters 2, 8 and 9, and, rather than blinding readers with long lists, I suggest as starting-points the authors (and publishers) referred to specifically in the notes on these chapters. Marx's original comments are found in *Kritik des Gothaer Programms.* Of course, it was not the Federal Republic alone which suffered from class-justice: the laws it took over from the pre-1914 years and from the Weimar Republic showed the same inherent features. This was analyzed by Ernst Fränkel (1968²) – a reprint which caused the work to be widely read by the student generation. Kirchheimer's approach to the general question of what constitutes political justice remains an important contribution to the field. See: Ooyen & Schale (2011, pp. 199–224).

Any serious history of the Federal Republic will include an outline of the early history of the state and explain the *passing of the* ***Grundgesetz*** and the foundation of the BVerfG. The standard commentaries on the *Grundgesetz* also summarize this history. I have referred in particular to: Bruno Schmidt-Bleibtreu & Franz Klein (1993⁸). Here we find the claim of the BVerfG's 'teleological function' – i.e. reading the entire legal code as if it were leading up to the *Grundgesetz*, in the same manner that the Old Testament was to be read in the light of the New (pp. 97, 99). Individual studies of the BVerfG are listed below. The place of judicial review in German legal history is discussed in: Kommers (1976), and by: Möllers (2014). For a view of the BVerfG and its relationship to basic rights see Galay (1964², pp. 159–98). Galay also closely examines the role of federalism in the *Grundgesetz*.

Two substantial accounts of *the BVerfG*, the first focused on structures and procedures, the second institutional, focused on court personnel and cases: Kommers (1997²); Collings (2015). For a comparative approach see: Rogowski & Gawron (2012). The comparison is conducted in terms not of structures, but of the two courts' historical function in giving stability to their respective countries: cf. especially p. 7 f. In this volume too the essay to which Chapter 1 refers: Alfred Rinken, pp. 55–90. Out of the considerable literature in German I have used especially: Ooyen & Möllers (2006). Also (from a left of centre perspective) Joachim Perels (1976). The most heated confrontation between the BGH and the BVerfG occurred in the early 1950s, when the conservative (not to say at times unreconstructedly Nazi) BGH tried to thwart the more radically democratic decision of the BVerfG concerning the absorption of NS civil servants (and their pensions) into the FRG (see: Frei, 1999, pp. 69–100). The most readable account of the court's history is: Uwe Wesel (2004) – a book epitomized by a readiness to critique the court's judgments. Typical of Wesel's approach is the comment that lawyers often get things right for the wrong reasons, 'just as a correctly argued case can lead to the wrong outcome' (2004, pp. 119–20). None of these studies are complete, in the sense of treating *all* the court's judgments. Wesel is the most successful in marking historical trends. The judgments of the court can be found in *BVerfG E*: they can also be found in the *Neue Juristische Wochenschrift*, though in neither case is it easy to find individual cases, for German law-cases are not designated with reference to the litigants.

Introductions to German law in English include: Horn, Kötz & Leser (1982). (This volume includes a pretty exhaustive list of abbreviations used in German legal documents, pp. 326–31). Helpful on the comparative aspect of the Federal Republic's law: Gessner, Hoeland & Varga (1996). The concept of a 'gapless system of legal propositions' is part of Max Weber's analysis of the rationality of the modern state. See the extract from Weber's 'Economy of Law' in the above volume, pp. 69–73, here 69. See also the legal sections of: Schweitzer, Karsten et al. (1984), pp. 80–112 (The Judiciary) and 113–37 (Basic Rights and Constitutional Review).

Two helpful comparisons between the *common law* (particularly in its American form) and *civil (or statute) law*: Benjamin Kaplan (1960); and Joseph Dainow (1966–67).

Readers will find two types of argument on the *fundamental aspects of the Rechtsstaat*. With the catastrophes of German history in mind, German legal commentators have a tendency to idealize the British concepts and practice of common law, and thus to play up the distinctiveness of statute law. Cf. Gessner, Hoeland & Varga (1996, pp. 69–73, 141–43); this view is critiqued by Zimmermann (1996). Dworkin resists a simple division of legal systems into 'interpretivist' and 'non-interpretivist' (1986, p. 359f). See also: Watson (1981). Collings points out – less problematically – that in the 19th century *Rechtsstaat* had meant little more than that law was substituted for democracy (2015, p. xxxiii). See also Otto Kirchheimer (1967).

On the innate *conservativeness of judges* in the Federal Republic, their potential openness to political influence and their traditional dependence on the paragraphs of the law (*Begriffspositivismus* or *Begriffsjurisprudenz*), see: Horn, Kötz & Leser (1982), pp. 37–50; and Heribert Prantl (1996). See also: Donald R. Kommers (1976, p. 50 f). It is informative to compare this discussion with the categories set up by Cass R. Sunstein (2015). Without descending into the 'legal realism' according to which a court's verdict depends on 'what a judge had for breakfast' (Dworkin, 1986, p. 36), Cass summarizes judicial personalities, from 'hero', 'soldier' and 'activist' downwards. (Sunstein, reviewed by Jeremy Waldron in *NYRB*, 24.03.2016, p. 23 f.) There is little doubt where most German judges would land.

The intense *sociological* discussion of the composition of the German judiciary was initiated in the 1960s, notably by Ralf Dahrendorf (1968: Chapter 16). Previous to these studies the judges were all but untouchables. A follow-up work packed with statistical detail: Raymund Werle (1977).

On the historical tradition of *legal education* in Germany see: Joachim Rückert (1991). On a crass example of the long continuation of NS ideas in university law departments see also: Ewald Grothe (2008). Wassermann insists that in terms of legal education 1945 did not represent any break in continuity (1969, p. 310). Some commentators argue that the shift which the NS state brought about in the law – from 'the individualism of the BGB' to collective thinking in terms of the community – remains a feature of the West German system (cf. Fraisek 2008). Those universities (e.g. Bremen) which most strongly broke with traditional legal education had to consider that they might suffer negative consequences within the profession.

The most stimulating account of the *post-war development of the SPD* away from radicalism: Theo Pirker (1965). In English see Wikipedia. For the early period the classic text is: Carl E. Schorske (1983).

Background Notes to Chapter 1

Parts of this chapter are indebted to the *historical perspectives on Nuremberg* offered by the essays included in: Philippe Sands (ed.) (2003), in particular, the essays of Richard Overy and Andrew Clapham. For a legal-historical analysis with greater focus on the actual Nuremberg trials see: Reginbogin & Safferling (2006). Of particular interest for my text were the essays in this volume: Raymond M. Brown; David Cesarini; Rodger D. Citron; Sam Garkawe; and Rebecca Wittmann. In the last essay there is a close examination of the problem of the 'desk-top murderers' and of the debates about the statute of limitation (*Verjährung*). Relating to the so-called 'Nuremberg Principle' see: Hiromi Satō (2011). Of particular interest is chapter 3: Foundation of the 'Nuremberg Principle' (pp. 49–102; also his study of the further international influence of the Nuremberg trials (p. 103 f). The 'personal memoir' of Telford Taylor (1993) contains valuable insights and illuminating details. An excellent short account: Annette Weinke (2006).

Philippe Sands' remarkable *East West Street* (2016) examines in detail the background of two international lawyers – Hersch Lauterpacht and Rafael Lemkin – who were (respectively) close to and on the periphery of the Nuremberg court. Sands' focus is to contrast the role of two varying judicial concepts relevant to the NS period and to subsequent international criminal trials: the concept of a 'crime against humanity', in which the complaining party was not the Allies (and not the Jewish people), but what Telford Taylor called 'civilization' (1993, p. 289) and the concept of 'genocide' which Lemkin tried to promote. Taylor's study briefly mentions Lemkin as an academic source for knowledge about the Third Reich, but no mention is made of Lauterpacht –

which says something about the balance between US and British prosecution teams. In Chapter 7 we examine the problems which arose in the Frankfurt Auschwitz trial (1963) because of the absence of the concept of genocide in German law. Taylor's book also contains the full text of the charter of the IMT (1993, pp. 646–53).

On the other side, one hardly needs to emphasize that, for a very high percentage of German lawyers and judges, the Nuremberg court and its methods were an abomination. See e.g.: Judex (1963, p. 21 f). More surprising might be the tireless agitation of the churches against all efforts to punish NS criminals. See Weinke (2006, p. 105 f).

My account of the actual *proceedings in the Flick trial* bases on K. H. Thieleke (1965). This is a thorough and extensive documentation. For an account of the trial in the full context of Flick's activities during the Third Reich see: Bähr, Drecoll & Gotto (2008). Together with an account of the trial itself (pp. 559–645) there is a detailed account of Flick's take-over of the Petschek empire (p. 322f). For a detailed account of the trial from a later legal point of view see: Susanne Jung (1992), on whose work this chapter gratefully draws at a number of points. Another detailed study of Flick and his trial (certainly more outspoken in its portrayal of Flick himself) is: Frei, Ahrens, Osterloh & Schanetcky (2009). This account makes interesting claims for the influence of the Soviet Union and East German agencies on the trial, including the suggestion that the *Stasi* (East German security services) had placed its own source in Flick's Bonn office (p. 747f); also on Flick's team offering half a million dollars to get the judgment overturned (p. 429 f). Dix' remarks on protecting compliance with orders are quoted in Satō (2011, p. 78). A brief account of the Flick scandals in: Collings (2015, pp. 199–202).

Although the issues involved in the lenient treatment of Flick and other members of the technical-industrial elite (*Funktionselite*) did not simply become one of the central concerns of the International Criminal Courts after Nuremberg: they were absolutely central to the *Eichmann trial in Jerusalem* in 1961 and to the Auschwitz trial in Frankfurt a.M. which followed shortly after it. These questions are discussed further in Chapter 7.

The material discussed in the Introduction suggests good reasons why a huge amount of the *documentation from the NS years* was not kept in German archives, but was held on to by the allies, in the Berlin Document Centre, until the end of the *Verjährung* debates of the 1960s. Under public pressure the statute of limitation was modified, with the result that the prosecution of NS war criminals is still possible today (but increasingly unlikely, in view of the age of those who actively participated in the regime). There is no doubt that without the obstruction of large sections of the judiciary and the legal professions much more could have been done to prosecute war-criminals. Perhaps that was – paradoxically – one of the lessons of Nuremberg for the German judiciary: that such trials were potentially dangerous to them and should therefore be prevented in the future.

An *alternative view of Germany's economic ruin* and its subsequent 'economic miracle' in the FRG in: Schmiede (1976). The Basic Law left open questions of overall economic policy, permitting both private and public ownership of the means of production, and allowing a potentially significant role for the trade-unions, and Erhard's policies appeared to modify Flick's ruthless logic. Schmiede argues that, while German production capacity in the East had been reduced by Soviet demontage of industrial plants and their removal to the Soviet homeland, in the West that capacity remained proportionally more intact than pictures of the destructive effects of the war might suggest. One consequence of Allied bombing policy, for instance, was that industrial production – not being situated inside the cities which were the bombers' principal target – did not suffer the damage which befell civilian housing. Certainly, Flick's plants were gearing up enthusiastically for the requirements of peace-time production when Flick himself was most inconveniently arrested at the end of the war. No-one could imagine, for instance, that a magnificent cultural city such as Dresden, crammed with refugees fleeing from the advancing Soviet armies, contained significant industrial plant. Whatever its devastation achieved, it was not the reduction of industrial productivity.

Background Notes to Chapter 2

In choosing to write on the question of *the balance of judgments in BVerfG* cases, Rinken draws up a helpful list of cases. His account makes clear that my approach here can be justified in summarizing almost any phase in the history of the court. Rinken in: Rogowski & Gawron (2012, p. 65). I have taken *Lüth* (Chapter Three) as a counterbalance to the KPD ban. Equally one might have taken the BVerfG's rejection of Adenauer's proposal for a TV channel in which the government would have had a complete monopoly, or on the other side the celebrated Constanze case, in which in retrospect the BVerfG was felt unreasonably to have restricted a citizen's freedom of expression. See: Thomas Henne (2006, esp. pp. 145, 148 f).

An overview of the *Adenauer government's measures against the KPD* in: Alexander von Brünneck (1978). Here too a critical account of the KPD's policies over these years (pp. 20–51). Also: Dietrich Stratitz (1976). In the same volume (Blanke 1976) an earlier version of Brünneck's arguments. The Interior Ministry issued on September 20 1950 a decree controlling 'the political activity of members of the public service aimed against the basic democratic order'. The text of the decree in: *Gemeinsames Ministerialblatt*, 1,12, pp. 93–4 This forerunner of the Decree on Radicals of January 28 1972 (see Chapter 8) encouraged public bodies to take action against public servants who were members of the KPD, FDJ and eleven other groups.

Anti-Communism played a highly significant role in the twenty-year discussion which finally led to emergency legislation. Martin Diebel (2019) has shown how prevalent it was among the higher civil servants in the Federal Ministry of the Interior. Emergency legislation was planned explicitly to combat the Communists' ability to bring about a collapse in the social order, e.g. by a general strike; to counteract an invasion of police and *Volksarmee* forces from the Communist neighbour, the GDR; and to prepare for the possibility of a general attack on the FRG by the Warsaw Pact. No-one thought that emergency legislation would be needed to stop a right-wing coup, although it was in that direction that historical precedents obviously pointed.

Background Notes to Chapter 3

This chapter is based extensively on the excellent volume of *documentation*: Henne & Riedlinger (ed.) (2005). The volume includes full details of both the Harlan and the Lüth case. The judgment itself is also available in *BVerfG E* 7, p. 198 f. An extensive account of aspects of the case helpfully presented in parallel English-German texts can be found in: Raymond Young (2002[2], pp. 504–59). Young's commentary does little to highlight the central importance of this judgment beyond the category – Tort – under which it appears.

It is easy to get muddled with the proliferation of efforts by Adenauer's governments to achieve a blanket *amnesty for NS criminals*. The first amnesty proposal in 1949 was followed by a further amnesty in 1954 and by the whole debate on *Verjährung* in the 1960s. See: Frei (1999, pp. 29–54), who shows clearly which NS criminals profited from individual measures. A notable decision of the BVerfG qualified the restoration of full status and pension rights (on the basis of GG § 131) to civil servants who had served under the Nazis and was correspondingly controversial in a society which wanted to forget. While Adenauer's blunt call to put an end to 'sniffing out Nazis' and his protection of Globke might suggest that the CDU was the principal mover in the call for amnesty, it should not be forgotten that leading figures in the SPD and the churches – to say nothing of the DP and the FDP – were prominent in the campaign. In this, after 1950 at least, they were supported by a majority of the population. The *Spiegel Special* 1/2009 gives a lively overview of the topic.

A positive view of *Harlan* is presented by Ingrid Buchloh (2010). Buchloh emphasizes that Harlan had many Jewish friends, that he held liberal views on § 175, felt himself the scapegoat for a historical situation he could not control and was following genuine artistic ambitions in *Jud Süß*. Readers may find the author's identification of 'Jewish blood' among Harlan's detractors (2010, p. 201) less attractive.

Background Notes on Chapter 4

Details of the Hetzel case have been taken from a variety of sources, including on-line. A near contemporary account by one of the harshest critics of miscarriages of justice in the Federal Republic, Austria and Switzerland: Arnau (1967, pp. 116–28). Most evidence comes in the articles in *Der Spiegel* written by Gerhard Mauz: 'Ich muss ihr die Luft abgestellt haben' (14.02.1966); 'Mit dem Töten in näherem Verhältnis' (5.09.66); 'Alter Mann mit Strick beim Abendbrot' (7.10.68 – here the full account of Ponsold's Italian article); 'Noch Fragen zum Enddarm? (3.11.69); and 'Zu feige, die volle Wahrheit zu sagen' (10.11.69).

The Birmingham Six case was one of a number of *miscarriages* of British justice in the wake of the IRA campaigns of the 1960s and 1970s. Frank Skuse was the 'expert witness' in this case, claiming to have found traces of explosive on the hands of the accused. (The actual origin of these traces was, after the six had spent sixteen years in prison, proved to have been a new pack of playing-cards.) The redressing of this miscarriage of justice was largely due to the work of the journalist, subsequently member of parliament and minister, Chris Mullen. Another 'eminent' expert British forensic scientist active in the period up to the 1950s was Bernard Spilsbury: his reputation has been corrected by Andrew Rose (2007). The 1960s were not a happy time for expert witnesses. Franz Arnau gives many examples of cases in which defendants were 'executed' by a medical witness and where the 'expert witness [...] usurps the role of the judge' (1973, p. 18).

Out of the range of *texts on Rosemarie Nitribitt* I have used primarily: Erich Kuby. (1961). See also Helga Dierichs, (2003). Rosemarie is described as a 'mythological' figure in the article: Edelhure Rosemarie Nitribitt, in: *Spiegel*-Online. Rosemarie's story is intriguingly brought into the present-day in: Judith Kuckart (2006). The Wikipedia article on Nitribitt contains an extensive list of the films, articles and studies on the case. On the *Vera Brühne case* see: Michael Gramberg (2003) and: Ulrich Sonnemann (1974). On Maria Rohrbach: Arnau (1967, pp. 96, 200 f).

A murder and subsequent trials similarly expressive of the state of a whole nation involved the death of Catrine da Costa in Stockholm in 1984, the so-called *Styckmordet*. Accusations of a mis-trial, disturbing material and bizarre circumstances attracted the attention of crime-writers, including Stieg Larsson. Mauz' fight for justice is paralleled in other *Swedish cases*: for instance, more recently: Stefan Lisinksi (2017).

Background Notes to Chapter 5

On the *general issues* raised in this chapter see: Dagmar Herzog (2011); Michael Kandora (2002). Also: Heinemann (2011). An overall view of the cultural shifts in the early post-war years in: Steinbacher (2011). Steinbacher's study is particularly strong in showing up the work of church organizations in fighting against any form of liberalization in sexual matters.

On *legal aspects* of these social and attitudinal changes: Thomas Schlemmer, (2012). On the *historical dimensions of § 175*: Kurt Hiller (1927) (here accounts of Gustav Wyneken and the major campaigner Magnus Hirschfeld, including of the assassination attempt against him in 1920). For a general view of homosexuals' situation in the Weimar Republic see: Martin Lücke (2015). On homosexuals in war see Herzog (2011, p. 98).

The *historical background of § 218* in: Kristine von Soden (1996); and Kirsten Pontus (1996); Robert Jütte (1993) – especially useful here is Michael Gante (1993), whose essay covers the 20th century. In addition there are numerous books written at various points in the debates and subsequently overhauled by events, one example: Schroeder (1975).

On the place of *sexuality under fascism* see: Dagmar Herzog (2005). Eric N. Jensen's essay in this collection explores the persecution in concentration camps. Also the volume *'Das sind Volksfeinde'* (1998). On the fear of contagion, see: Herzog (2011, p. 73). On the enthusiastic Gestapo persecution of gays in particular districts see: Jürgen Müller (1998) and Frank Sparing (1998).

On perceived *anomalies* in the legislation: The Federal Republic, in common with the USA and most European countries, experienced a major public campaign in support of Lesbianism in the early 1970s. (See e.g.: *Der Spiegel* 1974/36, p. 60f). The issue came into the legal sphere in a sensational way in 1974, when Judy Andersen and Marion Ihns were put on trial for having hired a Danish man to murder Ihns' husband. The inflexibility of German law contrasted with the flexibility of Danish law (Andersen was a Danish national), for the two women were sentenced to life, while the man got sixteen years from a Danish court. With extraordinary openness, the trial highlighted the emotional problems of Lesbians and – despite some sensationalist reporting – created further sympathy for their cause. (See: *Die Zeit*, 11.10.74, reproduced in http://www.zeit.de/1974/42/mitleid-fuer-zwei-frauen.) German law had never criminalized Lesbianism, mirroring the strong tradition in anti-gay legislation of regarding sexual acts which imitated heterosexual intercourse as criminal and – apart from during the NS years – ignoring other homosexual activity. Yet the law-givers consistently behaved as if the moral offence was homosexuality itself and the failure to procreate. See: Kandora (2002, p. 94); and Ackermann (1963, esp. p. 157 f).

Background Notes on Chapter 6

For a brilliantly exciting approach to the connections between Suez and Budapest see the remarkable novel by the great German novelist Uwe Johnson (1934–1984) *Speculations about Jakob* (*Mutmaßungen über Jakob*).

I have drawn on *five principal sources*. The most complete is the two-volume study, edited by Alfred Grosser & Jürgen Seifert (vol. 1 1966) and by Thomas Ellwein, Manfred Liebel & Inge Negt (vol. 2 1966). Of the four following texts, the first emphasizes the parliamentary dimension of the Affair; the second focuses on Augstein's personality, the third was the first to appear in English (in the same year in which the German translation appeared) and the fourth is closest to an inside, blow-by-blow story. Theodor Eschenburg (1962) – here the allegations of Strauss' drunken state at the onset of the Cuban Missile Crisis (p. 11) and the ironic reminder that the German police were out of practice at conducting house-arrests and searches (p. 7); Gert Bergner (1964); David Schoenbaum (1968); Joachim Schoeps (1983). *Der Spiegel* is easily available on-line, and the original article can be read there.

Adenauer's *attack on Augstein* was, naturally, reinforced by the Springer Press, which accused *Der Spiegel* of having 'become the delivery boy of quotations for Ulbricht's propaganda' (Ulbricht was head of the Central Committee of the SED in East Germany, and from 1949 to 1973 the most important politician of the state) – quoted by Schoeps (1983, p. 210). More on the Springer Press in Chapter 8. Prime Minister Harold Wilson's public dislike of the press is documented in: Nicholas Wilkinson, who offers a full account of the Lohan-Affair (2007, pp. 283–342). It's interesting to compare what happened to Ahlers with the respect in which the military correspondent Anthony Verrier was held after writing a critical account of a major manoeuvre of the British Rhine Army in October 1961 (published in the *Journal of the Royal United Services Institute*, 1962, and quoted in *Der Spiegel* 1962/47).

Particularly useful on press-government relations and on *D-notices* and their danger of 'overspill' (i.e. misuse): Colin Seymour-Ure (1968). In the British context, Seymour-Ure comments wisely on parliamentary anger with the Press. It happens, he remarks, 'when it [parliament] is unsure of its own standing with the electorate' (1968, p. 164).

Background Notes to Chapter 7

There is a huge literature on the *Holocaust*, considerable amounts of it sparked by the Frankfurt trial. My own reading here has stayed with those accounts close to the trial and, where possible, to the times. The most immediate account of the trial, historically and in terms of personal involvement, is: Hermann Langbein (1965). Langbein was both head of the IAK and had himself been a detainee in Auschwitz. He not only offered assistance in the prosecution of Boger (assistance rejected by Stuttgart authorities, gladly welcomed by Fritz Bauer), but personally attended the whole of the trial. The extracts from the cross-examination of Boger and Mulka are taken from his account (1965, pp. 163 f, 210 f and 367 f resp.). I have also drawn extensively on: Raphael Gross & Werner Renz (2013). This includes Johannes Schmidt's account of legal issues in the trial. Strongly to be recommended: Devin O. Pendas (2006). A close analysis of the legal issues in the trial (contextualized by comparison with American law) can be found here (2006 pp. 53–79). Sands (2016) includes much historical detail, filtered through his distinctive approach.

On the person and career of *Fritz Bauer*: Ronen Steinke (2013). Here esp. an account of Bauer's failure with the euthanasia trial (2013, p. 192f) and his ethical approach to the prosecution of war-criminals (p. 152f). A major biography: Irmtraut Wojak (2009^2), discussed in: Jochen Vogt (2014). Fritz Arnau gives a full account of the failure of Bauer's euthanasia trial and discusses Globke's protection of the accused in such trials (1967, pp. 55–61). In English: Paterson (2016). One small indication of the moral impact of the euthanasia programme on post-war generations is the frequency with which the policy is referenced in present-day quality crime fiction, e.g. by Ulrich Ritzel and Ute-Maria Heim.

The *amnesty* story is best told by Frei (1999) for the period up to 1955. See also: Wolfrum (2005, p. 346 f); and Hannover (1991, p. 22 f).

The *BGH verdict* had an unusual prehistory, starting from the so-called 'bath tub' case. This came to court in 1940, and raised what from the start was recognized as a sensitive question of law. Two sisters had drowned a new-born baby. Despite arguments to the contrary, the court initially determined that only the woman who actually held the baby in the water was guilty of murder. The fact that she was doing so with the encouragement of her sister (the mother of the child) was not relevant and did not make her merely an accomplice to murder. In fact, what the literature identifies as this 'subjective view' finally prevailed and the woman was spared the death-penalty. Quite remarkably the BGH took this view further in 1962, when it determined that a professional assassin, who had been sent by the KGB to murder a Ukrainian dissident in the Federal Republic, was not guilty of murder. The court ruled that his murderous action was not 'his own' but that 'of another party' (i.e. the head of the KGB) – those were the exact terms in which the bath tub verdict had been reached – and the assassin was thus merely an accomplice to murder. It's hard to see any other reason for their decision except its implications for the trials of NS criminals which the creation of the ZSL was expected to bring about. (See: *BGHSt* 18, 87 for the Stachynskij judgment, which Pendas calls 'infamous' (2006, p. 70). See also: Krey (2005, p. 13 f).

Background Notes to Chapter 8

I occasionally use the word *'victim'* to denote the subjects of this chapter, not in order to harvest sympathy, but because it is hard to find a more appropriate word. In the initial hearings they were the accused; at appeal they acted in the role of claimant, but, when the state appealed against decisions which had gone against it, they were once again defendants. When the case went to the BVerfG they and the state were – in legal terms at least – equal in status, if not in resources.

As the text of this chapter makes clear, the volume of literature in this field is considerable, but seldom mainstream. In their search for public support, some people experiencing the *Berufsverbot* produced informal *basic documentation*. This was occasionally collected by local support groups, trade-unions, regional or national committees against the *Berufsverbot* and international bodies such as the Russell Tribunal, and some of these collections were reissued, again in cyclostyled or basic form. A certain number of books was published, but the climate was such that many individuals felt discouraged from becoming involved in other people's cases and reluctant to publicize their own. Apart from the volumes of individual case documentation, frequent themes of the publications on the *Berufsverbot* included a statistical overview of the extent of the measure (on this point the federal states were not encouraged to pool their statistics and it was difficult to obtain precise figures) and surveys of the different approaches taken in the individual states. This information was more important for those threatened than any statistics for the FRG as a whole, because the individual cases were always conducted by individual states as the prospective employers. There was no shortage of evidence that those states with an SPD government were as enthusiastic in applying the *Berufsverbot* as those with CDU or CSU governments. On the SPD's anxiety to 'act tough' at this time see Pirker (1967, pp. 317–41).

At the end of the 1970s the *Berufsverbot tended to fade* from public attention. Terrorist movements had pushed it out of the headlines, but there can be little doubt that the *Berufsverbot* remained a significant aspect of the alienation of the student generation from the state. At any rate, the publications of the early 1980s–rather than documenting a flood of known cases, which they presented as an affront to democracy – more usually emphasized the fact that the *Berufsverbot* was continuing and endeavoured to ensure that the public was not losing interest. General literature I have directly used for this chapter includes: Metscher & Meyer (1976); and *Ohne Zweifel für den Staat.* (1982). This documentation includes several of the legal texts and judgments relevant to the issue and details of many individual cases. In English: Gerard Braunthal (1990). An excellent short account of the measure is given by the one-time vice-president of the Free University in Berlin, law-professor and member of the Russell-Tribunal, Uwe Wesel (2002, p. 220 f).

The only three post-hoc accounts explicitly *supportive of the Berufsverbot* which I have found are: Löhnig & Preisner (2012); also: Fuchs & Jesse (1978); and Kriele (1978). Even these authors critique not only the lack of unified (i.e. federal) guidelines – these were not issued until May 19 1976: text quoted by Funke (1978, pp. 577–8) – but the lack of transparency of the legislation used and the scandalous fact that neo-Nazis were effectively exempt from the measure. It is striking how opposed to the *Berufsverbot* was Mauer (1972)'s mainstream response in *NJW*, sharply criticizing the state for penalizing ideas rather than punishing *actions*.

In one small question *the judgment brought clarification*. The BVerfG recommended that, since the post of *Referendar* was temporary but the only way for lawyers to complete their professional training, even if subsequently they did not intend to enter the public service, ways should be found to relax the issue of candidates' political loyalty to the state for this period of training. The unsuitable could be weeded out *after* their two years as *Referendar*. Whatever comfort that recommendation might have brought to future legal trainees, it contained nothing positive for teachers such as Offergeld and Gingold: the state's monopoly on education ensured that there were virtually no career opportunities for teachers outside the state system. (A private secondary education system, such as Ireland or Britain has established, is all but unknown in the Federal Republic.)

The involvement of the *Trades Union movement in questions of emergency legislation* goes back to the late 1950s. Following the Bad Godesberg reforms, the SPD had been kept informed – albeit at arm's length – about the planning for that legislation. TU circles were horrified at officials' indifference both to any parliamentary control and to fundamental civil rights, but, for reasons we mentioned in Chapter 2, not at all worried about any danger the Communists posed to public order. The irony of emergency legislation and the trigger function it had in the events of the late 1960s was that the plans had been drawn up consistently by civil servants in the Ministry of the Interior who had been highly placed in the NS administration, and not just behind a desk in Berlin, but in the Gestapo (Bargatzky) and in police headquarters in occupied Poland (Köttgen). Very clearly these officials' c.v.s were not examined closely – or perhaps they were. (Full details of the discussions and their champions: Diebel 2019).

Background Notes to Chapter 9

The standard book on the *Baader-Meinhof* movement is Stefan Aust (2008). Also: Jillian Becker (1977). My chapter draws heavily on the volume on the Berlin trial edited by the 13 defendants: Johann Agnoli u. dreizehn andere (1977). Here the full text of Mescalero's text. Also: Berliner-Prozess-Info Nr. 2 März 1979 – Hans-Litten-Archiv eV. See also Heinrich Hannover (2001, pp. 85–102).

It is a major undertaking to analyze the work of the *defence counsels both of the Baader-Meinhof* and its associated groups and of defendants in *Berufsverbot* cases. The names of Klaus Croissant, Kurt Groenewold, Heinrich Hannover and Otto Schily are inexorably tied in with these events. Groenewold says of his approach to the RAF-trials, for instance: 'My theme is justice in court procedures, not the truth – [...] the trial itself was clearly an instrument of domestic politics' (2010, pp. 105–38, here 105, 108). Ingo Müller discusses the short-term effects of the liberalization of court procedures in the so-called *Kleine Strafreform* (April 1965) and their annulment in the *Erstes Strafverfahrensreformgesetz* of December 1974 (in: Drecktrah 1996, pp. 95–103). Aspects of the more exotic forms of the subversion of court-procedure in these years are discussed by Requate (2008, p. 192 f). Basten (1983) covers both the liberalization of legal instruments in 1968 and their subsequent strengthening.

Specifically on *the Stammheim complex* from the viewpoint of defence counsels see: Hannover (1991); Groenewold (2010, pp. 105–38). Also Ingo Müller (1996). Wesel (involved as defence counsel for Otto Schily) (2002, p. 275 f). Wesel compares StPO § 231a with Nazi laws. More on the legal pressure on defendants in: Fransiska Osterholzer (2012); and Hürter (1996).

The intransigence of the authorities and *polarization* of the situation meant – according to Thomas Henne – that the state missed out on the chance of negotiating with Schleyer's kidnappers (2010, p. 183). The difficulty for the defence teams was to keep a balance between respecting legal conventions in order to help their clients and over-identifying with their clients. Constantly the defence lawyers were attacked in the Springer press for the difficulties which the state had in 'dealing with' the B-M suspects. A typical comment: 'The problems come from the left, only from the left. And when the present alarm and man-hunts are over, the defence counsels with their dirty hands will stand up and blame the whole system of late capitalism for the troubles which they themselves helped to bring about'. (*Welt am Sonntag*, May 28 1972). Scheuermann (2011, p. 236) describes the legal position as 'legalized anti-communism'.

The *'German Autumn'* was a phrase current in the late 1970s to summarize the despondency which had descended onto the country, some of it a mourning for the wasted lives of the B-M group (a feeling usually, but not always, to be distinguished from whole-hearted support for urban terrorism). The many films which capture that atmosphere include *Die bleierne Zeit* (director Margarethe von Trotta) and *Deutscher Herbst* itself (whose directors included Erich Reitz, Rainer Werner Fassbinder, Alexander Kluge and Volker Schöndorf).

Background Notes to Chapter 10

The topic of this chapter is less focused than (I hope) the other chapters and contains fewer spectacular trials. As the chapter argues, the structure of environmental legislation tended to aim at the *avoidance* of litigation, and the relatively few trials on these topics were fragmentary, rather than – as happened with the *Berufsverbot* or terrorism – developing any real continuity. Three factors add to the openness of the chapter. First: the understanding of what is meant by the 'environment' has shifted repeatedly and radically since 1945 and is shifting as I write. Secondly, the environmental aspect of national legislation came late and had constantly to reinvent itself, invariably after the event. Thirdly: national law was constantly overshadowed by supra-national legislation, not only that of the European Community, later the EU, but by international agencies and the UN. The topic of *international environmental law* is highly complex and continuously evolving and does not always dovetail with an account of national legislation. In eight hundred pages Philippe Sands and Jacqueline Peel (2012) outline the evolution of International Law in this field, and while my chapter references this work at a number of points, I have neither attempted to summarize this aspect of the theme, nor to point to all the landmark international agreements which have shaped global thinking in this field (Stockholm, Rio, Paris, for instance, to name but a few): I know, however, that the reader will feel their relevance to the issues discussed and will repeatedly find guidance and bibliographical help from Sands and Peel. A useful discussion of different balances of environmental law within statute and common law in: Rehbinder (2010).

Details of the various actual and planned *nuclear plants* mentioned in this section are best found on-line. On Gorleben see in particular: Anselm Tiggemann (2004). This is a major and exhaustive study. An interesting account of Gorleben from the perspective of local politicians: Klaus Poggendorf (2008). On the Gorleben Hearing: Hatzfeldt, Hirsch & Kollert (1979). This contains a detailed account of the debates at the Hearing, especially those concerning safety, and the full text of the declaration by Ministerpräsident Dr Ernst Albrecht on May 16 1979 (pp. 185–92).

The opposition to atomic energy was linked to the traditional *Easter marches*, held in protest at the stationing of nuclear weapons in the FRG.

Background Notes to Chapter 11

There is – hardly surprisingly, in view of the movement's long and dishonourable history – an extensive literature on the neo-Nazi organizations and *extreme right parties in Germany*. Cas Mudde (2000) contextualizes the German situation with his account of developments in Belgium and the Netherlands. Similar in scope are: Uwe Backes & Patrick Moreau (2012); and Peter H. Merkel & Leonard Weinberg (2003). William M. Downs (2012) gives a wider context for the problem and examines political strategies for dealing with 'pariah parties' of the right and left. More narrowly focused on electoral performance: Henrik Steglich (2005).

The literature on the *NSU and its place in the neo-Nazi scene* may be divided into the early work, some conducted before the trial opened and full of outrage at the slowness of the authorities to respond appropriately to the (then as yet incomplete) series of racist murders and desperate to prevent what it sees as the trivializing of these deaths, for instance: Laura Benedict (1998) (Her subject was a neo-Nazi who came to attention by murdering a policeman in Schleswig-Holstein), and: Hajo Funke (2015). Such works contrast to later studies, which lay claim to greater objectivity and academic reflection, but in fact do not appear to correct any substantial elements in the previous literature.

See in particular the more recent study: Matthias Quent (2016). To take a concrete example of the relationship between these two types of literature: reading in Hajo Funke (p. 74) the suggestion that the murdered policewoman Michèle Kiesewetter and her colleagues were close to, even members of, far-right KluKluxKlan circles, one might suspect an element of overstatement. As one searches for any explanation of police incompetence, such a theory would seem a little too convenient. However, the account given by Quent (2016, p. 281f) – a work striving for academic rigour and explicitly distancing itself from Funke – is exactly the same. Friedrich, Wamper & Zimmermann (2015) also try to get distance to their material, but the essays are of variable quality. Predictably hard-hitting in its condemnation of the political environment of both the murders and their investigation is the volume edited by the leader of the parliamentary party of DIE LINKE in the Thüringen state parliament: Bodo Ramelow (2013). A work by the author of the respected standard work on Baader-Meinhof: Stefan Aust & Dirk Laabs (2014). In English (focusing on Kai Diesner): Nicholas Fraser (2001, pp. 48–86).

For contrast one can look at the neo-Nazi movement of *the 'second wave'*, for instance: Rainer Fromm (1998). The Hoffmann group was banned in 1980.

All references to the *trial* (for which the judge determined there would be neither an official transcript nor an official recording: 16.05.13) are taken from the excellent dedicated web-site of the Bavarian Radio: http://www.br.de/nachrichten/nsu-prozess/nsu-prozess-wichtigste-verhandlungstage-ueberblick-102.html. It is easiest to follow this site through the trial dates, which I give in brackets as the reference.

Bibliography

Abtreibung, Zur Geschichte der. Unter anderen Umständen. Eine Publikation des Deutschen Hygiene-Museums (Dresden). Dortmund: edition ebersbach, 1996.

Ackermann, Heinrich, Zur Frage der Strafwürdigkeit des homosexuellen Verhaltens des Mannes, in: Bauer et al. (1963), pp. 149–60.

Adorno, Theodor Wiesengrund, Sexualtabus und Recht heute, in: Bauer et al. (1963), pp. 299–318.

Agnoli, Johann u. dreizehn andere: *'da ist nur freizusprechen!' Die Verteidigungsreden im Berliner Mescalero-Prozess.* Reinbek: Rowohlt, 1977.

Arendt, Hannah: *Eichmann in Jerusalem. A Report on the Banality of Evil.* (1963). Harmondsworth: Penguin, 1978.

Arnau, Franz: *Die Straf-Unrechtspflege in der Bundesrepublik Deutschland. Dokumente der Zeit.* Munich: Desch, 1967.

Arnau, Franz: *Schon vor dem Urteil verurteilt. Autopsie eines Straf-un-Rechts-Verfahrens.* Luzern: Thesaurus, 1973.

Auer, Franz von (ed.): *Der Fall Offergeld. Dokumentation des Konflikts zwischen Bayerns Kultusminister und einem gewerkschaftlich engagierten Lehrer.* Frankfurt a.M.: Fischer, 1974.

Aust, Stefan: *The Baader-Meinhof Complex.* Translated Anthea Bell. London: Bodley Head, 2008.

Aust, Stefan & Dirk Laabs: *Heimatschutz. Der Staat und die Mordserie des NSU.* Munich: Pantheon, 2014.

Backes, Uwe & Patrick Moreau: *The Extreme Right in Europe. Current Trends and Perspectives.* Göttingen: Vandenhoek & Rupprecht, 2012.

Bähr, Johannes, Axel Drecoll, Bernhard Gotto, et al.: *Der Flick-Konzern im Dritten Reich.* Munich: Oldenbourg, 2008.

Basten, Thomas: *Von der Reform des politischen Strafrechts bis zu den Anti-Terror Gesetzen.* Cologne: Ruegenstein, 1983.

Bauer, Fritz, Hans Bürger-Prinz, Hans Giese und Herbert Jäger (ed.s): *Sexualität und Verbrechen.* Frankfurt a.M.: Fischer, 1963.

Becker, Jillian: *Hitler's Children.* London: Michael Joseph, 1977.

Benedict, Laura: *Sehnsucht nach Unfreiheit. Der Fall Kay Diesner und die rechte Szene.* Berlin: edition ost, 1998.

Benz, Wolfgang: *Deutschland unter alliierter Besatzung 1945–1949.* Klett: Stuttgart, 2009.

Berg, Nicolas, Lesarten des Judenmords, in: Herbert (2002), pp. 81–131.

Bergner, Gert: *Rudolf Augstein und die Spiegel-Affäre.* Berlin: Stoedtner, 1964.

Beutin, Wolfgang et al.: *A History of German Literature.* London & New York: Routledge, 1993.

Bickel, Alexander M.: *The Least Dangerous Branch. The Supreme Court at the Bar of Politics.* New Haven & London: Yale University Press. 1986².

Bischoff, Eva & Daniel Siemens, Class, Youth and Sexuality in the Construction of the *Lustmörder*: The 1928 Murder Trial of Karl Hussmann, in: Wetzell (2008), pp. 207–25.

Bittner, Wolfgang, Verfassungsfeindlichkeit zur Disposition. Eine Reportage über den Fall Silvia Gingold, in: Funke (1978), pp. 376–86.

Blanke, Bernhard: *Die Linke im Rechtsstaat.* Bd. 1. *Bedingungen sozialistischer Politik.* Berlin: Rotbuch Verlag, 1976.

Blasius, Dirk: *Geschichte der politischen Kriminalität in Deutschland, 1800–1980. Eine Studie zu Justiz und Staatsverbrechen.* Frankfurt a.M.: Suhrkamp, 1983.

Böll, Heinrich: *The Lost Honour of Katharina Blum* (1974). Translated Leila Vennewitz. London: Vintage, 2000.

Böll, Heinrich, Radikalität und Hoffnung (1973), in: *Werke. Kölner Ausgabe.* Vol. 18. Cologne: Kiepenheuer, 2010, p. 243 f.

Boyd, Andrew: *The Informers. A Chilling Account of the Supergrasses in Northern Ireland.* Cork & Dublin: Mercier, 1984.

Bracher, Karl Dietrich: *Die Auflösung der Weimarer Republik. Eine Studie zum Problem des Machtverfalls in der Demokratie* (= *Schriften des Instituts für politische Wissenschaft*, Band 4). Stuttgart: Ring, 1955.

Bracher, Karl Dietrich, Die Panik des Mittelstandes, in: Duve & Kopitzsch (1976), pp. 58–61.

Bracher, Karl Dietrich, Bewährung und Anfechtung. Zum Streit um Demokratie und Verfassung in der Bundesrepublik, in: Funke (1978), pp. 422–35.

Braunthal, Gerald: *Public Service in West Germany. The 1972 Decree against Radicals and its Consequences.* Amherst: University of Massachusetts Press, 1990.

Brown, Raymond M., The American Perspective on Nuremberg: A case of cascading ironies, in: Reginbogin & Safferling (2006), pp. 21–30.

Brünneck, Alexander von, Politik und Verfolgung der KPD seit 1948, in: Blanke (1976), pp. 211–235.

Brünneck, Alexander von: *Politische Justiz gegen Kommunisten in der Bundesrepublik Deutschland, 1949–1968.* Frankfurt a.M.: Suhrkamp, 1978.

Brunner, Bernhard, Lebenswege der deutschen SIPO-Chefs in Frankreich nach 1945, in: Herbert (2002), pp. 214–42.

Buchloh, Ingrid: *Veit Harlan. Goebbels' Starregisseur.* Paderborn: Schönigh, 2010.

Bültmann, Alexandra & Frank Wätzold: *Der Vollzug von Umweltrecht in Deutschland. Ökonomische Analyse und Fallstudien.* Marburg: Metropolis, 2002.

Burnham, James: *The Managerial Revolution. What's happening in the World.* New York: Day, 1941.

Burschel, Friedrich, Entschleunigung, Leerlauf und Langmut. Nach 200 Prozesstagen im Münchener NSU-Prozess, in: Friedrich et al. (2015), pp. 65–81.

Buske, Sybille, Die Debatte über 'Unehelichkeit', in: Herbert (2002), pp. 315–47.

Byrnes, Deirdre, Jean Conacher, & Gisela Holfter (ed.s): *German Reunification and the Legacy of GDR Literature and Culture*. Leiden: Brill, 2018.

Cesarini, David, The International Military Tribunal at Nuremberg. British Perspectives, in: Reginbogin & Safferling (2006), pp. 31–38.

Citron, Rodger D., The Nuremberg Trials and American Jurisprudence: The decline of legal realism and the revival of natural law, in: Reginbogin & Safferling (2006), pp. 139–150.

Clapham, Andrew, Issues of complexity, complicity and complementarity – from the Nuremberg trials to the dawn of the new International Criminal Court, in: Sands (2003), pp. 30–67.

Claßen, Isabella: *Die Darstellung von Kriminalität in der deutschen Literatur, Presse und Wissenschaft. 1900–1930*. Frankfurt a.M.: Peter Lang, 1988.

Collings, Justin: *Democracy's Guardians. A History of the German Federal Constitutional Court 1951–2001*. Oxford: Oxford University Press, 2015.

Conradt, David P.: *The German Polity*. New York: Longmans, 2001[7].

Cooper, R. W.: *The Nuremberg Trial*. Harmonsworth: Penguin, 1947.

Cragin, Thomas: *Murder in Parisian Streets. Manufacturing Crime and Justice in the Popular Press, 1830–1900*. Lewisburg: Bucknell University Press, 2006.

Crawford, James, The Redrafting of the Rome Statute, in: Sands (2003), pp. 109–56.

Dahrendorf, Ralf: *Society and Democracy in Germany*. London: Weidenfeld, 1968.

Dainow, Joseph, The Civil and the Common Law. Some Points of Comparison, in: *The American Journal of Comparative Law*, XV/3 (1966–67), pp. 419–35.

'Das sind Volksfeinde'. Die Verfolgung von Homosexuellen an Rhein und Ruhr 1933–1945. ed. Centrum Schwule Geschichte, Cologne. Ausstellung, 1998.

Degler, Hans-Dieter & Dieter Uentzelmann (ed.s): *Supergift Dioxin. Der unheimliche Killer*. Reinbek: Rowohlt, 1984.

Diebel, Martin: *'Die Stunde der Exekutive'. Das Bundesinnenministerium und die Notstandsgesetze 1949–1968*. Göttingen: Wallstein, 2019.

Dierichs, Helga, Rosemarie Nitribitt – Tod einer Hure, in: Spitra (2003), pp. 36–59.

Diestelkamp, Bernhard & Michael Stolleis (ed.s): *Justizalltag im Dritten Reich*. Frankfurt a.M.: Fischer, 1988.

Diestelkamp, Bernhard, Die Justiz nach 1945 und ihr Umgang mit der eigenen Vergangenheit, in: Diestelkamp & Stolleis (1988), pp. 131–49.

Dohrn: *Spiegel* articles. Sterilisierung: Methode Dohrn (8/1961); Dohrn-Urteil: Der Lückenbüßer (45/1964); Fall Dohrn: Blauer Brief (49/1964); and Moritz Pfeil, Axel Dohrn und die Folgen (45/1964).

Dolder, Klaus-Peter, Klaus Hansmann, Stefan Paetow & Eberhard Schmidt-Assmann: *Verfassung – Umwelt – Wirtschaft. Festschrift für Dieter Sellner*. Munich: Beck, 2010.

Domeier, Norman, Rainer Nicolaysen, Maria Borowski, Martin Lücke & Michael Schwartz (ed.s): *Gewinner und Verlierer. Beiträge zur Geschichte der Homosexualität in Deutschland im 20. Jahrhundert.* Göttingen: Wallstein, 2015.

Domeier, Norman, Die deutsche Homosexuellenbewegung im Kaiserreich und ihre Niederlage im Eulenberg-Skandal (1906–1909), in: Domeier et al (2015), pp. 13–26.

Downs, William M.: *Political Extremism in Democracies. Combatting Intolerance.* Palgrave Macmillian: New York, 2012.

Drecktrah, Volker Friedrich (ed.): *Die RAF und die Justiz. Nachwirkungen des 'Deutschen Herbstes'.* Munich: Meidenbauer, 2010.

Duve, Freimut & Wolfgang Kopitzsch (ed.s): *Weimar ist kein Argument. Texte zu einer gefährlichen Geschichtsauffassung.* Reinbek: Rowohlt, 1976.

Dworkin, Ronald: *Law's Empire.* Cambridge Ma. & London: Belknap, 1986.

Elder, Sace, Prostitutes, Respectable Women and Women from 'Outside'. The Carl Grossmann Sexual Murder Case in Postwar Berlin, in: Wetzell (2008), pp. 185–206.

Elias, Norbert, On law and political development, in: *Complete Works*, vol. 2–3, Appendix xvi. Dublin: University College Press, 2009, p. 585 f.

Eschenburg, Theodor: *Die Affäre. Eine Analyse. Protokolle der 'Spiegel-Debatte' des deutschen Bundestags.* Sonderdruck. Hamburg: Die Zeit, 1962.

Etzel, Matthias: *Die Aufhebung von nationalsozialistischen Gesetzen durch den Alliierten Kontrollrat (1945–1948).* Tübingen: Mohr Siebeck, 1992 (*Beiträge zur Rechtsgeschichte des 20. Jahrhunderts*, Bd. 7).

Fanning, Bryan: *Immigration and Social Cohesion in the Republic of Ireland.* Manchester: Manchester University Press, 2011.

Fehler der Inlandsgeheimdienste und die Chancen des Strafprozesses. Ein Interview mit Yavuz Selim Narin zum Prozessauftakt gegen den NSU, in: Ramelow (2013), pp. 193–200.

Fekete, Liz, Why the NSU case matters. Structural racism and covert policing in Europe, in: Friedrich et al. (2015), pp. 49–64.

Fränkel, Ernst: *Zur Soziologie der Klassenjustiz* (1932). Darmstadt: Wissenschaftliche Buchgesellschaft, 1968².

Fraisek, Ralf, Göttinger Hegel-Lektüre, Kieler Schule und NS-Juristenausbildung, in: Schumann (2008), 45–64.

Frankenberg, Günther, Der Verwaltungsrechtsstreit als Parteiordnungsverfahren. Anmerkung zum Berufungsurteil gegen Charlotte Nieß-Mache, in: *Kritische Justiz* (1978/3), pp. 310–16.

Fraser, Nicholas: *The Voice of Modern Hatred. Encounters with Europe's New Right.* London: Picador, 2001.

Frei, Norbert: *Vergangenheitspolitik. Die Anfänge der Bundesrepublik und die NS-Vergangenheit.* (1996). Munich: dtv, 1999.

Frei, Norbert, Ralf Ahrens, Jörg Osterloh & Tim Schanetzky: *Flick: Der Konzern, die Familie, die Macht*. Munich: Blessing, 2009.

Friedrich, Sebastian, Regina Wamper & Jens Zimmermann (ed.s): *Der NSU in bester Gesellschaft. Zwischen Neonazismus, Rassismus und Staat*. Münster: Unrast, 2015.

Friedrichsen, Gisela, Ich brauche ein zweites Memmingen. *Spiegel*-Online, 01.04.1999.

Fromm, Rainer: *Die 'Wehrsportgruppe Hoffmann'. Darstellung, Analyse und Einordnng. Ein Beitrag zur Geschichte des deutschen und europäischen Rechtsextremismus*. Frankfurt a.M.: Lang, 1998.

Fuchs, Friederike & Eckhard Jesse, Der Streit um die 'streitbare Demokratie'. Zur Kontroverse um die Beschäftigung von Extremisten im öffentlichen Dienst, in: Funke (1978), 389–421.

Fulbrook, Mary: *A History of Germany 1918–2008*. Oxford: Wiley & Blackwell, 2009.

Funk, Nanette, Patriarchal Morality versus Democracy. The 1993 German Constitutional Court Decision on Abortion, in: Barbara Wejnert & Metta Spencer (ed.s): *Women in Post-Communism. Research on Russia and Eastern Europe*, vol. 2. Greenwich Ct. & London: JIA, 1996, pp. 225–46.

Funke, Hajo: *Staatsaffäre NSU. Eine offene Untersuchung*. Unter Mitarbeit von Ralph Gabriel. Münster: Kontur, 2015.

Funke, Manfred (ed.): *Extremismus im demokratischen Rechtsstaat. Ausgewählte Texte und Materialien zur aktuellen Diskussion*. Düsseldorf: Droste, 1978.

Gabriel, Adrian, & Hermann Schau, Der NSU-Mord in Kassel und der Verfassungsschützer 'Klein Adolf'. Warum es in Hessen keinen Untersuchungsausschuss zum NSU gab, in: Ramelow (2013), pp. 54–61.

Galay, John Ford: *The Founding of the Federal Republic of Germany*. Chicago & London: University of Chicago Press, 1964^2.

Gante, Michael, Das 20. Jahrhundert (ii). Rechtspolitik und Rechtswirklichkeit 1927–1976, in: Jütte (1993), pp. 168–207.

Garkawe, Sam, The role and rights of victims at the Nuremberg International Military Tribunal, in: Regenbogin & Safferling (2006), pp. 86–93.

Gessner, Volkmar, Armin Hoeland, Csaba Varga (ed.s): *European Legal Cultures*. Aldershot & Brookfield: Dartmouth, 1996.

Gilcher-Holtey, Ingrid: *Die 68er Bewegung. Deutschland. Westeuropa. USA*. Munich: Beck, 2001.

Godau-Schüttke, Klaus-Detlev, Entnazifizierung und Wiederaufbau der Justiz am Beispiel des BGH, in: Schumann (2008), pp. 189–212.

Gödecke, Petra, Criminal Law after National Socialism and the Beginnings of Penal Reform in West Germany, in: Wetzell (2008), pp. 270–301.

Gramberg, Michael, Lebenslänglich für Vera Brühne, in: Spitra (2003), pp. 60–90.

Grimm, Dieter: *Die Verfassung und die Politik. Einsprüche in Störfällen*. Munich: Beck, 2001.

Groenewold, Kurt, Der RAF-Prozess. Öffentlichkeit und Justiz aus der Sicht der Strafverteidiger, in: Drecktrah (2010), pp. 105–38.

Gross, Raphael & Werner Renz (ed.s): *Der Frankfurter-Auschwitz-Prozess. Kommentierte Quellenedition.* Frankfurt a.M. & New York: Campus, 2013.

Grosser, Alfred & Jürgen Seifert (ed.s): *Die Spiegel-Affäre.* Vol. 1: *Die Staatsmacht und ihre Kontrolle.* Vol. 2: *Die Reaktion der Öffentlichkeit*, ed. Thomas Ellwein, Manfred Liebel & Inge Negt. Olten & Freiburg i.B.: Walter, 1966.

Grosser, Alfred, Bonn ist nicht Weimar, in: Duve & Kopitzsch (1976), pp. 7–13.

Grossmann, Atina: *Reforming Sex. The German Movement for Birth-Control and Abortion Reform 1920–1950.* New York & Oxford: Oxford University Press, 1995.

Grothe, Ewald: *Geschichte und Recht. Deutsche Verfassungsgeschichtsschreiben 1900–1970.* Munich: Oldenbourg, 2005.

Grothe, Ewald, 'Strengste Zurückhaltung und unbedingter Takt'. Der Verfassungshistoriker Ernst Rudolf Huber und die NS-Vergangenheit, in: Schumann (2008), pp. 327–48.

Grützbach, Franz & Heinrich Böll (ed.s): *Freies Geleit für Ulrike Meinhof. Ein Artikel und seine Folgen.* Cologne: Kiepenheuer & Witsch, 1984.

Gür-Şeker, Derya, 'In Deutschland die Soko Bosporus, in der Türkei die Soko Ceska' in: Friedrich et al (2015), pp. 93–113.

Gunlicks, Arthur B. (ed.): *German Public Policy and Federalism. Current Debates on Political, Legal and Social Issues.* New York & Oxford: Berghahn, 2003.

Gusy, Christoph, Die Verfassungsbeschwerde, in: Ooyen & Möllers (2006), pp. 201–13.

Gysi, Gregor, Schock, Trauer und Empörung, in: Ramelow (2013), pp. 215–20.

Halsey, Mark, Against 'green' criminology, in: White (2009), pp. 244–63.

Hamann, Andreas, Andreas Hamann jr. & Helmut Lenz: *Das Grundgesetz für die BRD vom 23. Mai 1949. Ein Kommentar für Wissenschaft und Praxis.* Neuwied & Berlin: Luchterhand, 1970[3].

Hannover, Heinrich: *Terroristenprozesse. Erinnerungen und Erkenntnisse eines Strafverteidigers.* Hamburg: VSA, 1991.

Hannover, Heinrich: *Die Republik vor Gericht 1975–1995. Erinnerungen eines unbequemen Rechtsanwaltes.* Berlin: Aufbau, 2001.

Hariman, Robert: *Popular Trials. Rhetoric, Mass Media and the Law.* Tuscaloosa & London: University of Alabama Press, 1993.

Harmon, Louise, The doctors' trial at Nuremberg, in: Reginbogin & Safferling (2006), pp. 164–73.

Harrington, Christine & Lief H. Carter: *Administrative Law and Politics: Cases and Comments.* Washington: CQ Press, 2014[5].

Hatzfeldt, Hermann Graf, Helmut Hirsch & Roland Kollert (ed.s): *Der Gorleben-Report. Ungewissheit und Gefahren der nuklearen Entsorgung.* Frankfurt: Fischer, 1979.

Heilig, René, 'Piato' und der 'Bums'. Brandenburgs Verfassungsschutz drückt sich, in: Ramelow (2013), pp. 92–7.

Heinemann, Elizabeth: *Before Porn was Legal. The Erotica Empire of Beate Uhse.* Chicago & London: University of Chicago Press, 2011.

Henne, Thomas & Arne Riedlinger (ed.): *Das Lüth-Urteil aus (rechts)historischer Sicht. Die Konflikte um Veit Harlan und die Grundrechtsjudikatur des BVerfG.* Berlin: Berliner Wissenschaftsverlag, 2005.

Henne, Thomas, Smend oder Hennis – Bedeutung, Rezeption und Problematik der Lüth-Entscheidung des BVerfG 1956, in: Ooyen & Möllers (2006), pp. 141–50.

Henne, Thomas, Das BVerfG und die RAF, in: Drecktrah (2010), pp. 171–84.

Hennendorfer, Eckard & Horst Schneider, 50 Jahre Atomgesetz – eine Zwischenbilanz, in: Dolder, Hansmann et al. (2010), pp. 347–72.

Herbert, Ulrich (ed.): *Wandlungsprozesse in Westdeutschland. Belastung, Integration, Liberalisierung.* Göttingen: Wallstein, 2002.

Hermann, Kai, Freispruch für Kurras. Auftakt für neue Auseinandersetzungen in Berlin. *Zeit*-Online, 1967/47.

Herzog, Dagmar (ed.): *Sexuality and German Fascism.* New York & Oxford: Berghahn, 2005.

Herzog, Dagmar *Sexuality in Europe. A twentieth-century history.* Cambridge & New York: Cambridge University Press, 2011.

Herzog, Todd, Crime and Literature in the Weimar Republic and Beyond: Telling the Tale of the Poisoners Ella Klein and Margarete Nebbe, in: Wetzell (2008), pp. 226–44.

Hettche, Thomas: *Der Fall Arbogast. Kriminalroman.* Cologne: DuMont, 2001.

Hiller, Kurt: *§ 175. Die Schmach des Jahrhunderts!* Hannover: Steegemann, 1927.

Hodenberg, Christine von, Die Journalisten und der Aufbruch zur kritischen Öffentlichkeit, in: Herbert (2002), pp. 278–311.

Hönig, Dieter & Heinrich Amadeus Wolff (ed.s): *Grundgesetz für die BRD. Handkommentar.* Baden-Baden: Nomos, 2016[11].

Hogan, Gerard & Clive Walker: *Political Violence and the Law in Ireland.* Manchester & New York: Manchester University Press, 1989.

Horn, Norbert, Heinz Kötz & Hans G. Leser: *German Private and Commercial Law. An Introduction.* Translated by Tony Weir. Oxford: Clarenden, 1982.

Hürter, Johannes, Sicherheit, Recht und Freiheit. Zum Balanceakt der bundesdeutschen Anti-Terrorismus-Politik in den 1970er Jahren, in: Gessner, Hoeland & Varga (1996), pp. 267–78.

Jäger, Herbert, Strafrechtspolitik und Wissenschaft, in: Bauer et al. (1963), pp. 273–98.

Jensen, Eric N., The Pink Triangle and Political Consciousness: Gays, Lesbians and the Memory of Nazi Persecution, in: Herzog (2005), pp. 319–49.

Johnson, Uwe: *Speculations about Jakob*, in: *Speculations about Jakob and other writings*, ed. Alexander Stephan. London: Continuum, 2000. [*Mutmaßungen über Jakob.* Frankfurt a.M., Suhrkamp].

Judex: *Irrtümer der Strafjustiz. Eine kriminalistische Untersuchung ihrer Ursachen.* Hamburg: Kriminalistik, 1963.

Jütte, Robert (ed.): *Geschichte der Abtreibung. Von der Antike bis zur Gegenwart.* Munich: Beck, 1993.

Jung, Susanne: *Die Rechtsprobleme der Nürnberger Prozesse, dargestellt am Verfahren gegen Friedrich Flick.* Tübingen: Mohr, 1992.

Kahl, Joachim, Giuseppe Caizzone, Pierre Kaldor & Hans Wielek: *Effy, Peter und Silvia Gingold. Porträt einer Familie. Ein Bilderbuch über deutsche Zustände.* Cologne: Pahl-Rugenstein, 1978.

Kandora, Michael, Homosexualität und Sittengesetz, in: Herbert (2002), pp. 379–401.

Kaplan, Benjamin, Civil Procedure – Reflections on the Comparison of Systems, in: *Buffalo Law Review* 9,3 (Spring 1960), pp. 409–32.

Kießling, Friedrich: *Die undeutschen Deutschen. Eine ideengeschichtliche Archäologie der alten Bundesrepublik 1945–1972.* Paderborn: Schöningh, 2012.

Kirchheimer, Otto (1961): *Political Justice. The Use of Legal Procedures for Political Ends.* Princeton N.J.: Princeton University Press, 1961.

Kirchheimer, Otto, Über den Rechtsstaat, in: *Politische Herrschaft. 5 Beiträge zur Lehre vom Staat.* Frankfurt a.M.: Suhrkamp, 1967, pp. 122–51.

Kloepfer, Michael: *Zur Geschichte des deutschen Umweltrechts.* Berlin: Duncker & Humblot, 1994.

Knortz, Karl: *Walt Whitman und seine Nachahmer. Ein Beitrag zur Literatur der Edelurninge.* Leipzig: Heichen, 1911.

Kocka, Jürgen, German History before Hitler: The Debate about the German *Sonderweg*, in: *Journal of Contemporary History*, 23/1 (Jan. 1988), pp. 3–16.

König, René, Sittlichkeitsdelikte und Probleme der Gestaltung des Sexuallebens in der Gegenwartsgesellschaft, in: Bauer et al. (1963), pp. 337–62.

Kommers, Donald R.: *Judicial Politics in West Germany. A Study of the Federal Constitutional Court.* Beverly Hills & London: Sage, 1976.

Kommers, Donald R.: *The Constitutitional Jurisprudence of the Federal Republic of Germany.* Durham & London: Duke University Press, 1997².

Krey, Volker: *Deutsches Strafrecht – allgemeiner Teil: Täterschaft und Teilnahme.* Stuttgart: Kohlhammer, 2005.

Kriele, Martin, Verfassungsfeinde im öffentlichen Dienst – ein unlösbares Problem. „Es gibt keinen ‚Radikalenerlass'", in: Funke (1978), pp. 335–48.

Krüger, Heike, Die Notstandsgesetze im Spiegel ihrer Zeit, in: Löhnig, Preisner & Schlemmer (2012), pp. 325–38.

Kuby, Erich: (1961) *Rosemarie – des deutschen Wunders liebstes Kind.* Reinbek: Rowohlt, 1961. Tr. from *Rosemarie* (New York: A. Knopf, 1959).

Kuckart, Judith: *Kaiserstraße.* Cologne; DuMont, 2006.

Langbein, Hermann: *Der Auschwitz-Prozess. Eine Dokumentation.* 2 vols. Vienna, Frankfurt & Zürich: Europa Verlag, 1965.

Laternser, Hans: *Die andere Seite im Auschwitz-Prozess 1963/65. Reden eines Verteidigers.* Stuttgart: Seewald, 1966.

Linder, Joachim & Claus-Michael Ort (in Zusammenarbeit mit Jörg Schönert und Marianne Wünsch): *Verbrechen – Justiz – Medien. Konstellationen in Deutschland von 1900 bis zur Gegenwart.* Tübingen: Niemeyer, 1995.

Lisinski, Stefan: *Att ta ett liv. Fallet Kaj Linna. Kalamarksmordet.* Stockholm: Mondial, 2017.

Lochner, Louis: *Tycoons and Tyrant. German Industry from Hitler to Adenauer.* Chicago: Regnery, 1954.

Löhnig, Martin, Mareike Preisner & Thomas Schlemmer (ed.s): *Reform und Revolte. Eine Rechtsgeschichte der 1960er und 1970er Jahre.* Tübingen: Mohr Siebeck, 2012.

Löhnig, Martin & Mareike Preisner, Berufsziel: Staatlich alimentierter Berufsrevolutionär? Die Grundsätze zur Frage der verfassungsfeindlichen Kräfte im öffentlichen Dienst von 1972, in: M. L., M. P. & Schlemmer (2012), pp. 297–324.

Loewy, Hanno & Bettina Winter (ed.s): *NS-Euthanasie vor Gericht. Fritz Bauer und die Grenzen juristischer Bewältigung.* New York & Frankfurt a.M.: Campus, 1996.

Lotz, Roy Edward: *Crime and the American Press.* New York: Praeger, 1991.

Lozowick, Yaacov: *Hitler's Bureaucrats. The Nazi Security Police and the Banality of Evil.* Translated Haim Watzman. London: Continuum, 2000.

Lücke, Martin, Scheinerfolge und Emanzipationsstillstand. Männliche Homosexualitäten in der Weimarer Republik, in: Domeier, Nicolaysen, Borowski, Lücke & Schwartz (2015), pp. 27–44.

Luhmann, Niklas: *Law as a Social System.* Oxford & New York: Oxford University Press, 2008.

Maihofer, Werner, Politische Kriminalität (1975), in: Funke (1978), pp. 327–33.

Mann, Heinrich, Zola, in: *Essays über Franzosen.* Frankfurt/M.: Suhrkamp, 1981, pp. 150–231.

Maron, Monika: *Flugasche. Roman.* Frankfurt a.M.: Fischer, 1981.

Marwick, Arthur: *The Sixties: Cultural Revolution in Britain, France, Italy, and the United States, c. 1958–c. 1974.* Oxford: Oxford University Press, 1998.

Mauer, Hartmut, Die Mitgliedschaft von Beamten in verfassungsfeindlichen Parteien und Organisationen, in: *NJW*, 25/14 (April 4 1972), pp. 601–6.

Maunz, Theodor & Günther Dürig: *Grundgesetz. Kommentar.* Loseblattsammlung. Munich: Beck, 1958 f.

McAdams, James: *Judging the Past in Unified Germany.* New York: Cambridge University Press, 2001.

Mehring, Reinhard: *Carl Schmitt. A biography.* Translated Daniel Steuer. Cambridge: Polity, 2009.

Merkel, Peter H. (ed.): *The Federal Republic at Fifty. The End of a Century of Turmoil.* Houndsmills: Macmillian, 1999.

Merkel, Peter H. & Leonard Weinberg (ed.s): *Right-Wing Extremism in the Twenty-First Century.* London & Portland Or.: Cass, 2003.

Metscher, W. & Beutin Meyer: *Berufsverbot. Ein bundesdeutsches Lesebuch.* Fischerhude: Atelier im Bauernhaus, 1976.

Möllers, Christoph, Scope and Legitimacy of Judicial Review in German Constitutional Law – the court versus the political process, in: Pünder & Waldhoff (2014), pp. 3–25.

Mudde, Cas: *The ideology of the extreme right.* Manchester & New York: Manchester University Press, 2000.

Müller, Ingo, Nazi Jurisprudence, in: Gessner, Hoeland & Varga (1996), pp. 217–21.

Müller, Jürgen, 'Sonderaktionen' gegen Kölner Homosexuelle im Sommer 1938, in: *'Das sind Volksfeinde'* (1998), pp. 103–20.

Müller-Heidelberg, Till Ulrich Finckh, Wolf-Dieter Narr & Marei Pelzer (ed.s): *Zur Lage der Bürger- und Menschenrechte in Deutschland.* Reinbek: Rowohlt, 1998.

Neumann, Franz: *Behemoth. The structure and practice of National Socialism 1933–1944* (1942). Washington D.C.: Rowman & Littlefield, 2009.

Nicholls, A. J.: *The Bonn Republic. West German democracy 1945–1990.* London: Longmans, 1991.

Nietzsche, F. W.: *The Uses and Abuses of History* (1874). New York: Cosimo, 2005.

Ohne Zweifel für den Staat. Die Praxis zehn Jahre nach dem Radikalenerlass, ed. Komittee für Grundrecht und Demokratie. Reinbek: Rowohlt, 1982.

Ooyen, Robert Chr. van & Martin H. W. Möllers: *Das BVerfG im politischen System.* Wiesbaden: Verlag für Sozialwissenschaften, 2006.

Ooyen, Robert Chr. van, Das Parteiverbotsverfahren vor dem BVerfG, in: Ooyen & Möllers (2006), pp. 333–49.

Ooyen, Robert Chr. van & Frank Schale: *Kritische Verfassungspolitologie. Das Staatsverständnis von Otto Kirchheimer.* Baden-Baden: Nomos, 2011.

Orwell, George: *James Burnham and the managerial revolution.* London: Polemic, 1946.

Osterholzer, Fransiska, Änderungen der StPO im Zuge der Terroristenbekämpfung, in: Löhnig, Preisner and Schlemmer (2012), pp. 243–65.

Ott, Sieghart: *Der Fall Dr Dohrn. Eine Dokumentation zur Frage der Schwangerschaftsverhütung und der guten Sitten.* Munich: Szcesny, 1964.

Overy, Richard, The Nuremberg Trials: International law in the making, in: Sands (2003), pp. 1–29.

Packard, Vance: *The Hidden Persuaders.* New York: McKay, 1957.

Panek, Leroz: *The Origins of the American Detective Story.* Jefferson NC & London: McFarland, 2006.

Papadakis, Elim: *The Green Movement in West Germany.* London: Croom Helm, 1984.

Papadakis, Elim: *Environmental Politics and Institutional Change.* Cambridge: Cambridge University Press, 1996.

Parkes, Stuart: *Understanding Contemporary Germany.* London: Routledge, 1997.

Paterson, Tony, Recognition for forgotten first Nazi hunter. *The Independent*, 22.02,16.

Patzelt, Werner J., Germany's Latent Constitutional Crisis, in: Gunlicks (2003), pp. 110–134.

Peck, Christoph, HCH und die armen Schweine, in: Degler & Uentzelmann (1984), pp. 83–7.

Pendas, Devin O.: *The Frankfurt Auschwitz Trials 1963–1965. Genocide, History and the Limits of the Law*. Cambridge & New York: Cambridge University Press, 2006.

Perels, Joachim: Das BVerfG in der Ära Adenauer, in: Blanke (1976), pp. 185–94.

Perels, Joachim, Die Rechtslehre vor und nach 1945, in: Schumann (2008), pp. 123–40.

Pfeiffer, Gerd & Hans-Georg Strickert (ed.s): *Der KPD-Prozess. Dokumentarwerk zu dem Verfahren über den Antrag der Bundesregierung auf Feststellung der Verfassungswidrigkeit der KPD vor dem Ersten Senat des BVerfG.* Sonderdruck des Urteils vom 17.08.1956. Karlsruhe: C. F. Müller, 1956.

Pfeil, Sigurd Graf von: *Das Kind als Objekt der Planung. Eine kulturhistorische Untersuchung über Abtreibung, Kindestötung und Aussetzung.* Göttingen: Schwartz, 1979.

Pirker, Theo: *Die SPD nach Hitler. Die Geschichte der sozialdemokratischen Partei Deutschlands, 1945–1964*. Munich: Rütten & Loening, 1965.

Poggendorf, Klaus: *Gorleben. Der Streit um die nukleare Entsorgung und die Zukunft einer Region.* Lüneburg: 2008.

Pontus, Kirsten, 'Ein Staat, der seine Kinder nicht ernähren kann, hat nicht das Recht, ihre Geburt zu fordern'. Abtreibung in der Nachkriegszeit, 1945 bis 1950, in: *Abtreibung* (1996), pp. 73–85.

Porch, Douglas: *Counterinsurgency. Exposing the Myths of the New Way of War.* Cambridge & New York: Cambridge University Press, 2013.

Prantl, Heribert, The Justice Administration in the Cage of Politics, in: Gessner, Hoeland & Varga (1996), pp. 358–60.

Prozess, Der. Justiz in der Bundesrepublik Deutschland am Beispiel Peter-Jürgen Boock 1982–1984 zu Stuttgart-Stammheim, ed. by Komitee für Grundrechte und Demokratie. Sensbachtal, 1985.

Pünder, Hermann & Christian Waldhoff (ed.): *Debates in German Public Law.* Oxford & Portland Or.: Hart, 2014.

Quent, Matthias: *Rassismus, Radikalisierung, Rechtsterrorismus. Wie der NSU entstand und was er über die Gesellschaft verrät.* Weinheim & Basel: Beltz Juventa, 2016.

Raabe, Wilhelm (1884): *Pfisters Mühle. Ein Sommerferienheft.* Stuttgart: Reclam, 1980.

Ramelow, Bodo: *Schreddern, Spitzeln, Staatsversagen. Wie rechter Terror, Behördenkumpanei und Rassismus aus der Mitte zusammengehen.* Hamburg: VSA, 2013.

Rauschning, Hermann: *Germany's Revolution of Destruction*. London: Heinemann, 1939.

Reginbogin, Herbert R. & Christoph J. M. Safferling: *The Nuremberg Trials. International Criminal Law since 1945. Die Nürnberger Prozesse. Völkerrecht seit 1945.* Munich: Saur, 2006.

Rehbinder, Eckard, Kodifikation des Umweltrechts in Europa – rechtsvergleichende Betrachtungen, in: Dolder, Hansmann et al. (2010), pp. 89–106.

Requate, Jörg: *Der Kampf um die Demokratisierung der Justiz. Richter und Öffentlichkeit in der Bundesrepublik.* Frankfurt a.M. & New York: Campus, 2008.

Richter, Hans Werner: *Lesebuch der Gruppe 47.* Munich: dtv, 1993^2.

Ridley, Hugh, Intellectual Freedom in Germany's 1848 Revolution – the Trial of Gustav Adolf Schlöffel, in: *German Life and Letters*, N.S. 32/4 (July 1979), pp. 308–17.

Riedlinger, Arne, Vom Boykottaufruf zur Verfassungsbeschwerde, in: Henne & Riedlinger (2005), pp. 149–86.

Rinken, Alfred, The German Constitutional Court and the German political system, in: Rogowski & Gawron (2012), pp. 55–90.

Robertson, Geoffrey, Fair Trials for Terrorists, in: Wilson (2005), pp. 169–83.

Rogowski, Ralf & Thomas Gawron (ed.s): *Constitutional Courts in Comparison. The US Supreme Court and the German Federal Constitutional Court.* New York & Oxford: Berghahn, 2012.

Rose, Andrew: *Lethal Witness: Sir Bernard Spilsbury, the Honorary Pathologist.* London: History Press, 2007.

Rowbotham, Judith, Kim Stevenson and Samantha Pegg: *Crime News in Modern Britain. Press Reporting and Responsibility 1820–2010.* London: Palgrave Macmillan, 2013.

Rückert, Joachim, Zur Rolle der Fallgeschichte in Juristenausbildung und juristischer Praxis zwischen 1790 und 1880, in: Schönert (1991), pp. 285–311.

Sack, Peter G., Reflections on the Relation between English law and the English language, in: Gessner, Hoeland & Varga (1996), pp. 63–67.

Sands, Philippe (ed.): *From Nuremberg to the Hague. The Future of International Criminal Justice.* Cambridge: Cambridge University Press, 2003.

Sands, Philippe, After Pinochet, in: Sands (2003), pp. 68–108.

Sands, Philippe & Jacqueline Peel, with Adriana Fabra and Ruth MacKenzie: *Principles of International Environmental Law.* (1996). Cambridge: Cambridge University Press, 2012^3.

Sands, Philippe: *East West Street.* London: Weidenfeld & Nicolson, 2016.

Sarotte, Marie Elise: *The Collapse. The Accidental Opening of the Berlin Wall.* New York: Basic Books, 2005.

Satō, Hiromi: *The Execution of Illegal Orders and International Criminal Responsibility.* Heidelberg, Dordrecht & London: Springer, 2011.

Schandurteil von Karlsruhe, Das. Ein Entscheid gegen FREIHEIT, EINHEIT und RECHT. Erwiderung auf die Begründung des Verbots der KPD durch das BVerfG vom 17. August 1956. Berlin: Dietz, 1957.

Schedler, Jan & Alexander Häusler (ed.s): *Autonome Nationalisten. Neonazis in Bewegung*. Wiesbaden: VS Verlag für Sozialwissenschaften, 2011.

Scheuermann, William E., Politische Justiz im Zeichen des 'War on Terror', in: Ooyen & Schale (2011), pp. 225–47.

Schilling, Jan Moritz (2010): *Deutscher Grundrechtsschutz zwischen staatlicher Souveränität und menschenrechtlicher Europäisierung. Zum Verhältnis zwischen BVerfG und dem Europäischen Gerichtshof für Menschenrechte*. Tübingen: Mohr Siebeck, 2010.

Schlemmer, Thomas, Sexualstrafrecht und Wertewandel, in: Löhnig, Preisner & Schlemmer (2012), pp. 231–42.

Schmidt, Johannes, Einführung zu den juristischen Erläuterungen, in: Gross & Renz (2013), pp. 91–104.

Schmidt, Manfred G.: *Political Institutions in the Federal Republic of Germany*. Oxford: Oxford University Press, 2003.

Schmidt-Bleibtreu, Bruno & Franz Klein: *Kommentar zum Grundgesetz*. Neuwied & Berlin: Luchterhand, 1993^8.

Schmiede, Rolf, Das deutsche 'Wirtschaftswunder' 1945–1965, in: Blanke (1976), pp. 107–38.

Schoenbaum, David: *The Spiegel Affair*. New York: Doubleday, 1968.

Schönert, Jörg (ed.): *Erzählte Kriminalität. Zur Typologie von narrativen Darstellungen in Strafrechtspflege, Publizistik und Literatur zwischen 1770 und 1920*. Tübingen: Niemeyer, 1991.

Schönert, Jörg, Bilder vom 'Verbrechermenschen', in: Schönert (1991a), pp. 497–531.

Schoeps, Joachim: *Die Spiegel-Affäre des Franz Josef Strauss*. Reinbek: Rowohlt, 1983. (*Spiegel*-Buch).

Schorske, Carl E.: *German Social Democracy, 1905–1917. The Development of the Great Schism*. Cambridge Ma.: Harvard University Press, 1983.

Schroeder, Friedrich-Christian: *Das neue Sexualrecht. Entstehung – Analyse – Kritik*. Karlsruhe: Müller, 1975.

Schütz, Erhard: *Romane der Weimarer Republik*. Munich: Fink, 1986.

Schumann, Eva (ed.): *Kontinuitäten und Zäsuren: Rechtswissenschaft und Justiz im 'Dritten Reich' und in der Nachkriegszeit*. Göttingen: Wallstein, 2008.

Schweitzer, Carl Christoph, Detlev Karsten, et al.: *Politics and Government in the Federal Republic of Germany. Basic Documents*. Leamington Spa: Berg, 1984.

Sendler, Horst, Krümmel-Urteil und atomrechtliche Änderungsgenehmigung, in: Klaus Hansmann, Stefan Paetow & Manfred Rebentisch (ed.s): *Umweltrecht und richterliche Praxis. Festschrift für Ernst Kutscheidt*. Munich: Beck, 2003, pp. 59–75.

Seymour-Ure, Colin: *The Press, Politics and the Public. An Essay on the Role of the National Press in the British Political System.* London: Methuen, 1968.

Shortt, Linda (2015): *German Narratives of Belonging: Writing Generation and Place in the Twenty-first Century.* Oxford: Legenda, 2015.

Sicko, Corinna: *Das Kopftuchurteil des BVerfG und seine Umsetzung durch die Landesgesetzgeber. Zur Vereinbarkeit des an Lehrkräfte gerichteten Verbots religiöser Bekundungen im Dienst mit den Vorgaben des Grundgesetzes.* Frankfurt a.M.: Lang, 2008.

Sling (Paul Schlesinger): *Richter und Gerichtete.* Berlin: Ullstein, 1929.

Soden, Kristine von, §218 – streichen, nicht ändern. Abtreibung und Geburtenregelung in der Weimarer Republik, in: *Abtreibung* (1996), pp. 36–50.

Somerville E. Œ. and Martin Ross: *Experiences of an Irish RM.* London: Longmans, 1899.

Sonnemann, Ulrich: *Der bundesdeutsche Dreyfus-Skandal. Rechtsbruch und Denkverzicht in der Justizsache Brühne-Ferbach.* Wollerau: Lentz, 1974.

Sparing, Frank, 'Merken Sie nicht, dass wir beobachtet werden?' Die Vorgehensweise der Gestapo gegen die Düsseldorfer Homosexuellen, in: *'Das sind Volksfeinde'* (1998), pp. 121–40.

Spiegel, Der: (1978) 'Dat ham wir uns so nicht vorjestellt', 1978/44, pp. 38–57.

Spitra, Helfried (ed.): *Die großen Kriminalfälle. Deutschland im Spiegel berühmter Verbrechen.* Munich: Piper, 2003.

Steglich, Henrik: *Die NPD in Sachsen. Organisatorische Voraussetzungen ihres Wahlerfolgs 2004.* Göttingen: V&R unipress, 2005.

Steinbacher, Sybille: *Wie der Sex nach Deutschland kam. Der Kampf um Sittlichkeit und Anstand in der frühen Bundesrepublik.* Munich: Siedler, 2011.

Steinbacher, Sybille, Die Geschichte des Konzentrations- und Vernichtungslagers Auschwitz-Birkenau: 1940–1945, in: Gross & Renz (2013), pp. 17–54.

Steinke, Ronen: *Fritz Bauer, oder Auschwitz vor Gericht.* Munich & Zürich: Piper, 2013.

Stöß, Richard, Rechtsextremismus im vereinten Deutschland [...], in: *Deutschland-Archiv*, 2 (March-April 2000), pp. 181–92.

Stolleis, Michael: *The Law under the Swastika. Studies on Legal History in Nazi Germany.* Chicago: University of Chicago Press, 1998.

Stolleis, Michael, The Reluctance to Glance in the Mirror – The Changing Face of German Jurisprudence following 1933 and since 1945, in: *Academia Scientiarum Fennica Vuosikirja – Year Book* (2001), pp. 137–152

Stolleis, Michael: *A history of public law in Germany, 1914–1945*, translated Thomas Dunlap. Oxford & New York: Oxford University Press, 2004.

Stolleis, Michael, Die Staatsrechtslehre der fünfziger Jahre, in: Henne & Riedlinger (2005), pp. 293–300.

Stratitz, Dietrich, KPD und kalter Krieg bis 1950, in: Blanke (1976), pp. 195–210.

Sunstein, Cass R.: *Constitutional Personae.* New York & Oxford: Oxford University Press, 2015.

Taylor, Telford: *The Anatomy of the Nuremberg Trials.* London: Bloomsbury, 1993.

Tergit, Gabriele: *Wer schießt aus Liebe? Gerichtsreportagen*, ed. Jens Brüning. Berlin: Das neue Berlin, 1999.

Thieleke, K. H. (ed.): *Fall 5. Anklageplädoyer, ausgewählte Dokumente, Urteil des Flick-Prozesses.* Berlin: Verlag der Wissenschaften, 1965.

Tiggemann, Anselm: *Die 'Achillesferse' der Kernenergie in der BRD. Zur Kernenergiekontroverse und Geschichte der nuklearen Entsorgung von den Anfängen bis Gorleben 1955–1985.* Lauf an der Pegnitz: Europaforum Verlag, 2004.

Trotsky, Leon (1975): *The Struggle Against Fascism in Germany*, ed. Ernest Mandel. Harmondsworth: Penguin, 1975.

Viereck, Peter: *Metapolitics. From Wagner and the German Romantics to Hitler.* (1941) New York: Transaction, 2003^2.

Vogt, Jochen, Ein unbekannter Gründervater. Endlich gibt es eine Biographie von Fritz Bauer, in: J.V..: *Erinnerung, Schuld und Neubeginn. Deutsche Literatur im Schatten von Weltkrieg und Holocaust.* Oxford & Bern: Lang, 2014, pp. 221–30.

Vogt, Jochen, *Die Ermittlung* im Kontext. Eine Rückblende, in: *die horen. Zeitschrift für Literatur, Kunst und Kritik*, 61,262 (2016), pp. 70–9.

Wagner, Helmut, Die Risiken von Wissenschaft und Technik als Rechtsproblem, in: *NJW*, 1980/ 13, pp. 165–72.

Wagner, Patrick, Die Resozialisation der NS-Kriminalisten, in: Herbert (2002), pp. 179–213.

Wahl, Rainer, Lüth und die Folgen. Ein Urteil als Weichenstellung für die Rechtsentwicklung: in: Henne & Riedlinger (2005), pp. 371–97.

Wassermann, Rudolf (ed.): *Erziehung zum Establishment. Juristenausbildung in kritischer Sicht.* Karsruhe: C. F. Müller, 1969.

Watson, Alan: *The Making of the Civil Law.* Cambridge Ma. & London: Harvard University Press, 1981.

Weber, Max, Economy of Law, in: Horn, Kötz & Leser (1982), pp. 69–73.

Weigel, Gerd, Abgründe des Staatsversagens. Ein Jahr NSU-Untersuchungsausschuss im Bundestag, in: Ramelow (2013), pp. 22–40.

Weinke, Annette: *Die Nürnberger Prozesse.* Munich: Beck, 2006.

Weinke, Annette: *Eine Gesellschaft ermittelt gegen sich selbst. Die Geschichte der ZSL.* Darmstadt: Wissenschaftliche Buchgesellschaft, 2008.

Weinreb, Lloyd L.: *Natural Law and Justice.* Cambridge Ma. & London: Harvard University Press, 1987.

Weisbrod, Bernd, Die 'Vergangenheitsbewältigung' der NS-Prozesse: Gerichtskultur und Öffentlichkeit, in: Schumann (2008), pp. 247–70.

Wells, Christina E., CIA v. Sims: Mosaic Theory and Government Attitude, in: *Administrative Law Review*, 58 (2006). (*University of Missouri-Columbia School of Law Legal Studies Research Paper* No. 2006-22).

Werle, Raymund: *Justizorganisation und Selbstverständnis der Richter.* Kronberg Ts.: Kronberg, 1977.

Wesel, Uwe: *Geschichte des Rechts in Europa. Von den Griechen bis zum Vertrag von Lissabon.* Munich: Beck, 1997.

Wesel, Uwe, Wenn die Linken Schlipse tragen, in: *Zeit*-Online, 1998/49.

Wesel, Uwe: *Die verspätete Revolution. 1968 und die Folgen.* Munich: Blessing, 2002.

Wesel, Uwe: *Der Gang nach Karlsruhe. Das BVerfG in der Geschichte der Bundesrepublik.* Munich: Blessing, 2004.

Wetzell, Richard F. (ed.): *Crime and Criminal Justice in Modern Germany.* New York & Oxford: Berghahn, 2008.

White, Rob: *Crimes Against Nature. Environmental Criminology and Ecological Justice.* Cullompton: Willan, 2008.

White, Rob: *Crimes Against Nature. Environmental Criminology and Ecological Justice. A reader.* Cullompton: Willan, 2009.

Wilkinson, Nicholas: *Secrecy and the Media. The Official History of the United Kingdom's D-Notice System.* London & New York: Routledge, 2007.

Wilson, Edmund: *To the Finland Station. A Study in the Writing and Acting of History* (1940). New York: NYRB Classic, 2003.

Wilson, Richard Ashby (ed.): *Human Rights in the 'War on Terror'.* Cambridge: Cambridge University Press, 2005.

Wittmann, Rebecca, The Normalization of Nazi Crime in Post-war German Trials, in: Reginbogin & Safferling (2006), pp. 209–15.

Wojak, Irmtraut: *Fritz Bauer. Eine Biographie.* Munich: Beck, 2009[2].

Wolf, Marcus: *Man without a Face. The Memoirs of a Spymaster.* London: Jonathan Cape, 1997.

Wolfrum, Edgar: *Die Bundesrepublik Deutschland – 1949–1990.* Stuttgart: Klett, 2004.

Wulf, Angela: *The Invention of Nature. The Adventures of Alexander von Humboldt. The Lost Hero of Science.* London: John Murray, 2015.

Wulf, Josef: *Theater und Film im Dritten Reich.* Gütersloh: Mohn, 1963.

Young, Raymond: *Source Book on German Law.* London, Sydney & Portland: Cavendish, 2002[2].

Zimmermann, Ekkart, Right-wing extremism and xenophobia in Germany: Escalation, exaggeration, or what? in: Merkel & Weinberg (2003), pp. 220–50.

Index

References to the notes are given with an n following the page number; b following the number indicates a reference to the background notes in the Appendix. Not all bibliographical references are taken up in the index.

Abortion legislation (§ 218)
  Seismograph of the law's humanity 107
  Overview of legal aspects 119, 286b
  History in Weimar Republic 110; 'Your body belongs to you' 110; § 218 in NS 110 f
  Immediate post-war change of policy 111
  FRG and GDR concerns with population growth 112, 120, 121
  Future of *Roe v. Wade* 129
  Three trials:
    a) Dohrn 118f. Attempted use of RGB § 14 119f; state's interest in women's fertility 120
      Church attitudes 120; court's clear opposition to sexual pleasure 122
    b) Public campaigns in 1960s 125 f. Parliament offers solution 1974 125; sabotaged by BVerfG 76, 125 f; parliament's second solution 126
    c) Memmingen trial in 1994 127 f. Hypocrisy of judges 128. Abortion rights diminished for women from GDR 128
Action, direct 230 f; not seen as a democratic right of citizens 230; in context of anti-Atom protests 242, 247 f, 249 f; taken vs old Nazis 206 f
Adenauer, Konrad Chancellor of the FRG 1949–1963 5, 12, 23, 56, 133, 267
  Lack of interest in tackling NS crimes 147: impatience with 'sniffing out Nazis' 284b; appointing NS compromised people to his staff 45
  Threat of loss of face if A. did not act on Auschwitz 152
  A.'s 1950 measure to exclude radicals from public service 198 f, 283b
  BVerfG seen as a lackey of A. 62
  A.'s hatred of KPD (Wesel's theory) 56
  Growing press suspicions of A. 80 A.'s plan for state TV channel thrown out by BVerfG 88, 283b
  A.'s unfounded attack on Augstein in *Spiegel* Affair 140
Adorno, Theodor Wiesengrund 113, 116 f
Ahlers, Conrad 131 f, 134, 141
Albrecht, Ernst 246; modifying scientific concept of safety 246
Allgemeines Landrecht (ALR) Not superseded by new legislation in 1848 178 f
Allied Control Council 278b. Intervention in FRG law-making 21
  Law no. 1, annulling NS laws 213; significance of Law no. 10 to IMT 3, 27, 157. Uneven application in RGB §14 case (eugenics) 119
  Relation to StGB § 90a 82n
  Intervention of Allies in arrest of Goebbels' successor 278b
Amnesty 151 f, 284b first amnesty laws 1949 69
  No will to tackle NS crimes 147, least of all from Adenauer who appoints NS compromised staff 45, 147n
  Effect of amnesties on Auschwitz trial 151f. Bath-tub case 288b. See also Statute of Limitation
Andersch, Alfred 'Artikel 3,3' poem claiming FRG as fascist state 209, 215; school experiences of proto-fascist authority 192
Anomalies, judicial and historical inconsistencies 20–23; law moves more slowly than society 179
  As a product of the structure of federal law 21; as result of banning of NS

laws 21; Tillessen case 21 f; NS laws better than no laws 115; in legislation on sexual behaviour 119 f, 286b; in 1871 law used in Auschwitz trial 155, 168
C19 example 177 f; reawakening of archaic laws in *Berufsverbot* 193 f; anachronism in GG § 33.5 on civil service 197; reviewing of StGB § 90a taken from pre-1933 versions 220; later effect of *Strafrechtsänderungsgesetz* 220
Anti-Communism Long reach of Adenauer's views 267; anti-communism of emergency legislation 284b; 'legalized anti-communism' 290b; of StGB § 90a 220. Widely used principle in W.R. and post-war period 29
Archives 282b
Arendt: Hannah View of totalitarianism 147; banality of evil reporting on Eichmann trial 149; view of Oppenheim 169n
Arnau, Franz 102, 103
Arndt, Adolf 70, 72, 74
Army Exhibition Vernichtungskrieg 148n
Arnau, Franz 103n
Arnold, Martin 256
Aschenauer, Rudolf 164
Asylum 1992 law and subsequent disunity 254, 260
Augstein, Rudolf 132 f, 140 f. Not accusing Strauss in Brühne affair 96
Auschwitz Institution and structure of Auschwitz-Birkenau 150 f: difference to concentration camps on German soil 151
All levels of society implicit in the system which produced A. 147
A. Trial in Frankfurt 152–76, within context of international approaches to crimes against humanity and genocide 146, 152 f, 158; effect of BGH judgment in bath-tub case 169, 171, 288b; representing generational shift in public attitudes 148
Previous Polish trials of A. personnel 151
Threat to Adenauer if he does not act, intensified by pressure from Eichmann trial 150, 152
Choice of legal code 154–58; failure in FRG to evolve suitable legislation for NS crimes 156; no lessons drawn from IMT 159; intended 'class action' affected by failure of catch-all concepts e.g. conspiracy, genocide 171 f; *Handlungseinheit* never wider than individual murder 171 f
Shortcomings with StGB § 211 155, 168 when related to anonymous and large-scale murder-machine 155, desk-top murderers 149
Place of trial 172
Bauer's ambition for trial: education, not collective guilt 161; 162 f
Central role of IAK & recently founded ZSL 159 f
Poor quality of defence counsels 165, 167 f
Size 160 f and representativeness of trial 153, numbers of witnesses 161 f
Was A. the product of an identifiable legal system? 156
Public effects of trial 174 f
Course of trial 163 f
Example 1 Boger 163 f
Example 2 Mulka 166 f; sentences 173 f
Comparison to later NSU trial 273
Außerparlamentarische Opposition (APO) 180 f; and trades-unions 180 f
Austrian Supreme Court 13

Baader, Andreas 210
Baader-Meinhof See Terrorism, urban
Baer, Richard 154
Baldwin, Hanson W. 138
Barbie, Klaus 207
Basic Law (Grundgesetz) early history 9, 12 f; GG part of FRG's public image 79; 'teleological' function 19, 72, 279b; elements of Weimar constitution in GG 12. View of political parties 51

Basic Law (Grundgesetz) (cont.)
GG § 3 Andersch poem 215; GG § 5 215; contrast to KPD ban & *Berufsverbot* 198; GG § 9 198 f; in *Berufsverbot* 204, 205
Pre-eminence over BGB explicitly asserted by BVerfG 71 f, 73
Implications of GG §§ 2,1 & 3.3 for citizens' sexual orientation 114. § 101 on choice of judges 113
No explicit right to strike 61. No reference to freedom of the press in GG 75, 143. Role of GG §9 in *Berufsverbot* 60, 198 f; definition of civil service in § 33,5 197
No initial reference to environment 226; GG § 20a on environment 226 f. Guarantee of freedom of movement in § 11 250
Failure to vote on GG in united Germany 254. Claim of collective nature of GG 281b
Bath-tub case details 288b; impact of BGB decision (Stachynskij) on Auschwitz trial 169, 171, 288b
Bauer, Fritz 116, 163, 175n, 288n. Clearing name of July 20, 1944 conspirators 159
Educative hope for Auschwitz trial 160 f. Doesn't attend trial 168. Admiration for Radbruch 159. Identifies location of Eichmann 172. See also Auschwitz, Euthanasia, Homosexuality, RSHA
Bavaria Rejection of GG 12 f, 135. Typified in Strauss 135. Early liberality of B. legislation 21
Abolition of RGB § 14 119; prosecution of Hitler 192; chances of legal appeals 97n
No protection for press sources 135
Role in Offergeld case 188 f
Place of religion in B. education 188 f. Crucifix vs. Kopftuch 254
Hostility to migration 260. See also Political Parties / CSU
Benn, Gottfried 67
Berufsverbot 177–203. Documentation 289. Victims 64, 288b; historical overview 289b
Early experience with Adenauer's 1950 measure to exclude radicals 199, 283b
Not mentioned in some histories 201
Legal basis, structure and administration 185 f; typical unfolding of cases 186, 288b
Case 1 Silvia Gingold 187 f;
Case 2 Rüdiger Offergeld 188 f; rejoinders to legal arguments 192 f;
Case 3 Christine Nieß-Mache 189
Clarification of legal training dilemma 289b
Tabooed radical causes 189
Unchallengeable role of security service evidence 100, 198, 202
Conflict of BVB practice with GG §3 and usefulness of GG §9 in banning political groups 191
BVerfG judgment 195 f; non-involvement in assessing personal applications 198 f (did that include war-records on c.v.? 199) dissenting judges 199 f
Final assessment 201. Rare defences of measure 289
'Youthful indiscretions' 203n
Distracting security forces from serious work 265
BGB 70n
BGB See Federal Court of Justice
Bhopal 227
Bickel, Alexander 63, 76
Biddis, Michael 24
Bismarck, Otto v. 50, 81
Blasius, Dirk 5, 212
Boehringer & dioxin 232 f
Boger, Wilhelm 158, 163, 173
Böhnhardt, Uwe 256, 269n, 274
Böll, Heinrich 10, 148; on Auschwitz trial 150; as opponent of BILD 82, 213; as 'sympathizer' 214 f; trying to get differentiation into 1970s 218, 295b

Börner, Holger 238
Boock, Peter-Jürgen 207
Boulgarides, Theodoros 256
Boycott 70, counterproductive effects 71
Bracher, Karl Dietrich 24n, 51n, 192
Brandt, Tino 266
Brandt, Willy 25, 159, 182. 'more democracy' 7; act of contrition in Warsaw 161; in exile 163 & vilified by Strauss 163; triumph & resignation 125; election 183 & turning on the left 183 f
Braun, Werner v. 29
Brecht, Bert 153, 253
Britain (England) Brexit iv. Comparison with legal system of FRG 16 f; negative experiences with expert witnesses 90
 Echoes of Christine Keeler scandals 93, 104
 Miscarriages of justice 285b
 Different approach to human rights 75n
 Use of D-Notices 139 f; military expertise in British press 142; Lohan affair 137, 287b; Anthony Verrier's revealing of military secrets 287b
 Politicians' frustration with press 287b
 Threatened prosecution of Pinochet in rejection of 'state function' defence 170. British neo-Nazis operating in FRG 261
 Parallels between Stephen Lawrence scandal and NSU investigation 264
 British security forces in N. Ireland, cf with BfV in NSU 266n, 271; specific cases 266n
 Wolfenden Report 117
Brokdorf 29; BVerfG judgment 249 f
Brückner, Peter 217, 223
Brühne trial Political sex-scandal 95 f; rumours of involvement of Strauss 96 f; insensitivity of judge 96
Brüning, Heinrich 13, 221; KPD attack on, equating B. and Hitler 58; can't reverse emergency legislation 204
Buback, Siegfried 10n, 210, 211 f, 222
Bürgerinitiativen Citizens' initiatives 239, 250, 251; differentiation from B-M 229, and from populism 251
Bundesamt für Verfassungsschutz (BfV) See Security forces
Burnham, James 47
BVerfG see Constitutional Court

Capote, Truman 103
Caroline, Princess of Monaco 77 f
Carson, Rachel 227
Chapeaurouge, Edmund 191
Chernobyl 227
Churches 80, 106. General geographical distribution in FRG 107; confessional differences Munich / Hamburg 134 f
 Role of religion in FRG re §§ 175 & 218 112, militant 'Volkswartbund' 112; *Roman Catholic*: opposition to § 218 120n; Schumacher's view of R.C. 46n
 Church's role in Offergeld case 188 f
 'Re-Catholicizing' of FRG 112
 Bismarck's ban on R.C. 50.
 Protestant: 120n
 Churches' role in pressing for amnesty for NS criminals 282b. Role in CASTOR protests 248
Citron, Rodger 43
Civil Service Broad definition of civil servants in FRG 44, 185
 Required loyalty of civil servants to the state 193; situation under Hitler 193
 GG traditional definition of service 197; BVerfG reference to 'the civil service of Adolf Hitler' 193
 Not supposed to fight for environment 230
 Judge and jury in safety measures 247. See also generally *Berufsverbot*
Clapham, Andrew 43, 156
Claßen, Isabella 83
Cohn-Bendit, Daniel 177
Collective Guilt Not among Bauer's guide-lines in Auschwitz trial 161
Collings, Justin 16, 142n

COMECON 258
Common Law Contrast to statute law 16 f
Conspiracy 27, 37, 41, 98, 269; in Flick 34 f, 172
Conspirators of July 20, 1944 44, Bauer's rehabilitation of them 159, 262n. See also Remer
Constitutional Court (BVerfG) 279b.
  Founding and early history 13 f
  Non-appellate 13; power of court 14; place in politics 15; nomination of judges 14, cf. to US Supreme Court 62 f; overwork 17; delays in delivering judgement: KPD 60, *Lüth* 71; image in 1950s 72 f; judges' self-understanding 19, 72 f; early insistence on unanimity of judgment 19; belated introduction of minority judgments 134
  Personal appeal to court (*Verfassungsbeschwerde*) 17
  Judicial review 18 f
  Exclusive right to ban political parties 51; judgment on KPD 56–59; refuses judgment on NPD 59, 270 f
  View of constitution's relation to statute law 63, 74
  A lackey of Adenauer? 62; balance of judgments 283b; blocking Adenauer's plans for state TV channel 283b; critique of phone-tapping perhaps as balance device for court 275
  More positive image in 1950s 65
  Chancellor Schmidt accuses BVerfG of overreaching itself 76
  Prestige drawn from opposition to NS legacy 77
  Challenge on natural justice 102, exception in view of § 175 114 f
  Intervention on § 218 and unacceptable, 'arrogant' outcome 118, 125
  BVerfG view of *Spiegel*-Affair 142 f
  Judgment on *Berufsverbot* 195 f
  Conflict with BGH on civil service 197
  Ambiguous judgment of parties 198 f; dissenting judges on *Berufsverbot* 199 f. Brokdorf judgment seen as arrogant 250
  Natural focus of court tends to ignore administrative issues 144, 200
  General cf. with US Supreme Court 126
  Election funding judgment 65
Crimes against humanity 27 f, 40. Ground on which Harlan is charged 69; used in IMT but not Auschwitz trial 157
  Sands' account 281b, 288b. See Lauterpacht, also Arendt
Croissant, Klaus 290
Culpability for war-crimes 36, white collar crimes 37; Wharton 39, 162
  Ordinary citizens left out of IMT 30. Asymmetry of responsibility and actual action 154
  Need under German law for accused to know something is a crime 156
  See also IMT, retroactive legislation, and superior orders defence

Dahrendorf, Ralf 6
Dainow, Joseph 20
Democracy *Passim*. Need for democratic law after NS 4 f
  Defence of democracy by undemocratic means 61, 204; 'militant' democracy 77, 197, 198, 202, 204, 220
  Mauz asks what democratic justice means in practice 99 f
Demonstrators, rights of 249 f
Denazification Failure of process for legal profession 278b
  US questionnaire 51
  Rare Allied interventions 278b
  Harlan's easy route through process 68 f
  Failure to re-frame StGB § 90a 220 f
Denunciation Part of the spirit of 1950s 158. Globke denouncing colleague 158
Desk-top murderers In Flick trial 37, 44, 46
  Supra-individual nature of Auschwitz 149, 155 f

GDR desk-top killers at frontier 254, 281b. See also Eichmann
Detective story Function in popular understanding of the law 80 f
Hettche's re-working of Hetzel case 102 f
Interest of law reformers in genre 81; Wulffen 80, 102n
Crime story/crime link in Sweden 285b
Spy fiction's enlightenment function 139 f
Diestelkamp, Bernhard 9
Differentiation Of terminology in order to break polarization, e.g. relating to violence by Glotz 217 f; and to fascism 161n, 205, 215; terrorism differentiation 207, 217 f
Ambition of Sympathizers 213 f; Böll on need for differentiation 218
Cheapening of political language 219
Dix, Rudolf 36, 38n
D-Notice 139, 140, 287b
Dönitz, Großadmiral Karl 31, 88n (here claim of *Tu quoque*)
Dohrn, Axel 118–24, 118n, 221
Dreher, Eduard Consistent critic of BVerfG 9, 14, 46, 76, 77, 248
Drenkmann, Günter von 10n
Dreyfus, Affair 25, 85, 99, 137
Importance stressed by Wesel 85n; Brühne affair compared to 95
Dutschke, Rudi 183 f
Dworkin, Ronald 64 f, 83

Easter Marches 247
EDC 14n, 54, 89
EDIFICIA 237
Eichmann, Adolf E. trial & execution 43, 149 f, 282
Arendt's reading of trial 147n; E.'s claim to have liked Jews and to have killed no-one 154
Bauer informs Israel of E.'s whereabouts 172 & wanted E. trial to be held in Germany 161
Einsatzgruppen 37, 46
Eisenhower, Dwight D. 31
Elias, Norbert 20
Eliot, Thomas Stearns 252
Emergency legislation Anti-communist background 284n
Insistence on passing e. legislation in 1967 181; emergency legislation as cheap justification of security measures in fight against B-M 268
Carl Schmitt's view 208
Spiegel-Affair prepares public hostility to emergency legislation 144 f
Brüning's situation illustrates problems 204, 221, 268
Trades-union engagement in opposing 284b
Environmental Law National and international focus 291b
Environmental law aims to prevent, not punish environmental crime 234, 235; financial drawback to preferred system of self-regulation 235 f
Complex relationship between state, community and polluter 236, 243, 245; Papadakis on 'circularity' of this relationship 237
Difficulty of law keeping up with scientific opinion 237, 243
Scientific and political understanding of safety 245, 246n. *Individual cases:*
a) situation in C19 as reflected in Raabe's novel and ecology in the work of Alexander von Humboldt 224 f;
b) forests, and destruction of forests (*Waldsterben*); importance of forests in German mind 231; acid rain 228;
c) slow emergence of national legislation in this field 226; no initial legal reference to environment 226; GG § 20a on environment 226 f importance of NS law on environment 226;
d) immediate post-war neglect of environment in FRG & GDR 228 f
e) shifts in world opinion & major industrial accidents 227

Environmental Law (cont.)
- *f*) role of European legislation, cf. Sands and Parr 227 f, 291;
- *g*) German cultural obsession with environment and forests 228 f;
- *h*) links with politics, rise of the Greens 229;
- *i*) protests at Frankfurt airport 230 f;
- *j*) nationalism and the environment 231, 242;
- *k*) dioxin pollution 231 f; accident at BASF Ludwigsburg 232; USA accidents and Soveso 232; waste-dump in Hamburg 232 f; solutions too expensive to carry through, view commented by Sands & Peel 233; dioxin in food chain 234 f; boomerang effect of pollution 234;
- *l*) EMAS 235 f;
- *m*) Grube Messel: waste dump or nature reserve 237–43; regional vs. local planning 238, 241; state gives in 241;
- *n*) radioactivity 243–51; popular protests 245 f, 248 f. Allied view of a nuclear FRG 243; internal security fears: Traube affair 244. DWK 244, 246; Gorleben 229, 244, 245; closeness to GDR 245 *'G. is everywhere'* 245; 249, 250; Gorleben Hearing & coincidence with 3-Mile Island accident 243, 245, 246, 292b; fast breeder 246; BVerfG on Atom Law in Kalkar judgment 246 f; new assessment of risk 246n; Wackersdorf 247, 248; CASTOR transports 245, 250; interrupted by Lüneburg court judgment 249; rights of demonstrators eventually settled by Brokdorf judgment 249 f

Erhard, Ludwig 180, 283b
Erminger, André 271, 274
Eschenburg, Theodor 135, 138
Eulenberg, Prinz v. E.-Hertefeld 108
EURATOM 243
European Court of Human Rights Tailpiece to *Lüth* 77 f; non-involvement on §§ 175 & 218 128
Euthanasia trials 112, 175, 288b; Bauer's failures 163. Perennial interest of theme 288b. See Loewy et al. (1996)
Expert witness in Hetzel trial 90, 92, 100; in Rohrbach trial 96; conspiracy of silence 98
Extreme right classification of 255

Fallex NATO exercise 131
Federal Court of Justice (Bundesgerichtshof, BGH) Post-war FRG's most senior appellate court 14
- Controversial pension judgment 187, 214, 217, 279n, 284b
- Defence of civil service 152n
- Use of natural law 106 in justifying NS 279b
- View taken of *Spiegel*-Affair 134
- Negative effects of notorious Stachynskij judgment (bath-tub case) 169, 171, 288b, contradicting Nuremberg Principle 169
- Judgment in StGB 90a 221. Hostility to ZSL 14n

Federal Republic of Germany General history 277b; sequence of generations 1. Political pressures from geopolitical situation 5; acceptance of democracy 6; state of the country after 1945 6 f; a) political 8, b) economic 8, 46 f, 283b; 'Economic Miracle' 226, 283b; economic miracle leaves real problems behind 226, 232; IMT means there are no economic crimes 40 f, 226n; social market economy 283b. c) Cultural problems 8 f; the *Stunde Null* 9, 277b
- Low priority of legal reform after 1945 88
- 'Restoration' rather than new beginning 11, 46
- Role of the law in stabilizing the country 49
- Adenauer's insistence on West orientation & the EU 54
- Legal aspects of remilitarizing 14

Obsession with the danger from the left 24
Smug materialism in late 1950s 124
'Re-Catholicizing' of Germany 112
Domestic and international political scene 1956–1962 130 f
Failure to adopt legal code suitable for trying genocide 172, despite support for international law 55
Divisions and crises in late 1960s 180 f; alienation of younger generation 216. Grand Coalition 180 f
Visit of Shah 181 f
Brandt's détente in foreign policy 183
Munich Olympics 184, 210
'German Autumn' 215, 269, 291b
Single party rule: CDU 58, SPD 212
Possible inflexibilities in handling terrorism 207
Shift of power from parliament to executive 208
Was FRG a fascist state? 147, 204, 209 f
Problems with right-wing extremism 292, mob-violence vs. migrant communities 257
Kohl and fortuitous unification 252
Possible disappointment with re-unification 252, yet unification seen as victory for FRG 201
Difficulties for Chancellor Merkel 256, 268 f, specifically in security forces' failure to handle NSU murders properly 269. See also Nazi past

Fekete, Liz 264
Fibag Affair 136
Flick Trial 26–48; 169, 192, 254, 282b
Trial details 32 f; charges 33; subsequent political scandals with Flick money 33, 268n
IMT court procedures 35; failure of conspiracy charges 37, 41
US hostility to trusts 32; sentencing 39 f and response 41 f law's attitude to 'economic crime' 40 f
'Fiasco' for Telford Taylor 39 f
Forest, dying (*Waldsterben*) On account of pollution 228, 231
Frank, Hans 29, 44
Freedom of thought Fears for 72
Frei, Norbert 9, 11
Freisler, Roland 44
Fried, Erich 220
Fromm, Heinz Head of BfV resigns 270
Führer principle Replacing legal hierarchy? 156; effect on retroactive legislation 157
Fukushima 227

Galay, John Ford 75, 144
Gerlach. Holger 271
Genocide In IMT preparations 43, 281b. Inapplicable concept in Auschwitz trial 170 f
German Democratic Republic Post-war demontages 49, 283b
Regular critique of FRG judges 49 f; using Auschwitz trial to denounce FRG 161 f
Falling behind FRG economically 54
Early changes of policy on §218 112; RGB § 14 quickly annulled 119; view of abortion 128n
Source of independent expert witness in Hetzel trial 101
GDR seen as militaristic by FRG 141
Relation to Baader-Meinhof 182n
Careless of environment 227; nuclear dump at Morsleben 248
Trial of Honecker does not take place 253; trials of those responsible for shootings on the German-German frontier 253 f
Particular circumstances of that anti-migrant racism which originates in GDR 257 f; inexperience of multi-ethnic society 259
Methods of the *Stasi* in NSU investigations 265
Gierth, Magdalena 89 f
Gingold, Silvia 187 f, 195, 204. Cf. Kahl (1978)
Globke, Hans 147n, 284b, 288b
Protected by Adenauer 148, denouncing friend 158. Protecting NS criminals 288b

Glotz, Peter 217, 255n
Goethe's sexual practices A new norm 101
Gollwitzer, Helmut 214 f
Göring, Hermann 28, 31, 34
Gorleben See Environmental Law, *section n*: radioactivity
Götzl, Manfred 254n, 271, 272n
Grabner, Maximilian 164, 165
Grand Coalition Formation 180; and emergency legislation 181
  Possible effect on political extremes 259
  Involvement of many parties means all are implicated in government mistakes 268
Grass, Günter 148
Grimm, Dieter 15, 64, 71 f, 75
Groenewold, Kurt 11, 212; on Stammheim 290b
Gross, Fritz 100, 101
Grosser, Alfred 192
Guantanamo Bay Shared torture methods with Auschwitz 164
Guillaume, Günter 190, 212

Habermas, Jürgen 38n
Hallstein Doctrine 54, 148; implies FRG to be 'successor state' to NS 8
Halsey, Mark 231, 242
Hannover, Heinrich 11, 75n, 278b, 288b, 290b; 'friend-foe' thinking in legal establishment 207n
Hariman, Robert 68 f
Harlan, Veit 68 f, denazification process 69 f; then riding post-war antisemitic wave 71
Harmon, Louise 42n
Heidegger, Martin 67
Heinemann, Elisabeth 91n, 101
Heinemann, Gustav Reforming minister of justice, then president of FRG 107, 117, 125, 195
Henne, Thomas & Arne Riedlinger 74
Herbert A.P. 20n
Herzog, Dagmar 109, 117, 128
Hettche, Thomas 102 f
Hetzel Trial Trial details 89 f, 122, 285b
  Press and official sensationalism 90; role of expert witness 90, 92, 96, 100; sexual inhibitions in the conduct of case 91, 101
  Efforts for a retrial 97 f; involvement of *Der Spiegel* 98 f
  Picked up by Hettche into novel 102 f; echoes of Wulffen 102n
Heuß, Theodor President of FRG 14, 71, 89
Heydrich, Reinhard 46
Himmler, Heinrich 41, 67, 109, 192
Hirschfeld, Magnus 117
Historikerstreit (historians' public debates on nature of NS) 38n, 159n, 277b; *Sonderweg* 6, 209, 277b
History, academic Nietzsche's view of history 24 f, in cf. to law 25
  Level of historical understanding of NS in 1947 30 f; court role for historians 23; in Flick trial 30, 47; recognition of historians' role in founding ZSL 158 f, 159n, 168
  Bracher's influence on *Berufsverbot* – 'self-destruction of liberalism' 192
  Fears of history repeating itself 178
  Historical justification of *Berufsverbot* countered by Offergeld 192
  Irish parallels in Foyle Fisheries Case 24n. See also Archives
Hitchcock, Alfred 103n
Hochhuth, Rolf 174
Hoeness, Uli 252 f
Höss, Rudolf 29, 151
Holocaust 287b. Holocaust deniers 261. See also Auschwitz, Eichmann
Homosexuality (§175) Issue acting as seismograph to indicate the humanity of a legal system 107. Relationship to 'natural' justice 44
  A little C19 background 108 f, 286b
  Artistic homosexuality 108n
  §175 under NS 109 f
  NS origin of anti-gay groups in FRG 110
  Student movement frees up debate on homosexuality 110
  Conservative hostility to Kinsey report's view 110

A judge who loves sentencing gays 113
Adorno & Bauer's counterarguments 116 f
Frankfurt homosexuality trials 112 f
BVerfG judgment on §175 114 f
Heinemann's liberalization 117
Honecker, Erich 253
Human Rights legislation 5, 11, 43; KPD trial context 51, 52, 190, 215, 272
BVerfG diagnoses GDR's respect for 254
Galay's critique: general 75 f; in context of *Spiegel*-Affair 144; in context of *Berufsverbot* 200. See also GG §5,
Humboldt, Alexander von 225
Hussein, Saddam 130

IAK International Auschwitz Committee 159 f
International Military Tribunal (IMT – Nuremberg Trials) 281b
IMT opens the post-war period 8
Influence on future of war-crimes legislation 26, 29 f, 43; challenging view that international law does not tie individuals 36
Nuremberg Principle 36, 169, 281b, contradicted by BGH 169, 171, 288b
Trials' legitimation for Allies 27, 38; pre-history – Allied differences 27; formal legal issues 282b
Follow-up cases 28 f, military 31, industrialists 31 f, lawyers 44
No role for victims in IMT 30 f; different role in Eichmann & Auschwitz trials 146; 161; lack of interest in homosexual victims 40
Ignoring role of 'ordinary' NS members 29
Flick case 26–48
Less than water-tight legal basis of IMT 156
Continuing relevance of IMT list of suspects 44n
IRA Activity in FRG 210; 216, 266n, 285b
Ireland British use of undercover agents 267n, 271
Referenda on same-sex marriage and abortion 128. Inexperience with multi-ethnic society 159 f
Israel, State of Effect on NS trials 31; kidnapping & trial of Eichmann 149, 175
Lüth's desire for improved relations with 74. FRG payments to Israel 152
Emigration to Israel takes away potential trial witnesses 69
Bauer informs Israel of Eichmann's whereabouts 172

Jackson, Robert H. 26, 29, 32, 39
Jäger, Herbert 117
Johnson, Uwe 286b
Johst, Hanns 67
Judges and denazification 16, 278b; Status and attitudes 7, 17, conservatism 7, sociology of 280b
Applying rather than developing law in BVerfG 18, 19, 72
Judges identify with civil servants 44 f; attitude to women shown in Brühne case 96
Responding to relaxation of formality after 1968, then reversing policy 194 f. Circularity of judges' arguments to establish fairmindedness of judgments 221 f. Time allowed for written judgement 254
New generation of lawyers 10, 45, 109, 133, 148, 206
Jud Süß (film) 68 f
Jünger, Ernst 67
Jurisprudence history of 271b. English-language history 277b, 280b. General history in FRG 18, 280b; writing its history 1, 3, 6 f; in relation to other history 3
Introduction to system of German law 284b; traditional idea of the *Rechtsstaat* 17, 280b
Statute and common law 17 f, 280b
Federal structure of law in Germany 16, 21
Legal positivism in German system 18; legal education not case-work based 18; non-adversarial trial structures 82 f

Jurisprudence (cont.)
Need for popular involvement and understanding of law 7
Law and politics 4 f
New generation of lawyers untouched by NS 45
Strafrechtsänderungsgesetz (1951) 23, 61, 65, 220
FRG support for international laws 55
Law's resistance to change, yet forced to cope with radical changes in German society 7, 179, 207 f
Miscarriages of justice 102; law on appeals 97
Meaning of 'democratic justice' 99 f; educational function of trials (Auschwitz) 160
Gustav Heinemann's liberal policies in 1960s 107, 117, esp. in preventing further repression in E162 107
Failure to adopt legal code suitable for trying genocide 172; failure of catch-all concepts e.g. conspiracy, genocide 171, *Handlungseinheit* never more than individual murder 172
Liberalization at end of 1960s: *kleine Strafreform* 290b; then accelerating backlash in BVB 184, 194, 201, 206; tightening of terror laws 207; difficulties for defence counsels 208; hardening of prison conditions 208 f; Stammheim 291b
End of heroic period of German law 252. See also Judges, NS Justice, Anomalies, Marxism

Kachelmann, Jörg 253
Kalkar Fast breeder 229, BVerfG judgment 246 f
Kaltenbrunner, Ernst 29n, 31
Kaul, Friedrich In KPD trial 56; in Auschwitz trial 161 f
Keeler, Christine 93, 104
Keitel, Feldmarschall Wilhelm 31
Kessler, Heinz 254
Khrushchev, Nikita 53
Kiesewetter, Michèle 256, 270, armoury of NSU 261n
Kiesinger, Kurt Georg 180, 183, 206
Kiliç, Habil 256
Kinsey Report Back-up for liberalization in Hetzel case 101; ideological hostility to 110, 122; attacked by Schelsky 116n
Kirchheimer, Otto 278b, 279b, 280b
Kisch, Egon Erwin 83n
Klarsfeld, Beate 206 f
Kleist, Heinrich v. 81n
König, René 121n
Kogon, Eugen 11n
Kohl, Helmut Chancellor 1983–1998 1, 130, 159n, 250, 252
Korean War 220
Krupp, Alfred & Gustav 31, 32 f, 160
Kubaşik, Mehmet 256
Kuby, Erich 104
Kurras, Karl-Heinz 182

Labour Court (Arbeitsgericht) Role in *Berufsverbot* trials 83, 196; exemplary procedures 196. Contrast to US labor courts 192
Langbein, Hermann 174, 287b
Laternser, Hans 168
Lauterpacht, Hersch 169, 281b
Lawrence, Stephen 260
Lemkin, Raphael 42, 281b
Lesbianism 126 f, 286b
Ley, Robert 28
Limitation, Statute of (Verjährung) 45, 46, 152, 281b, 282b. See also Amnesty
Lisinski, Stefan 285b
Lochner, Louis 32n
Lockheed Starfighter World-wide scandal and implication for FRG 136, 144
Lohan Affair 137, 287b
Luhmann, Niklas 6
Lüth trial 70–78. Contrast to KPD trial 96
Background 68 f; calling for boycott of Harlan 70
Verdict & retrospective view of BVerfG judge 71 f; wider implications 74 f; taken up in ECHR 77; relevance to

Spiegel-Affair 142; positive link to 'militant democracy' 197 f
Relevance to *Berufsverbot* judgment in minority opinion 200; argument used in Brokdorf judgment 250

Mahler, Horst 11
Maihofer, Werner ix; resignation over Traube affair 244
Mann, Heinrich 85 f, 102
Marburg resolution On abortion 111
Maron, Monika 227
Marschner, Rolf 274, 279b
Marxism Revival in 1960s 10 f
Suspicions of GG 54; view of the law 10; class justice 279b, in FRG 10 f, continuing problem 253, also in Mescalero 223; view of Flick judgment 41. Marxism as action not philosophy 57
Analysis of fascism prevailing at the time of IMT 31; attempted use by Kaul in Auschwitz trial 162
Marx & Schöffel 178
Mauz, Gerhard 98 f. Not accusing Strauss in Brühne affair 96
McAdams, James 254
McCarthyism Anti-communism in West 29; as label for BVB 65, 190
Idea of 'Communist sympathizer' 212 f; affects spirit of follow-up IMT trials 29. See Anti-communism
McNamara, Robert 131
Meadows, Donella H. & Dennis L. *The Limits of Growth* 227
Meinecke, Friedrich 25
Meinhof, Ulrike Justification of violence 205
Mescalero An article and its consequences 211 f;
consequences for other 'sympathizers' 212 f, 217 f; punishment of student unions 217; involvement of academic staff 217
Inappropriate use of StGB § 90a at trial in Berlin 219 f
Courts finally decide article to be 'deradicalization' 223

'Migrant' communities Chancellor Merkel's difficulties exacerbated by NSU trial 256, 268 f
Court judgments on head-scarf 254; dual nationality of many 'migrant' communities 254; deliberate targeting of 'migrants' by NSU 256 f; politicizing of migrant question through the sharing-out of migrants across the federal states 260
GDR inexperience with ethnic diversity 259. Bavarian objections to migrants 260
Milch, Feldmarschall Werner 35
'Militant democracy' Commitment of law to the upholding of democracy 77, 78; *Berufsverbot* in comparison to *Lüth* 197, 198, 202, 204, 220
Mitterand, François 191
Moral Order Conservative appeal for law to replace shaken moral order post-war 11. BGB appeals to it in § 826 70; difficulty of identifying moral consensus in Hetzel case 91; same difficulty for BVerfG re § 175 45, & re § 218 120, 123; and in Dohrn case 121
Difficulty of converting moral judgment into legal judgment: Flick 54 f & Auschwitz 154
Historical nature of moral order not recognized 123
Morgenthau, Henry 27
Mosaic theory of secret information 140 f
Müller, Hermann 27
Müller-Meiningen, Ernst 88n
Mulka, Robert 154, 166 f, 173
Mundlos, Uwe 256, 269n, 274

NATO 14n, 54; in *Spiegel*-Affair 130 f, 139; 202, 243
Natural Justice Differing responses to IMT in US and FRG 43 f; 74, 106, 114, 124.
Applied to §§ 218 and 175 107n
BGH as upholder of natural justice 106, view fundamentally challenged by BVerfG 106

Natural Justice (cont.)
- Concept used in assessment of insults to state 221, overlap with judges' search for 'fairmindedness': two cases 219
- Dangers of natural justice in environmental cases 231
- Weinreb's view 44

Nazi Justice Overview 278b, 286b
- On sexual matters 285b
- Utter failures of NS justice 4 f, 9. *Volksgerichtshof* 9, 44
- NS view of homosexuality 109 f. Attempted use of NS laws in Dohrn case 119; uneven removal of § 14 from statute books in British Zone 119 f
- View of § 90a 219, 220
- *Reichsnaturgesetz* 226. See also Anomalies

Nazi Past Bias in judging NS criminals 278b
- NS past makes democratizing of law absolutely essential 4 f
- Adenauer & NS past 278b
- Allied involvement in de-nazification 278b; overlaps with post-war policies, e.g. anti-communism 29 f
- Blood and Soil 231
- Nuremberg Race Laws 9, 191
- Röhm Putsch seen as anti-homosexual measure 109
- Adenauer's appointing of ex-Nazis 45
- Difficulties of dealing with NS artists and intellectuals 67
- Film in NS 68
- Slave labour 34, 39 f
- Demonizing of NS convenient way to avoid general responsibility 149
- Shifts in public opinion in dealing with NS crimes 71
- Not seen as a danger to FRG 24, 267
- NS law 'better than no law' 115
- Claimed by Burnham as equivalent to Soviet Union (also in *Historikerstreit*) & US New Deal 47 f

Neo-Nazism 292b. Established in middle-classes 258 in East and West Germany 260
- Particular circumstances in GDR 257 f; hatred of FRG even among former opponents of GDR 258
- 'Second wave' of right-wing extremism 293; 'third wave' 292b; previous events of right-wing violence 257; mob violence against migrants 257n
- Cult of Hitler 261; international dimensions in GB and USA 261
- Fluid cell-structure similar to that of Baader-Meinhof 261 f
- Various neo-NS groups banned 262
- Neo-NS politicans attending NSU trial 272
- Damage to FRG reputation abroad 272
- Stolpe cf. with Auschwitz 257; See also Parliamentary commissions of enquiry

Neumann, Franz 30, 47

Neurath, Otto 69

Nieß-Mache, Charlotte 189, 196

Nietzsche, Friedrich 24 f, 201, 255

Nipperdey, Hans Carl 83n, 196n

Nitribitt trial 92 f. N.'s celebrity clients and similarities with Christine Keeler 93; personal life history 94. General suspicion of cover-up 93

Northcliffe, Lord (= Alfred Harmondsworth) 80

NSU trial 292b, 293b. Opening 255 f; list of murders 256, conduct of trial 270 f, 271 f, 293
- Götzl judge 271, 254n, 272n
- Information excluded from trial by BfV 274
- Arms cache of NSU 261n
- Cf. to Auschwitz trial 273
- Legal view of use of agents 59, 262, 270; influence of agents on trial 265, 274
- See also Neo-Nazism

Nuclear plants in Germany 292

Oberländer, Theodor 147n, 148

Offergeld, Rüdiger 187 f, 192, 204

Ohlendorf, Otto 37

Ohnesorg, Benno 181, 201, 212, date 182

Oppenheim, Lassa F. L. *International Law* 169

Orwell, George (=Eric Blair) 47 f, 73, 123, 196
Osborn, John 252n
Ossietzky, Carl v. 82n, 83n, 134
Ottwalt, Ernst (=Ernst Gottwalt Nicolas) 87 f
Overy, Richard 43
Özüdoğru, Abdurrahim 256

Packard, Vance 73
Papadakis, Elim 229n, 237
Parliamentary commissions of enquiry into NSU. 264 f, 268; lack of commission in Hessen 268n
Parliamentary Council Prior to founding of FRG 12 f, 19. KPD membership of PC 12. Effect of civil service membership of PC 197
Peel, Jacqueline 229, 233, 292b
Pendas, Devin 155n, 287b
Petereit, David 272
Petschek expropriation Flick's antisemitic crime untouched by IMT 34, 40, 282b
Pfeil, Sigurt 125
Pincher, Chapman 142
Pinochet, Augusto 170
Pitival C18 text 2, 80
Pius XII 174
Police 278b. Close links to NS police & Gestapo 45, 275n
 Recruitment from ranks and officers of NS police 263
 Perhaps less conservative than their duties require 10
 Possible effects on NSU trial 265, 274
 Incompetence in Praun murder 95 f; and in *Spiegel*-Affair 138
 Schumacher's view of police 46n
Political Parties GG view of parties in contrast to Weimar 51
 Individual parties:
 AfD 260
 CDU see also under Adenauer. CDU & Flick scandal 45. Brief decline in late 1960s 180, end of shabby compromises 183. Established in the former GDR 262. Dominance in BVerfG nominations 76
 CSU Attitude to *Spiegel*-Affair 133; to migrants 260
 DKP 52, 59; 'with a touch of pink' (Wesel) 204; S. Gingold 187, 189, 202; Nieß-Mache 189. Why the BVerfG never banned it 195 f, 198
 DP 52, 284b
 DVU 255, 262
 FDP 260. Actively recruiting old NS members 52, 262, Dreher a member 14. Attitude to § 218 121. Attitude to *Spiegel*-Affair 133. *Spiegel*'s tendency towards party 135; only opposition during Grand Coalition 180, re-entering coalition 238
 Greens 229, in Hamburg 233; in Hessen 238 f; in Lower Saxony 248, 254 f
 KPD ban 49–66; 184, 198, 270. Opposition to Hitler 50, 53, 54 f, 57 f. Arrogance 58; Adenauer's hatred of KPD 56, 283b. Relationship to SPD and trades-unions 55; as a unity party 57; freedom to stand in national elections post-unification 57; no longer believing in own programme (Wesel) 203n.
 NPD 38, 180. Part of move to right 255, not seen as a threat 270n. BVerfG refuses to ban as for KPD 59, 262, 270, activity of BfV agents in party 271.
 PDS 258
 REP 262
 SED 258, 262. FDJ banned 60, 283b
 SPD early attitude to BVerfG 19; attitude to Flick 33. Slow on NS crimes on amnesty 20n. Bad Godesberg reforms 11, 133, 180, 183. Kept informed after 1958 on emergency legislation 290b. First entry into government 180. Ambiguity towards NS crimes 147. Attitude to *Spiegel*-Affair 133. General

Political Parties (cont.)
disappointment with SPD 186.
Talking tough with BVB 289b.
Offergeld's membership 187 f.
Overtaken by Greens on ecology 231, 233; shifting attitudes to atomic power 248 f; working with Greens on dual-citizenship arrangements 254; yet individuals critique migration policy 260
SRP ban 52, 60, 255, 262
Ponsold, Albert 90, 92, 100, 202
Ponto, Jürgen 210
Potsdam Agreement 56
Porch, Douglas Counter-insurgency 60n, 266n
Praun, Otto 95, 96
Press and Media General history of court-reporting 80, 277b; involvement of media in law 79 f
No reference to freedom of the press in GG 75
Pitival 80 and modern detective stories as part of knowledge of law 82 f; courtroom dramas 81
Shortcomings of press in post-war period 88; exceptions Gerhard Mauz 98 f & Ernst Müller-Meiningen 88n
Implications of Hetzel trial for role of media 90, 97, 98 f
Press suspicions of Adenauer 148; expressed generally in wake of Nitribitt murder enquiry 93 f;
Adenauer's plan for state TV channel 88
Limited military expertise in German press 141 f.; attitude of press to *Spiegel*-Affair 164; uneven press reporting of Auschwitz trial 174; press response to Mescalero 212. Böll vs. BILD-*Zeitung* 82, 213 f. Student protest at Springer press power 182; general intellectual opposition to Springer 182
Patchy reporting of *Berufsverbot* 190
Cheapened reporting of NSU through ethnic stereotypes 264n
Prokop, Otto 101
Proportionality 56, 59, 217, 242
Protest, right to Rights of demonstrators settled by Brokdorf judgment 250

Raabe, Wilhelm 224 f, 231
Radbruch, Gustav 81n, 85, 86n, 109. Bauer's admiration for 159
Radikalenerlass See *Berufsverbot*
Raeder, Großadmiral Erich 24
Ratzinger, Joseph 188
Rauschning, Hermann 31, 47
Realism, legal Superseded in USA through IMT experience 43, 106, 296b, Dworkin 43, 280b
Rechtsstaat 2, 11, 17, 18, 280b. Different public perceptions of law in *Rechtsstaat* 24, 82
Reichsgericht 12, 192. Judgment on § 218 110
Reichsfront Section of SRP 52
Remer, General Otto Ernst 262n
Requate, Jörg 9, 154
Restoration As a consequence of *Rechtsstaat* 11. Harlan as its cultural symbol 69
Retroactive legislation Issue in Flick trial 36
Secrecy legislation essentially retroactive 141; retroactivity in *Berufsverbot* practices 198; effort to avoid retroactivity in setting up Auschwitz trial 156 f; attempt to avoid retroactivity in dealing with German-German border shootings 254
Richter, Thomas (=Corelli) 269
Riedlinger, Arne 72n
Riefenstahl, Leni 68
Rinken, Alfred 64 f
Robertson, Geoffrey 207
Rohrbach, Maria 96, 102
Ronimi, Kurt 114
Rosenberg, Alfred 67
Rosenberg, Ethel & Julius 138
RSHA 45, 152n. Trials 149, 152, 193, 267
Desk-top murderers 46 f; bad publicity from failure of trial 153; problems

with StGB § 211 191. Ulm trial 152, 158 f
Vulnerability to same type of charge as in *Berufsverbot* 193 f
Rückert, Joachim 81
Rühe, Volker 260
Rupp-von-Brünneck, Wiltraut 125, 195, 200
Russell Tribunal & other international protest movements 190, 289b

Sack, Peter G. 75n
Safety, environmental 246. Reflection on risk following BVerfG judgment 246n
Sands, Philippe 170, 226, 244, 281b, 292b
Satō, Hiromi 169, 281b
Schacht, Hjalmar 38
Scharf, Bishop Kurt 214
Schelsky, Helmut 116
Schilly, Otto 11, 290b
Schleyer, Hanns-Martin 210. Could have been saved by negotiation 207, 291b
Schmidt, Helmut, Chancellor of FRG 76, 125, 134
Schmidt, Johannes 171
Schmitt, Carl 156, 208. Cf. Mehring (2009)
Schöffel, Adolf 178 f, 219
Schönert, Jörg 81n
Schröder, Gerhard, Chancellor of FRG 254, 260
Schubart, Alexander 230
Schulze, Carsten 271, 274
Schumacher, Kurt 46 f, 59, 220. Views on police and on Catholic church 46n
Secrecy Ambiguous post-war international view of military secrecy 137–42, 287b
Peculiarities of FRG secrecy legislation 138 f, 140 f; relation to freedom of expression 137: 'mosaic' theory 140 f; essentially retroactive material/formal understandings of secrecy 141
Transparency in military procurement 138, 143 f
Security forces Praun's relationship to BND 95
BND has no objection to *Spiegel*-Article 131 f
BfV's role in the *Berufsverbot*, and simultaneous failure on national security 190, 199
Unchallengable nature of their evidence 187
BfV's role in NSU trial 265 f, 274; shredding of material damaging to itself 266; possible explanation of behaviour 59, 266 f; use of paid informants & placing agents in Neo-Nazi groups 265; practice rejected by BVerfG 271
Self-justifying reference to emergency 268
Non-collaboration with police 267; resignation of BfV heads 270
Lack of government control 272
Discrediting in Traube affair 244
Seehofer, Horst 260
Sendler, Horst 237
Sexuality General attitudes to sexuality 285b
'The' sexual revolution 94
Mixture of repression and commercialization of sexuality 91, 92, 101; sex scandals and murders 90, 92 f, 95 f; public views of sexuality 115, 285b
Courts' general dislike of subject in Dohrn case 123
CDU plans for further repressive legislation, criminalizing adultery in Plan E162 107n, 116, 117; protests from intellectuals 116 f
NS views of sexuality 286b; legal aspects of §§ 175 & 218 110 f
Millennial 'new sexual conservatism' (Herzog) 128
Seymour-Ure, Colin 287b
Sherlock Holmes 81
Shortt, Linda 1
Şimşek, Enver 256
Skuse, Frank 190
Sling (Paul Schlesinger) 86 f, 99, 206
Snowdon, Edward & secrecy 137
Social Media Law's difficulty countering power of 253
Sonderweg 6, 209, 277b

Soveso 227
Soviet Union Withdrawal from Control Commission 5n
Stabilizing effect on post-war Europe 49
Role in IMT 6, 27, 34, 37, 38, 47
Role in GDR 8
Popular Front 55, 189; role of SU in KPD 53, 54 f
Possible influence on Flick trial 282b
Attitudes to homosexuality and abortion 109
Cold War 130, 134; Budapest 286b; Prague Spring 181
Legacy of Soviet bloc states to post 1989 world 255
Speer, Albert 39n
Spiegel-Affair 130–145, 287b. The *Spiegel*-magazine 134 f
Strauss' previous attacks on *Spiegel* 136
Lüth & freedom of expression in Affair 137, 143
Offending article by Ahlers 131 f; *Spiegel*'s habitual lack of interest in military matters 141
Imprisonment of editor & journalist 132 f
Peculiarities of secrecy legislation 137 f, 140 f: 'mosaic' theory 140 f; material/formal understandings of secrecy 140 f
Augstein's appeal to BVerfG (*Verfassungsbeschwerde*) 142 f. BVerfG view of *Sp.*-Affair 134, 142 f
Surprising intervention of BGH judge 133 f; BGH's formal place in case 142 f. Parliamentary debate & Adenauer's attack on Augstein 133
General effects of the Affair 133 f, 144 f; dangerous overlap of Affair with Cuban crisis 130 f
Springer press and *Spiegel* 287b
Spilsbury, Bernhard 90
SS (Schutzstaffel) Membership of SS seen as punishably criminal in Flick case 39, 41; not so in Auschwitz trial 157; challenge to view of inflexible hierarchy in which individuals could not avoid participating in crimes against humanity 172 f
Stalin, Josef 27, 30, 52 f, 87, 161n, 208
Steinbacher, Sibylle 92, 109
Steinbrinck, Otto 35, 41
Stoll, Peter 211
Stolleis, Michael 4, 18. English-language short history of jurisprudence post 1945 277b. See also Gödecke (2008)
Stolpe, Manfred 257
Stolting, Hermann II 167 f
Strafrechtsänderungsgesetz 23, 61, 65, 220
Strauss, Franz-Josef (political influence) Head of CSU. minister president of Bavaria
Debasing of political language with populism 219, 220; playing with regionalism 135. Attacks on opponents of NS 163
Rumours of involvement of in Brühne affair not shared by Mauz & Augstein 95. Strauss grants Brühne early pardon 96. See *Spiegel*-Affair
Streicher, Julius 27, 31, 69n, 157
Streletz, Fritz 254
Student revolt May 1968 Radicalized by *Spiegel*-Affair 144 f
Search for contact with the masses 182, 183, 216
Tactic at its end 183; effect of repression & unemployment 205
Threats to archaic structures of university 18, 182 f, 200, 217
SDS 183
Widening of horizons from the narrowly political & materialistic 202, 251
Frees up debate on homosexuality 110
Superior orders defence Offending against the 'Nuremberg Principle' 130, 162, 169, 170; but successful for Harlan 68 f & partially for Flick
Wharton 39, 162; further development in State function defence, example Pinochet 170; re-legitimation of defence in BGH's Stachynskij judgment 169, 170, 171 f; contrast with Kaltenbrunner's defence on grounds

of irresistible 'hypnotic power of NS 171
Sympathizers 212–15

Taşköprü, Süleyman 256
Taylor, Telford 26, 32n, 42, 82n, 281b
Temme, Andreas 272
Tergit, Gabriele (=Elise Reifenberg) 3, 86 f, 93, 98, 104 f
Terrorism, urban Baader-Meinhof; 289b
Corresponding radicalization of the law 184
Alleged rationale of terrorism. 205
Spiral of violence in 1970s 206; murders of Siegfried Buback, Jürgen Ponto & Hanns-Martin Schleyer 210; trivializing of violence 206; participants behaving as in an action film 215
Reactions on the left 201 f
Using trials as attack on state 207
On defence counsels of terrorists 208, 290b; dilemma of over-reaction in counter- t. measures 207; cf. with British counter-terrorism problems cf. Porch (2013). Relation to *Berufsverbot* victims 205
Conservative efforts to smear SPD and FDP with links to terrorism 214
Böll insists on his distance to B-M 214. 2nd June talisman 182
Model for neo-Nazi structures 262
Teufel, Fritz 206
Thälmann, Ernst 278b
Theissen, Horst 127 f
Three Mile Island 227
Tillessen, Heinrich 21 f
Tito, Marshall 70, 225
Totalitarianism 147, 209
Trades-Unions GEW, ÖTV in Offergeld case 188n, 192; role in constitution 55, 61, 181. View of emergency legislation 290b
Traube, Klaus 244
Trotsky Critique of Stalin 30
Truman, Harry S. 27
Tu quoque Unspoken element in IMT deliberations 38; in Auschwitz trial 127, 157, 175; significant role in *Historikerstreit* 38n
Turgut, Mehmet 256
Turing, Alan 30

Ulm-Trial (1958) 158 f. See also RSHA
Universities Inclusion of universities into codified law 17
Inappropriate power of professors 90
Radicalization of students and staff 184; threatened in BVB 190, 214; general critique from student movement esp. of law faculties 202
University law departments' support for NS law 45, 278b, 281b
BVerfG adjustment of effect of BVB on law training opportunities 289b
USA Legal realism pre-1947 43, 56, 106
Post-war hostility to trusts 32
American Civil Liberties Union intervention in Homosexual trials 114
Constitution compared to GG 126
Office of Strategic Information 139
Active role of Labour Courts in US *Berufsverbot* cases 196
Problems with dioxin 233 f
US Supreme Court Structural comparison with BVerfG 13, 62 f, 82
Election of judges 14
Reflections on relations to politics: *Brown vs the Board of Education* 63; *Marbury vs Madison* 63 f; *McCutcheon vs. Federal Election Committee* 65 f. Avoidance of 'authoritarian judicalism' (Bickel) 76

Violence Perceived need to redefine 293 f; concept of counter-violence 214
Violence in ecological protest 231 f
B-M definition of function of violence 205
K-Gruppen 251
Mescalero's approach to B-M violence 211 f; court finds this view to be 'de-radicalization' 223
Vogt, Jochen 159, 175

Wackersdorf 229, 247, 248
Wahl, Rainer 77 f
Wand, Walter Rudi 195, 200, 204
Weber, Max 146, 280b; ineffectual German admiration for English methods 139n
Weimar Republic General desire for legal reform, yet not carried through 108, 109, 25; Wulffen 82f; Radbruch 81n, 85, 86n
Cultural golden age 8
Early attempts at reform of §§ 175 & 218 110; role of public intellectuals in the law 85
Legal journalism and court-reporting in W.R. 85 f
Class justice in W.R. 279b
elements of W.R. constitution taken over into GG 12; problem with its imprecise language 278b
Political murders in W.R. 192
Centrality of question why W.R. failed 23; would banning NSDAP have saved it? 50
Bracher's diagnosis 192
Judicial review in W.R. 13. View of parties 51
Role of emergency legislation in destroying W.R. 181
Weinreb, Lloyd on normative nature of law 44
Weiss, Bernhard 40, 41
Weiss, Peter 55n, 175n, 174 f
Weizsäcker, Richard von 19, 233
Wells, Christina 140
Wesel, Uwe 56, 59, 76n, 177n, 203n, 207n, 209, view of BVerfG 280b, 289b, 291b on DKP 204; judges understanding Ireland 266
Wetzell, Richard 7
Wharton's Criminal Law 39n, 162
White, Rob 234
Whitman, Walt 108
Wiesenthal Simon Discredited by FRG officialdom in order to hamper his efforts to identify NS criminals 174n
Wilde, Oscar 108 f
Wilson, Harold 133, 297b
Wilson, Richard Ashby 204, 207
Wohlleben, Ralf 271, 273
Wolf, Friedrich 110
Wolf, Marcus 182
Wolfenden Report 117
Wulffen, Erich 102n. Reform and detective stories 81

Yaşar, Ismail 256
Yozgat, Halit 256, 272

Zola, Émile 85, 98
Zschäpe, Beate 255 f, 271, 273
ZSL (Zentrale Stelle der Landesjustizverwaltungen Ludwigsburg) Historical institute dedicated to preparing cases on NS crimes 158 f, 278b. Hostility of BGH 14n